EXPORT QUALITY MANAGEMENT

A GUIDE FOR SMALL AND MEDIUM-SIZED EXPORTERS

SECOND EDITION

Geneva 2011

ABSTRACT FOR TRADE INFORMATION SERVICES

ID=42653 2011 F-09.03 EXP

International Trade Centre (ITC)
Physikalisch-Technische Bundesanstalt (PTB)
Export Quality Management: A Guide for Small and Medium-sized Exporters. Second edition.
Geneva: ITC, 2011. xii, 270 pages

Guide seeking to provide small and medium-sized exporters with a comprehensive understanding of quality-related issues linked to the quality infrastructure – consists of questions and answers related to quality control, technical requirements (standards, technical regulations, sanitary and phytosanitary measures), management systems, conformity assessment (testing, inspection, certification), metrology, accreditation, and the WTO Agreements on Technical Barriers to Trade and the Application of Sanitary and Phytosanitary Measures; answers to questions are followed by relevant bibliographical references and web resources.

Descriptors: **Quality Control, Quality Management, Standards, Conformity Assessment, Inspection, Testing and Exports, Certification, Metrology, Accreditation, SPS, TBT**.

English, French, Spanish (separate editions)

ITC, Palais des Nations, 1211 Geneva 10, Switzerland (www.intracen.org)

P247.E/DBIS/EC/11-XI

ISBN 978-92-9137-399-4
United Nations Sales No. E.12.III.T.2

Foreword

Quality is a prerequisite for successful market access and for improving the competitiveness of exporters. However, meeting technical requirements is a challenge for many exporters, especially in view of the proliferation of standards. Countries impose a growing number of standards to protect the health and safety of their citizens and to meet demands of buyers for their specific needs. This has been confirmed by research conducted by the International Trade Centre (ITC), which has found that most problems faced by exporters are a result of non-tariff measures due to technical regulations, conformity assessment procedures, and sanitary and phytosanitary measures.

Enterprises intending to export their products need up-to-date information about the applicable technical requirements, both voluntary and mandatory, in their target markets. After obtaining this information, they have to adapt their products and processes to satisfy export market requirements and demonstrate compliance with them. They may not readily have access to recognized conformity assessment service providers for this purpose, as the quality infrastructure in their country may not be fully developed. They may have to use foreign certification bodies that are recognized in the export market thereby increasing their cost.

Given this context, ITC and Physikalisch-Technische Bundesanstalt (PTB – the National Metrology Institute of Germany) saw fit to revise the guide for managers of small and medium-sized enterprises (SMEs) in developing countries and transition economies dealing with export quality management. The initial guide, developed in 2001, was based on a global survey to determine the top 100 questions that exporters ask about quality management. This revised guide has taken into account international trade developments during the last decade. It also has built on the tremendous success of the previous edition, with 15 customized versions tailored to the needs of 18 countries, in eight languages. The new edition is based on a survey carried out to determine the relevance of the questions in the first edition and to include additional questions.

The book provides answers to questions on quality, technical requirements (standards, technical regulations, sanitary and phytosanitary measures), management systems, conformity assessment (testing, inspection, certification), metrology, accreditation, and the WTO Agreements on Technical Barriers to Trade and the Application of Sanitary and Phytosanitary Measures.

We hope that this book, which forms part of the ITC Trade Secrets series of question-and-answer guides, will be useful to small and medium-sized firms in their endeavour to export.

Patricia Francis
Executive Director
International Trade Centre

Ernst Otto Göbel
President
Physikalisch-Technische Bundesanstalt

Acknowledgements

This updated publication was made possible through the expertise, experience and knowledge of many individuals and organizations; they are noted below with thanks and appreciation.

Partner

Physikalisch-Technische Bundesanstalt (PTB), Germany's national metrology institute, partnered with the International Trade Centre (ITC) in the release of this second, updated edition of the publication that was first released by ITC in 2001. PTB's technical cooperation work, including its contribution to this publication, is funded by the German Federal Ministry for Economic Cooperation and Development (BMZ).

Technical development

The book was developed by a technical team headed by Shyam Kumar Gujadhur, Senior Adviser on Standards and Quality Management, in close collaboration with Ludovica Ghizzoni, Adviser on Export Quality Management, Hema Menon, Trade Training Officer, at ITC; Uwe Miesner, Project Coordinator, Technical Cooperation, at PTB, with the following experts: Subhash Chander Arora, Digby Gascoine, John Gilmour, Martin Kellermann and Eberhard Seiler.

The cooperation of Stefan Wallerath, Martin Stavenhagen and Martin Kaiser at PTB are deeply appreciated.

Review

The technical review was conducted by various individuals from DCMAS, STDF, the Secretariats of the WTO Committees on TBT and SPS, as well as Navin Dedhia in an individual capacity.

Contributions

ITC extends deep gratitude to the many people who responded to the survey conducted to validate the publication outline. Individuals responded from a variety of trade support institutions (including national standards bodies), as well as experts in their individual capacity.

Shirin Abrar, Associate Librarian at ITC, contributed to the research of the information sources.

Flavia Alves and Eu Joon Hur, interns at ITC, contributed to the survey of SMEs and researched sources of information.

Natalie Domeisen, manager of ITC's publications programme, coordinated the publication production and promotion.

Evelyn Jereda at ITC provided administrative support.

Editing and layout

The publication was edited and reviewed by Leni Sutcliffe. Isabel Droste and Carmelita Endaya edited the sources throughout the book. The layout was done by Carmelita Endaya. The cover was designed by Kristina Golubic.

Contents

Note

Unless otherwise specified, all references to dollars ($) are to United States dollars. The term 'product' ('products') is used to mean both goods and services wherever appropriate and particularly in the chapters on product certification, quality management and ISO 9000.

The following abbreviations are used:

APLAC	Asia Pacific Laboratory Accreditation Cooperation
ASEAN	Association of Southeast Asian Nations
ASQ	American Society for Quality
ASTM International	Formerly known as American Society for Testing and Materials
AWI	Australian Wool Innovation Limited
BCI	Better Cotton Initiative
BIPM	International Bureau of Weights and Measures
BIS	Bureau of Indian Standards
BMZ	Federal Ministry for Economic Cooperation and Development (Germany)
BQF	British Quality Foundation
BRC	British Retail Consortium
CAC	Codex Alimentarius Commission
CIPM	International Committee for Weights and Measures
CLP	Classification, Labelling and Packaging
CQI	Chartered Quality Institute
CSA	Canadian Standards Association
EA	European co-operation for Accreditation
EC	European Commission
ECHA	European Chemicals Agency
EFQM	European Foundation for Quality Management
EN	European Standard
EOQ	European Organization for Quality
EPTIS	European Proficiency Testing Information System
EU	European Union
EURAMET	European Association of National Metrology Institutes
FAO	Food and Agriculture Organization of the United Nations
FDA	United States Food and Drug Administration
FLO	Fairtrade Labelling Organizations International
FSC	Forest Stewardship Council
GEN	Global Ecolabelling Network
GFSI	Global Food Safety Initiative
GLOBALG.A.P.	Global Good Agricultural Practices
GOTS	Global Organic Textile Standard
HACCP	Hazard analysis and critical control points
IAAC	InterAmerican Accreditation Cooperation
IAF	International Accreditation Forum
IATF	International Automotive Task Force
IEC	International Electrotechnical Commission
ILAC	International Laboratory Accreditation Cooperation
IPPC	International Plant Protection Convention
IRCA	International Register of Certificated Auditors

ISO	International Organization for Standardization
ITC	International Trade Centre
MLA	Multilateral Recognition Agreement
MRA	Mutual Recognition Agreement
NANDO	New Approach Notified and Designated Organisations
NCB	National certification body
NIST	National Institute of Standards and Technology
NLAB	National Laboratories Accreditation Bureau
NSB	National standards body
OECD	Organisation for Economic Co-operation and Development
OIE	World Organisation for Animal Health
OIML	International Organization of Legal Metrology
PTB	Physikalisch-Technische Bundesanstalt
QMS	Quality Management System
REACH	Registration, Evaluation, Authorisation and Restriction of Chemicals
RoHs	Restriction of Hazardous Substances
SAAS	Social Accountability Accreditation Services
SABS	South African Bureau of Standards
SADCA	Southern African Development Community Accreditation
SAI	Social Accountability International
SDoC	Supplier's declaration of conformity
SMEs	Small and medium-sized enterprises
SPS	Sanitary and phytosanitary (measures)
STDF	Standards and Trade Development Facility
TBT	Technical barriers to trade
TPO	Trade promotion organization
UNCTAD	United Nations Conference on Trade and Development
UNECE	United Nations Economic Commission for Europe
UNIDO	United Nations Industrial Development Organization
WRAP	Worldwide Responsible Accredited Production
WTO	World Trade Organization

INTRODUCTION

Quality infrastructure – a prerequisite for business

Standards and quality have been part of human society since ancient times. Not only are they likely to stay, but experience also shows that they increasingly shape commercial prospects for developing and transition economies.

In one form or another, they have always underpinned trade and business. Standards support compatibility and can drive down costs through the use of common parts, specifications and methods. They can facilitate the creation of new industries and allow new technologies to be exploited. They are also crucial to realizing and maintaining market access.

Over the past decades, standards and related concepts have gained in importance and have become subject to more and more scientific and technological scrutiny and definitions. At the same time, the business world and society have been changing rapidly. Because of global trade, many of today's products are built with components sourced from around the world, which must fit together and perform as expected. Product life cycles are becoming shorter and the pace of technological development is accelerating. Consumers are demanding ever higher levels of safety, performance, reliability and sustainability. All these have to be facilitated by an effective and efficient network of service providers known as the quality infrastructure (QI).

What is a quality infrastructure?

The national quality infrastructure (NQI) can be understood as the totality of the institutional framework (public or private) required to establish and implement standardization, metrology (scientific, industrial and legal) and the accreditation and conformity assessment services (inspection, testing, and product and system certification) necessary to provide acceptable evidence that products and services meet defined requirements, whether these are imposed by the authorities (in technical regulations and sanitary and phytosanitary measures) or the marketplace (i.e. contractually or inferred).

A simplified model identifies five main components of an NQI: standardization, testing, metrology, certification and accreditation, which are closely related and depend on each other (see figure).

National quality infrastructure

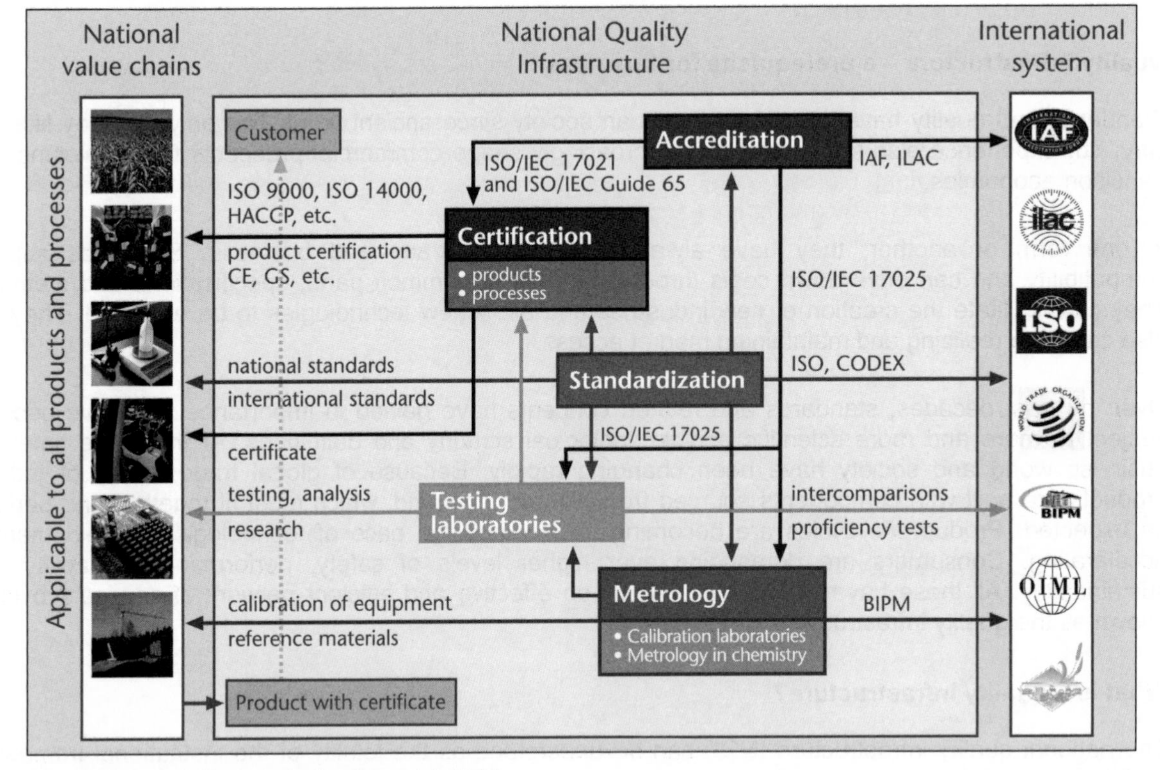

Source: Physikalisch-Technische Bundesanstalt (PTB).

Note: CE and GS refer to the European Union's CE mark and to the German *Geprüfte Sicherheit or 'tested* safety' certification mark respectively.

Enterprises need to manufacture products according to the **standards, technical regulations** and **sanitary and phytosanitary measures** prevailing in their export markets; they need to be able to use **testing laboratories** to determine compliance of their products; these laboratories should have access to **metrology and calibration services** to ensure that their test equipment are giving reliable results; the products/systems may be **certified by third parties** to give confidence to the buyers and regulatory bodies that the relevant requirements are being consistently met. The certification bodies and laboratories **have to be accredited** to demonstrate their technical competences. The manufacturer may use a supplier's declaration of conformity (SDoC) instead of third-party certification.

Why a quality infrastructure?

Industrialized countries as well as economies in transition and developing countries have much to gain from a quality infrastructure: international partnership, transfer of knowledge, increased trade and development, and a higher standard of living. The many benefits of a functional QI are detailed below:

- **It helps to overcome challenges from free trade and globalization.** QI is essential to breaking down technical barriers to trade by harmonizing import and market access requirements. It is thus the key to greater integration of countries into the international trading system.
- **It enables access to international markets and preserves domestic markets.** Agreements among nations or regions on the mutual acceptability of requirements, assessment methods, inspection or test results can all help to reduce or remove technical barriers to trade, thus strengthening domestic markets and opening up foreign markets.

- **It promotes innovation and competitiveness.** Since manufacturing and service delivery are strengthened in terms of quality, safety and compatibility, which ultimately leads to higher customer desirability, suppliers who can take advantage of QI services are empowered to become more innovative and competitive.
- **It protects consumers.** Consumers benefit from conformity assessment because it provides them with a basis for selecting products or services: they may have more confidence in products or services that bear a mark or certificate of conformity attesting to quality, safety or other desirable characteristics. Legally binding technical regulations are particularly important in the areas of health, safety and environmental protection. Sanitary and phytosanitary measures, which are mandatory, are crucial for food safety and animal and plant health.
- **It assists regulators and service providers.** Regulatory bodies responsible for enforcing governmental health, safety and environmental legislation, and service providers such as national metrology institutes, testing institutes and calibration services can rely on the existing infrastructure. In this way, they can avoid duplicating facilities and services, particularly in countries with limited resources.
- **It advances economic development.** QI helps to promote sustainable development by providing opportunities to make domestic products and services more competitive in both national and international markets. QI thus paves the way towards further integration of the partner countries in the interests of a fairer global trade regime, and establishes institutions and influences the enabling environment at the national level.
- **It encourages regional integration.** A dialogue initially focusing on technical issues can promote confidence-building and lead to sharing QI capacities – technical expertise, testing and calibration laboratories, among others, and thus reduce costs.

For all these benefits to materialize, international recognition of the NQI is essential. It is in every country's interest to participate in the relevant international forums so as to facilitate this recognition and avoid multiple standards, regulations, tests and accreditation, and work towards the ultimate goal of 'inspected once, tested once, certified once – accepted everywhere' for a worldwide acceptance of shared standards.

Sanitary and phytosanitary measures (SPS)

One important sector-specific application of an NQI is to ensure safety of food and agricultural products as well as animal and plant health through sanitary and phytosanitary measures and to support the export of these products. Market access for animals and plants is dependent on the absence of specific pests and diseases in the exporting and importing countries. Therefore a country needs to have competent bodies for food and agricultural products, i.e. a food safety authority, a veterinary service and a plant protection organization. They can certify exports and control imports to protect domestic plants and animals from new pests and diseases which can also threaten exports.

QI from a business perspective

In view of the relevance of standards, technical regulations, sanitary and phytosanitary measures and conformity assessment to international trade, it is obvious that businesses – and especially small and medium-sized enterprises – have a strong interest in a functioning QI. In this context, the business community has different roles to play in order to strengthen the development of this infrastructure:

- As customer, enterprises need to lobby for internationally recognized QI services within their country. This is particularly true for SMEs, as unlike large companies, they tend not to have any calibration or testing capacities of their own. Instead, they rely on the support of national QI organizations. One key motivating factor for the lobby is the fact that enterprises are enabled to increase sales of their product by being able to provide proof of its quality.

- As partner, businesses are called upon to cooperate actively with government and civil society organizations such as consumer associations in order to develop the national QI. One prominent example is standardization, which is based on collaborative efforts and inputs from different interested parties. In addition, the business community could assist government in international trade negotiations, e.g. by providing information on national priorities for the international recognition of the NQI and mutual recognition agreements.
- As provider, businesses could exploit the commercial potential of conformity assessment services, e.g. by establishing testing, inspection and certification facilities for external customers. Although this usually applies to larger companies, private provision of QI services is a viable option not only in developed countries but also in developing countries where the public sector may not be able to offer services that are recognized on international markets. Thus, the private sector becomes a key stakeholder of the national quality infrastructure.

This publication seeks to provide small and medium-sized exporters with a comprehensive understanding of crucial quality-related issues linked to the quality infrastructure, for them to improve continually and succeed in international and regional export forums.

We hope the publication will also contribute to maintaining the dialogue and the exchange of experience between ITC, PTB, and our partner institutions in the field of export quality management, where issues evolve rapidly and will continue to challenge developed and developing countries.

FOR MORE INFORMATION

- Physikalisch-Technische Bundesanstalt (PTB). Quality Infrastructure in almost 5 minutes. 2009. http://www.ptb.de/en/org/q/q5/_index.htm

  This movie presents the most important institutions of quality infrastructure and shows its significance for society, the economy and consumers in three illustrative examples.

- Sanetra, Clemens and Rocío M. Marbán. The Answer to the Global Quality Challenge: A National Quality Infrastructure. Physikalisch-Technische Bundesanstalt (PTB). 2007. http://www.ptb.de/de/org/q/q5/docs/OAS_EN07.pdf

  This publication illustrates how a national quality infrastructure relies on five main components, how these relate to each other and how, in turn, the national infrastructure relates to the international quality system.

- International Trade Centre. Innovation in Export Strategy. 2005. http://legacy.intracen.org/tdc/Export%20Quality%20Handbooks/32756_InnovationsQualityAssuranceWeb.pdf

  This publication provides a practical approach to developing a strategy for setting up a suitable quality infrastructure in developing countries.

UNDERSTANDING QUALITY

1. What is quality?

A quick Internet search will provide you with an interesting insight into the meaning of quality. For the *Oxford English Dictionary*, for example, quality is “the standard of something as measured against other things of a similar kind; the degree of excellence of something”. The *Business Dictionary* defines manufacturing-related quality – our main focus here – as “a measure of excellence or state of being free from defects, deficiencies and significant variations, brought about by the strict and consistent adherence to measurable and verifiable standards to achieve uniformity of output that satisfies specific customer or user requirements”. Finally, ISO 9000 defines quality simply as “the degree to which a set of inherent characteristics fulfils requirements”. These requirements are the needs or expectations, generally implied or obligatory, of interested parties such as customers, suppliers and society.

For us, the quality of a product or service depends on an exchange between two persons, one supplying the product or service and the other receiving the product or service. The supplier and the customer can have different views on what quality is and this may lead to misunderstandings and disputes. In that sense, quality can be understood as “the conformance with customers' requirements or fitness for purpose”.

The first point to note is that it is the customer who defines whether a product is fit for use or not. If the characteristics of a product or service do not match those required by the customer, it will not be a quality product for the latter. For example, a limousine with high gas consumption will not be a quality product for someone looking for a small car with low gas consumption. A supplier can prepare specifications for his/her product based on what is perceived as the requirements of customers and manufacture products conforming to those specifications. However, if the conforming products are found to be unfit for use by the users, they would be considered defective products; in this case, the specifications have failed to take fully into account the needs of the consumers. This brings us to the adage that the customer is king. Quality is not absolute but relative. A product may be of good quality for someone, but of poor quality for someone else. For instance, one person may be comfortable with high-heeled shoes while another may prefer flat shoes. As pointed out by Snyder, quality is all about the customer's perception of excellence and our response to that perception. It is measured solely by its utility to one audience – the customer.

The second point to note is that customers' requirements change over time as purchasing power increases or as more innovative products are made available on the market. A customer who was satisfied with a black-and-white television set in the past now goes for a colour television set with a flat screen.

Quality or fitness for purpose is usually defined by quality of design and quality of conformance (see question 2). However, for products with a long life such as computers and refrigerators, which require after-sales service, there are two other parameters. These are the availability for use (the product should not break down often and should work for a reasonable period before breaking down again) and field service, which should be prompt and performed with integrity by competent personnel.

When talking about quality, the term ‘grade’ comes to mind; it is defined in ISO 9000 as the “category or rank given to different quality requirements for products, processes or systems having the same functional use”.

Some examples are the class of airline ticket and category of hotel in a hotel guide.

Quality has many dimensions and these have been defined by Garvin (1987) as follows:

- Performance, which refers to a product's main operating characteristics;
- Features, which are extras that supplement the main characteristics;
- Reliability, which reflects the probability of a product malfunctioning or failing within a specified period;
- Conformance, which is the degree to which a product's design and operating characteristics meet established standards;
- Durability, which is the amount of use before the product deteriorates;

- Serviceability, which is dependent on the service team's speed, courtesy, competence and the product's ease of repair;
- Aesthetics, which is linked to appearance and impression;
- Perceived quality, which is linked to the reputation of the brand.

The ISO 9000 definition of quality, i.e. "degree to which a set of inherent characteristics fulfils requirements"', is equally applicable to a service. While it is easy to define and measure the characteristics of a hardware item, the service being an intangible item is difficult to define and measure. Parasuraman, Zeithaml and Berry (1988) have defined the following generally acceptable service characteristics and have given them the acronym RATER:

- Responsiveness: willingness and/or readiness of employees to help customers and to provide prompt service, timeliness of service.
- Assurance: knowledge and courtesy of your employees and their ability to convey trust and confidence, viz. competence, trustworthiness, inspiring confidence.
- Tangibles: physical appearance of the service such as facilities, tools, equipment, appearance of servicing personnel and communication materials.
- Empathy: provision of caring, individualized attention to the customer, giving the customer information in a language he or she understands, understanding the customer's specific needs.
- Reliability: the ability to perform the promised service dependably and accurately, e.g. performing the service right the first time, giving accurate information in the billing.

In the marketplace, the winners will be those who can give products or services that are better (in terms of quality), cheaper (in terms of costs) and supplied more efficiently (delivered in time or provided with a timely after-sales service).

FOR MORE INFORMATION

- Zirek, Mehmet. Qualitopia, the Quest for Perfection Through Quality Management Principles. 6 January 2010. Available at SSRN: http://ssrn.com/abstract=1550639

  This paper is about the quest for universal utopia; it focuses on how quality principles in general and quality management principles in particular show us the way to proceed towards 'Qualitopia'.

REFERENCES

Business Dictionary. www.BusinessDictionary.com

Garvin, David A. Competing on the Eight Dimensions of Quality. Harvard Business Review, November-December 1987.

International Organization for Standardization. ISO 9000:2005, Quality management systems – Fundamentals and vocabulary. Obtainable from ISO or ISO members (list at www.iso.org)

Juran, J. and F. Gryna. Quality Planning and Analysis. McGraw-Hill, New York. 1980.

Oxford Dictionaries Online. www.oxforddictionaries.com

Parasuraman, Zeithaml and Berry. Studies PBZ90 and PBZ 91. 1990. Cited in George R. Milne, Mark A. McDonald (eds.). Sport marketing: managing the exchange process, 1999, pp. 10-114 (cited at http://en.wikipedia.org/wiki/Service_quality).

Snyder, I. G. The Quality Revolution. *Quality Progress*, vol. 18, No. 10, October 1985, pp. 63-66.

2. Will a quality product or service cost more and what are the benefits of manufacturing quality products or providing quality service?

Cost of a quality product or service

Paradoxically, the answer to the first part of the above question is both 'yes' and 'no'. How can that be possible? It depends on what aspect of quality we are talking about.

If you want to have a limousine with many gadgets, it will cost you more than a small car with basic amenities. Likewise, if you want to stay in a five-star hotel, it will cost you more than a two-star hotel. Here we are talking about 'quality of design', which is related to the features of the product or the service delivery. Costs are higher for products or services with additional features, and lower for products or services with a lower quality of design. When manufacturers or service providers say that 'quality costs more', they have the quality of design in mind.

'Quality of design' needs to be differentiated from 'quality of conformance', which is the level at which products or services conform to the quality of design. A higher quality of conformance can be achieved by the application of quality management (see question 4). In our car example, after the design of the vehicle, a limousine or a small car, the application of quality control during the manufacturing process will minimize scrap and rework. By adopting a preventive approach, you will have more conforming products and less product recalls, resulting in lower costs. Thus, achieving a higher quality of conformance costs less as it reduces waste due to rework or discarding defective parts.

Quality costs that refer to the quality of conformance are divided into prevention costs, appraisal costs and failure costs. These are detailed below:

- Prevention costs. These are associated with activities designed to prevent poor quality in products and services. For example, a car company may decide to implement a quality improvement project, or to invest in education and training to avoid poor quality in the manufacturing line.
- Appraisal costs. These are associated with measuring, evaluating or auditing products and services to measure their conformance with requirements. For example, our car company wants to inspect the parts coming from suppliers to make sure they meet its quality requirements.
- Failure costs. These are associated with products or services not conforming to requirements or customer needs. Failure costs are divided into: a) internal failure costs, which occur prior to the delivery of the product or service; and b) external failure costs which occur after the product is shipped or while the service is being delivered. For the car company, an internal failure cost would be reworking a door which does not fit when the car is assembled. An external failure cost would result from a customer complaint following the malfunctioning of the gearbox.

You can measure your quality costs. These are actually not the costs of producing quality products but the costs associated with poor quality. They result from deficiencies in the product or service provided to customers and the associated activities which contributed to them. Briscoe and Gryna (2002) summarized the data on quality costs in medium-sized and large firms as follows:

> *The quality related costs are much larger than are shown in the accounting reports. For most companies in the manufacturing and service sectors, these costs usually vary from 10 to 30 % of sales revenue or between 25 to 40 % of operating expenses. Some of these costs are visible; some of them are hidden. Such profit leaks help to justify an improvement effort.*

By focusing on activities related to prevention, you can significantly reduce your appraisal and failure costs; these will result in a drop in your total quality cost and a rise in your profit.

Benefits of manufacturing a quality product or delivering a quality service

After designing your product for a particular market segment, you can attain a higher quality of conformance by applying quality control techniques (see question 8) and quality management (see question 4). By aiming to produce 'right the first time and every time', you will reduce waste and thus lower costs. You will have more satisfied customers who will have fewer problems with your product or service. Customers will come back for more of your product and business will grow as your brand name gets established. If your product or service is under warranty, costs will be minimized because you will have fewer calls for repairs during the after-sales service period. All these will bring about a rise in productivity and a reduction in costs.

You can make use of part of the savings resulting from the higher quality of conformance to add features to your product or service at no real extra cost and no added cost for the customer. You would thus raise your quality of design without a price increase. This would have a major effect on your sales revenue, improve your market share and engender in your customers a higher level of satisfaction. You can thus have cycles of continual improvement through higher quality of conformance, followed by higher quality of design, again followed by higher quality of conformance, and so on.

FOR MORE INFORMATION

- Dhawan, Sanjeev. Cost of Quality (COQ). http://www.tqmschool.com/articles/TQM%20-%20Cost%20of%20Quality.pdf

  A four-page document detailing a business approach to the cost of quality. Briefly discusses what, why, when and the benefits of COQ.

- Kajiwara, Takehisa. Factors Influencing the Use of Quality Costs in TQM Environments: Evidence from Japan. December 2009. AAA 2010 Management Accounting Section (MAS) Meeting Paper. Available at SSRN: http://ssrn.com/abstract=1444763

  This paper examines some of the factors that influence the use of quality costs in TQM (Total Quality Management) environments; it is based on survey data collected from Japanese manufacturing firms.

- Keogh, William and others. Data Collection and the Economics of Quality: Identifying Problems, 2006. http://mams.rmit.edu.au/kh85606qs2qn.pdf

  This paper illustrates the problems that arise in collecting appropriate data for a cost of quality exercise and evaluating the economic cost of quality.

- Ryan, John. Making the Economic Case for Quality. An ASQ white paper. 2004. Downloadable at: http://faculty.mercer.edu/burtner_j/documents/ASQWhitePaperEconCaseQuality.pdf

  This is a review of current knowledge about the economic impact of an organizational focus on quality/quality improvement. It reveals the impact of quality management practice on almost every area of organizational performance, including bottom-line measures, market measures and internal operating measures.

REFERENCES

American Society for Quality. Basic Concepts – Cost of Quality (COQ). Downloadable at: http://asq.org/learn-about-quality/cost-of-quality/overview/overview.html

Briscoe, Nat and Frank M. Gryna. Assessing the Cost of Poor Quality in a Small Business. Downloadable at: www.qimpro.com

Brust, Peter J. and Frank M. Gryna. Quality and Economics: Five Key Issues. October 2002. Downloadable at: www.qualityprogress.org, free for members of the American Society for Quality or at a price for others.

3. What is quality management and what are its four components?

The term 'quality management' (QM) is defined in ISO 9000 as "coordinated activities to direct and control an organization with regard to quality".

To direct and control an organization, its management should first set out its quality policy and related quality objectives and then specify activities related to quality planning, quality control, quality assurance and quality improvement.

The objective of QM is to ensure that all company-wide activities necessary for enhancing the satisfaction of customers and other stakeholders are carried out effectively and efficiently. QM focuses not only on product/service quality but also on the means for achieving it.

The four components of QM are briefly explained below.

1. Quality Planning (QP)

Quality Planning is "a part of quality management focused on setting quality objectives and specifying necessary operational processes and related resources to fulfil quality objectives." (ISO 9000:2005 3.2.9)

QP is a systematic process that translates quality policy into measurable objectives and requirements and lays down a sequence of steps for realizing them within a specified time frame. The results of QP are presented, for use by all concerned, in the form of a quality plan, a document specifying which procedures and associated resources will be applied by whom and when. Such quality plans are prepared separately for specific processes, products or contracts.

2. Quality Control (QC)

Quality Control is "a part of quality management focused on fulfilling quality requirements." (ISO 9000:2005 3.2.10)

QC helps in evaluating the actual operating performance of the process and product and, after comparing actual performance with planned targets, it prompts action on the deviations found, if any.

QC is a shop-floor and online activity that requires adequate resources, including skilled people, firstly to control the processes and then to carry out timely corrections when process and/or product parameters go beyond prescribed limits.

3. Quality Assurance (QA)

Quality Assurance is "a part of quality management focused on providing confidence that quality requirements will be fulfilled." (ISO 9000:2005 3.2.11)

Both customers and management have a need for an assurance of quality because they are not in a position to oversee operations themselves.

QA activities establish the extent to which quality will be, is being or has been fulfilled. The means to provide the assurance need to be built into the process, such as documenting control plans, documenting specifications, defining responsibilities, providing resources, performing quality audits, maintaining records, reporting reviews. QA is more comprehensive than QC, which is part of it.

4. Quality Improvement (QI)

Quality improvement is "a part of quality management focused on increasing the ability to fulfil quality requirements." (ISO 9000:2005 3.2.12)

Remaining static at whatever level you have reached is not an option if your organization is to survive. To maintain your performance and your position in the market, you will have to carry out quality improvement activities on a continual basis. Such improvement activities include refining the existing methods, modifying processes first to reduce variations and second to yield more and more by consuming less and less resources. If you want to have a breakthrough, this will often require new methods, techniques, technologies, processes.

The figure below shows the evolution from quality control to quality management.

Conceptualization of quality management as defined in ISO 9000:2005

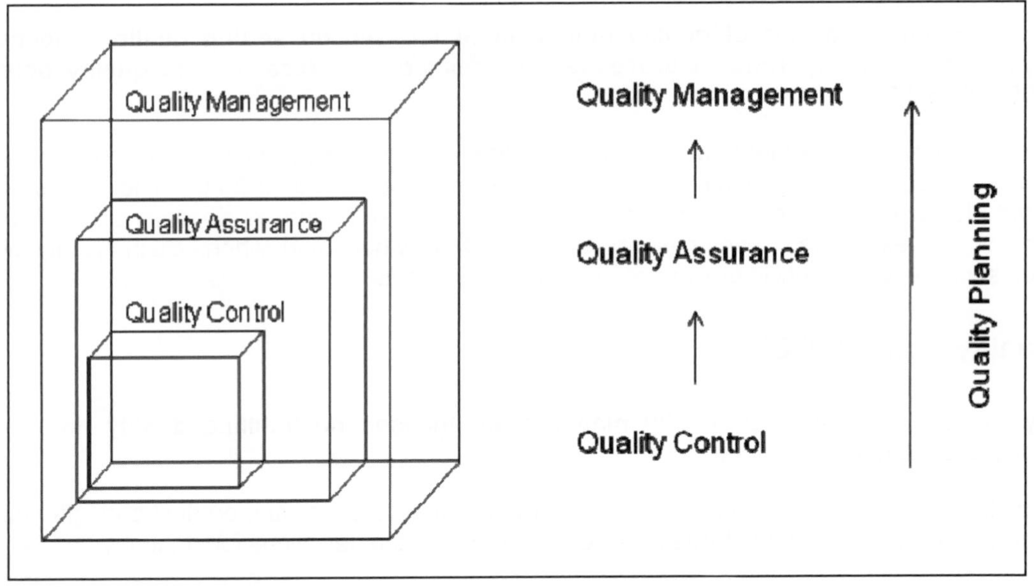

Source: S.C. Arora, India.

The illustration shows that quality control (QC) is the core activity within QM. When you carry out QC within a defined system, you have upgraded your QC to quality assurance (QA). If you then continue carrying out quality improvement activities based on the analysis of the data resulting from the measurement of processes/product as well as of data on customer feedback, you have moved towards QM. In that sense, quality planning remains an integral part of all steps in quality management.

To put it simply, the four components of QM mean:

- Quality planning – Can we make it OK?
- Quality control – Are we making it OK?
- Quality assurance – Will we continue making it OK?
- Quality improvement – Could we make it better?

Quality control, being the core activity of quality management, should be established first by an organization. It will, inter alia, require the availability of equipment and machines of the requisite capability, skilled persons, accurate measuring instruments and basic support services. Without these, it will not be possible to exercise proper quality control and then to move towards quality assurance and quality management.

FOR MORE INFORMATION

- Dale, Barrie and Jim Plunkett. Managing Quality. Blackwell's Publishing. Blackwell's Online Bookshop, Blackwell's Extra, 50 Broad Street, Oxford OX1 3BQ, United Kingdom, Email: bob.online@blackwell.co.uk Internet: http://blackwell.co.uk

  Provides an appreciation of the concepts and principles of total quality management (TQM).

- International Organization for Standardization. Quality management principles. This brochure can be freely downloaded as a PDF file from ISO (www.iso.org).

  This document introduces the eight quality management principles on which the quality management system standards of the ISO 9000 family are based. These principles can be used by senior management as a framework to guide their organizations towards improved performance.

- Lakhal, Lassâad and others. Quality management practices and their impact on performance. *International Journal of Quality & Reliability Management*, vol. 23, Issue 6, 2006, pp. 625–646. http://www.emeraldinsight.com/journals.htm?articleid=1562387&show=html

  This paper aims to explore the relationship between quality management practices and their impact on performance.

- Office of the Secretary of Defense. Small Business Guidebook to Quality Management. Quality Management Office. Washington, D.C. 20301-3016. This guide book is freely downloadable from http://dodreports.com/pdf/ada310869.pdf

  The aim of this guidebook is to help small businesses make the transition to a quality culture. It was developed by the United States Federal Government and the Department of Defense to enable small businesses to catch up with the rapidly spreading quality movement.

REFERENCES

International Organization for Standardization. ISO 9000:2005, Quality management systems – Fundamentals and vocabulary. Obtainable from ISO or ISO members (list at www.iso.org).

Price, Frank. Right First Time – Using quality control for profit. Gower Publishing (Customer Service). 1986. A priced publication of Book Point Limited, 130 Milton Park, Abingdon, Oxon OX14 4SB, United Kingdom. Email: orders@bookpoint.co.uk, Internet: www.gowerpub.com

4. How do quality control system activities relate to quality management? Should I start with a quality control system before setting up a quality management system?

Quality control system (QCS) activities focus on all functions that need to be performed to produce a conforming product. These include providing an adequate infrastructure and work environment, setting up specifications for raw materials and finished product, developing work instructions for employees, procuring raw materials and components of the right quality, controlling the production processes, proper handling and storage of materials and products, carrying out stage and final inspection of the product, timely maintenance of the process hardware and testing equipment. The interaction of QCS activities is depicted in the QCS model in the figure below.

QCS model

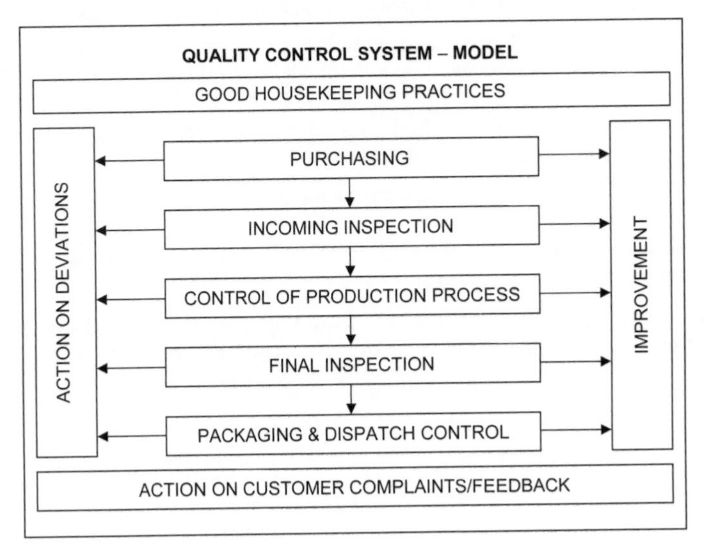

Source: S.C. Arora, India.

Quality control is one of the most important components of quality management (see question 3). If quality control is not properly conducted, quality management will not be effective. Therefore, before establishing a quality management system (QMS), it will first be necessary to have an effective quality control system (QCS) in place. Once the QCS stabilizes, then you can add the other requirements of QMS (see question 32). Even before you set up a QCS, it is also advisable to set up good housekeeping practices, by using the Japanese 5S for example (see question 10).

You should review your current QCS and carry out the following activities as a minimum, if they are not already being done:

a. **Provide adequate infrastructure.** This includes providing and maintaining building equipment and machines, utilities, facilities, support services. For example, a food handling or processing plant should have hard paved roads inside the premises, an efficient drainage system, walls up to a height of 1.3 meters of smooth surface (tiled), self-closing doors, toilets, hand-washing and changing facilities for personnel, pest control facilities.

b. **Establish a proper work environment and hygiene.** This means ensuring adequate lighting, proper ventilation, temperature and humidity control, proper noise/vibration levels. It also means adhering to good personal hygiene practices (using head gear/masks, abstaining from chewing gum and the use of loose jewellery during production in a food processing plant).

c. **Make workers aware of quality practices.** For example, make sure your workers understand the job clearly before they start. They should handle the product carefully to prevent damage and avoid mixing defective items with good ones.

d. **Make available easy-to-understand raw material and product specifications.** Unless specifications are clearly drawn and understood by all concerned, no amount of checking will help. For example, the types of defects that should not be allowed must be clearly known to your workers and checkers.

e. **Make available easy-to-understand instructions for performing work.** If the competency level of your employees is inadequate, they will need verbal or written work instructions (preferably in the local language) which should make generous use of graphics rather than text only. Sometimes, a sample of the item or component to be made (in case of leather products or garments, for example) can serve the purpose better.

f. **Purchase raw materials of acceptable quality from suppliers.** Buying only at the lowest price without looking into the quality of raw materials and other supplies is not a good practice. Dealing with a few suppliers with whom you had good experience in the past is better than looking for a large number of new suppliers. It is good to verify the credentials of the suppliers through your own survey of their business premises or by obtaining feedback from other companies doing business with them. To receive products of acceptable quality from suppliers, it is equally necessary for you clearly to explain to them in advance your product specifications and your procedures for accepting supplies from them.

g. **Store your raw materials and other supplies properly to prevent mix up and spoilage.** To run your business you will need some inventory of raw materials and other consumable items. These items should be handled carefully and stored properly to prevent a mix up and spoilage. For example, in food processing companies, food and non-food items (like oil, lubricants, detergents, chemicals, machinery spares) should be isolated from each other. Hazardous materials will require extra precautions during storage. Proper temperature control of food items (through the use of freezers and cold storage) is required to prevent spoilage.

h. **Check or inspect raw materials and other supplies before use.** You should check raw materials ordered from suppliers on receipt to determine whether they meet your equirements. For example, when raw produce from farms arrive at the plant for grading or processing, it should not be accepted if it contains extraneous substances, is decomposed, etc.

i. **Maintain your machines, building and production facilities regularly.** You should plan and carry out regular preventive maintenance of your machines to ensure that they are in a fit state when production starts. Preventive maintenance will also reduce chances of machine breakdowns. For example, in the case of food processing, a programme for cleaning and disinfecting all parts of the building, facilities and equipment should be drawn up and followed. Holes, drains and other places from where pests may come should be examined regularly to ensure that they remain sealed.

j. **Maintain measuring instruments and check their accuracy (calibration).** If you use instruments like thermometers, pressure gauges, viscosity meters, micrometers, they should be checked periodically and repair and maintenance work should be undertaken as required. The accuracy of these instruments may be affected over a period of use. You would therefore need to calibrate your instruments by comparing them with other instruments of known accuracy.

k. **Follow proper production process steps.** First you should analyse your production process and each step of the process should be documented in the form of a process flow diagram. This will help your workers to follow the steps, preventing errors and thus reducing the need for reprocessing.

l. **Control the process to achieve product specification.** Some steps in the production process will need controls, for example, weight control, temperature control, time control, pH control, Brix control, colour control, visual control. You should set limits for such controls and monitor them.

m. **Prevent the manufacture of defective products.** For this you need to carry out proper checks on the process and keep checking the product intermittently. If any deviation is observed after these checks, you should take timely action. In this way you can improve the chances of producing a defect-free product. This also means that you are close to performing 'right the first time'.

n. **Make use of statistical techniques, such as sampling plans and control charts for process control, and other QC tools.** There are various quality control tools which can help you systematically to collect and record process control and product inspection data and then to analyse the data with a view to taking actions on the root causes of problems should they occur (refer to question 8). The check sheet is a simple but useful tool for tracking your products' most common defects.

o. **Conduct stage inspection during manufacturing.** In addition to certain checks on the product being carried out by your operators either visually or with the help of simple instruments, a stage inspection (on 100% or sampling basis) may be carried out by your supervisor or QC inspector after completion of each process step or group of process steps. This will ensure that defective products, if any, are detected and set right at the earliest possible time.

p. **Conduct final inspection of the finished product and packaging against set specifications.** This is your last opportunity to check your product. After this, the product leaves your factory and if any defect is found by the customer or user, it will not be good news, as you will need much time and money to correct the situation. Therefore, the final check on your product should be performed carefully; this may involve conducting certain tests in the laboratory. You should also decide on the person who will release the product to the customer. If, during final inspection, you come across some deviation from specifications, you may either reprocess the product or, if reprocessing is not possible, reject it. Alternatively, you could decide to release a product with deviations or concessions, but you should first inform the customer of this and obtain his/her approval before shipping the product.

q. **Handle the product with care both during internal processing and during delivery to the customer.** A good product may be damaged by mishandling during production, not being stored properly (e.g. at the required temperature), not being packed correctly or during shipment to the customer. It is therefore necessary for you to take proper care of the product at all stages.

r. **Obtain feedback on the findings of the final inspection and take appropriate action.** The results of the final inspection, including deviations found by you if any (as at P. above), should be shared with your production workers so that they can ensure that such deviations will not occur again.

s. **Analyse customer complaints or feedback and take action to remove the causes of complaints.** If you get customer complaint(s), the first thing for you to do is to acknowledge and accept the complaint and provide relief to the customer, either by repairing the product or by replacing it free of charge. Your action will depend on the nature of the complaint and your contractual obligations. The matter should not end there. Now, internally, you should try to find the root cause of the complaint and, if necessary, make changes to the process that contributed to the complaint. Such action will ensure that you do not get the same type of complaint again. Some customers are also likely to give a positive feedback or make suggestions to you. You should thank them for these and then find out whether the suggestions can be used to improve your process or processes. In that case, the identified process should be so improved.

t. **Take corrective action on deviations found, if any.** You may find opportunities for taking corrective action in the deviations found in the raw materials received from suppliers, deviations revealed during process controls and during stage and final inspections; you may also see such opportunities in customer complaints. To decide on a corrective action, you will need to analyse the problem and find its root cause. Once the root cause or causes have been identified, action should be taken to eliminate them in a way that will prevent the problem from occurring again.

For you to be successful in quality control, workers at all levels must cooperate actively. This means that continual development of your workers will be necessary. The Japanese 'revolution in quality' is largely the result of comprehensive education and training for all functions and staff levels, from top management to the workers.

Initially while setting up the quality control system, you may find that additional expenditure may be required. However, the costs of reprocessing, repairing and rejecting products internally will fall considerably when the system is up and running. Furthermore, the costs of withdrawing your product from the market, handling customer complaints and providing replacements will also be reduced, resulting in overall savings.

The above model of a quality control system was implemented by selected small and medium-sized enterprises (SMEs) in the light engineering products sector in Bangladesh (2009-2010) under the joint UNIDO-ITC Bangladesh Quality Support Project. Selected SMEs first implemented the Japanese 5S and, after achieving some promising results (e.g. one SME increased its productivity by 30%), they developed and implemented the QCS. Enterprises producing leather goods implemented 5S (see question 10) and obtained interesting results after some of them were trained in understanding, implementing and auditing the ISO 9001 quality management system.

FOR MORE INFORMATION

- Caplen, R.H. A Practical Approach to Quality Control. 5th ed. 1998. A priced publication of Random House Business Books Ltd, 20 Vauxhall Bridge Road, London SW1V 2SA, United Kingdom, Email: enquiries@randomhouse.co.uk, Internet: http://randomhouse.co.uk

  This book gives an introduction to the practical aspects of quality control, showing how suitable techniques can be identified and integrated into a cost-conscious system.

- Office of the Secretary of Defense. Small Business Guidebook to Quality Management. Quality Management Office. Washington, D.C. 20301-3016. This guide book is freely downloadable from http://dodreports.com/pdf/ada310869.pdf

  The aim of this guidebook is to help small businesses make the transition to a quality culture. Developed by the United States Federal Government and the Department of Defense, it helps small businesses to keep up to date with the rapidly spreading quality movement.

- Webber, Larry and Michael Wallace. Quality Control for Dummies. Publisher for Dummies ISBN 0470069090. Can be purchased from www.amazon.com

  This book provides expert techniques for introducing quality methods to your company, collecting data, designing quality processes, and more. This hands-on guide gives you the tools you will need to enhance your company's quality.

REFERENCES

International Organization for Standardization. ISO 9001:2008, Quality management systems – Requirements. Obtainable from ISO or ISO members (list at www.iso.org).

5. What is the quality management approach to managing the sustained success of an organization?

As defined by ISO 9004, sustained success is the ability of an organization to achieve and maintain its objectives in the long term.

The immediate objective of any organization is to satisfy customers by consistently giving them products and services meeting their requirements. Effective implementation of ISO 9001 will help you to achieve this objective. However, if you wish to attain your long-term objective of economic survival, you should use ISO 9004, which supports companies seeking sustained success. ISO 9004 can be used by any organization regardless of its size, type or activity.

ISO 9004 provides a wider focus on quality management than ISO 9001. While ISO 9001 addresses the needs and expectations of customers, ISO 9004 takes into account the needs and expectations of all relevant interested parties. Customers need and expect product quality, an acceptable price and delivery performance; employees search for a good work environment and job security; society expects a commitment to ethical behaviour and environmental protection; owners and shareholders push for sustained profitability. Meeting all these needs and expectations will help you achieve sustained success.

The important elements of ISO 9004 include:

- *Managing for the sustained success of an organization* – covering processes required for sustained success, the organizational environment, the needs and expectations of interested parties.
- *Strategy and policy* – including its formation, deployment, and communication.
- *Resource management* – including financial resources, people, suppliers and partners, infrastructure, work environment, knowledge, information technology and natural resources.
- *Process management* – including process planning and control and process responsibility and authority.
- *Monitoring, measurement, analysis and review* – including key performance indicators, internal audit, self-assessment and benchmarking.
- *Improvement, innovation and learning* – covering small-step continual improvement in the workplace and significant improvements in the entire organization, innovation in order to meet the needs and expectations of interested parties, and encouraging improvement and innovation through learning.

ISO 9004:2009 complements ISO 9001:2008 (and vice versa). If you have not implemented ISO 9001 earlier and you wish to use ISO 9004 straight away, you can do so. As ISO 9004 is a guidance standard, it is not intended for certification, regulatory or contractual use, or as a guide for the implementation of ISO 9001. Annex C to ISO 9004 provides a clause-by-clause correspondence between ISO 9001:2008 and ISO 9004:2009.

The self-assessment tool, given in Annex A to ISO 9004:2009, can help you to assess the performance of your organization and the degree of maturity of its management system. The results of the self-assessment can also help you to identify areas for improvement or innovation and determine priorities for subsequent actions.

FOR MORE INFORMATION

- Al-Dabal, Jamal K. Is Total Quality Management Enough for Competitive Advantage? Realities in Organizations Implementing Change Initiatives: with examples from the United States and the Developing World. 15 March 1999. ISBN 1-58112/126/1. http://www.bookpump.com/dps/pdf-b/1121261b.pdf

  Presents a discussion on realities in organizations when it comes to implementing major change initiatives. TQM's fit for the services sector is discussed with emphasis on customer satisfaction.

- From Certification to Excellence, Quality Management to Sustained Success. http://www.cii-iq.in/events/QS_09/ppts/Mark%20Fraser.pdf

  A didactic PowerPoint presentation by Mark Fraser, Group Product Manager – Sustainability, British Standards Institution (BSI). Good visual summary of ISO 9004:2009.

- IRCA INform. Issue 23, 2009. http://www.irca.org/inform/issue23/DHoyle.html

  This carries an article titled 'ISO 9004:2009 – Towards sustained success' by David Hoyle, in which the author explains the changes that have been made in ISO 9004 and what they could mean for ISO 9001.

- Powell, Thomas C. Total Quality Management as Competitive Advantage: A Review and Empirical Study. *Strategic Management Journal*, vol. 16, pp. 15-37, 1995. http://www.business.uzh.ch/professorships/som/stu/Teaching/FS10/MA/som/Powell_1995_TQM_practices.pdf

  This article examines TQM as a potential source of sustainable competitive advantage, reviews existing empirical evidence and reports the findings of a new empirical study of TQM's performance consequences.

REFERENCES

International Organization for Standardization

- ISO 9004:2009, Managing for sustained success of an organization – A quality management approach. Obtainable from ISO or ISO members (list at www.iso.org).
- ISO 9001:2008, Quality Management Systems – Requirements. Obtainable from ISO or ISO members (list at www.iso.org).
- New edition of ISO 9004 maps out the path forward to 'sustained success'. ISO press release (Ref. 1263 of 2009) freely downloadable from http://www.iso.org/iso/pressrelease.htm?refid=Ref1263

6. What are national quality awards? Are they relevant for SMEs?

National quality awards (NQA) play an important role in promoting and rewarding excellence in organizational performance. In the short history of the development of NQAs, three awards have played a key role. They are the Deming Prize (Japan, 1951), the Malcolm Baldrige National Quality Award (United States, 1987) and the EFQM (European Foundation for Quality Management) Excellence Award (Europe, 1992). Many countries have modelled their award programmes on these three awards.

Quality awards are now popular in all parts of the world. For example, there are NQAs in Australia, almost all countries of Latin America and the Caribbean, in the Middle East (Egypt and Israel), in Asia (Hong Kong SAR, India, Malaysia, Singapore, Sri Lanka), and in Africa (Mauritius, South Africa).

Some governments have shown strong commitment to ensuring the successful implementation of NQAs. For example, the Malcolm Baldrige National Quality Award and its associated awards were established by the Malcolm Baldrige National Quality Improvement Act of 1987 and the awards are given by the President of the United States. Another example is the National Quality Award of Argentina, which was also established by law and is supported by government funds.

NQAs are designed to promote quality awareness, understanding of the requirements for quality excellence, and the sharing of information on successful strategies and their benefits. NQAs typically contain 7 to 10 criteria for performance excellence (with 20 to 30 subcriteria). The 10 usual criteria elements are as follows:

- Leadership
- Strategic planning
- Customer and market focus
- Information and analysis
- Human resource focus
- Process management
- Business results
- Impact on society
- Resources
- Performance and management of suppliers/partners

For example, the European Foundation for Quality Management has nine criteria elements which are divided into two categories: enablers and results (see figure below). The enabler criteria are concerned with how the organization conducts itself, how it manages its staff and resources, how it plans its strategy and how it reviews and monitors key processes. The organization's results are what it achieves. These encompass the level of satisfaction among the organization's employees and customers, its impact on the wider community and key performance indicators.

The EFQM Excellence Model Framework

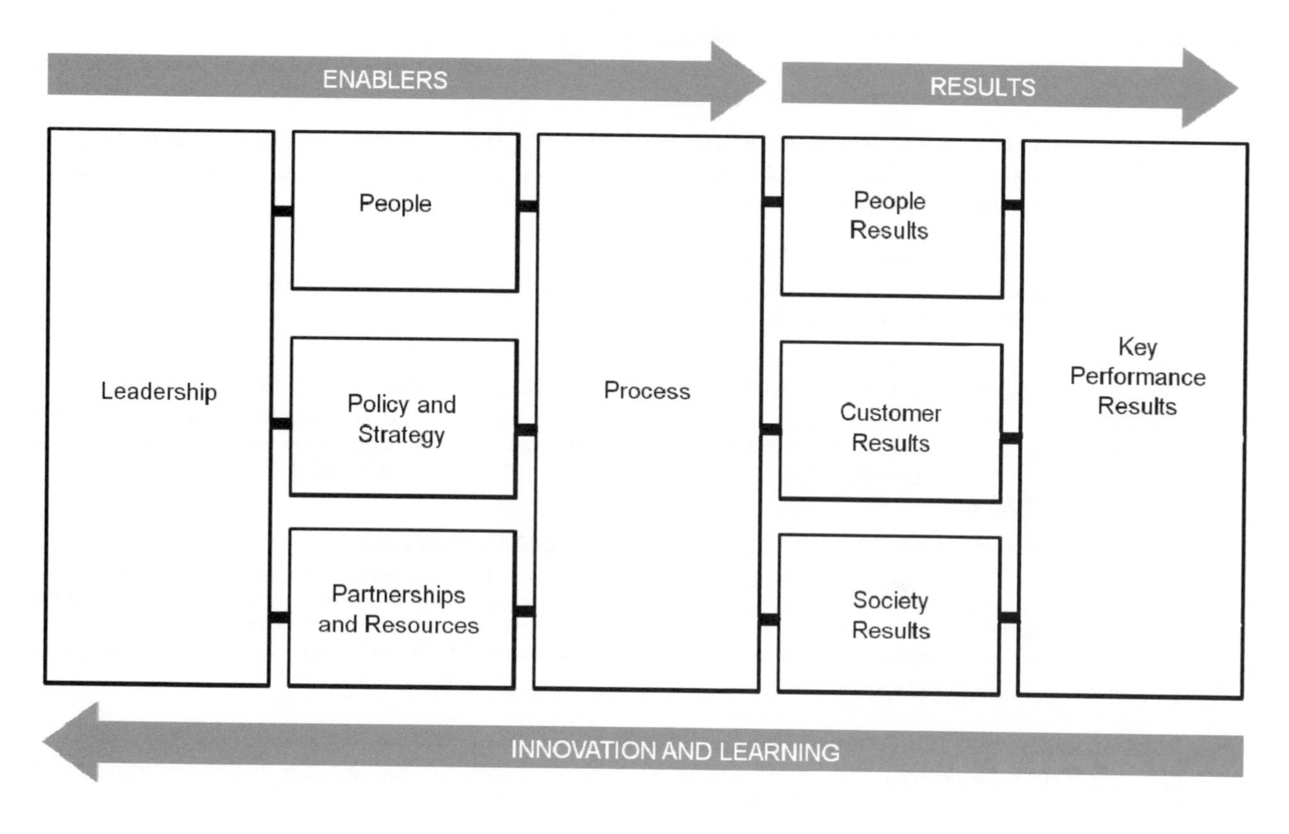

Source: British Quality Foundation.

The British Quality Foundation (BQF) has also developed a software tool called 'BQF snapshot' which will run on most Windows-based computers. It provides a quick and simple way of finding out how your organization measures up to the characteristics of excellence.

The general assessment process for the selection of the winners of an NQA involves preliminary scrutiny and assessment of the applicants' data for preliminary selection, followed by site visits and then final selection by a panel of judges. Feedback reports on the findings of the entire review process, covering among others the applicants' strengths and areas for improvement, are also given to the applicants. The names of the winners are displayed on the website of the NQA administering organization and the awards are given to the winners in a ceremony which receives huge publicity.

Separate awards are given by most countries for different sizes and sectors of industry. For example, in the case of the Malcolm Baldrige Award, the categories awarded include manufacturing, small business, health care, non-profit activities and education.

SMEs are becoming increasingly crucial to national competitiveness and job markets (in the United States, SMEs contribute with more than half of the country's total value produced, while the proportions attributed to SMEs in Singapore and Hong Kong SAR are 91% and 98%, respectively). Several countries/areas have modified their award criteria for SMEs; for example, the national quality award organizations of Australia, Chile, India and Hong Kong SAR have simplified their NQA criteria for SMEs.

SMEs can also apply for an NQA. Such an award will boost the image of an SME on both domestic and international markets.

FOR MORE INFORMATION

- Australian Business Excellence Awards. www.businessawards.com.au/

  The Awards are open to any organization operating within Australia. This includes any private or public company, multinational subsidiaries, government and non-government organizations.

- European Foundation for Quality Management (EFQM). EFQM Excellence Award: www.efqm.org/en/tabid/132/default.aspx

  Portal of the EFQM, which is the custodian of the EFQM Excellence Model, a framework that is helping over 30 000 organizations around the globe to strive for sustainable excellence.

- Malcolm Baldrige National Quality Award. http://www.nist.gov/baldrige/

  Presents a full explanation of the Malcolm Baldrige National Quality Award, the advantages of taking the Award; also provides a thorough explanation of the Award by sector.

- National Quality/Business Excellence Awards in different countries. http://www.nist.gov/baldrige/community/upload/National_Quality_Business_Excellence_Awards_in_Different_Countries.xls

  *The link gives a list (with websites wherever available) of 103 national quality/business excellence awards in different countries; the list is based on research undertaken on behalf of the National Institute of Standards and Technology (NIST) by Musli Mohammad (*m.mohammad@massey.ac.nz*) and Robin Mann (*r.s.mann@massey.ac.nz*), Centre for Organizational Excellence Research,* www.coer.org.nz

- Rajiv Gandhi National Quality Award (India). http://www.bis.org.in/other/rgnqa_geninfo.htm

  The Rajiv Gandhi National Quality Award was instituted by the Bureau of Indian Standards in 1991, with a view to encouraging Indian manufacturing and service organizations to strive for excellence and giving special recognition to the leaders of the quality movement in India. This award is intended to generate the interest and involvement of Indian industry in quality programmes, drive India's products and services to higher levels of quality and equip India's industry to meet the challenges of the domestic and international markets.

- Singapore Quality Award. http://www.spring.gov.sg/QualityStandards/be/bea/Pages/singapore-quality-award.aspx#what

  Launched in 1994 with the Prime Minister as its patron, the Singapore Quality Award is an award conferred on organizations that demonstrate the highest standards of business excellence.

- Sri Lanka National Quality Award. http://www.slsi.lk/national-quality-awards.php

  The Sri Lanka National Quality Award is an annual Award to recognize Sri Lankan organizations that excel in quality management and quality achievement. The quality award programme is organized and implemented by the Marketing and Promotion Division of the Sri Lanka Standards Institution (SLSI).

REFERENCES

British Quality Foundation. http://www.bqf.org.uk/ex_framework.htm

Tan, Kay C. A comparative study of 16 national quality awards. *The TQM Magazine*, vol. 14, Issue 3, pp. 165–171. Available free from http://pessoas.feb.unesp.br/vagner/files/2010/03/Quality-Awards_comparative-study.pdf

7. What is the concept of 'triple role' in quality management?

Everyone in an organization can be seen in a triple role, i.e., as a customer, a processor and a supplier.

Quality is meeting customer expectations (see question 1) and is achieved by coordinating and managing many interrelated activities, market research, design, purchasing, production, testing, inspection, packaging and shipping. As pointed out by John Ruskin (1819-1900): "Quality is never an accident; it is always the result of intelligent effort." To meet the expectations of our customers, we must obtain the product specifications from these customers, and produce and supply according to these specifications. Managing this supplier-customer interface is a key element in managing quality.

We have a tendency to view suppliers and customers as being external to our organization. Suppliers provide us with raw materials, spare parts and information, and customers purchase our products and services. We tend to forget that we also have suppliers and customers inside our organization. For example, the marketing department identifies the characteristics demanded by users. Now acting as a supplier, the marketing department communicates this information to the design department, which is its internal customer. The design department, taking on the role of processor, prepares specifications based on this information, and passes the completed specifications on to the production department, its internal customer. Here the design department acts as supplier to the production department. In this example, the design department has performed a triple role, acting as customer, processor and supplier in turn.

The concept of 'triple role' is evident in the process approach in quality management. An activity that uses resources and is managed in order to convert inputs into outputs can be considered a process. Inputs are provided by a supplier to a customer who transforms these inputs into outputs to be given to another customer. Transformation of the inputs into outputs is done by the former customer acting as a processor. The figure below illustrates the supplier-customer chain:

Customer-supplier chain

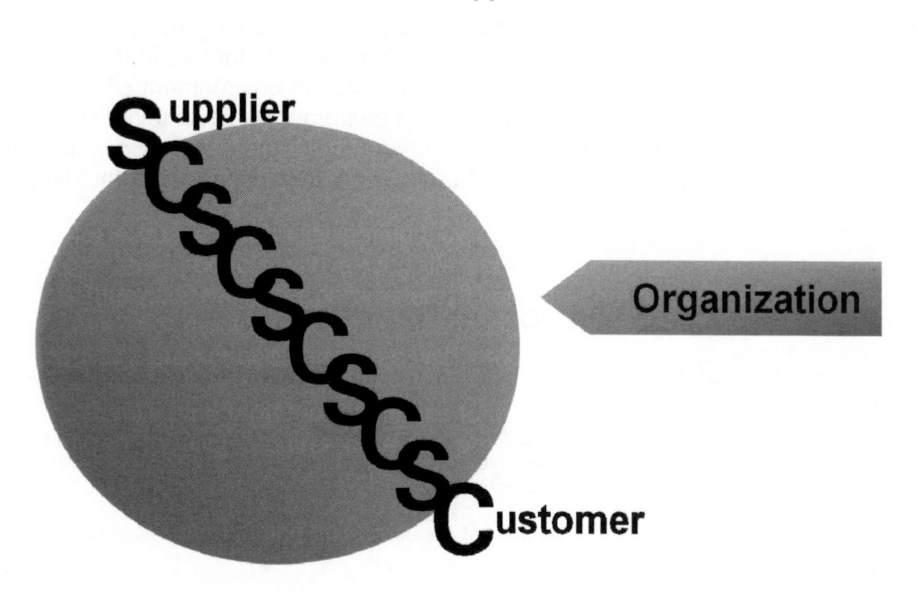

Source: Oakland (2003), adapted.

All organizations have what is known as quality chains of customers and suppliers. It is important to ensure that these quality chains are not broken at any point so that the expectations of the customer can be met. Otherwise, the organization will be faced with customers irritated by the delivery of a defective product or service because of a failure at one of the quality chains. For example, if you ordered a vegetarian meal for a flight through your travel agent and he did not communicate this to the airline, you will not get your special meal and the air hostess will have to put up with your displeasure.

At each supplier-customer interface in the organization, it is important to agree on the requirements as there is no point in receiving products that are not fit for use. This will ensure that proper inputs are received for processing, which should then be carried out in such a way as to keep variation in the process to a minimum. The outputs should match the specifications agreed with the next customer. At each interface, customers should refuse to accept nonconforming products, which should be sent back to the suppliers. This will give a message that only conforming products are accepted, reduce waste, and minimize customer complaints and product recalls. The 'triple role' concept will promote a culture of making the product right the first time and every time.

Ideally, each person in the organization should adopt the 'triple role' concept, identify his/her suppliers and customers, take ownership of his/her process, and reduce variation in the process to a minimum.

As a customer, ask questions such as:

- Who are my immediate suppliers?
- Have I communicated my real requirements to them?
- Have I agreed the manner of checking the conformity of their inputs with them?

As a supplier, ask questions such as:

- Who are my immediate customers?
- Have they communicated their real requirements to me?
- Have they agreed with me the manner of checking the conformity of my outputs to them?

As a processor, ask questions such as:

- Is my process capable of meeting the requirements of my immediate customers?
- If not, how can my process be improved to meet these requirements?

An organization has to put its own house in order first by consolidating its quality chains of internal suppliers and customers before involving its external suppliers and customers in the concept of the 'triple role'. Creating a culture that promotes the concept will establish an environment of trust between internal suppliers and customers. Successful internal supplier and customer quality chains will lead to successful external supplier and customer interfaces. In such an environment, there will be constant and immediate feedback resulting in reduction of waste, improved customer satisfaction and continual improvement of processes.

FOR MORE INFORMATION

- Department of Trade and Industry, United Kingdom. Total Quality Management in the series on 'From Quality to Excellence'. http://dti.gov.uk/quality

  This document explains that external and internal customer-supplier interfaces form the core of total quality management. It highlights the processes at each interface and the need for commitment to quality, communication of the quality message and recognition of the need to change the culture of organizations.

- Gašparík, Josef and Sylvia Szalayová. Quality Management System in Construction Firm. http://huog.hr/sesta/Gasparik.pdf

  Explains the triple role as it applies to the construction sector.

REFERENCES

Hutchins, David C. Just in Time. Gower Publishing Ltd., 1999. www.gowerpub.com

Oakland, John S. Total quality management: Text with cases. Butterworth-Heinemann, 2003. www.elsevierdirect.com

8. What are the 'Seven Tools of Quality Control' and how do they assist in solving quality-related problems?

The 'Seven Tools of Quality Control' are a set of graphical/pictorial techniques to assist you in troubleshooting quality-related issues.

Kaoru Ishikawa, known as the Japanese father of quality, formalized the Seven Basic Tools of Quality Control. Ishikawa believed that 95% of a company's problems could be solved by using these seven tools and that, with the exception of control charts, they could easily be taught to any member of the organization. Their easy-to-use approach combined with their graphical nature makes statistical analysis easier to understand and apply. The seven tools are described below.

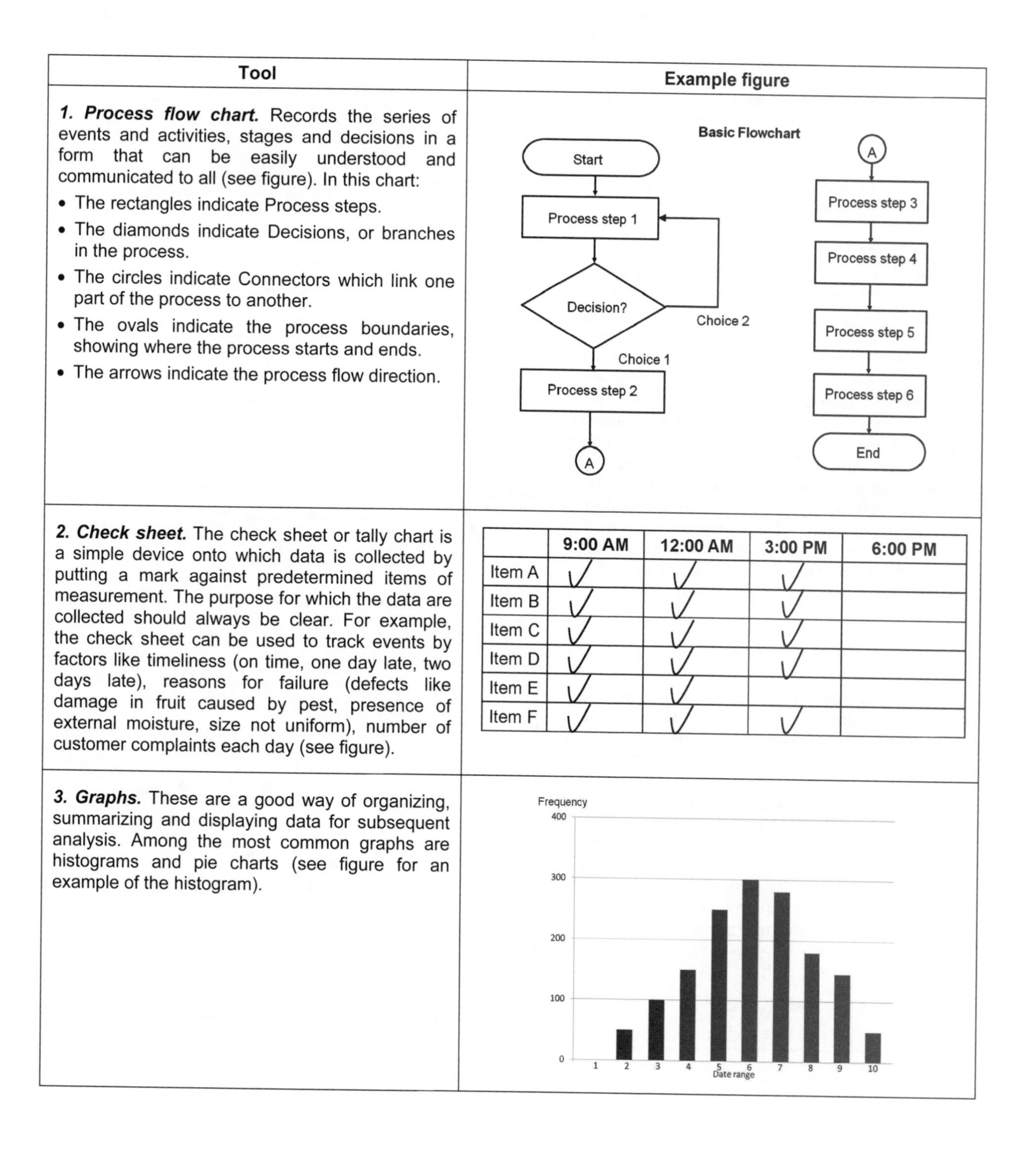

Tool	Example figure
1. Process flow chart. Records the series of events and activities, stages and decisions in a form that can be easily understood and communicated to all (see figure). In this chart: • The rectangles indicate Process steps. • The diamonds indicate Decisions, or branches in the process. • The circles indicate Connectors which link one part of the process to another. • The ovals indicate the process boundaries, showing where the process starts and ends. • The arrows indicate the process flow direction.	Basic Flowchart
2. Check sheet. The check sheet or tally chart is a simple device onto which data is collected by putting a mark against predetermined items of measurement. The purpose for which the data are collected should always be clear. For example, the check sheet can be used to track events by factors like timeliness (on time, one day late, two days late), reasons for failure (defects like damage in fruit caused by pest, presence of external moisture, size not uniform), number of customer complaints each day (see figure).	(check sheet below)
3. Graphs. These are a good way of organizing, summarizing and displaying data for subsequent analysis. Among the most common graphs are histograms and pie charts (see figure for an example of the histogram).	Histogram

	9:00 AM	12:00 AM	3:00 PM	6:00 PM
Item A	✓	✓	✓	
Item B	✓	✓	✓	
Item C	✓	✓	✓	
Item D	✓	✓	✓	
Item E	✓	✓		
Item F	✓	✓	✓	

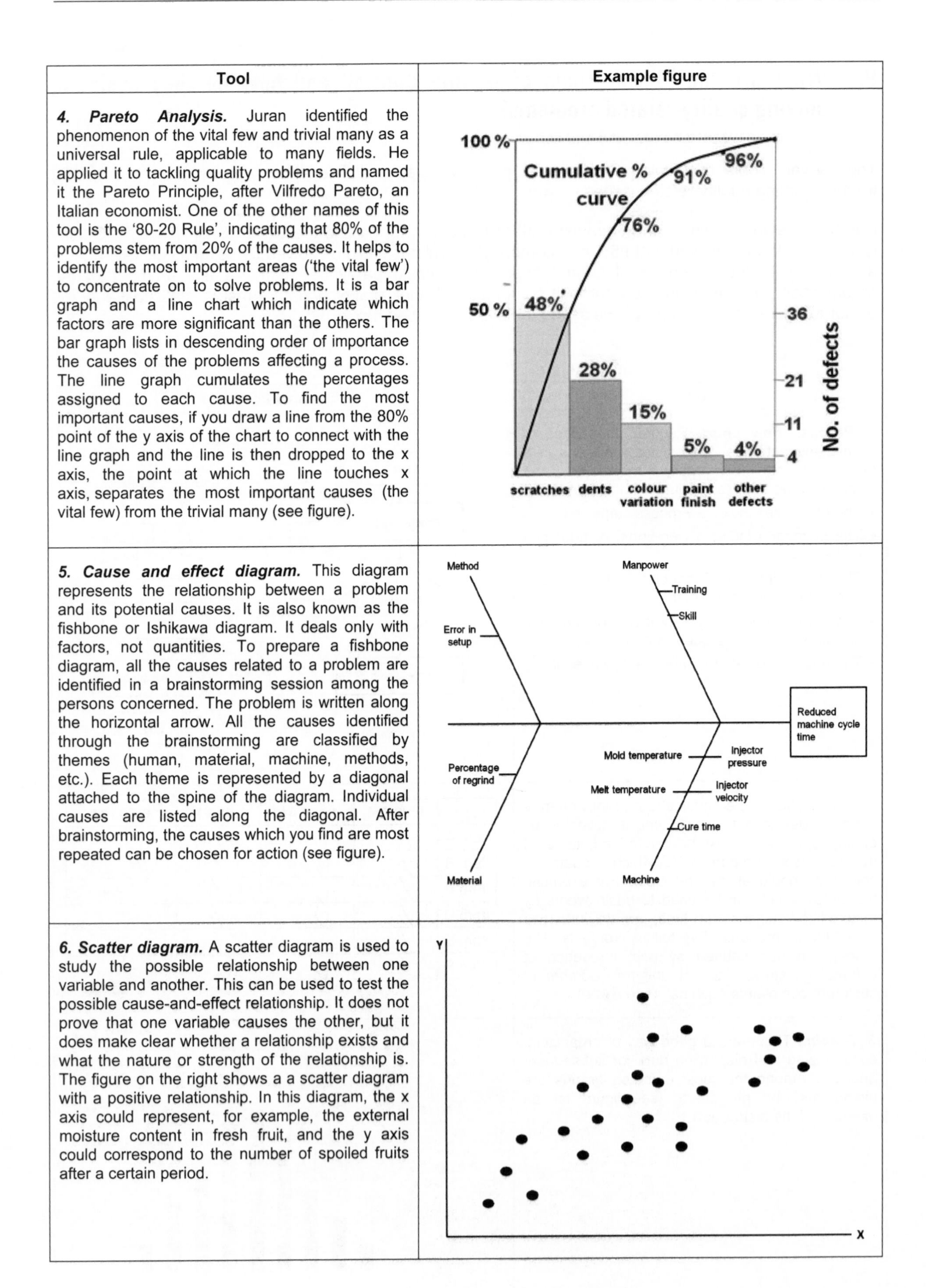

Tool	Example figure
4. Pareto Analysis. Juran identified the phenomenon of the vital few and trivial many as a universal rule, applicable to many fields. He applied it to tackling quality problems and named it the Pareto Principle, after Vilfredo Pareto, an Italian economist. One of the other names of this tool is the '80-20 Rule', indicating that 80% of the problems stem from 20% of the causes. It helps to identify the most important areas ('the vital few') to concentrate on to solve problems. It is a bar graph and a line chart which indicate which factors are more significant than the others. The bar graph lists in descending order of importance the causes of the problems affecting a process. The line graph cumulates the percentages assigned to each cause. To find the most important causes, if you draw a line from the 80% point of the y axis of the chart to connect with the line graph and the line is then dropped to the x axis, the point at which the line touches x axis, separates the most important causes (the vital few) from the trivial many (see figure).	
5. Cause and effect diagram. This diagram represents the relationship between a problem and its potential causes. It is also known as the fishbone or Ishikawa diagram. It deals only with factors, not quantities. To prepare a fishbone diagram, all the causes related to a problem are identified in a brainstorming session among the persons concerned. The problem is written along the horizontal arrow. All the causes identified through the brainstorming are classified by themes (human, material, machine, methods, etc.). Each theme is represented by a diagonal attached to the spine of the diagram. Individual causes are listed along the diagonal. After brainstorming, the causes which you find are most repeated can be chosen for action (see figure).	
6. Scatter diagram. A scatter diagram is used to study the possible relationship between one variable and another. This can be used to test the possible cause-and-effect relationship. It does not prove that one variable causes the other, but it does make clear whether a relationship exists and what the nature or strength of the relationship is. The figure on the right shows a a scatter diagram with a positive relationship. In this diagram, the x axis could represent, for example, the external moisture content in fresh fruit, and the y axis could correspond to the number of spoiled fruits after a certain period.	

Tool	Example figure
7. Control charts. Control charts are graphical representations of variations found in a process of measurement or observations that are plotted on graphs against time. These charts comprise two lines called UCL (upper control limit) and LCL (lower control limit). These are not the same as specification tolerances. If the results of measurements exceed these limits, then the 'cause' needs to be investigated and action taken on it immediately. To reduce the variations found in the process, fundamental changes would need to be made in methods, machines, materials or other factors. Control charts can be plotted for variable or continuous data (like weight of bag, temperature of a cold storage, time of baking, speed of a conveyor). Control charts for variables consist of mean and range charts. Control charts can also be plotted for attributes or discrete data (such as the number of defects found in a lot, the number of cracks in a piece, the number of missing stitches in a leather purse, percentage delays in shipments or percentage delays in responding to customer complaints). The two most popular charts for attribute data are the np chart (for the number of defective items in a lot) and the p chart (for the proportion of defective items). Control charts help to monitor and control quality by acting as 'traffic lights' and are valuable in all types of activities.	UCL Center line LCL

FOR MORE INFORMATION

- Ishikawa, Kaoru. Guide to Quality Control (Industrial Engineering & Technology). Asian Productivity Organization. ISBN-9283310357.

  The book covers the fundamental tools of quality control, including data collection, control charts, histograms, scatter diagrams, cause-and-effect diagrams, probability studies, check sheets, sampling, Pareto diagrams, graphs. Simply written and self-teaching, it encourages workers to seek applications of the tools in their work. Includes practice problems.

- Office of the Secretary of Defense. Small Business Guidebook to Quality Management. Quality Management Office. Washington, D.C. 20301-3016. This guide book is freely downloadable from http://dodreports.com/pdf/ada310869.pdf

  The aim of this guidebook is to help small businesses make the transition to a quality culture. Developed by the United States Federal Government, and the Department of Defense to help small businesses to familiarize themselves with the rapidly spreading quality movement. The book has a chapter on the seven quality tools.

REFERENCES

BreezeTree Software. http://www.breezetree.com/flow-charts/flowchart.htm – source for figure of flow chart.

Cause and effect diagram, source: http://thequalityweb.com/cause.html

Ho, Samuel K. TQM: An Integrated approach. ISBN 0749415614. A priced publication obtainable from Dr. Samuel Ho, Leicester Business School, De Montfort University, Leicester LE1 9BH, United Kingdom. Email SKHCOR@dmu.ac.uk

Seven QC Tools: Q-BPM. http://en.q-bpm.org/mediawiki/index.php/Seven_QC_Tools – source for figures except flow chart and cause and effect diagram.

9. What is Six Sigma?

Six Sigma is a data-driven structured problem-solving methodology for dealing with chronic issues facing a business by reducing variations in the business processes.

The Six Sigma methodology, started and popularized in 1987 by Motorola in the United States, provides techniques and tools to improve the process capability and reduce the defects in any process. Six Sigma essentially has two elements: the 'voice of the customer' and the 'voice of the process'. It entails reducing the gap between the two voices and ensuring that they match. Six Sigma efforts target three main areas:

- Improve customer satisfaction
- Reduce cycle time
- Reduce defects

Six Sigma aims at virtually error-free business performance. Achieving the goal of Six Sigma requires more than small incremental improvements – it demands a breakthrough in every area of the business.

Sigma is a Greek letter symbolized by 'σ'. It is used to designate the standard deviation of a process. In other words, sigma is a measurement used to determine how good or bad the performance of a process is, i.e. how many mistakes a process makes. Traditionally, Six Sigma stands for 'six standard deviations' from process mean. The table below gives process yields at various sigma levels.

Process yield at various sigma levels

Sigma level	Product meeting requirements: %	Defects per million opportunities (DPMO)*
1	68.26	697,672.15
2	95.45	308,770.21
3	99.73	66,810.63
4	99.9937	6,209.70
5	99.999943	232.67
6	99.9999998	3.40

Source: David Hoyle, ISO 9000 Quality Systems Handbook, 6th ed. 2009.

*DPMO with a 1.5 Sigma shift.

DPMO is the result of DPU (defects per unit) multiplied by 1 000 000 divided by opportunities for errors in a unit. For example, if a purchase order has 50 opportunities for errors and assuming that the data entry operator who prepares purchase orders makes 1 defect on average, the DPMO in this case will be 1 multiplied by 1 000 000 divided by 50 or 20,000.

Suppose that you run a business that delivers pizzas to nearby offices. You have a reputation for making good pizzas and you have many customers. According to your contract with customers, pizza will be delivered to them fresh and hot between 11.45 am and 12.15 pm. This allows them to receive their orders in time for lunch (their 'requirements'). You have also agreed that if a pizza is delivered before 11.45 am or after 12.15 pm (a defect), you will discount their next order by 50%. Because your staff gets a bonus for on-time delivery, you are all very motivated to deliver the pizza during the half-hour window.

Here is how Six Sigma, as a measure, could play a part in this simple process. If you deliver about 68% of your pizza on time, your process is only at the 1 sigma level. If you deliver it 99.73% on time, which sounds good, you are operating at only the 3 sigma level of performance. To be a 6 sigma pizza shop, you would need to have on time pizza delivery 99.9999998% of the time. That is practically perfect. In fact, for every million pizzas you make, you would end up with only three or four late deliveries.

The first step in calculating sigma or in understanding its significance is to grasp what your customer expects. In the language of Six Sigma, customer requirements and expectations are called CTQ (critical to quality).

In the pizza example, one of the key customer requirements is timely delivery; other requirements are likely to be related to the temperature of the pizza, the accuracy of the order, tastiness and so on. In fact, one of the keys of Six Sigma is to understand better and assess how well a process performs on all CTQs, not just one or two.

Companies operating at three or four sigma typically spend between 25 per cent and 40 per cent of their revenues fixing problems. This is known as the cost of quality, or more accurately the cost of poor quality. Companies operating at Six Sigma typically spend less than five per cent of their revenues fixing problems. Depending on the size of a company and the volume of its production, the dollar cost of this gap can be huge. For example, the gap between three or four sigma and six sigma was costing General Electric between US$ 8 billion and US$ 12 billion per year.

Six Sigma uses a handful of proven methods and tools. But the tools are applied within a simple performance improvement model known as DMAIC (Define-Measure-Analyse-Improve-Control).

An important feature of Six Sigma is the creation of an infrastructure to ensure that performance improvement activities have the necessary resources. A small percentage of managers are assigned full time to the identification and execution of Six Sigma improvement projects. They are popularly called Six Sigma Black Belts, Green Belts or Champions. Effectively, Six Sigma has been the first quality initiative to bring line managers into action in addition to quality managers, quality engineers and auditors, allowing them to become Black Belts, Green Belts or Champions. The requirements are high; for example, a Black Belt should have a college level background in mathematics, know the basic tools of quantitative analysis, and undergo 160 hours of classroom training plus one-on-one project coaching from a Master Black Belt.

To ensure access to needed information for initiating improvement projects, Six Sigma activities should be closely integrated with the organization's information systems. Obviously, the acquisition of skills and training of Six Sigma Black Belts must be enabled by investment in software and hardware.

FOR MORE INFORMATION

- De Mast, Jeroen. Six Sigma and Competitive Advantage. *Total Quality Management*, vol. 17, No. 4, May 2006, pp. 455-464. http://hera.ugr.es/doi/1651967x.pdf

  This paper studies the validity of the claim that Six Sigma provides a competitive advantage by positioning it among the paradigms provided by the literature on competitive strategy.

- International Organization for Standardization. ISO 13053:2011, Quantitative methods in process improvement – Six Sigma. Obtainable from ISO or ISO members (list at www.iso.org).

  The new standard deals exclusively with the application of Six Sigma to ameliorate existing processes. It is published in two parts: ISO 13053-1:2011, Quantitative methods in process improvement – Six Sigma – Part 1: DMAIC methodology, and ISO 13053-2:2011, Quantitative methods in process improvement – Six Sigma – Part 2: Tools and techniques.

- Pande, P. and others. The six sigma way: How GE, Motorola and other top companies are honing their performance. McGraw-Hill Companies, 2 Penn Plaza, New York, NY 10121-2298. ISBN 0-07-135806-4.

  This book is organized for use by a variety of readers, from Six Sigma novices to people right in the thick of improvement. Part One of the book gives an executive summary of Six Sigma; Part Two deals with gearing up to and adopting Six Sigma; and Part Three deals with implementing Six Sigma, providing the road map and the tools for it.

- Pande, P. and L. Hollp. What is Six Sigma? McGraw-Hill Companies, 2 Penn Plaza, New York, NY 10121-2298. ISBN 0-07-138185-6.

  This book provides a simple introduction to Six Sigma.

REFERENCES

Chowdhury, Subir. The Power of Six Sigma. Pearson Education (Singapore) Pte Ltd, Indian branch 482, FIE, Patparganj, Delhi 110092. ISBN 81-7808-437-6. Obtainable from www.pearsonapac.com/

Hoyle, David. ISO 9000 Quality Systems Handbook, 6th ed. 2009. ISBN 978-1-85617-684-2. It is a priced publication of Butterworth-Heinemann, Linacre House, Jordan Hill, Oxford 0X2 8DP, United Kingdom. Also available from www.amazon.com.

Pyzdek, Thomas. The six sigma revolution. This article is freely available in Quality America magazine on their website: www.qualityamerica.com/knowledgecente/articles/PYZDEKSixSigRev.htm

10. What is Japanese 5S and what are its benefits?

The Japanese 5S is a good housekeeping tool which is described by five Japanese words, Seiri, Seiton, Seiso, Seiketsu and Shitsuke.

The use of this tool was started in 1972 by Henry Ford in the United States as the CANDO programme: Cleaning up, Arranging, Neatness, Discipline and Ongoing improvement. The technique was popularized as 'Japanese 5S' in 1980 by Hiroyuki Hirano.

You may be thinking that 'housekeeping' is simple work and that you are already doing it. Yes, it is simple, but if it is carried out systematically, it produces results in the long term and may save you money.

The Japanese 5S consists of the following steps:

The five steps of Japanese 5S

Seiri *Sort*	*Distinguish* between necessary and unnecessary items. *Remove* the latter.
Seiton *Set in order*	*Enforce the dictum* 'a place for everything and everything in its place'.
Seiso *Shine*	*Clean up* the workplace and look for ways to keep it clean.
Seiketsu *Standardize*	*Maintain* and monitor adherence to the first three Ss.
Shitsuke *Sustain*	*Follow the rule* to keep the workplace 5S-right. Hold the gain.

Source: S.C. Arora, India.

Each step is briefly explained below. Suggested methods, examples of actions to be taken and the benefits of each step are also outlined.

1. SEIRI – SORT

This means distinguishing between or sorting out wanted and unwanted items at the workplace and removing unwanted items.

Suggested method and examples:

- You first decide what is necessary and what is unnecessary (unnecessary items may be found on the floor, in shelves, within lockers, in the storehouse, on the stairs, roofs, notice boards, etc).
- You should put a red tag on unnecessary items and keep them in a separate area.
- You may discard or throw away items that have not been used in the past year. Things used once in 6 to 12 months may be stored at a distance from the work station, and things used more than once a month should be available at a central point in the workplace.
- It will be good to keep things used hourly/everyday/once a week near the work station; some items may be worn by or kept in the pocket of, your workers at the work station.

Benefits of SEIRI:

- Useful floor space is saved; the time searching for tools, materials and papers is reduced; work flow is improved; the inventory cost of unnecessary items is cut.

2. SEITON – SET IN ORDER

While Seiri helps in determining which items are needed, Seiton enables one to decide how they are to be kept. You arrange items in such a manner that they are easy to use, labelling them so that they are easy to find and put back. In effect, Seiton demands that there be a place for everything necessary and that everything should be in its place. Seiton puts an end to 'homeless' items.

Suggested method and examples:

- You first identify the right places for everything and put all materials and equipment at the places allocated to them with proper labels and signs. For example, you could draw outlines on tool boards, making it easy to see where each tool belongs.
- You could use floor paint marking to define working areas, paths, entrances, exits, safety equipment, cart or trolley locations, and colour coding for pipelines for steam, water, gas, drainage.
- You should display clearly written warnings, messages, instructions at proper places at the right heights. You can also use alerts or indicators to prevent out-of-stock positions.

Benefits of SEITON:

- It becomes easy to keep and take out things; you make fewer mistakes; searching time is reduced; the work environment is safer.

3. SEISO – SHINE

This means removing dirt, stains, filth, soot and dust from the work area. It includes cleaning and caring for equipment and facilities and inspecting them for abnormalities.

Suggested methods and examples:

- Decide on cleaning points, order of cleaning, type of cleaning, cleaning aids required; display cleaning schedule; during cleaning look out for defective conditions (loose bolts, vibrations, excessive noise, high temperatures, fallen tools) and correct them.

Benefits of SEISO:

- The workplace becomes free of dirt and stains which is the starting point for quality; equipment life is prolonged; the number of breakdowns falls and accidents are prevented.

4. SEIKETSU – STANDARDIZE

Seiri, Seiton and Seiso are easy to do once but they are very difficult to maintain because they call for a systematization of practices. This means ensuring that whatever level of cleanliness and orderliness has been achieved, it should be maintained. This requires the development of a work structure that will support the new practices and turn them into habits.

Suggested methods and examples:

- Everyone in your company should use the same names for items, the same sizes, shapes and colours for signals, floor markings, etc. To achieve this, you could write guidelines for the first 3Ss and carry out periodic evaluations with the aid of checklists.

Benefits of SEIKETSU:

- Activities are simplified; consistency in work practices increases; mistakes are avoided.

5. SHITSUKE – SUSTAIN

Sustain also means 'discipline'. It denotes your commitment to maintaining orderliness and to practice the first 3S as a way of life. It requires your employees to show a positive interest in, and overcome their resistance to, change. For this, you should create awareness and publicize the first 3S.

Suggested methods/examples:

- Use 5S news releases, posters, slogans, etc. Your management should support Shitsuke by providing resources and leadership and you should reward and recognize the best performers.

Benefits of SHITSUKE:

- Promotes the habit of complying with workplace rules and procedures, creates a healthy atmosphere and a good workplace.

Before starting quality control activities (see question 4), it is crucial first to set your housekeeping in order. Systematic housekeeping is the foundation for quality control.

FOR MORE INFORMATION

- Harper-Franks, Kathy. The 5S for the Office User's Guide. Published by MCS Media Inc., 888 Ridge Road, Chelsea MI 48118, United States (info@theleanstore.com). ISBN 978-0-9799665-4-5. Can be purchased from www.amazon.com

  This book provides an organization with the forms, worksheets, and checklists necessary to ensure a 5S project is well planned from the start as well as its sustainability over time. The guide focuses on how 5S principles apply to both the physical desktop (paperwork, desk layout, drawer organization) and the PC desktop (folders, files, emails, shortcuts).

- The 5S Implementation Process in Detail.
  www.tpmonline.com/articles_on_total_productive_maintenance/leanmfg/the5sindetail.htm

  An article on 5S freely downloadable from the Lean Expertise website.

REFERENCES

Hirano, Hiroyuki. 5S for Operators: 5 Pillars of the Visual Workplace. Created by The Productivity Press Development Team, Productivity Press, Portland, Oregon (service@productivityinc.com). ISBN 1-56327-123-0.

Ho, Samuel K. TQM: An Integrated approach. ISBN 07494 1561 4. A priced publication obtainable from Dr. Samuel Ho, Leicester Business School, De Montfort University, Leicester LE1 9BH, United Kingdom. Email SKHCOR@dmu.ac.uk

11. How can I motivate my subordinates to achieve quality?

Even if you have a well-designed quality system, you will not achieve the desired level of quality without a motivated workforce. One of the eight quality management principles in ISO 9000 emphasizes the involvement of people: "People at all levels are the essence of an organization and their full involvement enables their abilities to be used for the organization's benefit." You can use some of the requirements of ISO 9001 (see question 29) to motivate your employees by:

- Ensuring that your quality policy is communicated and understood within your organization;
- Using measurable and consistent quality objectives to meet requirements for your product;
- Defining and communicating responsibilities and authorities within your organization;
- Building the competence of your employees;
- Providing adequate infrastructure and work environment;
- Initiating improvements, e.g. by implementing your employees' suggestions.

Recent research on motivation summarized in an article by Nohria *et al* (2008) paves the way to a powerful new model for employee motivation. People take into account four basic emotional needs, or drives: to acquire (e.g. social status), to bond (e.g. form connections with co-workers), to comprehend (e.g. satisfy our curiosity), and to defend (e.g. ourselves, our ideas and beliefs against external threats).

A reward system based on performance which differentiates between good and average or poor performers and which matches the pay of your competitors can take care of the emotional need **to acquire**. This will promote an environment where workers are treated fairly and equitably. The productivity of workers increases when they perceive the caring attitude of managers rather than when there is a positive change in the working environment.

An organizational culture which encourages trust and friendship among co-workers, values collaboration and teamwork, and encourages sharing of best practices can satisfy the emotional need **to bond**. Quality circles, where small groups of workers meet periodically to solve problems, leading to improvement in quality and productivity and cost reduction, are a good vehicle for promoting this culture. They enable workers to satisfy their social, self-esteem and self-fulfilment needs, which are inherent in human beings, as described in the hierarchy of human needs elaborated by Abraham Maslow.

Job enrichment by designing jobs that are meaningful and add value to the organization can fulfil the emotional need **to comprehend**. Jobs can be designed in such a way that decisions are taken at the appropriate level (e.g. strategic decisions are made by managers, while subordinates are allowed to decide matters at the operational level without constant interference from managers). An example of empowerment took place in a Corning plant where management developed a partnership with employees who were called 'associates' and were given the authority to shut down the process when it was producing defective products if this was necessary to fix the problem definitively.

One of the means to address the emotional need **to defend** is through fair, trustworthy and transparent processes in the organization, e.g. for performance management and resource allocation. Workers like to work for an organization that promotes justice, that has clear goals and that allows workers to express their ideas and opinions. They will be motivated in an environment where they are not afraid to speak the truth and where they are not driven to hide problems under the carpet. This would satisfy one of the elements of W.E. Deming's philosophy of management, i.e. to drive out fear from the workplace. This environment can be enhanced if a factual approach to decision-making is adopted; the approach should be based on data analysis using statistical methods. In this environment, workers would not be blamed for problems that can be solved only by management.

Some models for employee motivation focus on the mindset of management. For instance, you can motivate your workers by believing in their capability to produce quality products. Douglas McGregor propounded two theories of management. According to Theory X, the average human being has a dislike of work and responsibility and needs a 'carrot and stick' approach. Theory Y says that the average human being has as much a liking for work as for play and seeks to accept responsibility for his/her work. By emphasizing Theory Y, you can motivate your workers. You should beware of the Pygmalion effect with its self-fulfilling prophecy: if you believe that your workers will produce a high level of defective products, they will do so to reinforce the message you are sending to them.

There is always a better way of doing things in manufacturing or service. Your workers are best qualified to find this way as they are closer to the work itself. You can motivate them to do this if you provide them with tools, support, training and encouragement.

You can also motivate your workers by making them adopt the 'triple role' concept, in which everyone is considered a customer, processor and supplier (see question 7). This will bring back the direct notion of supplier and customer within the organization instead of thinking exclusively of suppliers and customers outside the organization. It will also promote a feeling of satisfaction in your workers who will have satisfactory inputs from their immediate suppliers and give satisfactory outputs to their immediate customers. Adopting the concept of 'triple role' will create an environment of trust in your organization.

Daniel Freeman and Jason Freeman, in their book *Use Your Head: A Guided Tour of the Human Mind,* have listed eight of the most significant incentives, a distillation of more than a century's worth of research into employee motivation. They are the following:

- A job that meets the emotional, practical, social and intellectual needs of your workers.
- A job that suits the personality of your worker and that is compatible with his/her values.
- A work environment that helps your workers to grow and develop their skills.
- Demanding but achievable goals.
- Rewards that your workers really want for meeting those goals.
- Feeling that your worker is being rewarded fairly in relation to his/her peers.
- A work environment that strengthens the belief of your workers in their own abilities.
- Workers believing that the management they are working for are honourable, honest and trustworthy.

FOR MORE INFORMATION

- Lester, John. ISO 9001 and Personal Quality Development. Chartered Quality Institute (CQI). http://www.thecqi.org/Knowledge-Hub/QW-express/archives/Quality-updates/ISO-9001-and-personal-quality-development-/

  Looks at the application of ISO 9001 to personal quality development; includes an interesting enneagram that matches different types of personality, needs, belief systems, knowledge and leadership.

- Thareja, P. Each One is Capable (A Total Quality Organisation Thru' People). (14 October 2009). *FOUNDRY*, Journal For Progressive Metal Casters, vol. 20, No. 4, July/August 2008. Available at SSRN: http://ssrn.com/abstract=1488690

  This paper presents people as the backbone of the organization. It discusses how organizations can synergize people's competencies to close the gaps in an individual's capabilities.

- Thomas, Kenneth and Walter Tyman Jr. Bridging the Motivation Gap in Total Quality. *Quality Management Journal*, vol. 4, No. 2, January 1997, pp. 80-96. www.asq.org

  This article points out that total quality management requires a shift in motivational emphasis from extrinsic rewards and punishments to intrinsic motivation of workers. Intrinsic motivation is based on positively valued (rewarding) experiences that individuals get directly from their work tasks. This article provides an integrative model for intrinsic motivation and discusses practical implications for its measurement and enhancement.

REFERENCES

Feigenbaum, A.V. Spring into Action. *Quality Progress*, November 2009. www.qualityprogress.org

Freeman, Daniel and Jason Freeman. Use Your Head: A Guided Tour of the Human Mind 2010. John Murray, 2010. ISBN 978-1-84854-325-6.

Heller, Robert. Motivating People. Essential Managers Collection. Dorling Kindersley, 1998.

International Organization for Standardization

- ISO 9000 Quality Management Systems. Obtainable from ISO or ISO members (list at www.iso.org).
- ISO 9001:2008, Quality management systems – Requirements. Obtainable from ISO or ISO members (list at www.iso.org).

Nohria, Nitin and others. Employee Motivation: A Powerful New Model. *Harvard Business Review*, July-August 2008, www.hbr.org

12. How do I keep abreast of developments related to quality?

Some possible ways of keeping abreast of developments related to quality are listed below. Most of the organizations with which we suggest membership collect small annual fees. They will provide you with an opportunity to network with people with similar interests and keep abreast of developments which can help you to improve your business.

- Your organization can become a member of the quality association or institute of your country. If you are from a large country, there may be several quality associations and you may choose to become a member of one of them. You may obtain the contact details of the quality association through your national standards body, chamber of commerce and industry, exporters' association or trade promotion organization. The websites of the American Society for Quality, the European Organization for Quality and the Asia Pacific Quality Organization provide contact details of various quality organizations.
- You can become a member of well-established organizations such as the American Society for Quality and the Chartered Quality Institute of the United Kingdom. You will receive their monthly journals and have access to further information from their websites. Even if you are not a member of a well-established quality organization, you can scan their websites as parts of these are accessible to the public.
- You can participate in the annual conferences held by organizations such as the American Society for Quality and the European Organization for Quality.
- You can subscribe to journals such as *Quality World* (Chartered Quality Institute of the United Kingdom), *Quality Progress* (American Society for Quality), *ISO Focus* (International Organization for Standardization; PDF versions of *Focus* are now freely available from the ISO web page) and to newsletters published by your national standards body.
- You can also scan the web pages of journals such as *Quality Progress,* which provides free access to some articles. Web pages of other organizations such as the Juran Institute also give free access to news and selected articles and case studies.
- The ISO website contains a 'News and Media' section which provides information on developments in the quality field, especially with respect to international standards under preparation and new standards published. Articles and case studies from ISO magazines like *ISO focus* (from 2004 onwards) and *ISO Management Systems* (from 2001 to 2009) can also be freely accessed from the 'News and Media' section. In addition to these, various ISO brochures, videos and guidance documents are also freely accessible.
- Regular participation in the seminars and training events on quality subjects organized by the quality association, national standards body, chamber of commerce and industry, exporters' association or trade promotion organization in your country will also keep you abreast of developments taking place in the quality field.
- You can purchase a copy of *Juran's Quality Handbook: The Complete Guide to Performance Excellence* which is in its sixth edition and has been a reference book on quality for more than 50 years. It presents up-to-date methods, research and tools related to quality. The 1999 version of this book (fifth edition) is currently available online (**see**: For More Information, below).
- For information on the quality of specific products or systems, please refer to questions 23, 24, 74 and 77.
- You can obtain information on other subjects associated with quality such as standardization, accreditation and metrology by consulting the website of the International Bureau of Weights and Measures (BIPM), which has links to metrology institutes, accreditation bodies, standards bodies, testing laboratories, etc.
- You can consult the website of DCMAS, the Network on Metrology, Accreditation, and Standardization for Developing Countries. DCMAS was established by the principal international organizations mandated to strengthen technical infrastructures and deliver capacity building in metrology, standardization and conformity assessment (including accreditation). Its website provides links to the websites of these organizations.

- You can consult the website of STDF, the Standards and Trade Development Facility, a joint initiative in capacity building and technical cooperation aiming at raising awareness of the importance of sanitary and phytosanitary issues, increasing coordination in the provision of SPS-related assistance, and mobilizing resources to assist developing countries to enhance their capacity to meet SPS standards. Its website provides links to the websites of its partner organizations.

FOR MORE INFORMATION

- Juran, Joseph and Blanton Godfrey. Juran's Quality Handbook, 5th ed. McGraw-Hill, 1999. www.pqm-online.com/assets/files/lib/juran.pdf

  A reference work on quality engineering and management practices, this handbook covers planning and control methods and results in the field of quality.

- Quality Magazines. http://thequalityportal.com/q_mags.htm

  Provides links to other resources on quality management.

REFERENCES

American Society for Quality. www.asq.org

Asia Pacific Quality Organization. www.apqo.org

Chartered Quality Institute. www.thecqi.org

European Organization for Quality. www.eoq.org

International Bureau of Weights and Measures. Useful links at www.bipm.org/en/practical_info/useful_links/

International Organization for Standardization. www.iso.org

Juran Institute. www.juran.com

Juran, Joseph and Joseph De Feo. Juran's Quality Handbook: The Complete Guide to Performance, 6th ed. McGraw-Hill Professional. 2010.

Network on Metrology, Accreditation and Standardization for Developing Countries (DCMAS), www.dcmas.net.

Quality Progress magazine. www.qualityprogress.org

Standards and Trade Development Facility (STDF). www.standardsfacility.org

TECHNICAL REQUIREMENTS

13. What is a standard?

A standard is a document that pins down the characteristics of a product or a service. These characteristics may cover design, weight, size, performance, environmental requirements, interoperability, materials, production process or service delivery or even the protocols that allow computers or mobile phones to connect to each other. The standard may include or deal exclusively with terminology, symbols, packaging, marking or labelling requirements as they apply to a product, process or production method. There are also other types of standards, such as measurement standards which are dealt with in question 1.

Standards are generally divided into public standards and private standards. Public standards are developed and published by recognized organizations, usually standardization organizations. This takes place at the international, regional and national levels. The figure below cites examples of public and private standards at the various levels.

Diversity of standards

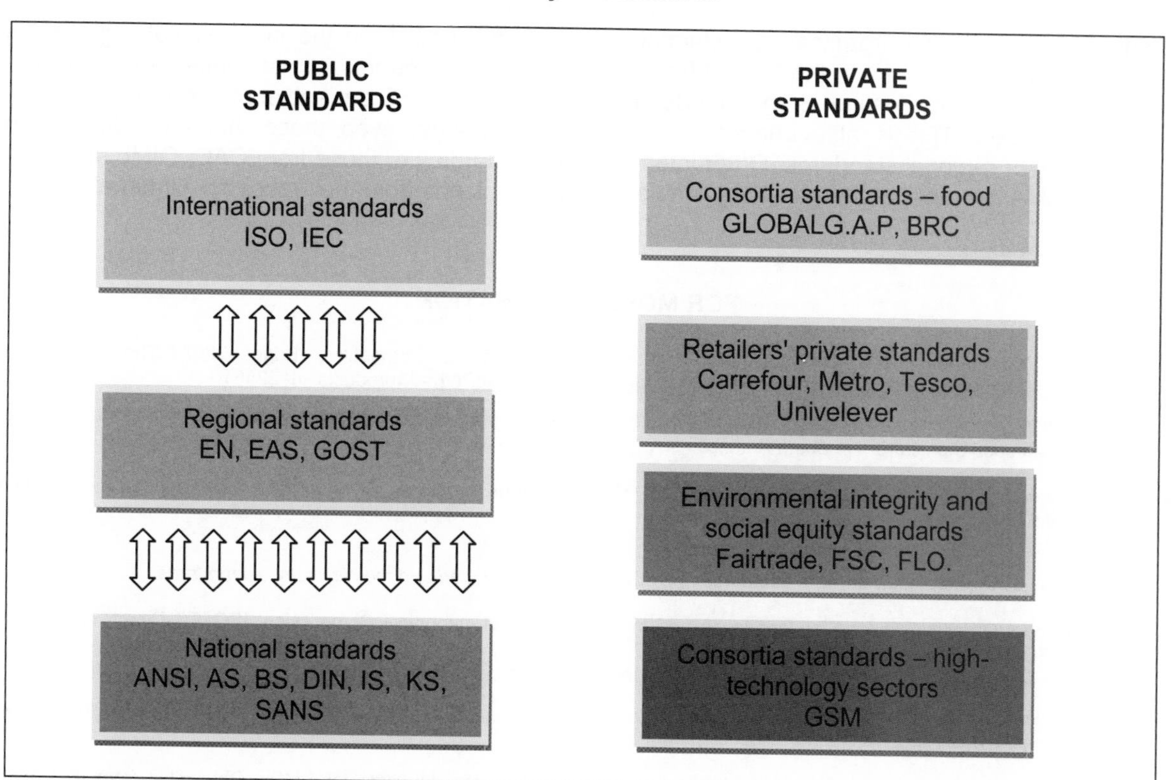

Source: Martin Kellermann, South Africa.

Note: The full names of the standards and standardization bodies listed are given further below as well as in question 14, which discusses private standards.

When public standards are developed, the needs and wishes of many stakeholders are taken into consideration, i.e. they are developed with consensus principles in mind. This implies that the standards will make the same demands on all suppliers and on all consumers, and that externalities such as health, safety and environmental considerations have been considered.

Among the typical international standards are those published by the International Organization for Standardization (ISO), the International Electrotechnical Commission (IEC), the International Telecommunication Union (ITU), the Codex Alimentarius Commission (CAC), the World Organisation for Animal Health (OIE), the International Plant Protection Convention (IPPC) and others. Probably the best known regional standards are the harmonized standards (EN) of the European Union, but there are other standards such as the State Standards (GOST) of the States of the former Soviet Union and the East African Community standards (EAS).

National standards are published by more than 150 countries worldwide, and are far too numerous to list here. Among the typical national standards are those of the American National Standards Institute (ANSI), the Australian Standards (AS), British Standards (BS), the standards of the German Institute for Standardization (DIN), Indian Standards (IS), Korean Industrial Standards (KS) and South African National Standards (SANS). It is difficult to quantify the number of public standards in the world, but Perinorm, a bibliographic database, for example, has a list of more than 700,000 standards, which covers only the most important public standards. Hence, public standards are everywhere in today's world, defining much of the way people, products and processes interact with each other and with their environment.

Standards are developed by technical committees established by national standards bodies, regional and international standardization organizations, representing all the stakeholders. The way in which standards are developed is guided by ISO/IEC Directives and by the requirements of Annex 3 of the WTO Agreement on TBT (see question 93). National technical committees are useful vehicles for ensuring that the interests of the suppliers are considered, but it means that such suppliers have to become members of the committees and actively participate in their proceedings. The same applies to regional and international technical committees.

Standards are available from national standards bodies, or direct from the international organizations mentioned above. They are in the form of hard copies or are in electronic format, either as a CD-ROM or as PDF files accessible online. Standards developed by ISO and IEC are subject to copyright, and have to be purchased. This is also true of most national standards, even those that are adopted from international or regional standards. Other international standards, i.e. those from CAC, OIML and similar intergovernmental organizations, are obtainable as free downloads from their respective Internet sites.

FOR MORE INFORMATION

- Gausch, Luis and others. Quality Systems and Standards for a Competitive Edge. 2007. The World Bank. http://publications.worldbank.org/index.php?main_page=product_info&cPath=0&products_id=22561

  Publication containing many examples that deals with the nature of standards and quality systems, their importance in trade and the situation then current in South America.

- International Organization for Standardization and United Nations Industrial Development Organization. Fast Forward: National Standards Bodies in Developing Economies.
  2008. www.iso.org/iso/fast_forward.pdf/

  Provides useful information on what standards are, how they are developed and the hierarchy of standards.

- International Organization for Standardization and International Electrotechnical Commission. ISO/IEC Directives – Parts 1 and 2, ISO, 2009.
  www.iso.org/iso/standards_development/processes_and_procedures/iso_iec_directives_and_iso_supplement.htm

  These Directives cover the principles and methodology for developing international standards. Many national standards bodies use them as a basis for their standards development processes.

- International Organization for Standardization. 10 good things ISO standards do for SMEs. Obtainable from ISO or ISO members (list at www.iso.org).

  Managers of small businesses in 10 countries from around the world explain how ISO standards contribute to their success in this new ISO brochure.

- Maur, Jean-Christophe and Ben Shepherd. 'Product standards'. *In* Jean-Pierre Chauffour and Jean-Christophe Maur (eds.), Preferential Trade Agreement Policies for Development. A Handbook. The World Bank. 2011.
  http://siteresources.worldbank.org/INTRANETTRADE/Resources/C10.pdf

  Overview of the relationship between product standards and trade, the policy measures available for dealing with standards in preferential trade agreements, and broader issues of institutional coordination and regional cooperation.

- United Nations Industrial Development Organization. Role of standards: A guide for small and medium-sized enterprises. Working Paper. Vienna, 2006.
  http://www.unido.org/fileadmin/media/documents/pdf/tcb_role_standards.pdf

REFERENCES

International Organization for Standardization

- International standards and 'private standards'. A freely downloadable brochure published by ISO. http://www.iso.org/iso/private_standards.pdf
- ISO 9000:2005, Quality management systems – Fundamentals and vocabulary. Obtainable from ISO or ISO members (list at www.iso.org).

International Organization for Standardization and International Electrotechnical Commission. ISO/IEC Guide 2:2004, Standardization and related activities – General vocabulary. Obtainable from ISO or ISO members (list at www.iso.org), and from IEC or IEC National Committees (list at www.iec.ch).

Perinorm. *www.perinorm.com*

World Trade Organization. Agreement on Technical Barriers to Trade, Annex 1: Terms and their definitions for the purpose of this Agreement, and Annex 3: Code of good practice for the preparation, adoption and application of standards, 1994. www.wto.org/english/res_e/booksp_e/analytic_index_e/tbt_02_e.htm#article15

14. What are private standards and what is their impact on trade?

Many standards are developed outside the auspices of national, regional, and international standards bodies (see question 13). The reasons for the development of these standards are many and varied. Organizations such as major retail chains apply detailed requirements to the products they wish to trade in, the oil industry operates worldwide on similar technical requirements and the vehicle manufacturers of the United States developed common standards for the supply of certain parts (i.e. SAE standards – SAE being the Society of Automotive Engineers). Suppliers band together to gain market advantages in supplying products with similar technology. For instance, the music CD was a joint Philips-Sony standard, and the GSM standards (Global System for Mobile Communications) for mobile phones are agreed to by a few manufacturers. These standards are generally known as private standards. Some private standards eventually end up as public standards if their growing market relevance warrants it, or the marketing advantage is no longer an issue for the originators.

Private standards are developed by specific non-government groupings, i.e. sectoral organizations including non-governmental organizations, consortia, certification bodies or major retailers. Private standards are generally geared to meet the needs of those who develop and publish them and are not intended for mandatory application by the government. Private standards usually require certification (see question 75) of suppliers, because a self-declaration of conformity (see question 57) is generally not accepted by the market. On the other hand, none of the private standards are enforceable by the government under law. Hence the decision by a supplier to obtain certification is always a business decision, depending on whether it will be profitable to do so.

Private standards can be loosely divided into four groups:

- **Consortia standards in the food and horticulture domains.** Examples are the European Retailer Group's good agricultural practice (GLOBALG.A.P.) and the British Retail Consortium (BRC) standards (see also question 15). They are important because the European Union is one of the largest importers of food in the world. These standards have been developed by consortia of European and British retailers that wish to ensure that their suppliers meet all the regulatory food safety requirements, as well as the additional requirements set by the retail organizations themselves, including social accountability. For these standards, sophisticated certification systems have been established and if you wish to export food and horticultural products to EU, certification may help you to gain market share or increase profitability. Certification, however, is not cheap, nor is it mandatory. Deciding to seek it is a pure business decision based on the level of competitiveness that the exporter wishes to achieve.
- **Retailers' private standards.** Sometimes called niche standards, retailers' private standards have a huge impact on suppliers to the large multinational retail chains such as Carrefour, Metro, Tesco, Unilever and Wal-Mart. These companies have developed their own standards for agricultural produce and processed food for competitive or brand protection purposes; they may expand their standards into other areas in the future.

  They apply highly detailed standards to their purchases for a number of reasons. Among these are: to ensure that products coming from suppliers are in the form that will minimize costs and maximize their profits; to ensure that they are selling only products that conform with official requirements (public standards, technical regulations and SPS measures); to minimize their liability for legal action by dissatisfied customers; to ensure that products conform with the ethical views of their clients on matters such as animal welfare and environmental protection; and to persuade customers that the goods being offered for sale are better because they are safer or of higher quality as a consequence of the use of private standards.

  If a supplier wishes to provide products to these major retail organizations, then these products will have to comply with niche standard requirements. The impact of such niche standards on trade can be enormous. On a positive note, these retail organizations frequently provide substantial support to SMEs in meeting their standards. However, fulfilling the requirements of one purchaser may not guarantee that the requirements of other purchasers will be met.

- **Standards related to environmental integrity and social equity.** Private standards are important in the more developed markets where many consumers are concerned about issues such as child labour, environmental protection, fair trade, genetically modified foods and similar matters (see also question 17). Buyers may insist that products destined for such markets have been produced in a manner that does not violate their social or environmental concerns. Relevant recommendations come from organizations like Social Accountability International, with its SA 8000 standard, for good social conduct in industry, the Forest Stewardship Council (FSC) for standards in the wood and paper industries, and the Fairtrade Labelling Organizations International (FLO). Demonstrating compliance, i.e. through certification, to such private standards is therefore important to gain a competitive edge.
- **Consortia standards in high-technology sectors.** A fourth group of private standards are important in specific, usually high-technology, sectors; the GSM standards for the mobile-phone industry are an example of such standards. The compliance and certification demands of these sectoral private standards are as varied as the standards and the sectors themselves; hence, a proper study of the requirements of the sector is indicated before any decisions are made.

Buyers like retail chains specify the attributes that they want in the goods they purchase. They argue that by doing so they are more able to meet their customers' requirements. However, international trade problems arise, especially where purchasers like the big retail chains in developed countries wield enormous market power in comparison with small-scale suppliers in developing countries. These problems are exacerbated when different purchasing organizations apply different private standards on the same suppliers, or if there is a significant cost to the suppliers in demonstrating that they are meeting the purchasers' standards.

In part because of concerns raised by developing countries that multiple private standards raise the costs of compliance, private-sector retail organizations have moved to consolidate the standards of individual companies into industry-wide standards in order to avoid unnecessary adverse impacts on international trade.

FOR MORE INFORMATION

- International Trade Centre
  - Standards Map: www.standardsmap.org

    Standards Map is the web-based portal of ITC's Trade for Sustainable Development (T4SD) programme; it is a partnership-based effort to enhance transparency in voluntary standards and to increase opportunities for sustainable production and trade.
  - *Export Quality Management Bulletin* No. 86, Directory of marks and labels related to food safety, environmental integrity and social equity. www.intracen.org/exporters/quality-management/Quality_publications_index

REFERENCES

British Retail Consortium (BRC). www.brcglobalstandards.com

Fairtrade Labelling Organizations International (FLO). www.fairtrade.net

Forest Stewardship Council (FSC). www.fsc.org

Global Good Agricultural Practices (GLOBALG.A.P.). www.globalgap.org

International Organization for Standardization (ISO). International standards and 'private standards'. A freely downloadable brochure. www.iso.org/iso/private_standards.pdf

Social Accountability International (SAI). www.sa-intl.org

UNIDO. Making private standards work for you: A guide to private standards in the garments, footwear and furniture sectors. Vienna, 2010. www.unido.org/fileadmin/user_media/Uploads/Documents/UNIDO_%20Guidelines_web.pdf

World Trade Organization. World Trade Report 2005: Exploring the links between trade, standards and the WTO. 2005. www.wto.org/english/res_e/booksp_e/anrep_e/world_trade_report05_e.pdf

15. Which standards are required to export food and agricultural products?

Exports must always conform with the official requirements imposed by the government of the importing country (mandatory requirements), and with the commercial requirements of the importer (purchaser's requirements).

It is difficult to elaborate exhaustively on specific standards owing to the wide range of products in the food and agricultural sectors. These are subject to sanitary and phytosanitary controls and technical regulations and standards that vary from country to country and sector to sector.

According to the WTO Agreement on SPS, countries are encouraged to base their requirements on international standards, for example those of the Codex Alimentarius Commission, OIE, IPPC.

The Codex Commission was created by FAO and WHO to develop food standards, guidelines and related texts such as the codes of practice under the Joint FAO/WHO Food Standards Programme. It aims to protect the health of consumers, ensure fair trade practices in the food trade, and promote coordination of all food standards work undertaken by international governmental and non-governmental organizations. Some of the important Codex Committees are the Codex Committee on Contaminants in Foods, Codex Committee on Fish and Fishery Products, Codex Committee on Food Additives, Codex Committee on Food Hygiene, Codex Committee on Food Import and Export Inspection and Certification Systems, Codex Committee on Food Labelling and the Codex Committee on Fresh Fruits and Vegetables.

Many countries have adopted HACCP as a mandatory requirement in the preparation of various food products. Question 42 explains what the Hazard Analysis and Critical Control Points (HACCP) are and why they are important for SMEs in the food sector.

The World Organisation for Animal Health (OIE) is the intergovernmental organization responsible for improving animal health worldwide. Its mission is, inter alia, to safeguard world trade by publishing health standards for international trade in animals and animal products to ensure transparency in the global animal disease situation and to collect, analyse and disseminate veterinary scientific information.

The International Plant Protection Convention (IPPC) is an international agreement on plant health which aims to protect cultivated and wild plants by preventing the introduction and spread of pests. IPPC allows countries to analyse risks to their national plant resources and to use science-based measures to safeguard their cultivated and wild plants.

The International Organization for Standardization's Technical Committee on food products, ISO/TC 34, deals with standardization in human and animal foodstuffs. It covers the food chain from primary production to consumption, as well as animal and vegetable propagation materials. It works particularly with, but is not limited to, terminology, sampling, methods of testing and analysis, product specifications, food and feed safety and quality management, and the requirements for packaging, storage and transportation.

ISO 22000, developed by ISO/TC 34, harmonizes the requirements for food safety management systems. Question 44 explains the difference between HACCP and ISO 22000. Question 45 lays out the steps involved in the implementation of ISO 22000.

In view of the proliferation of private standards for food and agricultural products, the Global Food Safety Initiative (GFSI), a non-profit foundation created under Belgian law, benchmarks existing food standards against food safety criteria. It is also looking to develop mechanisms for exchanging information in the supply chain, to raise consumer awareness and to review existing good retail practices. Within GFSI, benchmarking is a "procedure by which a food safety-related scheme is compared to the GFSI Guidance Document."

Question 22 discusses the relationship between the mandatory legal requirements imposed by governments in importing countries and the private standards that a buyer may impose. Only the buyer can provide definitive information on the private standards that will be applied. Usually the buyer will also want to be assured that the products being traded will meet mandatory government standards as well, because otherwise it may not be possible for the purchased goods to enter the importing country.

Question 23 provides guidance on where to obtain information on the official requirements of the importing country. These may include food standards such as hygiene rules and limits on residues of agricultural chemicals. They may also impose restrictions related to the protection of animal and plant health (freedom from specified pests and diseases in the exporting country, quarantine controls at the point of entry into the importing country, and so forth). There may be only a few applicable requirements or many, according to the nature of the food and the particular circumstances of the importing and exporting countries.

FOR MORE INFORMATION

- International Trade Centre. *Export Quality Management Bulletin* No. 86, Directory of marks and labels related to food safety, environmental integrity and social equity. www.intracen.org/exporters/quality-management/Quality_publications_index.
- Will, Margret and Doris Guenther. Food Quality and Safety Standards, as required by EU Law and the Private Industry: A Practitioners' Reference Book. 2nd ed. 2007. GTZ. http://www2.gtz.de/dokumente/bib/07-0800.pdf

  Reference book on food quality management systems, covering legislative and private industry market requirements in the European Union for selected product groups such as fresh and processed fruits and vegetables.

REFERENCES

Codex Alimentarius Commission. www.codexalimentarius.net

Færgemand, Jacob and Dorte Jespersen. ISO 22000 to ensure integrity of food supply chain. ISO. 2004. www.iso.org/iso/tool_5-04.pdf

Global Food Safety Initiative (GFSI). www.mygfsi.com

International Organization for Standardization (ISO). www.iso.org

International Plant Protection Convention (IPPC). www.ippc.int

World Organisation for Animal Health. www.oie.int

16. Which standards are required to export textile products?

Considering the broad span of textile producing and manufacturing activities, it is useful to make a distinction between those that can easily be conducted by SMEs, and those that need a large amount of finance and technology. For natural fibres the activities include: (i) growing and harvesting; (ii) ginning or other preparation of the fibres to make them suitable for use in spinning; (iii) spinning of the fibres into yarns; (iv) weaving of the yarns into fabric; (v) manufacture of final product (e.g. blouse, tablecloth); and (vi) labelling and packaging. The activities covering synthetic (man-made) fibres are similar, except for the fact that the fibres do not come from plants that have to be grown and harvested. Many textile products are combinations of natural and man-made fibres.

The early stages of fibre production, spinning, weaving and dyeing (i.e. the textiles) are capital intensive, hence they are usually confined to large-scale operations and big organizations. They are also subject to more mandatory technical requirements than the later stages. The final products, e.g. clothing, tablecloths, napkins, cushions, on the other hand are labour intensive, and although large manufacturers are quite common, there are an immense number of SME-type operations in many countries manufacturing clothing and other products made from textiles.

At each stage of the production process, the outputs may have to comply with technical requirements and have to be tested and certified. Many public and private textile and clothing standards (see questions 13 and 14) have evolved over the years, but only a few, mostly related to textiles, have been declared mandatory. Hence, market forces determine to a large extent which standards must be applied by manufacturers of clothing and other products made from textiles.

International and other technical requirements

The International Organization for Standardization (ISO) has developed and published hundreds of international standards on textiles. These can be found in the ISO online catalogue. The list is very helpful, and referring to the four main ISO committees involved might ease the search further. These are TC 38 Textiles, TC 94/SC 13 Protective clothing, TC 219 Floor coverings and TC 221 Geosynthetics. In spite of the existence of these international standards, few if any have been adopted by all countries. Many national and regional standards remain.

National and private standards bodies also publish extensive collections of standards for textiles and textile products. Here are two examples:

- In China, a whole suite of new standards for textiles was published in 2008 for implementation, replacing many outdated standards.
- The American Society for Testing and Materials (ASTM) has published two handbooks with a collection of more than 350 textile-related ASTM test methods, practices and specifications covering the uses of textiles, nomenclature, characteristics and properties.

Some of the mandatory technical requirements for textiles and clothing in the European Union are to be found in the REACH Directive (see question 27 for a full discussion). This Directive, for example, disallows the use of certain products in the manufacture of textiles and clothing such as azo dyes, organotin compounds, dimethyl fumarate substances and the like. In the United States, the US Consumer Product Safety Commission has been given the mandate to implement safety requirements for marketed textile products, e.g. fire resistance and the banning of certain types of children's upper body garments that incorporate drawstrings as these are considered a 'substantial product hazard'.

It is therefore extremely important for suppliers to obtain correct information about standards or technical regulations for the target market. The local NSB or TPO may be of help in identifying these (see also question 23).

Purchaser requirements

Clothing and other goods manufactured from textiles is big business, and the large retail organizations and specialized trading companies will have their own ideas regarding standards for these goods. These may relate to the design of the clothing, the technical requirements for the fabric and manufacturing processes, labelling and packaging and other matters. This contrasts with the general lack of mandatory technical requirements for clothing in almost all countries, quite unlike textiles which have to comply with a number of technical regulations.

The exporter therefore has to find out exactly what these buyer-specific requirements are, and which testing and certification regimes are demanded. Mandatory technical requirements for textiles cannot be ignored by the clothing manufacturers either. They will have to ensure that the cloth, yarn and other manufacturing inputs do comply with the mandatory requirements, otherwise the clothing fashioned from them may not be allowed in the marketplace.

As regards conformity assessment, some of the major retail organizations operate their own textile testing laboratories, whereas others rely on independent accredited laboratories and certification organizations for these services. Many national standards bodies in textile-producing countries have established textile laboratories.

Labelling

Some countries have technical regulations requiring the proper labelling of textiles. In the United States, for example, any product that is exclusively composed of textile fibres, or a product containing at least 80% by weight of textile fibres, has to carry a label indicating the fibre content, e.g. cotton 80% polyester 15% nylon 5%. The types of names that must be used are also prescribed. Some products that contain textile fibre are exempt from these requirements, including tobacco pouches, footwear, sails, oven gloves. The European Union has similar fibre content requirements in place.

The other information that must appear on labels has to do with how the textile products are to be cared for. Examples are how warm they can be washed; whether they should only be dry-cleaned; whether they can be spin-dried or ironed, and if so at what temperatures. These labels differ slightly from country to country. Hence, the correct pictograms have to be obtained for each market. Typical examples are shown in the figure below. Some countries (for instance, China, Egypt, Indonesia, Malaysia, Pakistan and Switzerland) have no national labelling requirements and purchaser requirements have to be considered.

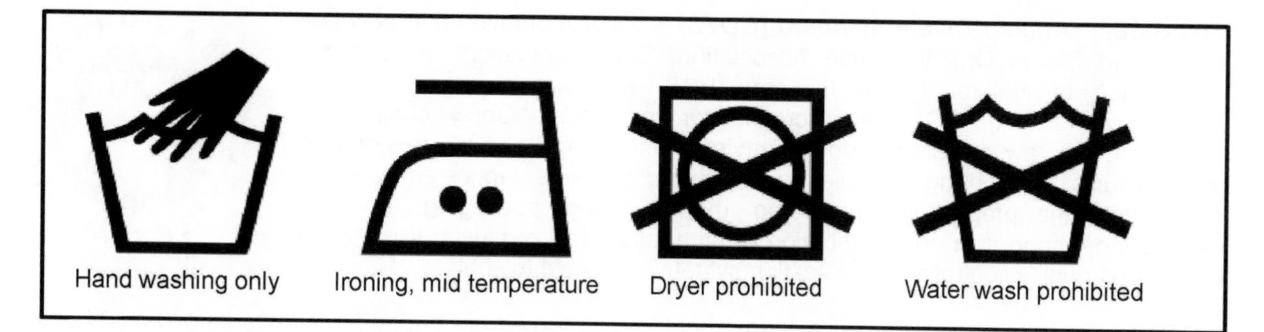

Clothing sizes

No recognized international system for clothing sizes has been implemented so far, hence clothing has to be marked specifically for the market it is destined for. A man's dress shirt marked 15 in the United States would be the equivalent of a size 38 shirt on the European continent. For women, a 12 in the United States would translate roughly into a 14 in the United Kingdom and a 42 in France.

In the European Union, two mandatory standards have been in operation since 2006 to replace the many national systems, namely: EN 13402-1: Terms, definitions and body measurement procedure and EN 13402-2: Primary and secondary dimensions. In contrast, there is no mandatory standard in place in the United States, and a whole series of customs and practices have evolved over the years, starting with the US standard clothing sizes which are slowly being replaced by US catalogue clothing sizes.

A few countries make use of the ISO standards on clothing sizes. These are ISO 3635:1981 Size designation of clothes – Definitions and body measurement procedure, ISO 8559:1989 Garment construction and anthropometric surveys – Body dimensions, and ISO/TR 10652:1991 Standard sizing systems for clothes.

Packaging

The packaging of individual products as well as the bulk packaging of textiles and clothing has to comply with many standards and technical regulations. See question 28 for more detail.

Private certification standards

Probably no consumer product is more affected or targeted by social, ethical and environmental demands than textiles and clothing. Hence certification to SA 8000 (social accountability), Fairtrade (ethical considerations) and WRAP (environmental concerns) may be required to gain market acceptance. These are fully discussed in questions 17 and 77. Quite a few eco-labelling type schemes exist that could be applied to textiles and clothing (see also question 78) and in some markets these are important parameters for marketing success. A few additional schemes and programmes specific to textiles and clothing are shown below. There are many of these; hence the supplier will have to determine very carefully which one of the many systems is relevant from a market perspective in the chosen export market.

Woolmark

The ***Woolmark*** is one of the most recognizable textile labels worldwide. It is owned by Australian Wool Innovation Limited (AWI). The company operates a global licensing programme to ensure that any product bearing the Woolmark logo meets strict wool quality and performance criteria. To become a licensee, you should contact the local AWI office (a list of offices can be found on the AWI website). An application fee has to be paid, and the products have to be tested in AWI laboratories to ensure they meet the standards. If successful, a licence is granted to use the Woolmark. Labels and merchandising support material are provided to licensees.

Global Organic Textile Standard (GOTS)

The ***Global Organic Textile Standard (GOTS)*** is a collaborative effort between the United States Organic Trade Association, Soil Association, International Association of Natural Textile Industry (IVN), and Japan Organic Cotton Association (JOCA). GOTS sets criteria for the entire supply chain from harvesting the raw materials, through environmentally and socially responsible manufacturing, to labelling. It applies to fibre products, yarns, fabrics and clothes, and covers the production, processing, manufacturing, packaging, labelling, exportation, importation and distribution of all natural fibre products. It is thus a continuous quality control and certification system from 'field to shelf'.

GOTS carries detailed social criteria: there should be no forced or bonded labour; workers should not be required to lodge deposits or identity papers with their employers; there should be no child labour; workers should be free to leave after reasonable notice; working conditions should be safe and hygienic. The requirements for waste water treatment include the measurement and monitoring of sediment quantities, waste water temperature and waste water pH. GOTS certification is awarded only to natural fibres; it is not applicable to synthetic fibres.

More information on GOTS, as well as a list of, and links to, the certification organizations that are accredited to provide GOTS certification can be found on the GOTS website.

Textile Exchange

The ***Textile Exchange (previously Organic Exchange)*** is a non-profit organization with a global multi-stakeholder approach to developing markets in the textile value chain. It has over 230 global organizational members, including many of the world's best known brands and retailers, whose total sales amounted to over US$ 755 billion in 2009.

The Exchange covers the entire value chain, from the farm or producer through manufacturing to retail. It thus concerns itself with building both demand and supply simultaneously. Its demand efforts focus on the brand and on retail sales. Brand promotion gives suppliers incentives to increase production and helps stabilize both short- and long-term production schedules. The Exchange provides models and tools for collaborative planning, problem solving, product development and sourcing, and consumer education.

Information on Textile Exchange activities can be obtained from its website.

Better Cotton Initiative (BCI)

The ***Better Cotton Initiative (BCI)*** is a fairly new initiative to make cotton production better for the people who produce it, better for the environment it grows in, hence better overall for the sector. During the start-up implementation phase, the BCI geographical focus is on four regions: Brazil, India, Pakistan and West and Central Africa (Benin, Burkina Faso, Cameroon, Mali, Senegal and Togo). These regions have a diversity of climatic conditions, farm sizes, agricultural practices and environmental and social issues. BCI will also provide access to materials, tools and guidelines to enable any country to grow Better Cotton.

The Better Cotton System will build on farm and supply chain data and employ strong monitoring, evaluation and learning mechanisms. The System will be externally reviewed at the end of 2012 to evaluate whether it has delivered the desired results and impacts. BCI wants to learn from three years of implementation to make any necessary adjustments to improve both the Better Cotton System and the way the Initiative works.

Oeko-Tex

Oeko-Tex (also written Őko-Tex) is another textile and clothing certification scheme based on a catalogue of harmful substances that could be deleterious to human health. This catalogue is updated frequently in accordance with the latest scientific results. Responsibility for the Oeko-Tex Standard 100 is shared by 17 test institutes which make up the International Oeko-Tex Association. The Association has branch offices in more than 40 countries. With a total of over 51 000 certificates issued for millions of different individual products, and over 6 500 companies involved worldwide, the Oeko-Tex Standard 100 has become one of the better known labels for textiles tested for harmful substances.

The test samples are tested by the independent Oeko-Tex institutes, for example, for their pH value, formaldehyde content and the presence of pesticides, extractable heavy metals, chlorinated organic carriers and preservatives such as pentachlorophenol and tetrachlorophenol. The tests also include checks for any MAC amines in azo dyestuffs and allergy-inducing dyestuffs.

FOR MORE INFORMATION

- Centre for the Promotion of Imports from developing countries (CBI). Website at www.cbi.nl

  Provides information on textiles and clothing in relation to European Union markets; offers market information and information on sectors, suppliers, supporters, buyers.

- United States Consumer Product Safety Commission. www.cpsc.gov

  Provides information and publications relevant to business and products that pose a fire, electrical, chemical, or mechanical hazard or can injure children.

- US Consumer Product Safety Improvement Act. Guidance for Small Manufacturers, Importers, and Crafters of Children's Products. http://www.cpsc.gov/about/cpsia/smbus/manufacturers.html

  Explains how certification requirements affect small manufacturers, importers and crafters of children's products.

REFERENCES

ASTM International. www.astm.org

Australian Wool Innovation Limited (AWI). www.wool.com

Better Cotton Initiative (BCI). www.bettercotton.org

Global Organic Textile Standard (GOTS) certification. www.global-standard.org

Hong Kong Trade Development Council (HKTDC). Textile Safety Update, 2008. www.hktdc.com/info/mi/a/psls/en/1X0014YQ/1/Product-Safety-Laws-And-Standards/Textile-Standard-Update-China-Market.htm

International Organization for Standardization (ISO). www.iso.org.

Oeko-Tex. www.oeko-tex.com/OekoTex100_PUBLIC/index_portal.asp

Textile Exchange. www.textileexchange.org/

Wikipedia, Oeko-Tex Standard information. http://en.wikipedia.org/wiki/Oeko-tex_standard

17. Which standards are required by some purchasers to address social, environmental and ethical concerns?

Ethical, environmental and social concerns arising from the design, manufacture and supply of products have risen steeply over the last few decades. Suppliers can no longer ignore these concerns, and in many markets products have to be shown to comply with technical requirements related to such issues. The technical requirements may be provided in public as well as private standards, and in some cases have found their way into technical regulation and SPS measures. A few examples are discussed below.

Social responsibility

Social responsibilities are addressed in SA 8000:2008, a private standard published by the New York based Social Accountability International. This is the third issue of SA 8000, an auditable standard for a certification system, setting out the voluntary requirements to be met by employers in the workplace, including workers' rights, workplace conditions and management systems. The normative elements of this standard are based on national law and human rights as defined by the United Nations and the conventions of the International Labour Organization. The SA 8000 standard can be used along with the 'SA 8000 Guidance Document' to assess the compliance of a workplace. The Guidance Document helps to explain SA 8000 and how to implement its requirements; provides examples of methods for verifying compliance; and serves as a handbook for auditors and for companies seeking certification of compliance with SA 8000. The standard can be downloaded free of charge from the SA 8000 website, whereas a fee has to be paid for the Guidance Document.

At the international level, ISO launched 'ISO 26000:2010, Guidance on social responsibility'. ISO 26000 provides guidance for all types of organizations, regardless of their size or location, on:

- Concepts, terms and definitions related to social responsibility;
- Background, trends and characteristics of social responsibility;
- Principles and practices relating to social responsibility;
- Core subjects and issues of social responsibility;
- Integrating, implementing and promoting socially responsible behaviour throughout the organization and, through its policies and practices, within its sphere of influence;
- Identifying and engaging with stakeholders; and
- Communicating commitments, performance and other information related to social responsibility.

ISO 26000 is a voluntary guidance standard that is not to be used for certification, unlike ISO 9001:2008 (quality management) and ISO 14001:2004 (environmental management), which can be used for certification.

Ethical concerns

Fairtrade is a set of standards covering mostly ethical trade issues. They endeavour to provide farmers in developing countries at the beginning of the production chain a better deal when trading with developed markets.

There are two distinct sets of Fairtrade standards, which acknowledge different types of disadvantaged producers. One set of standards applies to smallholders who work together in cooperatives or other organizations with a democratic structure. The other set applies to companies with hired workers who are paid decent wages and are guaranteed the right to join trade unions.

Fairtrade standards also cover terms of trade. Most products within the scope of the standards have a Fairtrade price, which is the minimum that must be paid to the producers. These producers get an additional sum, the Fairtrade Premium, to invest in their communities. Full details can be obtained from the Fairtrade website.

Many other sector-based private standards cover ethical concerns or social responsibility issues to a smaller or greater extent. A typical example is the Global Organic Textile Standard (GOTS), which has requirements for fair wages and covers non-bonded workers in textile manufacturing plants (see question 16 for more details).

Environmental standards

The ISO 14000 environmental management series is probably the best known collection of standards dealing with environmental issues. They require an organization to ensure that, within a formal management system, it will:

- Take stock of its impact on the environment;
- Commit itself to effective and reliable processes and to the prevention of pollution;
- Establish objectives and targets to continuously improve its position; and
- Demonstrate that it complies with all the environmental legislation of its country.

There are quite a number of standards already published within the ISO 14000 series, and the number is growing, even though the publishing tempo is not as frenzied as it was a decade ago. Many of the standards are under review as is normal practice in standards development. Suppliers therefore must ensure that they always obtain the latest version of the relevant ISO 14000 series of standards.

The figure below shows some of the standards, their relationship to each other and how they fit into a holistic view of environmental management. An overview of all the standards can be found in the ISO publication *The ISO 14000 Family of Standards,* available as a free download from ISO. Questions 38 to 41 provide further explanations on environmental management systems. For a discussion on certification related to environmental concerns, see question 78.

ISO 14000 series of standards

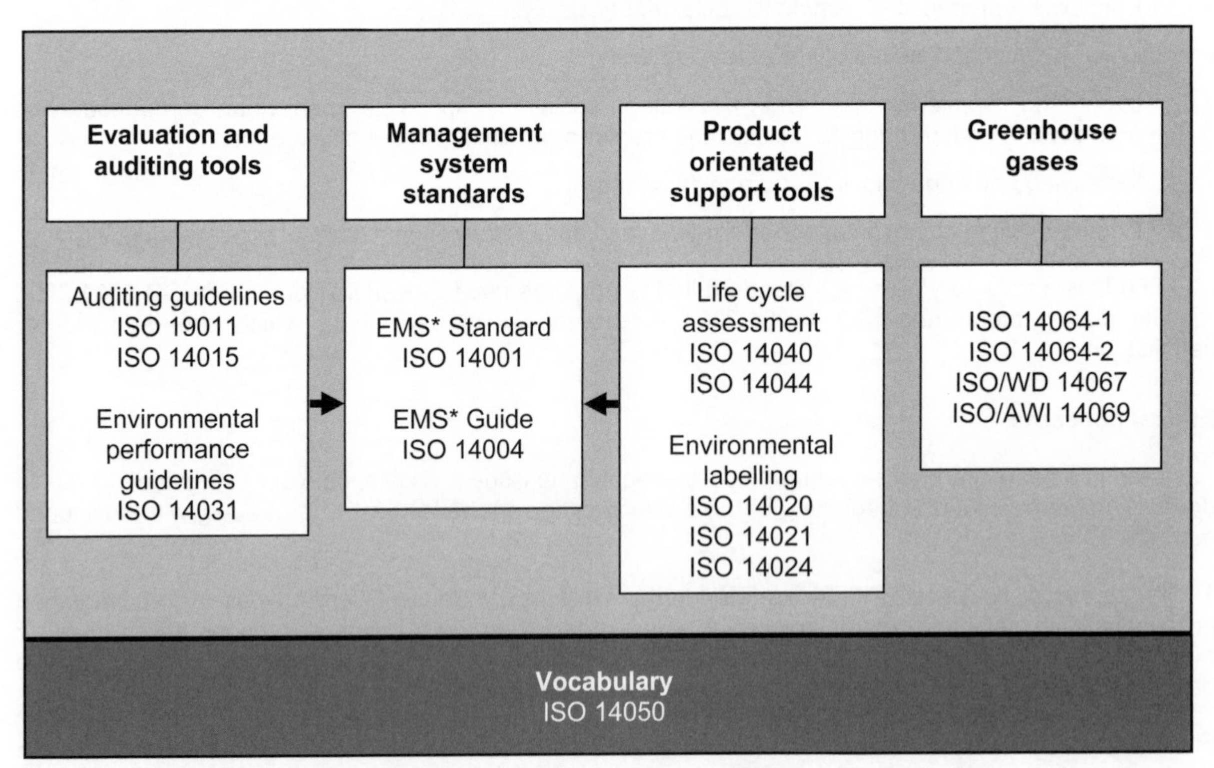

Source: International Organization for Standardization, adapted by Martin Kellermann.

* Environmental Management System.

Companies that wish to demonstrate compliance have to be certified to ISO 14001. There are many certification bodies that offer such a service. It is important, however, to choose one that is accredited to provide certification (see question 71 for more details on the choice of certification body). The economic importance of ISO 14000 is gradually increasing and a growing number of companies are obtaining certification to ISO 14001, as can be seen from the annual ISO worldwide review of management system certificates.

There are also quite a number of private standards that deal with environmental issues, and these are related to the certification schemes that have cropped up in developed countries. They are frequently closely related to eco-labelling (see question 78). Two typical examples are itemized below:

- GREENGUARD. GREENGUARD has developed proprietary indoor air-quality pollutant guidelines based on guidelines from government and industrial bodies. It was launched in 2000 by the Atlanta-based (United States) Air Quality Sciences (AQS).
- Cradle to Cradle. This standard leads to certification that a product uses environmentally safe and healthy materials. It has an energy, water and social responsibility component. Cradle to Cradle's strength is in material chemistry. All ingredients in a product are identified down to 100 parts per million and assessed according to 19 human and environmental health criteria.

FOR MORE INFORMATION

- International Trade Centre. Standards Map. www.standardsmap.org

  Provides online access to ITC's detailed database on private standards and presents academic, scientific and research articles on private standards issues in global value chains. Standards Map operates in a web-based interactive environment and enables comparisons of the requirements of private standards at various levels of analysis, from general social and environmental requirements to detailed criteria and indicators for food safety and carbon emission, as well as labour rights and gender issues.

REFERENCES

Cradle to Cradle. http://mbdc.com/detail.aspx?linkid=2&sublink=8

Fairtrade Labelling Organizations International (FLO). www.fairtrade.net

FLO-CERT. www.flo-cert.net/flo-cert/

GREENGUARD. www.greenguard.org

International Organization for Standardization

- Environmental Management – The ISO 14000 family of International Standards. www.iso.org/iso/free_pubs#MANAGEMENT_STANDARDS
- International Organization for Standardization. ISO 26000:2010, Guidance on social responsibility. Obtainable from ISO or ISO members (list at www.iso.org).

International Trade Centre. Standards Map: www.standardsmap.org

18. What is a technical regulation?

Products may fail and so endanger the health and safety of people, or they may have a negative effect on the environment, or they may be offered in such a way that consumers are seriously deceived. To deal with such issues, governments implement official controls. Such controls are called technical regulations as defined in the WTO TBT Agreement (see question 92). Technical regulations are not standards, but these two are sometimes confused with each other because they seem alike (see question 13). Technical regulations could be stand-alone documents, but they could also be based on standards or may reference them. Whereas standards are considered voluntary in principle, i.e. suppliers can choose to implement them or not, technical regulations are mandatory in nature, i.e. everybody has to comply with them by law.

A technical regulation is a document or legislation that lays down *product characteristics* or their related processes and production methods. A technical regulation may also include or deal exclusively with terminology, symbols, packaging, marking or labelling requirements as they apply to a product, process or production method. In all cases, a technical regulation would include the *administrative measures* required to implement it. For example, it can identify the regulatory authority, list the conformity assessment requirements, and provide for market surveillance responsibilities and the implementation of sanctions in case of non-compliance. The building blocks of a typical technical regulation are shown in the figure below.

Building blocks of technical regulations

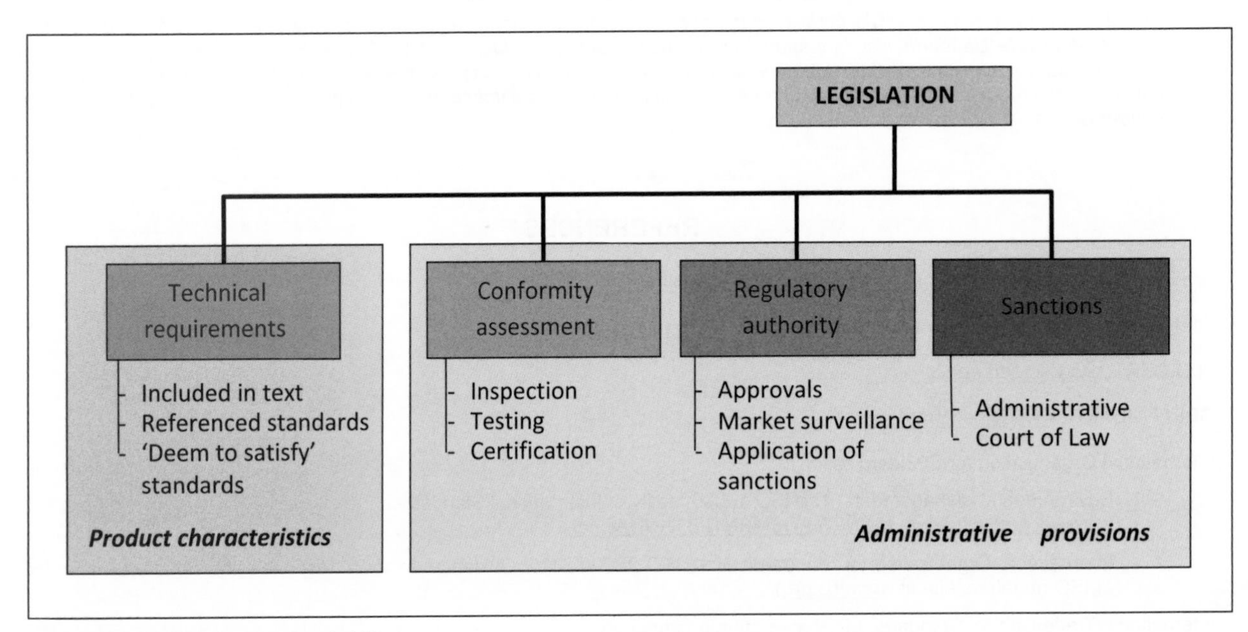

Source: Martin Kellermann, South Africa.

Technical regulations are formulated and implemented by a variety of government ministries or regulatory agencies or both, depending on the practices and legal system of the country. They are generally not developed according to consensus principles, but in some countries stakeholders are given opportunities to provide comments and influence regulations at a draft stage.

Technical regulations are given a range of different names. In the European Union, they are called Directives, Regulations, Decisions. In some countries, they are called Compulsory or Mandatory Standards, sometimes even Compulsory Specifications or just simply Regulations. A further complication arises from the fact that technical regulations have been around for decades, some of them dating back 70 or more years, and finding information about the old regulations may be a challenge. They may even be technically outdated, but they still have the force of law and have to be complied with.

Technical regulations can apply to all industrial and agricultural products. An agricultural product may therefore be subject to both technical regulations and SPS measures (see question 19). It also happens frequently that a specific product is subject to more than one technical regulation, e.g. a fax machine may be subject to electrical safety requirements, to electromagnetic interference (EMI) requirements and to connectivity requirements with regard to the communication network of the country. Furthermore, these three technical regulations may even be administered by three different regulatory agencies.

The spread of information on technical regulations, the diversity of the regulatory agencies responsible for their administration, and the variety of inspection, testing and certification requirements – all these factors may make it difficult for a supplier to obtain relevant information and to ensure compliance with all the requirements for the product that is to be exported or marketed. Although the WTO Agreement on TBT endeavours to ensure that technical regulations do not act as unnecessary barriers to trade and are harmonized with international standards as much as possible, the world is still far from attaining that goal. Suppliers therefore have to ensure that they obtain the correct information on their products for their target market before marketing and shipping them in order to prevent major disappointments, unanticipated costs or financial losses (see question 21).

FOR MORE INFORMATION

- European Commission. Guide to the Implementation of Directives Based on the New Approach and the Global Approach. 2008. http://ec.europa.eu/enterprise/policies/single-market-goods/files/blue-guide/guidepublic_en.pdf

  Although focussing on explaining the EU's New Approach Directives, this Guide contains useful information on technical regulations in general.

- World Trade Organization. Agreement on Technical Barriers to Trade. 1994. www.wto.org/english/res_e/booksp_e/analytic_index_e/tbt_02_e.htm#article15

  Presents the full text of the WTO TBT Agreement (as well as all the other WTO Agreements), together with information on its interpretation and the various trade disputes related to the Agreement that have been resolved.

REFERENCES

Physikalisch-Technische Bundesanstalt and International Trade Centre. Technical Regulations, Recommendations for their Elaboration and Implementation, Guide 1/2009, Alex Inklaar, 2009.
www.ptb.de/de/org/q/q5/docs/broschueren/broschuere_Guide1_Technical_regulations_e.pdf
www.intracen.org/exporters/quality-management/Quality_publications_index/

World Trade Organization

- Technical Barriers to Trade Gateway. www.wto.org/english/tratop_e/tbt_e/tbt_e.htm
- World Trade Report 2005: Exploring the links between trade, standards and the WTO, 2005. www.wto.org/english/res_e/booksp_e/anrep_e/world_trade_report05_e.pdf

19. What are sanitary and phytosanitary measures?

Sanitary and phytosanitary (SPS) measures are requirements imposed on goods by governments to control certain kinds of risks to human, animal or plant life and health. Most SPS measures are concerned with the maintenance of food safety, and the protection of animal and plant health against pests and diseases. Sanitary measures deal with the protection of the life or health of humans or animals; phytosanitary measures deal with the protection of the life or health of plants.

The function performed by governments in keeping out exotic animal and plant pests and diseases of plants and animals is often called biosecurity. According to FAO (Food and Agriculture Organization of the United Nations), biosecurity is a strategic and integrated approach encompassing the policy and regulatory frameworks for analysing and managing risks in the sectors of food safety, animal life and health, and plant life and health, including the associated environmental risks.

The WTO Agreement on the Application of Sanitary and Phytosanitary Measures (the SPS Agreement) defines sanitary and phytosanitary measures as any measure applied to:

- Protect human life or health from risks arising from additives, contaminants, toxins or disease-causing organisms in food and beverages, or from diseases carried by animals or plants or their products, or from pests;
- Protect animal life or health from risks arising from additives, contaminants, toxins or disease-causing organisms in feedstuffs, or from diseases carried by animals or plants, or from pests, diseases or disease-causing organisms;
- Protect plant life or health from pests, diseases or disease-causing organisms; and
- Prevent or limit other damage to a country from the entry, establishment or spread of pests.

The measures also cover those taken to protect the health of fish and wild fauna, as well as forests and wild flora. Environmental provisions to protect consumer interests or the welfare of animals other than as defined above do not fall within the purview of the SPS Agreement.

The measures include all relevant laws, decrees, regulations, requirements and procedures. These may stipulate end product criteria; processes and production methods; testing, inspection, certification and approval procedures; quarantine treatments and requirements for the transport of animals or plants, and for the materials necessary for their survival during transport. They may also impose obligations in regard to statistical methods, sampling procedures and methods of risk assessment. Finally, they may prescribe packaging and labelling requirements directly related to food safety.

Food standards enforced by government agencies to ensure the safety of foods, and biosecurity controls enforced at international borders to keep out exotic animal and plant pests and diseases are typical SPS measures.

FOR MORE INFORMATION

- International Trade Centre. 'Quality & Standards.' *International Trade Forum Magazine*, Issue 3, 2010, www.tradeforum.org

  The 'Quality & Standards' issue looks, inter alia, at standards, technical regulations, SPS measures and their role in the promotion of exports from developing countries. It is available in English, French and Spanish.

- Standards and Trade Development Facility (STDF). www.standardsfacility.org/en/index.htm

  Joint initiative in capacity building and technical cooperation aiming at raising awareness of the importance of sanitary and phytosanitary issues, increasing coordination in the provision of SPS-related assistance, and mobilizing resources to enhance the capacity of developing countries to meet SPS standards.

- World Trade Organization. Sanitary and Phytosanitary Measures. www.wto.org/english/tratop_e/sps_e/sps_e.htm

  The site provides many resources to help deepen understanding of the meaning of the SPS Agreement and to facilitate its implementation by WTO Members.

REFERENCES

Food and Agriculture Organization of the United Nations (FAO). www.fao.org/

World Trade Organization. Sanitary and Phytosanitary Measures.
www.wto.org/english/res_e/booksp_e/agrmntseries4_sps_08_e.pdf

20. What is the relationship between standards, technical regulations, and SPS measures?

The terminology of standards, technical regulations and SPS measures is frequently a source of confusion. Common usage of these expressions in many countries does not necessarily correspond to the specific legal meanings given to them in the TBT and SPS Agreements. For example, many countries have official food standards that must be obeyed, whereas the TBT Agreement says that compliance with 'standards' (as defined in that Agreement) is not mandatory. Furthermore, the word carries different meanings even in the SPS and TBT Agreements. To understand the relationship between the various terms in the context of the WTO rules, it is necessary to look at the Agreements separately.

It is important to understand that the TBT and SPS Agreements are complementary. The SPS Agreement applies to a defined set of official requirements, called SPS measures, concerning the control of certain risks to human, animal and plant life and health (see question 19). By their nature SPS measures are technical barriers to trade, but they are not covered by the TBT Agreement. The latter Agreement concerns itself with all other technical barriers to trade.

Differences between SPS and TBT measures

SPS measures typically deal with:	TBT measures typically deal with:
• Additives in food or drink • Contaminants in food or drink • Toxic substances in food or drink • Residues of veterinary drugs or pesticides in food or drink • Certification: food safety, animal or plant health • Processing methods with implications for food safety • Labelling requirements directly related to food safety • Plant and animal quarantine • Declaring areas free from pests or disease • Preventing disease or pests from spreading to or in a country • Other sanitary requirements for imports (e.g. in regard to the imported pallets used to transport animals)	• Labelling on composition or quality of food, drink and drugs • Quality requirements for fresh food • Volume, shape and appearance of packaging • Packaging and labelling of dangerous chemicals and toxic substances, pesticides and fertilizer • Regulations on electrical appliances • Regulations on cordless phones, radio equipment, etc. • Labelling of textiles and garments • The testing of vehicles and accessories • Regulations on ships and ship equipment • Safety regulations on toys

Source: World Trade Organization.

Under the TBT Agreement, a technical regulation is a document prescribing product characteristics or related processes and production methods. Compliance with this regulation is mandatory – that is, it is a legally binding condition for market access. The responsibility for developing, promulgating and enforcing technical regulations and SPS measures lies with the State and its authorities. Ultimately, these tasks are incorporated into the legal system and the decision on the way they are to be carried out is a State prerogative.

The TBT Agreement refers to documents that are similar to the above but which are not meant to have mandatory application as 'standards'. Standards are recommendations; the users of a standard may decide for themselves which standards are relevant for them and whether the benefits of implementation outweigh its costs. The responsibility for developing and publishing standards lies with recognized standards bodies. Approval of the standards is vested in the councils or boards of these standards bodies, which – in accordance with international good practices – consist of representatives of interested parties, including the State. The standards development process follows internationally agreed principles such as openness, consensus and transparency.

As has already been said, SPS measures are requirements imposed on goods by governments to control certain kinds of risks to human, animal or plant life and health. SPS measures are defined in the WTO Agreement on the Application of Sanitary and Phytosanitary Measures which came into force in 1995. The Agreement affirms the right of WTO Members to apply such measures provided that they conform to the provisions of the Agreement.

The SPS Agreement asks WTO Members to base their SPS measures on the international standards, guidelines and recommendations developed by specific organizations, namely the Codex Alimentarius Commission, the International Office of Epizootics and the Secretariat of the International Plant Protection Convention. These are intergovernmental bodies that develop international norms, including many standards that are intended for mandatory application by governments.

There is therefore, a strong relationship between standards, technical regulations and SPS measures, but there are also fundamental differences mostly related to their implementation and the responsibility for developing them. The technical content of technical regulations and SPS measures may be very similar to that found in standards. They may even be exactly the same, owing to the fact that the WTO SPS and TBT Agreements require regulations and SPS measures to be based on international standards where these are available. Countries do have the right, however, to deviate from international standards if reasons for doing so exist or can be demonstrated. In some countries, the national standard may even be declared mandatory, thereby elevating it to a technical regulation. These are known as mandatory standards, compulsory standards, or sometimes just regulations.

FOR MORE INFORMATION

- European Commission. Guide to the implementation of Directives Based on the New Approach and the Global Approach, 2008. http://ec.europa.eu/enterprise/policies/single-market-goods/files/blue-guide/guidepublic_en.pdf

  This information document contains an excellent discussion on the indirect referencing of the harmonized European standards (EN) in the New Directives.

- International Organization for Standardization. Using and referencing ISO and IEC Standards for technical regulations, September 2007. www.iso.org/iso/standards_for_technical_regulations.pdf

  This information document explains in detail the advantages of, and methodology for, direct and indirect referencing of the ISO and IEC standards in technical regulations.

- World Trade Organization
  - Understanding the WTO Agreement on Sanitary and Phytosanitary Measures. 1998. www.wto.org/english/tratop_e/sps_e/spsund_e.htm

    An introduction to the WTO SPS Agreement, with questions and answers.

  - Agreement on Technical Barriers to Trade, 1994. www.wto.org/english/docs_e/legal_e/legal_e.htm

    Provides the full text of the WTO TBT Agreement, as well as a fair amount of information about its interpretation and the use of standards in developing regulations.

REFERENCES

Physikalisch-Technische Bundesanstalt and International Trade Centre. Technical Regulations: Recommendations for their Elaboration and Implementation. Guide 1/2009, Alex Inklaar, 2009.
www.ptb.de/de/org/q/q5/docs/broschueren/broschuere_Guide1_Technical_regulations_e.pdf
www.intracen.org/exporters/quality-management/Quality_publications_index/

World Trade Organization. World Trade Report 2005: Exploring the links between trade, standards and the WTO. 2005.
www.wto.org/english/res_e/booksp_e/anrep_e/world_trade_report05_e.pdf

21. Are standards, technical regulations and SPS measures barriers to trade and how can these barriers be overcome?

Barriers to trade are measures in place in the country to which you wish to export which make it difficult or even impossible for you to export your product to it. They can take many forms but are generally classified in two broad categories: tariff barriers and non-tariff barriers. Technical regulations and SPS measures are considered non-tariff barriers.

The primary purpose of the WTO TBT and SPS Agreements is to minimize the negative impact on trade of technical regulations and SPS measures as barriers to trade by allowing legitimate restrictions while preventing the imposition of arbitrary or unjustified ones.

Where the technical regulations and SPS measures of an importing country are in conformity with the TBT and SPS Agreements, exporters seeking to access that market have no choice but to comply with the requirements. Trade may not be possible where, for example, it is beyond the capacity of the industry in a developing country to supply goods that meet the high technical requirements of an importing country at a competitive price. Similarly, an SPS requirement imposed by an importing country in order to protect its biosecurity, such as one prohibiting imports of animal products from countries that are known to have certain serious animal diseases, may also prevent trade with these countries.

Voluntary standards may be barriers to trade if buyers in an importing country are unwilling to purchase products that do not conform to the local norms promulgated by a standardization organization. Exporters can choose whether or not to conform to voluntary standards, but they must in any case meet buyers' specifications.

Since the advent of the General Agreement on Tariffs and Trade (GATT), negotiators have set up agreements with Members of GATT and later WTO to alleviate unnecessary trade barriers emanating from standards, technical regulations and SPS measures. The notion of internationally harmonized standards is fundamental to these agreements, which ask countries to adopt international standards as their national standards. Technical regulations and SPS measures should be based on international standards or their national adoptions.

The same applies to standards for the conformity assessment systems (see question 55) used to demonstrate compliance of products or services with international requirements. Mutual recognition among countries of the outcomes of inspection, testing and certification, even though they may be different in application, is strongly advocated by the WTO Agreements, provided that the different systems result in similar levels of product integrity.

How can barriers to trade be overcome? This can be achieved by WTO Members by taking advantage of the opportunities that are available to them to influence the contents of trade-restrictive measures in importing countries.

The transparency procedures under the TBT and SPS Agreements allow all WTO Members to have advance notice of proposed new or revised measures and to submit comments that must be taken into account by the notifying country. Consequently, each country should monitor the flow of notifications, which are regularly circulated by the WTO Secretariat, and promptly identify and act upon those notifications that may adversely affect its trade interests (see also question 25). The organization given the task of monitoring notifications should maintain close contact with the private sector bodies representing exporters in order to keep them informed of, and to obtain their views on, potential barriers to trade.

If an exporting country believes that a technical regulation or SPS measure imposed by an importing country is not legitimate in terms of the relevant WTO Agreement (TBT or SPS), a range of options is available to try to have the measure modified or removed. These options begin with discussions with the authorities of the importing country in order to obtain information about the precise nature of the impediment to trade and the reasons for its imposition. The national enquiry point of the importing country may be the first point of contact for this purpose, but other channels for bilateral communication can be used (see question 23). Such discussions may lead to the negotiation of mutually satisfactory amendments to the measure in question.

If appropriate, the matter can be raised in the multilateral forum of a meeting of the WTO Committee on Sanitary and Phytosanitary Measures or the Committee on Technical Barriers to Trade, with a request to the importing country to explain its measure publicly. Ultimately, the WTO's dispute settlement procedure involving formal intergovernmental consultations and a dispute settlement panel to hear the case is available to a complaining country.

The following measures should be pursued by authorities and industry alike in overcoming trade barriers:

- National standards bodies should be encouraged to ensure that their technical committees take cognizance of international standards in developing national standards. In fact, unless there are compelling reasons based on solid evidence, national standards should reflect international standards with as few deviations as possible.
- Industry and the national standards bodies should ensure that they participate actively in the relevant international technical committees that deliberate on international standards in order to 'protect' their countries' interests. That being said, it is far better to participate in a few selected technical committees dealing with a country's main exports than to try and participate in as many as possible.
- Authorities should be encouraged to utilize standards as a basis for developing technical regulations and SPS measures. The referencing method should be pursued vigorously, and authorities should be dissuaded from including specific technical requirements in the text of legislation. In this way they will ensure that international best practices are considered, stakeholders will have a say in the formulation of technical requirements through the development of standards, and acceptance of the technical regulations and SPS measures will be heightened.
- The industry and the authorities in developing economies should work together and do their utmost to develop control systems (particularly for food and feeds) that will satisfy the demands of sophisticated markets like the European Union. EU has a 'field to fork' approach to these products and insists on traceability, testing and certification of produce and processed foods from the time of planting until the time these products reach its consumer tables. The same applies to the establishment of the testing and certification capacity and its accreditation (see questions 87, 88 and 90).

FOR MORE INFORMATION

- European Commission. Guide to the implementation of directives based on the New Approach and the Global Approach. http://ec.europa.eu/enterprise/policies/single-market-goods/files/blue-guide/guidepublic_en.pdf

  Contains an excellent discussion on the indirect referencing of the harmonized European standards (EN) in the New Directives.

- Iacovone, Leonardo. Analysis and Impact of Sanitary and Phytosanitary Measures. Final Dissertation. http://www.cid.harvard.edu/cidtrade/Papers/iacovone.pdf

  Introduces the crucial elements that characterize regulations in general and SPS measures in particular, presents a synthetic overview of the institutional framework set by the WTO SPS Agreement, discusses the difficulties posed to economic analysis by domestic regulations, and offers an econometric method for measuring the effect of standards and domestic regulations on trade flows.

- Ignacio, Laura. Implications of Standards and Technical Regulations on Export Competitiveness. African Economic Research Consortium. June 2007. http://www.aercafrica.org/publications/item.asp?itemid=352

  This paper discusses how standards and technical regulations pose constraints to the competitiveness of exports and provides guidance on research as an aid to policy decisions.

- Magalhães, João. Regional SPS Frameworks and Strategies in Africa. Report for the Standards and Trade Development Facility. July 2010. http://www.standardsfacility.org/Files/Publications/STDF_Regional_SPS_Stategies_in_Africa.pdf

  Assesses the regional SPS policy frameworks and strategies in Africa. At the centre of the many challenges to addressing SPS issues is the absence of national strategies dealing with food safety, animal and plant health measures. Discusses how inadequate SPS measures, often without legislative basis, severely reduce export capacity and the ability to control imports, and what to do to change this scenario.

- United Nations Industrial Development Organization and International Organization for Standardization. The Conformity Assessment Toolbox. http://www.unido.org/fileadmin/user_media/Publications/Pub_free/building_trust_FINAL.pdf

  Discusses concepts, techniques and conformity assessment bodies; elucidates on how UNIDO can help set up a quality infrastructure, and presents some case studies.

REFERENCES

Physikalisch-Technische Bundesanstalt/International Trade Centre. Technical Regulations: Recommendations for their Elaboration and Implementation. Guide 1/2009, Alex Inklaar. 2009.
www.ptb.de/de/org/q/q5/docs/broschueren/broschuere_Guide1_Technical_regulations_e.pdf
www.intracen.org/exporters/quality-management/Quality_publications_index/

World Trade Organization

- Sanitary and phytosanitary measures. www.wto.org/english/tratop_e/sps_e/sps_e.htm
- Technical barriers to trade. www.wto.org/english/tratop_e/tbt_e/tbt_e.htm
- World Trade Report 2005: Exploring the links between trade, standards and the WTO, 2005. www.wto.org/english/res_e/booksp_e/anrep_e/world_trade_report05_e.pdf

22. What is the difference between mandatory requirements and buyers' commercial requirements?

The distinction between mandatory (official) requirements and buyers' commercial requirements is often subject to confusion. While mandatory requirements are imposed by governments and are enforceable by law, commercial requirements are normally determined by private sector organizations.

Typically, mandatory requirements take the form of technical regulations or SPS measures as defined by the WTO Agreements on TBT and SPS respectively, and they apply to goods that are to be placed on the market. Very often, the requirements are intended to protect health and safety, to prevent deception and fraud, or to avoid technical incompatibilities.

Commercial requirements are normally set by companies that purchase goods for further processing or for direct sale to their customers. Sometimes, these requirements may be specific to a single purchaser; or they may have been worked out collectively for application by buyers in a particular industry, such as retail supermarkets. Private requirements are often concerned with the quality rather than the safety attributes of products.

To illustrate the difference between mandatory and commercial requirements, consider a product like fresh apples. Mandatory requirements for imported apples may include absence of pesticide residues, and pests and diseases that might establish themselves in the importing country. Commercial requirements may specify variety, colour, size, flavour/sweetness, freshness, organic or conventional production methods, absence of superficial blemishes, treatments like washing and waxing, and so forth. The commercial requirements may also include provisions on environmental protection or labour conditions in the country of origin.

Increasingly, commercial requirements are being broadened to include matters that are also covered by mandatory requirements. This happens particularly when the laws of the importing country impose a legal obligation on importers and sellers to ensure that their products are safe for consumption or use.

Private companies are also keen to avoid any situation where their products might be found to be in violation of mandatory health and safety requirements and thus damage their reputation. Hence, commercial specifications for the purchase of fresh horticultural products, for example, may include a requirement for certification that good agricultural practices have been observed in production and harvesting, that pesticide use has been properly managed, that hygienic practices have been followed by field and packing-house workers. Such provisions minimize the risk that inspection of products on arrival in the importing country will reveal a violation of mandatory requirements.

The following should be borne in mind:

- **Mandatory requirements**, such as those set out in technical regulations (see International Electrotechnical Commission) and SPS measures (see question 19), have to be complied with by all suppliers placing a product on the market or bringing it into circulation, whether it is locally produced or imported, whether it is sold, given away or sometimes even used merely for one's own purposes. There is no choice in the matter; compliance is a legal obligation.
- **Commercial requirements** are determined by agreement, usually in the form of an official contract between a supplier and a major retail organization, or a formal order in the case of a direct sale from a supplier to an individual buyer. The contract may include extensive technical requirements very similar to those of a standard, and may even reference one or more standards. The contract may also detail the evidence of compliance (e.g. inspection, testing and certification) that the supplier has to provide to the purchaser before, during and after delivery of the product or service. If a prospective supplier chooses not to accept or is unable to fulfil these contractual requirements, there is no sale; in this sense, the requirements are 'mandatory' for the supplier.

Suppliers may choose whether or not to accept the contractual or commercial requirements of specific buyers and are free to sell their products to other buyers without breaking the law. They do not have this choice In the case of a mandatory requirement. Whoever the buyers are, and whatever their commercial requirements, mandatory requirements have to be fulfilled under pain of breaking the law.

Because of the high cost of conducting import inspection, factory surveillance and product inspection, the immense variety of products and the considerable expense of testing and certification, most regulatory authorities cannot inspect all products falling within the scope of technical regulations and SPS measures. In fact, they would be satisfied with being able to check even 5% of such products. Regulatory authorities therefore have to rely on suppliers to fulfil their obligations in the first instance. They may also conduct occasional market surveillance, i.e. do an audit in the marketplace of the products available (rather than carry out individual product approval inspections before specific products are placed on the market) and keep track of suppliers who do not have an acceptable record.

This is not good enough for the major retail organizations and other large purchasers – the risk of receiving non-compliant products is too high. These retail organizations have a brand to protect, and any non-compliant product from whatever source reflects badly on their name. Hence, many of them include the mandatory requirements of technical regulations and SPS measures in their contractual terms and demand that their suppliers provide evidence of compliance with these requirements.

The GLOBALG.A.P. and BRC standards (see question 14) are to some extent the result of decisions made by major European and British retailers. These standards incorporate the specifications of the European Food Law as well as a number of requirements that the retailers have agreed among themselves. Certification to these standards entails providing evidence that EU Food Law requirements have been fulfilled. Certification to ISO 14001, the international environmental management standard, also requires companies to provide evidence that they meet or exceed the obligations imposed by their countries' environmental laws.

FOR MORE INFORMATION

- BRC Global Standards. www.brcglobalstandards.com/

  The BRC Global Standards are a leading global product safety and quality certification programme used by certified suppliers in over 100 countries.

- Food and Agriculture Organization of the United Nations. Private standards in the United States and European Union markets for fruit and vegetables – Implications for developing countries, Part 2: Overview of existing analytical work on the impacts of private standards on trade. ftp://ftp.fao.org/docrep/fao/010/a1245e/a1245e03.pdf

  Provides an overview of existing analytical work on private standards and trade, with a focus on exports of fruits and vegetables from developing countries.

- GLOBALG.A.P. Certification. www.globalgap.org/cms/front_content.php?idcat=30

  GLOBALG.A.P. (formerly known as EUREPG.A.P) has established itself as a key reference for good agricultural practices (GAP) in the global marketplace. It is a private sector body that sets voluntary standards for the certification of production processes of agricultural (including aquaculture) products around the globe.

- International Organization for Standardization. International standards and 'private standards'. A freely downloadable brochure. http://www.iso.org/iso/private_standards.pdf

  This paper outlines the important role that ISO's international standards play in fostering trade while supporting the implementation of public policy and allowing good regulatory practice through performance-based, as opposed to prescriptive, technical regulations.

- Standards and Trade Development Facility. www.standardsfacility.org/en/TAPrivateStandards.htm

  STDF is a forum for information-sharing on SPS-related technical cooperation activities. It also aims to mobilize resources to address SPS issues which limit the trading possibilities of developing countries and so better protect human, animal and plant health from SPS risks.

- World Organisation for Animal Health (OIE). www.oie.int/international-standard-setting/implications-of-private-standards/

  OIE is the intergovernmental organization responsible for improving animal health worldwide. It is recognized as a reference organization by WTO. In 2011 it had 178 member countries and territories. This document presents the implications of private standards for the international trade in animals and animal products.

- World Trade Organization. Research and Researchers on Private Standards. 2008. www.standardsfacility.org/Files/PrivateStandards/GEN891.pdf

  Lists organizations confirmed by WTO that are active in research on the effects of private standards.

REFERENCES

EU Food Safety Legislation. http://europa.eu/pol/food/index_en.htm

International Organization for Standardization. 14001:2004, Environmental management systems – Requirements with guidance for use. Obtainable from ISO or ISO members (list at www.iso.org).

23. Where can I find information on the technical requirements for export?

You need two types of technical information to be able to export successfully. First, you need to find out whether a technical regulation or SPS measure is in place in the importing country for the produce, product or service to be exported. Compliance with these requirements is a legal obligation, and it is crucial for the source of this information to be reliable, i.e. an official source. Second, you have to determine what the commercial requirements for your product are, whether they are merely implied by the marketplace, whether they form part of the contractual requirements of major buyers (see question 22) or whether marketing advantages will be gained by complying with national standards.

This section provides some background on where you can find information on technical regulations, SPS measures, public standards and private standards. The role of trade promotion organizations (TPO) and how you can benefit from them is also discussed briefly.

Technical regulations

Each WTO Member has to establish and maintain a national TBT enquiry point to answer any questions on its current and proposed standards, technical regulations and conformity assessment regimes. This should be the first port of call for any supplier seeking information on technical regulations in an export market. There are a number of options available:

- If your country is a WTO Member, it will have been obliged to set up a TBT enquiry point. You can request this enquiry point to forward your information needs to its counterpart enquiry point in the country you wish to export to. You can also make direct inquiries with the enquiry points abroad. Either way is an effective means of obtaining information. Please see the last paragraph of this subsection for directions on how to obtain information about enquiry points from the WTO website.
- Even if your country is not a WTO Member, you can make direct contact with the enquiry point of the country you wish to export to. Although enquiry points are not legally obliged to provide information to non-WTO Members, they will rarely refuse to do so.
- If your target market is not a WTO Member and has not established a national TBT enquiry point, things get a bit more complicated. A good place to start your search for information is the trade attaché's office in the embassy of the country you wish to export to, or its trade ministry abroad. If they cannot provide answers, at least they may be able to point you in the right direction.
- Should all of the above fail, you will have to search for information from various official sources such as the ministries for trade, health, agriculture, transport, housing and communication, i.e. the ministries responsible for technical regulations in your target export market. This can be a time consuming and frustrating task. Sometimes your trade promotion organizations can help identify sources of official information. A partner resident in the export market or the large buyer you wish to deal with may also provide valuable assistance.

For about 60% of all WTO Members, the national TBT enquiry point is established within their national standards bodies (NSB). In some countries (approximately 15% of WTO Members), the enquiry point is shared between the NSB and the trade ministry. WTO keeps an up-to-date list of the national TBT enquiry points (and their contact details) established by its Members. This list is available as a free download from the WTO website at http://docsonline.wto.org/gen_home.asp. In the document symbol search field, type G/TBT/ENQ to obtain the updated list.

SPS measures

Each WTO Member also has to establish and maintain a national enquiry point to provide information on adopted or proposed SPS measures. These SPS enquiry points are usually found within the ministries responsible for agriculture and health. As for TBT enquiry points, WTO keeps an up-to-date list of the SPS enquiry points of its Members. This list is available as a free download from the WTO website at http://docsonline.wto.org/gen_home.asp. In the document symbol search field, type G/SPS/ENQ to obtain the updated list.

Some WTO Members maintain websites that list the SPS conditions applicable to imports of food and other animal and plant products. These sites are likely to be associated with the websites of the agriculture or health ministries.

For exports to non-WTO Members, it will be necessary to approach the relevant ministries in the importing country with a request for advice on the import conditions for a particular commodity. Local embassies may be able to offer guidance on how to seek information by this route or through other means.

Trading partners in an importing country may be able to provide helpful information too, but there is a risk involved in relying exclusively on information from unofficial sources without obtaining official confirmation from the authorities of the importing country.

Public standards

The first step is to contact the national standards body in your own country, which normally has a standards information centre. NSBs keep a collection of their own national standards, have access to international standards such as those of ISO and IEC, and frequently have commercial links with the national standards bodies of the main export markets. These links allow NSBs to provide suppliers with standards information from major trading countries. If the NSB does not have the relevant information at hand, it will certainly be able to source it from counterpart NSBs. NSB information centres offer an advantage in that they are usually staffed with knowledgeable personnel who can save you time in your search for information.

It is also possible to obtain information direct from the websites of many NSBs around the world. The Internet has become a powerful search tool for information on standards. More and more NSBs use the Internet to sell their standards online. A useful starting point to gain access to the websites of national, international and regional standardization organizations is the website of the World Standards Services Network (WSSN). Direct links are provided from this website to almost all standardization bodies in the world.

Standards are generally not available for free. International ISO and IEC standards are subject to copyright and have to be purchased. Standards from intergovernmental organizations such as OIML, CAC and others may be downloaded for free from their respective websites. Regional standards are seldom available from the regional organizations; they have to be purchased from the NSBs that are involved in their development. The European harmonized (EN) standards and the East African Standards are examples of regional standards. National standards normally have to be purchased, especially if they are adoptions of ISO and IEC standards. The price of standards varies widely, depending on whether the NSB sees standards as a source of revenue or not. It may be useful to shop around, especially for those that are adoptions of international standards.

Private standards

Information on private standards (see question 14) should be available from your trading partner in the country you wish to export to. In addition, some private standards, especially those utilized in certification, are available as free downloads from the websites of the respective organizations. Typical examples include the GLOBALG.A.P. standards, SA 8000 standards and the FSC standards. For other standards like BRC, a fee must be paid to download the documents. An Internet search will provide the necessary links quite quickly as these organizations are good at making their presence known on the Internet.

The role of trade promotion organizations

The fundamental role of TPOs is to provide information on actual and potential export markets to enable suppliers to export successfully, as well as to create the required linkages between exporters and importers. Hence, TPOs have gathered a tremendous amount of information on their countries' exports as well as information from their markets on requirements for these products. This could include information on market preferences, design preferences, quality requirements and the like. It will be useful for suppliers to contact their TPOs and find out how they can be of assistance in obtaining information on technical requirements.

FOR MORE INFORMATION

- EU Help Desk for Developing Countries. http://exporthelp.europa.eu

  The Export Helpdesk is an online service provided by the European Commission to facilitate market access to the European Union, particularly for developing countries. This free and user-friendly service provides information required by exporters interested in supplying the EU market.

- FAO, IPCC, WTO, OIE, CBD, Codex Alimentarius, WHO. International Portal on Food Safety, Animal and Plant Health (IPFSAPH). www.ipfsaph.org/En/default.jsp

  Interactive database on official information on food safety, animal health and plant health; contains standards, legislation, safety assessments, relevant contacts, and other information at the international, regional and national level in order to facilitate information exchange between countries and regions, and to facilitate the international food and agricultural trade.

- International Bureau of Weights and Measures. www.bipm.org/en/practical_info/useful_links

  BIPM acts in matters of world metrology, particularly concerning the demand for measurement standards of ever-increasing accuracy, range and diversity, and the need to demonstrate equivalence between national measurement standards. Its website has an extensive database on metrology institutes, regional metrology organizations and testing laboratories, among others.

- International Trade Centre

  - *Export Quality Management Bulletin* No. 72, Information retrieval on standards, technical regulations and conformity assessment procedures.
    www.intracen.org/exporters/quality-management/Quality_publications_index

    The Export Quality Management website of ITC enables you to retrieve bulletins and handbooks published by the organization; many of them are available in English, French, and Spanish. ITC Bulletin 72 gives directions on how to retrieve information on standards, technical regulations and conformity assessment procedures.

  - *Export Quality Management Bulletin* No. 81, Information retrieval on sanitary and phytosanitary measures (SPS). www.intracen.org/exporters/quality-management/Quality_publications_index

    Provides information on SPS measures, control, inspection and approval procedures; international standards; private standards; the International Portal on Food Safety, Animal and Plant Health; the SPS Information Management System (SPS IMS); and the European Commission's Export Helpdesk.

- Perinorm. www.perinorm.com

  Launched by AFNOR (France), BSI (United Kingdom) and DIN (Germany), Perinorm is a bibliographic database of standards and technical regulations. It is available on CD and online, on subscription from the three partners.

- World Trade Organization.

  - SPS Information Management System. http://spsims.wto.org

    Database of WTO information on SPS (notifications, concerns raised, other documents, enquiry points, etc).

  - TBT Information Management System. http://tbtims.wto.org

    Database of WTO information on TBT (notifications, concerns raised, other documents, enquiry points, etc).

REFERENCES

International Trade Centre and International Organization for Standardization. Building Linkages for Export Success. 2010.
Print versions can be obtained online from ITC's e-shop (www.intracen.org/about/e-shop/)
and ISO (http://www.iso.org/iso/standards_development_publications).
PDF files can be obtained at: www.intracen.org/exporters/quality-management/Quality_publications_index/
and at www.iso.org/e-products/standards_development_publications.htm

International Trade Centre. Innovations in Export Strategy: A strategic approach to the quality challenge. 2005.
http://www.intracen.org/exporters/quality-management/Quality_publications_index/

World Standards Services Network (WSSN). www.wssn.net

World Trade Organization. WTO Agreements on TBT and SPS. http://docsonline.wto.org. Once you enter in this link, type 'G/TBT/ENQ' and 'G/SPS/ENQ' to obtain the updated lists.

24. How can I keep abreast of changes in technical requirements of interest to me?

Keeping abreast of changes in technical requirements is of the same vital importance to the exporter as obtaining the original information. There are many examples of bankruptcy among industries in developed and developing economies alike because they did not keep track of the changes in the marketplace. This is especially true of fast-moving technologies such as electronics, but many and profound changes have taken place over the last decade even in such areas as food safety and building materials.

Public standards

Contact your country's national standards body (NSB), which can provide you with information on the standards that are currently under development or are being revised that may affect your business. The NSB should also be able to give you information on international or regional standards that are under development or revision, especially those that the NSB is involved in. If information in other regions is required, the NSB will be able to obtain the information from its counterparts worldwide.

NSBs of WTO Members have to provide information on standards under development in their countries every six months through the ISO/IEC Information Centre (www.standardsinfo.net). In the past, these were hard copy lists, but they are nowadays available on NSB websites. Hence, if you have Internet access, it may be useful to trawl through the websites of national and regional standardization organizations of interest to your business. Most standardization organizations maintain an updated list of the standards under development, information that is easily accessible to the general public. This is also a useful entry point for obtaining details when a draft standard is circulated for public comment before it is formally approved and published as a national standard.

Becoming a member of the relevant national technical committee is another means of keeping abreast of international, regional, and national developments on standards; in fact, it may be one of the best ways. Not only will you gain advance warning about possible revisions to existing standards, or the way things are developing in relation to a new standard, but you may also be able to influence the development of the standard in a way that suits your business or business sector.

Technical regulations and SPS measures

According to their obligations under the TBT and SPS Agreements, WTO Members have to notify the WTO Secretariat at least 60 days prior to the adoption of a new technical regulation or SPS measure. This is to give trading partners a chance to comment on the envisaged technical regulation or SPS measure in time to influence the final outcome. This information can be obtained in two ways.

You can access any of the notifications submitted under the WTO TBT and SPS Agreements on the WTO website. However, this is a time-consuming task, as the notifications are published in date order, and there is no other index to help you sift through them quickly. It means that once a week a person from your organization will have to spend a fair amount of time going through all the notifications. Once a notification has been spotted that may influence your business, i.e. it deals with your produce or product and it comes from one of your current or potential export markets, you will need to obtain details from the national enquiry point in the country concerned. The notifications are fairly brief, and only list the scope of the new technical regulation or SPS measure. The notification does, however, provide the contact details of the organization from which the full text and further information can be obtained.

Some national enquiry points run an early warning system on the TBT and SPS notifications submitted to the WTO Secretariat. It works briefly as follows: the enquiry point evaluates the notification posted by the WTO Secretariat on a weekly basis, and determines which notifications could be of interest to the country's industry and authorities. The results of this evaluation are then provided online to a predetermined list of interested organizations. If your NSB operates such an early warning system, it would be useful for you to become an addressee for the sector, produce or products you are interested in. Find out from your local enquiry points whether they have such a service and, if not, try to persuade them to provide the service. Information on how to find the enquiry point of interest to you can be obtained from the WTO website.

A third option would be for the business or manufacturing association to establish an early warning system for the sector, much as the enquiry point would do. The services of the trade promotion organization could also be requested in this regard. Electronic communication has made things easier, and you should develop innovative ways to use it to your full advantage.

Private standards

Keeping abreast of developments in private standards is a much more complex undertaking as the organizations concerned do not operate through the WTO or ISONET system. NSBs sometimes maintain information on private standards, but this is the exception rather than the rule. If you are a company certified to a private standard, the certifying organizations involved will usually be good at advising you on forthcoming revisions. Such revisions may require you to update your system to retain your certification, and the certifying organizations would not wish to lose you as a client.

The organizations developing private standards usually have active and up-to-date websites as part of their public face. Any revisions, changes or new developments are given generous space on these websites, and are therefore easy to track once you know where to look for them. This is another service that the business or manufacturers' association can provide to its members, especially if these are SMEs that find it difficult to access the Internet for whatever reason.

FOR MORE INFORMATION

- International Trade Centre. Standards Map: www.standardsmap.org

  Provides online access to ITC's most detailed database on private standards and presents academic, scientific and research papers on private standards issues in global value chains. Standards Map operates in a web-based interactive environment. It enables comparisons of the requirements of private standards at various levels of analysis, from general social and environmental requirements to detailed criteria and indicators for such matters as food safety and carbon emission, as well as specific requirements in regard to labour rights and gender issues.

- ISONET Directory. www.wssn.net/WSSN/RefDocs/isonetdir/introduction.html

  In its 'Related addresses' section, this Directory provides direct links to the regularly updated listings of ISO and IEC members on the ISO and IEC websites. Also included are the latest WTO listings of the names and addresses of the enquiry points established under the TBT and SPS Agreements.

- ISO/IEC Information Centre. www.standardsinfo.net

  Provides information on standardization and conformity assessment, standards and related matters; serves as a portal to the main information given on various pages of the ISO and IEC websites, e.g. the ISO and IEC standards and publications catalogues; offers an inquiry service and access to the websites of national standards organizations.

- National Institute of Metrology, Quality and Technology (INMETRO), Brazil. Exporter Alert! www.inmetro.gov.br/english/international/alert.asp

  Provides an early warning to suppliers that have subscribed to the service.

- Standards Council of Canada. Export Alert! https://alert.scc.ca/ExportAlert/

  Provides an early warning to suppliers that have subscribed to the service.

- World Trade Organization
  - SPS Information Management System (SPSIMS). http://spsims.wto.org

    Provides access to documents and records under the WTO Agreement on the Application of Sanitary and Phytosanitary Measures. The SPSIMS allows users to track information on SPS measures that Member Governments have notified to WTO, specific trade concerns raised in the SPS Committee, SPS-related documents circulated at WTO, Member Governments' SPS enquiry points and notification authorities, and the membership of WTO, Codex Alimentarius, IPPC and OIE.

  - TBT Information Management System (TBTIMS). http://tbtims.wto.org

    Allows users to track and obtain information on TBT measures that Member Governments have notified to WTO, on Member Governments' enquiry points, on standardizing bodies that have accepted the TBT Agreement's Code of Good Practice, on publications used to provide information on technical regulations, standards, conformity assessment procedures, and on statements on the implementation and administration of the TBT Agreement.

  - WTO Documents Online. http://docsonline.wto.org

    Database providing access to the official documentation of WTO, updated daily. Gives access to notifications related to the WTO Agreements on TBT and SPS.

25. Can I influence the preparation of standards, technical regulations and SPS measures?

This section provides information on how you can influence the preparation of standards, technical standards and SPS Measures:

Standards

You can certainly influence the preparation of standards. The fundamental principles for the development of standards require an open, transparent, impartial, stakeholder-driven and consensus-based process. For it to be stakeholder-driven, interested parties must be given a chance to provide meaningful input during the development process.

Almost all developed, developing and transition economies have a national standards body (or bodies) charged with responsibility for publishing national standards. The vast majority of these bodies are members of ISO and many are also members of IEC. The statutes of these international standardization organizations require members to follow the fundamental stakeholder consensus principles in developing their national standards. These principles are contained in the ISO/IEC Directives.

National standards bodies of WTO Members are required to follow the Code of Good Practice for the Preparation, Adoption and Application of Standards contained in Annex 3 to the WTO TBT Agreement. This Code of Practice also requires the standards-making process to be open and transparent. Members are therefore obliged to ensure that the national standards-making process is stakeholder-driven and consensus-based.

You can become involved in the standards-making process through your national standards body, whether it is governmental or non-governmental. Active participation is required in national technical committees, subcommittees or working groups that deliberate on the development of new national standards and the revision of old ones. You should apply to your national standards body to become a member of the national committees themselves or to participate in their work through a trade association relevant to your business.

Work in national committees feeds into the work of regional and international standardization bodies. If you are an exporter and you know that standards development work is under way at the regional or international level, you should persuade your national standards body, through the relevant national committee, to participate actively in the deliberations, preferably with the participation of representatives of the suppliers. In this way developing economies have been able to safeguard their industries against unnecessary and onerous requirements in regional and international standards that would have had negative consequences for those industries had they been adopted.

A good example is provided by the Malaysian natural rubber industry, which was able to forestall a ban on natural rubber surgical gloves in the revision of the then international standard by coming up with a new refining process that eliminated the problematic ingredient causing life-threatening allergic reactions in doctors and patients. This action ensured the continued use of natural rubber in the manufacture of surgical gloves.

Technical regulations

Technical regulations are not always developed according to consensus principles (see question 18). In that sense, it is more difficult to influence their development. However, things are changing even in this respect as many governments are trying to adopt a more open and transparent regulatory regime.

First, in many countries, technical regulations are based on standards and even reference standards in their totality (see question 18). Because the standards-making process is open and transparent, you can influence it as described above. This is another reason why active participation in the standards-making process is important to your business.

Second, many countries publish draft technical regulations for public comment long before implementation. These are normally published in the official gazette of the government or in newspapers. For you, it is therefore a question of keeping track of such developments. Business and manufacturing associations could also be useful allies in informing suppliers of any regulatory developments. Once the draft is published for comment, you should use the chance to make comments – if you don't, you will have to accept what others decide on your behalf.

At the international level, technical regulations have to be notified to WTO at least 60 days before they are implemented. An early warning system usually run by national enquiry points is a useful means of keeping track of such international developments (see question 24). When you receive early notice information, you should submit your comments to the enquiry point or to the ministries responsible for the TBT Agreement (usually the trade ministry), which will group the comments and forward them to the relevant authority in the importing country for consideration. If they are too complex, the concerns can be raised with the WTO TBT Committee in Geneva.

SPS measures

According to the SPS Agreement, WTO Members should base their SPS measures on international standards, guidelines, and recommendations developed by relevant international organizations, including the Codex Alimentarius Commission, the World Organisation for Animal Health, and international and regional organizations operating within the framework of the International Plant Protection Convention, without requiring Members to change their appropriate level of protection of human, animal or plant life or health. Therefore, the first opportunity for exporting countries to influence the SPS measures of importing countries arises through active participation in the work of these bodies and in particular in the preparation and adoption of international SPS standards. Since the work of the standardizing bodies is carried out by governments, private sector organizations and individuals should engage with their own governments in developing national policy positions that the national delegations will argue for in the expert and plenary bodies of Codex, OIE and IPPC.

A second opportunity to influence the SPS measures of importing countries is offered by the transparency procedures of the SPS Agreement. As mentioned above (see questions 21 and 24), these procedures entitle all WTO Members to have advance notice of proposed new or revised measures and to submit comments that must be taken into account by the notifying country.

Consequently, each country should monitor the flow of notifications, which are circulated regularly by the WTO Secretariat, and promptly identify and act upon those notifications of measures that may adversely affect its trade interests. The organization that is given the task of monitoring notifications should maintain close contact with the private sector bodies representing exporters in order to keep them informed of developments and to obtain their views on potential barriers to trade.

The coordinated national position should then be set out in a submission to the notifying country's notification authority. If appropriate, a Member that is commenting on the notification of a proposed new or revised SPS measure can ask the notifying Member to enter into discussions of the issues involved and the possible ways of minimizing adverse effects on trade.

It often happens in regard to trade that may present risks to animal or plant health that an importing country will want to develop SPS measures on the basis of its own risk assessments because international standards are not available or it considers these standards not suitable for the circumstances. To identify and assess risks, the importing country may require data from exporting countries. In these cases, a dialogue should be established between the importing and exporting countries. This is another opportunity for the authorities of an exporting country to influence decisions in importing countries on SPS risk management measures. Private sector bodies in the exporting country should assist the authorities in preparing submissions to their counterparts in the importing country.

FOR MORE INFORMATION

- Commonwealth Secretariat and International Trade Centre. Influencing and Meeting International Standards – Challenges for developing countries, Vol. Two, 2004. http://www.intracen.org/about/e-shop/

  Overview of the main international standardization bodies, and how they endeavour to support developing countries; contains case studies of a few countries, and how they go about influencing and implementing international standards. (Vol. 1: Background Information, Findings from Case Studies and Technical Assistance Needs.)

- International Organization for Standardization.

  - Joining in. Participating in International Standardization, ISO, 2007.
    www.iso.org/iso/free_pubs#STANDARDS_DEVELOPMENT

    Describes active and effective participation in international standardization; intended as a primer for the Enhanced Participation Course, and expands on the basic information given in the booklet 'My ISO Job'.

  - Supporting stakeholders – Disseminating ISO Documents to National Mirror Committees, 2009.
    www.iso.org/iso/free_pubs#STANDARDS_DEVELOPMENT

    Automated service that allows ISO members to disseminate all types of ISO committee documents within minutes to their national stakeholders. This brochure describes how the service works and what ISO members need to do to use it for the benefit of their stakeholders.

REFERENCES

World Trade Organization. Code of Good Practice for the Preparation, Adoption and Application of Standards. Annex 3 to the Agreement on Technical Barriers to Trade. www.wto.org/english/docs_e/legal_e/17-tbt_e.htm

26. What are RoHS regulations and what are their implications for the export trade?

This section discusses the European Union's Directive on the Restriction of Hazardous Substances (RoHS), its requirements, product coverage and its implementation. It also provides some information about RoHS regulations worldwide.

The European Union's Directive on the Restriction of Hazardous Substances

The European Union's 'Directive 2002/95/EC on the restriction of the use of certain hazardous substances in electrical and electronic equipment' (the RoHS Directive for short) is of great importance to manufacturers and suppliers of equipment. Its aim is to reduce the hazardous substances that are encountered in everyday life and that may enter the ecosystem. RoHS is generally the responsibility of EU equipment manufacturers, importers of equipment from outside EU and even those that rebadge equipment within the Union. Although the major focus of the RoHS regulation has been the reduction of lead within products, it restricts the use of six substances:

- Cadmium;
- Hexavalent chromium (also known as chromium VI or Cr6+);
- Lead;
- Mercury;
- Polybrominated biphenyls (PBB); and
- Polybrominated diphenyl ethers (PBDE).

Cadmium occurs naturally with zinc; if the zinc is not properly refined, non-compliances can occur. Hexavalent chromium has an oily-gold/green appearance and is still used as an anti-corrosive coating on metal parts by many manufacturers. PBB and PBDE are generally utilized as flame retardants in plastic.

Requirements and products covered by the RoHS

The RoHS Directive applies to equipment defined in EU 'Directive 2002/96/EC on waste electrical and electronic equipment (WEEE)'. The WEEE Directive aims to reduce waste arising from electrical and electronic equipment, and improve the environmental performance of all those involved in the life cycle of electrical and electronic products. It covers electrical and electronic equipment used by private consumers and for professional applications; they include:

- Large and small household appliances;
- IT equipment;
- Telecommunications equipment (infrastructure equipment is exempt in some countries);
- Consumer equipment;
- Lighting equipment;
- Electronic and electrical tools;
- Toys, leisure and sports equipment; and
- Automatic dispensers.

Maximum concentrations of 0.1% by weight of homogeneous material are set for all but cadmium, for which the maximum level is 0.01% as it is more toxic. These limits do not apply to just the whole product, but to any element, component or substance that can be separated from it. For example, the limits could apply to the solder used on a printed circuit board. It could equally apply to the plastic insulation of a wire. In effect, everything that is used in the construction of a product must be RoHS-compliant.

Among the main exemptions from the RoHS Directive are batteries, despite the high levels of substances they contain that would normally come under RoHS. Lead-acid batteries, nickel-cadmium batteries and mercury batteries are prime examples. Fixed industrial plant and tools are also exempted; compliance in this case is the responsibility of the company that operates the plant.

Implementation of RoHS Regulations

It is necessary for products within the relevant categories to show RoHS compliance before they can be marketed. Each EU country may have slightly different legislation in place, but generally, the manufacturer or supplier/importer has to:

- Ensure that the product placed on the market does not contain banned substances at levels above the maximum limit;
- Prepare technical documentation that shows that the products meet the requirements. Appropriate test reports from a competent laboratory would be part of this documentation;
- If requested by the regulatory authority, provide the technical documentation to the authority within a given time limit – usually about a month; and
- Ensure that the technical documentation is maintained for at least four years after the manufacturer has stopped placing the product on the market.

Although RoHS is more than just lead-free manufacturing, one of the main thrusts of manufacturers of electronic equipment has been to adopt soldering processes that are lead free to provide RoHS compliance. At one time lead was a major constituent of solder, and the legislation has meant that many new lead-free solders are being developed and used. As their properties are slightly different from those of solders containing lead, careful control of processes is required to ensure that the same high standard of solder joint reliability is maintained.

RoHS worldwide

RoHS regulations are contained in an EU Directive, and in view of the size of the EU market, countries that export products to EU need to be compliant. This makes its application far more wide-ranging, with countries around the globe being aware of it and having to manufacture goods that are RoHS compliant. Hence, many countries are adopting RoHS itself, or RoHS-like legislation and standards.

China has been introducing similar legislation, and many refer to its standards as 'China RoHS'. One of the main differences between the EU and the Chinese standards has to do with product coverage. In EU products are excluded if they are not specifically included in the coverage; in China the opposite is true. Hence, the China RoHS may cover some products that the EU excludes.

In the United States, the State of California has adopted RoHS legislation which took effect on 1 January 2007. The Californian RoHS Regulation is based on the EU RoHS Directive. In Japan, a slightly different approach is being followed. While Japan does not have RoHS legislation in place, Japan's recycling legislation has driven manufacturers to adopt lead-free processes. Additionally there is a significant 'green bonus' for manufacturers who adopt environmentally friendly manufacturing as this can be used as part of their advertising and sales pitch.

FOR MORE INFORMATION

- National Measurement Office, United Kingdom
  - RoHS-related website: www.RoHS.gov.uk

    Information on due diligence, enforcement, decision tree, RoHS exemptions, conformity.
  - RoHS Guidance – Producer Support Booklet, 2010.
    www.bis.gov.uk/assets/bispartners/nmo/docs/rohs/docs/23115-rohs-booklet-for-the-web.pdf

    This booklet provides guidance for the producer and/or importer on how to meet RoHS legislation.

REFERENCES

European Union. Directive 2002/96/EC, EUR-Lex.
http://eur-lex.europa.eu/LexUriServ/LexUriServ.do?uri=OJ:L:2003:037:0024:0038:EN:PDF

European Chemicals Agency (ECHA). http://echa.europa.eu/home_en.asp

Information on RoHS for California. www.dtsc.ca.gov/hazardouswaste/rohs.cfm

Information on RoHS for China. www.chinarohs.com/faq.html

Information on RoHS for Japan. www.rsjtechnical.com/WhatisJapanRoHS.htm

27. What are REACH regulations and what are their implications for the export trade?

This section discusses the European Community 'Regulation on Registration, Evaluation, Authorisation and Restriction of Chemicals' (REACH), its requirements, product coverage, implementation, guidance documentation, and the related Classification, Labelling and Packaging (CLP) legislation.[1]

Registration, Evaluation, Authorization and Restriction of Chemicals (REACH)

REACH is the European Community regulation on the registration, evaluation, authorization and restriction of chemicals. It entered into force on 1 June 2007 to streamline and improve the EU's fragmented legislative framework on chemicals and replaced about 40 pieces of legislation. From this perspective, it was a welcome change, but the implications of REACH for trade are immense.

REACH makes manufacturers bear greater responsibility for managing the risks that chemicals may pose to the health of the population and the environment, and requires industry to provide appropriate safety information to their users. In parallel, it foresees that the European Union can take additional measures on highly dangerous substances, where there is a need for complementing action at the EU level. REACH also created the European Chemicals Agency (ECHA) with a central coordination and implementation role in the overall process.

Requirements and products covered by REACH

In principle, REACH applies to all chemicals, not only the chemicals used in industrial processes, but also those present in day-to-day life, for example in cleaning products, paints, clothes, furniture and electrical appliances. It is therefore far-reaching in its application, and a short introduction like this one cannot list all the products affected. Suppliers must therefore obtain information relevant to their own products.

It is possible to search for this information on the ECHA website, which has a valuable tool called the Navigator to help you to do so. The Navigator is an interactive tool that enables companies to obtain answers to questions on their substance and to find out quickly what they need to do under REACH. If you do not have Internet access, contact your national enquiry point, your NSB, or your TPO for assistance (see question 23).

Other legislation regulating chemicals (e.g. in cosmetics, detergents) and related legislation (e.g. on the health and safety of workers handling chemicals, product safety, construction products) not replaced by REACH continue to apply. REACH has been designed not to overlap or conflict with other chemical legislation.

The regulation has been and will be implemented progressively over several years. For example, 30 November 2010 was the deadline for the registration of phase-in substances (i.e. those that were already being manufactured or placed on the market before the regulation came into force) manufactured or supplied at above 1 000 tonnes per manufacturer or company per year; the tonnage for substances that are carcinogenic, mutagenic or toxic to reproduction was set at 1 tonne or more and that for substances very toxic to the aquatic environment was 100 tonnes a year. The other deadlines are 31 May 2013 for quantities of 100 tons or more per year, and 31 May 2018 for volumes of 1 tonne or more per year.

Non phase-in substances do not benefit from the transitional regime provided for phase-in substances and need to be registered before they can be manufactured, imported or placed on the market in the European Union.

[1] Taken from http://guidance.echa.europa.eu/about_reach_en.htm and
http://guidance.echa.europa.eu/docs/guidance_document/registration_en.pdf?vers=31_01_11

Implementation of REACH

All manufacturers and importers of chemicals must identify and manage risks linked to the substances they manufacture and market. For substances produced or imported in quantities above 1 tonne per year per company, manufacturers and importers need to demonstrate that they have appropriately done so by means of a registration dossier, which is submitted to ECHA.

When the registration dossier has been received, ECHA will check that it is compliant with the Regulation and will evaluate testing proposals to ensure that the assessment of chemical substances will not result in unnecessary testing, especially on animals. Where appropriate, the authorities may also select substances of concern for a broader substance evaluation.

Manufacturers and importers must provide their downstream users with the risk information they need to use the substance safely. This has to be done via the classification and labelling system and safety data sheets (SDS), where relevant.

REACH also foresees an authorization system aiming to ensure that Substances of Very High Concern (SVHC) are adequately controlled, and progressively replaced by safer substances or technologies or used only where society will gain an overall benefit from this use. These substances are prioritized in the Candidate List on the ECHA website that is updated every six months. Once they are included, industry has to submit applications to the Agency for authorization to continue to use them. In addition, EU authorities may impose restrictions on the manufacture, use or placing on the market of substances causing an unacceptable risk to human health or the environment.

Substances can be exempted from all or a part of the obligations under REACH. Information on exemptions can be found through the Navigator on the ECHA website. Companies are strongly advised to use the Navigator to find out if their substance is covered by an exemption under REACH.

Guidance on the implementation of REACH

Guidance documents have been developed over the past few years for industry and the authorities to assist in the smooth implementation of REACH. The guidance documents were drafted and discussed within projects led by European Commission services, involving stakeholders from industry, Member States and non-governmental organizations. Finalized guidance documents are published on the ECHA website. National help desks have also been established in each EU Member State to provide advice to industry on its obligations and how to fulfil these obligations under REACH, in particular in relation to registration.

Classification, Labelling and Packaging (CLP) legislation

An important and far-reaching piece of EU legislation related to REACH are the rules on the classification, labelling and packaging of substances and mixtures contained in Regulation (EC) No. 1272/2008. The regulation obliges manufacturers and manufacturers of these products to submit classification and labelling information (the submission is referred to as a notification) to ECHA. The CLP notification procedure for substances became effective on 1 December 2010; the corresponding date for mixtures is 1 June 2015.

As a result of these procedures, ECHA will have a Classification and Labelling Inventory which will ultimately replace the previous three different lists maintained by EU authorities. If your product was classified according to one of the previous lists, you must have it reclassified and notified accordingly.

A series of extensive CLP guidance documents has been published on the ECHA website.

Manufacturers and importers needed to notify ECHA by 3 January 2011 of the classification of substances placed on the market that are:

- Subject to REACH registration (for substances that had to be registered by 30 November 2010, notification formed part of the registration dossier);
- Classified as hazardous (regardless of volume);
- In mixtures above certain concentration limits, which result in the need for classification.

You should note that substances or mixtures whose marketing and use are controlled by Directive 98/8/EC (on biocides) or by Directive 91/414/EEC (on plant protection products) are also subject to CLP. This means that a substance in the meaning of those Directives or a biocidal or a pesticidal product (mixture) containing such a substance should be labelled and classified under CLP as well.

FOR MORE INFORMATION

- ECHA. Navigator. http://guidance.echa.europa.eu/navigator_en.htm

  Tool for identifying whether a product falls within the scope of REACH and CLP; helps manufacturers, importers, downstream users, distributors of chemical substances, and producers or importers of articles to figure out their obligations under REACH.

- European Commission. Enterprise and Industry website on REACH. http://ec.europa.eu/enterprise/sectors/chemicals/reach/index_en.htm

  Provides information on REACH, how it works, registration, evaluation, authorization, restrictions, enforcement; gives information on CLP, how CLP works, dangerous preparations, safety data sheets, good laboratory practice.

REFERENCES

European Chemicals Agency (ECHA). http://echa.europa.eu/home_en.asp

Regulation (EC) No. 1272/2008 on classification, labelling and packaging of substances and mixtures. http://eur-lex.europa.eu/LexUriServ/LexUriServ.do?uri=OJ:L:2008:353:0001:1355:en:PDF

28. What are the packaging requirements for my products?

The subject of packaging requirements is complex, but generally these requirements have to be addressed from the marketing point of view and at the regulatory level for aspects related to legal metrology, packaging integrity and the environmental impact of packaging materials.

It is important to consider packaging requirements carefully. Mandatory requirements have to be fulfilled, as noncompliant exports may be denied entry at the country of destination or even on their way there. Goods have also been known to be returned to the country of origin, resulting in massive financial losses for the exporter.

This section discusses marketing requirements, trade metrology requirements, packaging integrity and the environmental concerns that you should pay attention to. It also presents some packaging standards you might consider, depending on your type of business and product destinations.

Marketing requirements

The actual design or look of the packaging plays an important role in your marketing success. Packaging is the first thing a potential customer sees, and good design is essential to grabbing his or her attention and directing it to your product among all the other products on offer. This usually means that you have to have your packaging designed by a specialist designer. Packaging institutes and many trade promotion organizations (TPOs) can be of assistance in this regard. Some even provide design services to support SMEs. It would therefore be useful for you to contact your national TPO or packaging institute. In addition, the major retailers often have very specific requirements for packaging and labelling, with which you as supplier need to comply.

Trade metrology requirements

There are quite a few mandatory metrology-related requirements in place in various countries for packaging. Most countries have established legal or trade metrology (sometimes called 'weights and measures') requirements for pre-packaged goods. These deal not only with weight, volume and other measurement quantities, but also with the packaging itself and specify, for instance, the maximum amount of space a package can have inside not filled with product.

These requirements are usually based on the Recommendations of the International Organization of Legal Metrology (OIML), which can be downloaded freely from the OIML website. It would, however, be prudent to obtain relevant information from the country you wish to export to (see question 23), because many countries modify the OIML Recommendations slightly to conform with local customs and practices. Your national legal or trade metrology department may also be able to provide information on requirements in major foreign markets.

Packaging integrity and environmental concerns

If technical regulations or SPS measures are in place for a produce or product, these often carry packaging requirements for the product or produce in question. You will have to study these requirements carefully and comply with them fully.

In addition, many countries impose general packaging requirements to ensure the continued integrity of packaging during transport and regulate the environmental impact of packaging when it is disposed of.

Some information is provided below on the packaging standards of the European Union. Furthermore, examples are given of standards developed by several organizations for packaging and transporting dangerous goods.

European Union

At the mandatory level, the European Union has promulgated 'Directive 94/62/EC of 20 December 1994 on Packaging and Packaging Waste' (with amending acts) and has published harmonized European standards (EN 13427 – EN 13432) which are 'deemed to satisfy' standards underpinning the implementation of the Directive. The requirements cover not only the bottle, plastic bag or box that the product is packed in but also extend to the cartons used for bulk packing, the wooden pallets on which these are stacked, and the plastic sheeting the whole lot is frequently wrapped with. Certain glues previously used for making boxes have been banned; printing inks are not allowed to contain lead, and wood used in pallets has to be acceptably treated to ensure that no wood worm and other pests are inadvertently introduced into the ecosystem (an SPS measure – see question 19) of the importing country.

The Green Dot scheme (see also question 78) is covered by the Packaging and Packaging Waste Directive and is binding on all companies if their products use packaging; the scheme requires manufacturers to contribute to the costs of packaging recovery and recycling through a Green Dot licensing fee and the imposition of other fees. According to the Directive, if a company does not join the Green Dot scheme, it must collect recyclable packaging itself, although this is almost always impossible for mass products and is only viable for low-volume producers. Regulatory authorities in individual countries are empowered to fine companies for non-compliance, although enforcement varies by country. Since its European introduction, the scheme has been rolled out in 23 European countries.

Packaging and transportation of dangerous goods

- **Air transport**

  Technical instructions for safe transport of dangerous goods by air. Document Sales Unit, International Civil Aviation Organization (ICAO). Montreal, Canada.
  www.icao.int/icao/en/m_publications.html

  Dangerous Goods Regulations. International Air Transport Association (IATA).
  www.iata.org/ps/publications/dgr/Pages/index.aspx

- **Europe**

  European agreement concerning the international carriage of dangerous goods by road (ADR) and protocol of signature, ISBN 92-1-139053-2 (Vol. 1) and ISBN 92-1-139054-0 (Vol. 2), United Nations Economic Commission for Europe (UN-ECE), info.ece@unece.org

- **Sea transport**

  International Maritime Dangerous Goods (IMDG) Code. ISBN 92-801-1465-4, International Maritime Organization, IMO Publishing Service www.imo.org/safety/mainframe.asp?topic_id=158

- **United Nations**

  Recommendations on the transport of dangerous goods: Model Regulations.
  ISBN 91-1-1-139067-2, United Nations. United Nations Publication Service, Palais des Nations, Geneva 10, CH =1211, Switzerland. Tel: +41 22 917 2613, Fax: +41 22 917 0027, E-mail: unpublic@unog.cg, Internet: www.unog.ch.

FOR MORE INFORMATION

- EN 13427:2004, Packaging – Requirements for the use of European Standards in the field of packaging and packaging waste. www.cen.eu/CEN/sectors/sectors/transportandpackaging/packaging/Pages/ppw.aspx

  Available from the national standards bodies of EU Members, or from your own national standards body.

- EN 13428:2004, Packaging – Requirements specific to manufacturing and composition – Prevention by source reduction. www.cen.eu/CEN/sectors/sectors/transportandpackaging/packaging/Pages/ppw.aspx

  Available from the national standards bodies of EU Members, or from your own national standards body.

- EN 13429:2004: Packaging – Reuse. www.cen.eu/CEN/sectors/sectors/transportandpackaging/packaging/Pages/ppw.aspx

  Available from the national standards bodies of EU Members, or from your own national standards body.

- EN 13430:2004, Packaging – Requirements for packaging recoverable by material recycling. www.cen.eu/CEN/sectors/sectors/transportandpackaging/packaging/Pages/ppw.aspx

  Available from the national standards bodies of EU Members, or from your own national standards body.

- EN 13431:2004, Packaging – Requirements for packaging recoverable in the form of energy recovery, including specification of minimum inferior calorific value. www.cen.eu/CEN/sectors/sectors/transportandpackaging/packaging/Pages/ppw.aspx

  Available from the national standards bodies of EU Members, or from your own national standards body.

- EN 13432:2000, Packaging – Requirements for packaging recoverable through composting and biodegradation – Test scheme and evaluation criteria for the final acceptance of packaging. www.cen.eu/CEN/sectors/sectors/transportandpackaging/packaging/Pages/ppw.aspx

  Available from the national standards bodies of EU Members, or from your own national standards body.

- International Trade Centre. Export Packaging website. www.tradeforum.org/news/fullstory.php/aid/159/ITC_92s_Export_Packaging_Bulletins.html

  Website with a number of documents on packaging for free download; provides links to marking and labelling regulations in various countries; gives environment-related references for a number of products.

REFERENCES

European Parliament and Council Directive 94/62/EC of 20 December 1994 on packaging and packaging waste. EUR-Lex, European Union. http://eur-lex.europa.eu/LexUriServ/LexUriServ.do?uri=CELEX:31994L0062:EN:HTML

Green Dot. Wikipedia. http://en.wikipedia.org/wiki/Green_Dot_(symbol)

International Air Transport Association (IATA). Dangerous Goods Regulations (DGR). www.iata.org/ps/publications/dgr/Pages/index.aspx

International Civil Aviation Organization (ICAO). www.icao.int/icao/en/m_publications.html.

International Maritime Dangerous Goods (IMDG) Code. International Maritime Organization, 2009. www.imo.org/safety/mainframe.asp?topic_id=158.

International Organization of Legal Metrology (OIML). www.oiml.org

United Nations

- Recommendations on the transport of dangerous goods: Model Regulations. 2009. www.unece.org/trans/danger/publi/unrec/rev16/16files_e.htm
- Recommendations on the transport of dangerous goods: Model Regulations, ISBN 91-1-1-139067-2. United Nations. Publication Service. www.unog.ch

MANAGEMENT SYSTEMS

A. QUALITY MANAGEMENT SYSTEMS

29. What is the ISO 9000 family of standards and how widely are the standards used? Do they help the export trade?

Background

It was in 1987 that the International Organization for Standardization (ISO) developed and published ISO 9001, 9002 and 9003 and other related guidelines on international standards. This gave birth to the currently popular 'ISO 9000 family of standards'. The first revision of the ISO 9001, 9002 and 9003 standards took place in 1994 without much alteration in their structure. The second major revision was done in 2000, when ISO 9001, 9002 and 9003 were replaced by a single standard – 'ISO 9001:2000 Quality Management Systems – Requirements'. This was revised again in 2008 as ISO 9001:2008. Both the 2000 and 2008 versions of the ISO 9001 standard promote the adoption of the process approach.

The ISO 9000 family

The ISO 9000 family of standards represents an international consensus on good quality management practices. It consists of standards and guidelines related to quality management systems (QMS) and supporting standards. The ISO 9000 family comprises of the following four main standards:

ISO standards and contents

Standard	Content
ISO 9000:2005	Gives the principles, fundamental concepts and terms used in the ISO 9000 family of standards.
ISO 9001:2008	Defines the requirements of QMS, the purpose of which is to enable an organization continually to satisfy its customers. It is the only standard in the ISO 9001 family against which organizations can be certified.
ISO 9004:2009	Provides guidelines on how an organization can achieve sustained success by applying quality management principles.
ISO 19011:2011	Provides guidance on the principles of auditing, managing audit programmes, conducting quality management system audits and environmental system audits, as well as guidance on the competence of quality and environmental management system auditors.

Source: S.C. Arora, India.

The adoption of all standards published by ISO, including standards in the ISO 9000 family, is voluntary in nature. Many countries have adopted the ISO 9000 family of standards as is and have also appropriated its numbering system for their national standards. For instance in the United Kingdom, ISO 9001 is referred to as BS EN ISO 9001:2008, with BS standing for British Standard and EN for European Norm. In Sri Lanka, the standard is numbered SLS ISO 9001:2008, with SLS denoting Sri Lankan Standard. The ISO standards can be purchased (hard or soft version) from ISO through its online store. Your country's bureau of standards may also sell ISO publications as well as its adopted version of these standards (you will probably pay less for the national version).

ISO 9001

ISO 9001 is applicable to all sectors of industry, including manufacturing and service, and to organizations of all sizes. It is not a product standard but a management system standard to demonstrate an organization's ability consistently to provide products or services that meet customer and regulatory requirements. ISO 9001 specifies 'what' is required to be done by an organization but does not indicate 'how' it should be done, thus giving you great flexibility in running your business.

Furthermore, ISO 9001 does not set any particular level of quality. You and your customers do that. The standard will only help you to achieve the level you want. For example, if you set an objective that 99% of the time you will meet your delivery commitments, the system will help you to achieve that.

At both national and international levels, certification[2] to ISO 9001 by accredited certification bodies has received wide acceptance. As of 31 December 2009, 1 064 785 certificates for ISO 9001 were issued in 178 countries. The highest share (47%) was achieved in Europe, followed by 37.4% in the Far East, 7.3% in Africa and West Asia, 3.4% in Central and South America and 1.0% in Australia and New Zealand[3].

ISO 9001 and the export trade

The ISO 9000 family of standards is increasingly becoming a symbol of quality in both the manufacturing and services industries. It engenders greater customer loyalty as implementation ensures that customer needs and expectations are continually met, giving customers less or no reasons to complain. More and more small and medium-sized firms are choosing to adopt the ISO 9000 family of standards – often because their customers expect them to have it. Adherence to the ISO standards can also be publicized to gain market access abroad, because many foreign buyers place a premium on these standards.

Guidance documents

In addition to the above international standards, there are a number of guidance standards and guidance documents which provide help in implementing and improving your QMS. These documents are listed below.

As with the ISO standards, these can be purchased online from the ISO website or from your national standards bodies.

Guidance standards	Guidance documents
ISO 10001, Quality Management (TQM) – Customer satisfaction – Guidelines for codes of conduct for organizations	*ISO 9001 – What does it mean in the supply chain http://www.iso.org/iso/iso_catalogue/management_and_leadership_standards/quality_management/more_resources_9000/9001supchain.htm http://www.iso.org/iso/9001supchain
ISO 10002:2004, Quality Management – Customer satisfaction – Guidelines for complaints handling in organizations	*Selection and use of the ISO 9000 family of standards http://www.iso.org/iso/iso_9000_selection_and_use.htm
ISO 10003:2007, Quality Management – Customer satisfaction – Guidelines for dispute resolution external to organizations	*Quality management principles http://www.iso.org/iso/qmp
ISO/DIS 10004, Quality Management – Customer satisfaction – Guidelines for monitoring and measuring	*Publicizing your ISO 9001:2008 or ISO 14001:2004 certification. http://www.iso.org/iso/publicizing_your_certification.htm
ISO 10005:2005, Quality management systems – Guidelines for quality plans	**ISO 9001 for Small Business – What to do: Advice from ISO/TC 176 http://www.iso.org/iso/pressrelease.htm?refid=Ref1329
ISO 10006, Guidelines for quality management in projects	**The integrated use of management system standards. 2008. http://www.iso.org/iso/pressrelease.htm?refid=Ref1144

[2] In some countries, the word 'registration' is used instead of 'certification' in the certification of management systems.

[3] http://www.iso.org/iso/pressrelease.htm?refid=Ref1363.

Guidance standards	Guidance documents
ISO 10007:2003, Quality management systems – Guidelines for configuration management	*1 Introduction and support package: Guidance on 'Outsourced processes' *2 Introduction and support package: Guidance on the documentation requirements of ISO 9001:2008
ISO/TR10013:2001, Guidelines for QMS documentation	*3 Introduction and support package: Guidance on the concept and use of the process approach for management systems
ISO 10014:2006, Quality management – Guidelines for realizing financial and economic benefits	*4 ISO 9000 Introduction and Support Package: Guidance on the Terminology used in ISO 9001and ISO 9004
ISO 10015:1999, Quality management – Guidelines for training	
ISO/TR 10017:2003, Guidance on statistical techniques for ISO 9001:2000	
ISO/DIS 10018, Quality management – Guidelines on people involvement and competencies	
ISO 10019:2005, Guidelines for the selection of quality management system consultants	
ISO/IEC 90003:2004, Software Engineering – Guidelines for application of ISO 9001:2000 to computer software	

*These documents can be downloaded for free from the ISO website
http://www.iso.org/iso/publications_and_e-products/management_standards_publications.htm

** These documents can be purchased from ISO.

*1 Can be downloaded for free from:
http://www.iso.org/iso/iso_catalogue/management_standards/quality_management/iso_9001_2008/guidance_on_outsourced_processes.htm

*2 Can be downloaded for free from:
http://www.iso.org/iso/iso_catalogue/management_standards/quality_management/iso_9001_2008/guidance_on_the_documentation_requirements_of_iso_9001_2008.htm

*3 Can be downloaded for free from:
http://www.iso.org/iso/iso_catalogue/management_standards/quality_management/iso_9001_2008/concept_and_use_of_the_process_approach_for_management_systems.htm

*4 Can be downloaded for free from:
http://www.inlac.org/documentos/N526R2-Guidance-on-the-Terminology-used-in-ISO-9001-and-ISO-9004.pdf

FOR MORE INFORMATION

- Grajek, Michal. ISO 9000: New Form of Protectionism or Common Language in International Trade? ESMT European School of Management and Technology. http://www.etsg.org/ETSG2007/papers/grajek.pdf.

  Reviews the literature considering the role of networks in reducing the information costs associated with international trade.

- International Trade Centre and International Organization for Standardization. ISO 9001 for Small Businesses – What to do: Advice from ISO/TC 176, ISBN 978-92-67-10516-1. Obtainable from ISO or ISO members (list at www.iso.org).

  This handbook gives guidance to small organizations on developing and implementing a quality management system based upon ISO 9001:2008. It offers some practical advice on different options should you wish to introduce a quality management system into your organization or update an existing one.

REFERENCES

International Organization for Standardization

- ISO catalogue. www.iso.org/iso/iso_catalogue
- ISO 9001:2008, Quality management systems – Requirements. Obtainable from ISO or ISO members (list at www.iso.org).
- Survey of ISO 9000 certificates issued as on December 2009. http://www.iso.org/iso/survey2009.pdf

30. What are the sector-specific versions of ISO 9001?

ISO/TC 176, the technical committee responsible for the development of the ISO 9000 family of standards had the view that ISO 9001, being a generic standard, could be used by any sector of industry, including the hardware, processed materials, services and software sectors. However, specific industry sectors, such as the automotive, telecommunications, aerospace, medical devices, oil and gas, and information technology sectors, felt the need for specific QMS requirements in addition to those included in ISO 9001. This led to the development of sector-specific QMS standards, both by ISO and by industry groups, as explained below.

Sector-specific standards published by ISO

1. *Automotive industry*

ISO/TS 16949:2009 – Quality management systems – Particular requirements for the application of ISO 9001:2008 for automotive production and relevant service part organizations

This technical specification (TS) was first developed in 1999 by the International Automotive Task Force (IATF), comprising representatives of nine large vehicle manufacturers in the United States and Europe and representatives of ISO/TC 176. Its latest version, ISO/TS 16949:2009, incorporates the ISO 9001:2008 requirements (as boxed texts) and details sector-specific supplemental requirements (noted outside the boxes) for employee competence, awareness and training, design and development, production and service provision, control of monitoring and measuring devices, and measurement, analysis and improvement. A common global certification scheme for this TS (different from that used for ISO 9001) has been developed by IATF for the certification of automotive suppliers.

2. *Medical devices*

ISO 13485:2003 – Medical devices – Quality management systems – Requirements for regulatory purposes

This standard is based on worldwide medical device regulations as well as QMS requirements in ISO 9001. It is intended for use by organizations involved in the design, production, installation and servicing of medical devices as well as their related services. A guidance technical report (TR) for the application of ISO 13485 has also been published by ISO as ISO/TR 14969.

3. *Primary packaging materials for medicinal products*

ISO 15378:2011 Primary packaging materials for medicinal products – Particular requirements for the application of ISO 9001:2008, with reference to Good Manufacturing Practice (GMP)

This international standard specifies requirements for a quality management system where an organization needs to demonstrate its ability to provide primary packaging materials for medicinal products which consistently meet customer requirements, including regulatory requirements and international standards for primary packaging materials. It is an application standard for the design, manufacture and supply of primary packaging materials for medicinal products. It can also be used for certification purposes.

4. *Petroleum, petrochemical and natural gas industries*

ISO/TS 29001:2010 – Petroleum, petrochemical and natural gas industries – Sector-specific quality management systems – Requirements for product and service supply organizations

This TS defines the quality management system for product and service supply organizations for the petroleum, petrochemical and natural gas industries. It is intended to ensure the safety and reliability of equipment and services throughout the supply chain of petrochemicals, oil and gas. It is meant for the use of manufacturers, purchasers and service providers of equipment and materials needed by the petrochemical, oil and gas industries.

All the above standards are fully compatible with ISO 9001:2008 (those compatible with ISO 9001:2000 are being revised to align with ISO 9001:2008). They have not diluted or modified the requirements of the ISO 9001 generic standard, but have added some sector-specific requirements, guidelines and clarifications.

Certification by accredited certification bodies is available for all the standards. By the end of 2009, a total of 41 240 certificates had been issued for ISO/TS 16949 and 16 424 certificates for ISO 13485. Details of the certification schemes for these standards can be obtained from the certification bodies or from their websites.[4]

Sector-specific guideline standards and IWAs published by ISO

In addition to the sector-specific standards which can be used for certification as well, ISO has developed the following guideline standards and international workshop agreements (IWAs). The latter are ISO documents produced through workshop meeting(s) and not through the technical committee process.

1. *ISO/IEC 90003:2004 – Software engineering – Guidelines for the application of ISO 9001:2000 to computer software*

   This provides guidance for organizations in applying ISO 9001:2000 to the acquisition, supply, development, operation and maintenance of computer software and related support services. (This guidance standard is under revision to align it with ISO 9001:2008.)

2. *ISO 16106:2006 – Packaging – Transport packages for dangerous goods – Dangerous goods packagings, intermediate bulk containers (IBCs) and large packagings – Guidelines for the application of ISO 9001*

   This gives guidance on quality management provisions applicable to the manufacture, measuring and monitoring of design type approved dangerous goods packagings, intermediate bulk containers (IBCs) and large packagings.

3. *ISO 22006:2009 – Quality Management Systems – Guidelines for the application of ISO 9001:2008 to crop production*

   This gives guidelines on the use and application of ISO 9001:2008 to the establishment and management of a quality management system by an organization involved in crop production. The standard has facilitated understanding of the language of ISO 9001:2008 for crop production applications.

4. *IWA 1:2005 – Quality management systems – Guidelines for process improvements in health service organizations*

   This provides guidance for any health service organization involved in the management, delivery or administration of health service products or services, including training and/or research, in the life continuum process for human beings, regardless of type, size and the product or service provided.

5. *IWA 2:2007 – Quality management systems – Guidelines for the application of ISO 9001:2000 in education*

   This gives guidelines to assist organizations that provide educational products of any kind to implement an effective quality management system that meets the requirements of ISO 9001:2000.

6. *IWA 4:2009 – Quality management systems – Guidelines for the application of ISO 9001:2008 in local government*

   This provides local governments with guidelines for the voluntary application of ISO 9001:2008 on an integral basis. It helps local governments to guarantee minimum conditions of reliability for the processes that are necessary to provide the services needed by its citizens in a consistent and reliable manner.

[4] http://www.iso.org/iso/pressrelease.htm?refid=Ref1363

The above guideline standards and IWAs do not add to, change or otherwise modify the requirements of ISO 9001:2000 or ISO 9001:2008 and are not intended for use in contracts for conformity assessment or for certification. However, they help the organizations concerned in developing ISO 9001 QMS for the above products and services and then to obtain certification against ISO 9001.

Sector-specific standards developed by other organizations

1. *Telecommunications industry: TL 9000*

   TL 9000 is a set of telecommunications-specific quality management system requirements, published by the Quality Excellence for Suppliers of Telecommunications (QUEST) Leadership Forum. The Forum provides its members with a set of performance-based documents useful for determining the 'best in class' for every product or service provided by suppliers.

2. *Aerospace Industry: AS 9100*

   AS 9100 was prepared by the International Aerospace Quality Group (IAQG) for use by the aviation, space and defence industries. It can be applied throughout the supply chain of these industries, including post-delivery and maintenance support organizations. This standard is based on ISO 9001:2008 and carries additional requirements for the above industries.

3. *Information technology: TickIT.*

   TickIT is a guide to software quality systems. It is supported by the United Kingdom and Swedish software industry for use in areas such as software development and services. It can be used only in combination with ISO 9001. TickIT covers the assessment and certification of an organization's software quality management system to ISO 9001.

Certification by accredited certification bodies is also available for all the above standards.

FOR MORE INFORMATION

- International Organization for Standardization. Quality Management Systems: Advice from ISO/TC 176 for Sector-specific applications. http://www.tc176.org/PDF/News_Articles/2006/2006_1.pdf

  PowerPoint presentation on ISO/TC 176's scope and QMS standards; ISO's sector-specific policies and directives; ISO's guidance documents for sector-specific QMS documents; assessment of sector-specific needs and technical support from ISO/TC 176.

REFERENCES

Hoyle, D. ISO 9000 Quality Systems Handbook, 6th ed. 2009. It is a priced publication of Butterworth-Heinemann, Linacre House, Jordan Hill, Oxford 0X28DP, United Kingdom. ISBN 978-1-85617-684-2. Also available from www.amazon.com

QuEST Forum. Details about TL 9000. www.questforum.org

International Aerospace Quality Group (IAQG). Details about AS 9100. www.iaqg.sae.org

ISO/TC 176 N881R3 'List of ISO 9001 Sector Applications' developed by ISO/TC 176, Quality Management and Quality Assurance. This list is updated by ISO/TC 176 on a periodic basis as information becomes available. www.tc176.org/pdf/N881R3SectorSpecificDocumentationList2008_06.pdf

International Organization for Standardization

- The ISO Survey of Certifications 2009. http://www.iso.org/iso/survey2009.pdf
- ISO/TS 16949:2009, Quality management systems – Particular requirements for the application of ISO 9001:2008 for automotive production and relevant service part organizations. Obtainable from ISO or ISO members (list at www.iso.org).
- ISO 13485:2003, Medical devices – Quality management systems – Requirements for regulatory purposes. Obtainable from ISO or ISO members (list at www.iso.org).
- ISO 15378:2011, Primary packaging materials for medicinal products – Particular requirements for the application of ISO 9001:2008, with reference to Good Manufacturing Practice (GMP). Obtainable from ISO or ISO members (list at www.iso.org).
- ISO/TS 29001:2010, Petroleum, petrochemical and natural gas industries – Sector-specific quality management systems – Requirements for product and service supply organizations. Obtainable from ISO or ISO members (list at www.iso.org).

TickIT: Details about TickIT. www.bsigroup.com

31. What are the costs and benefits of obtaining ISO 9001 certification?

There is no definite answer to this popular question, as the cost of ISO 9001 certification depends on various factors, e.g. how long it takes to develop a quality management system, how many staff members are involved and whether an external consultant is hired or not. In view of this, this section considers only the broad cost categories and lists major cost items by category. The broad categories include the cost of establishing and implementing a quality management system, the cost of maintaining it, and the cost of the initial certification and its maintenance.

Cost of establishing and implementing the QMS

- Training of one or two of your company managers by an external trainer (preferably from an industry association or chamber) to get them to understand the requirements of ISO 9001 and the QMS-related documentation needed by your organization.
- Assessing the current quality control practices and setting up additional routine test facilities if required.
- Revamping work space, equipment, machines, utilities, facilities support services, etc, if required. For example, additional test facilities may be required for conducting routine tests of the product during production and before dispatch to customers.
- Reviewing and providing lighting, ventilation, controls for temperature, humidity, noise and vibration, hygienic practices, as required.
- Reviewing and revamping arrangements for the proper and safe handling and storage of raw materials, semi-finished and finished products, as necessary. (At this point if you think it appropriate, you may implement good housekeeping practices or the Japanese 5S (see question 10).
- Reviewing current procedures/practices and listing new procedures, checklists and records to be prepared.
- Developing QMS-related documents (e.g. quality policy, quality objectives, QMS manual, procedures, quality plans, specifications and drawings, formats for record-keeping).
- Conducting awareness training for all persons who have roles and responsibilities for implementing QMS.
- Miscellaneous expenditures like word processing, stationery and other consumables required for the preparation of manuals, procedures and the like.

Cost of maintaining the QMS

- Checking periodically the condition of measuring instruments for their repair, maintenance and calibration.
- Training some of your managers to perform periodic internal audits.
- Performing periodic internal QMS audits, corrective actions and management reviews.
- Reorienting, raising the awareness of, and training your employees to keep them up-to-date on changes in QMS, continual improvement of QMS and other matters.

Many of the activities listed above can be carried out by your employees after studying ISO 9001 and the guideline standards and brochures published by ISO (see question 29). While they may not incur direct costs, they will involve indirect costs arising from your employees' efforts to educate themselves and to carry these activities out. To supplement their knowledge, you could ask one or two of your employees to undergo short training on the implementation of ISO 9001. Alternatively, you could outsource some of the above activities to consultants or experts known in the field.

Cost of initial certification and cost associated with the maintenance of certification

- Registration or certification fee payable to the certification body for a period of three years.
- Fees for the two-stage audit visit by the nominated certification body.
- Fee for periodic surveillance audits by the nominated certification body.
- Travel, board and lodging of auditor(s) from the certification body.

It may be added here that certification to ISO 9001 is not a mandatory step towards implementation of QMS. Your management should study whether it would be appropriate for strategic and other reasons for your company to implement ISO 9001 and to undergo certification before incurring the above costs.

Benefits of ISO 9001

If you implement and keep practicing the system well it will provide you with a number of benefits such as:

- Quality will be seen as everyone's responsibility instead of being the sole responsibility of the quality control inspector or manager.
- QMS will provide you with a means of documenting the company's experience in a structured manner (quality manual, procedures, instructions, etc).
- You will generate savings, as the costs of reprocessing, rework, repeat inspections, replacing products, penalties due to delayed deliveries, customer returns, customer complaints and warranty claims will gradually fall.
- You will be able to secure your customers' loyalty as their needs and expectations will be continually met, leading to more business opportunities for you.
- You can use ISO 9001 for publicity to win more sales.
- You get preferential treatment from potential customers who themselves have implemented ISO 9001.
- Export marketing will be easier for you, as many foreign buyers place a premium on ISO 9001 systems.
- You will have a level playing field with large companies when bidding for new contracts.
- Obtaining certification will reduce the frequency of audits of your system by different customers.

The biggest benefit to be gained from maintaining a QMS (which is an investment in preventing failures) is the huge savings you can make by considerably reducing the cost of failures (see question 2).

FOR MORE INFORMATION

- International Organization for Standardization
  - ISO 9000 Family – Global management standards (Video). This video is freely available from ISO website http://www.iso.org/iso/iso9000_video

    In this video ISO 9000 users speak from experience on management commitment, metrics, customer focus, continual improvement, knowledge transfer, cost savings and the eight quality management principles.
  - *ISO* Management *Systems* magazine database.
    http://www.iso.org/iso/iso-management-systems

    The electronic editions from 2001 to 2009 of the ISO magazine 'ISO Management Systems' are available for consultation and downloading free of charge from the 'News and Media' section of the ISO website. They cover news, issues and developments related to ISO's management standards and their implementation around the world.

REFERENCES

International Organization for Standardization. Selection and use of the ISO 9000 family of standards: This brochure is freely available from the ISO website http://www.iso.org/iso/iso_9000_selection_and_use-2009.pdf

International Trade Centre. ISO 9001:2008 Diagnostic Tool. www.intracen.org

32. How do I set up an ISO 9001 quality management system?

It is commonly believed that only large companies can implement ISO 9001, as it requires elaborate documentation that may be difficult for small firms. This is a misconception.

As a word of caution, before deciding to implement the system, your management should first be clear about the purpose for which the system is needed by your organization. If the only driver is to get on customers' tender lists or because your competitor has already got it, it is highly likely that your QMS will remain a set of documents for certification purposes only. The results obtained from such a strategy will not serve any useful purpose for you and will simply put a serious drain on your resources. Rather, your management should first set the specific objectives to be achieved through the QMS, such as providing confidence to customers that your organization is capable of meeting their requirements all the time.

Given the state of present quality management practices in SMEs in developing countries, the implementation of ISO 9001 should be taken up as a project, the sequence of steps for which is explained below.

Step 1: Team nomination

A small team consisting of a senior person from each of your functions should be appointed by your management for system development. One member of the team should be designated as the coordinator; the management representative could be given this role. The team should first undergo awareness and documentation training on the ISO 9000 family of standards with a professional training organization.

Engaging a good consultant to provide support for your team may be a worthwhile investment. A good consultant will make possible a speedy transfer of knowledge and skills to your people. However, hiring a consultant should not be regarded as an exercise in shifting the responsibility for establishing the system to someone else. Rather, your people should carry this out themselves with the help of the consultant in order to retain 'ownership' of the system.

Step 2: Gap analysis

For the gap analysis, a flow chart should be drawn, showing how information currently circulates, from order placement by the customer to delivery of the product or service. From this overall diagram, a flow chart of activities in each department should be prepared. Next, with the diagrams you have built, a list of existing procedures and work instructions for the most relevant activities can be formulated. You may also add other activities and processes that you consider relevant at this point, keeping in mind the requirements established by ISO 9001. Throughout the process just described, you may identify some infrastructural gaps such as:

- Need for additional building space, equipment and machines, utilities, facilities, support services or for revamping the current set-up.
- Need for adequate lighting, ventilation, temperature control, humidity control, proper noise and vibration levels, good hygienic practices (in food processing plants).
- Need for proper handling and storage of raw materials to avoid their mix up and spoilage.
- Need for additional test facilities for routine testing of the product during production and before dispatch to customers.
- Need for periodic check-ups of measuring instruments and subsequent repair, maintenance or calibration.
- Need for taking proper care of the product at all stages to avoid damage.

A time-bound action plan to close the gaps identified during this exercise should be prepared and action taken as planned.

Step 3: Documentation

QMS-related documents such as quality policy, quality objectives, process performance parameters, skills requirements, quality manual, quality plans, and procedures and work instructions should be prepared. It is good to involve all personnel concerned in the development of the procedures and work instructions applicable to their areas. The documentation on procedures and work instructions should reflect current practice and not your ideas of what should be implemented. Create new forms and checklists if they help you; otherwise adopt the existing ones to the extent possible.

Step 4: Training and implementation

Train all employees in 'how to use your QMS'. As the system gets developed (refer to step 3 above), the implementation phase should get going at the same time, i.e. supporting evidence like records, minutes of meetings and customer feedback data should be maintained.

Step 5: Internal audit and improvement

Some of your managers and staff members should be trained by a professional trainer to carry out internal auditing of the QMS. Your management representative may also carry out audit management activities. After the system has been implemented for about three months, your trained auditors should conduct an internal audit. Any gaps found during the audit should be corrected; any modification required in the system documents should be carried out; any need for additional awareness and skills training or improving the infrastructure should be taken care of. Once the system stabilizes, internal audits should be conducted at planned intervals, once every six months for example, or as needed.

You should also use internal audits, customer feedback data, process and product monitoring data, evidence of the attainment or not of quality objectives, corrective actions taken, etc. as resources for improving the system. Your management should provide financial and other resources for improvement projects and monitor the progress of improvement.

Step 6: Management review

Your management should review internal audit results, customer feedback data, status of quality objectives, analysis of process performance, product conformity trends, status of corrective and preventive actions. As a result of this review, management may decide to set new targets for quality objectives and to make the improvements needed in the QMS. Management reviews should be held at regular intervals, for example at least once every six months.

Step 7: Certification

Certification to ISO 9001 is voluntary; therefore the need for it should be decided by your management.

Once the system has been in operation for a few months and at least one internal audit and one management review has been conducted, you may consider making an application for certification.

Action plan

An action plan for developing QMS covering the above activities should be prepared. The plan should define the responsibilities of team members and management and set target dates. A total period of six to nine months will be required for the full development and implementation of the system. An example of an action plan is given in the table below.

ISO 9000 implementation action plan

Activities \ Month	1	2	3	4	5	6	7	8	9	Responsibility
Team nomination										Management
Gap analysis										Team
Documentation										Team
Training and implementation										All
Internal audit/ improvement										Audit manager
Management review										Management
Certification										Certification body

Source: S.C. Arora, India.

FOR MORE INFORMATION

- International Organization for Standardization. Selection and use of the ISO 9000 family of standards. This brochure is freely available from ISO http://www.iso.org/iso/iso_9000_selection_and_use-2009.pdf

  The brochure provides an overview of the standards in the ISO 9000 family and demonstrates how, collectively, they form a basis for continual improvement and business excellence. In addition to giving examples of the experience of users of the standards, it has sections on the following topics: description of the ISO 9000 core series standards; step-by-step process for implementing a quality management system; maintaining benefits and continual improvement; future of the ISO 9000 family.

REFERENCES

International Trade Centre and International Organization for Standardization. ISO 9001 for Small Businesses – What to do: Advice from ISO/TC 176, ISBN 978-92-67-10516-1. Obtainable from ISO or ISO members (list at www.iso.org).

International Trade Centre. ISO 9001:2008 Diagnostic Tool. www.intracen.org

33. What are quality objectives and how do they help an organization to accomplish the commitments made in its quality policy?

The quality policy is a statement of an organization's overall intentions and directions in regard to quality. One of the purposes of a quality policy is to remind your employees about what is expected of them to obtain customer satisfaction. In order to put the quality policy into practice, your management should also define quality objectives that are targeted to your employees. Therefore, while framing quality policy, your management should ensure that it can be easily translated into objectives. For example, a quality policy statement may read as follows:

'We are committed to satisfying the needs of our customers and will deliver defect-free products and services to them, on time and every time.'

From the policy above, the following objectives, among others, can be derived.

Policy	Objectives
We are committed to delivering defect-free products and services.	99% of monthly outputs to be defect-fee (measured from customer returns).
Delivery of products and service on time.	98% on-time delivery (measured from promised delivery vs actual delivery).

Quality objectives should be **SMART**, i.e.

S – **S**pecific	Relevant to the process or task to which they are being applied.
M – **M**easurable	Should be expressed in terms that can be measured using available technology.
A – **A**chievable	Within the resources that can be made available.
R – **R**ealistic	In the context of the current and projected work load.
T – **T**imely	Should have specific start and completion dates.

Note that objectives should be measurable. For example, an objective to 'do better', is not a measurable objective. With a measurable objective, you will be able to check if you are achieving it and, if not, decide what you are going to do about it. You will also need to set a target for the objective, keeping in mind your current performance and resource availability. For example, if you are currently achieving 75% on-time delivery and you propose a target of 85% to be achieved within a period of six months, you should first assess whether the resources and processes needed for this higher target are in place.

Some examples of objectives which will help you to improve customer satisfaction and your business performance are:

- Reduce errors or defects in the purchasing process from 1% to 0.5 % over a period of six months;
- Reduce the time needed to assemble each item in the assembly shop from the current 60 minutes to 45 minutes;
- Reduce finished product inventories from x million dollars to y million dollars over a period of six months;
- Ensure 98% on-time product delivery;

- Dispose of all complaints within 48 hours of their receipt;
- Answer all customer queries within 48 hours of their receipt;
- Ensure that working machines are available 90% of the time.

Your employees should know and understand the specific quality objectives that have been set for their function or level and how these objectives can be achieved. It will also be important to tell them from time to time how well these objectives are being met and where improvements are required.

For each objective, you should set up a clear plan defining how and by whom the objective is to be achieved as well as the resources needed. Objectives should be reviewed and revised from time to time as part of the continual improvement process.

FOR MORE INFORMATION

- Hoyle, David. ISO 9000 Quality Systems Handbook, 6th ed. 2009. ISBN 978-1-85617-684-2. It is a priced publication of Butterworth-Heinemann, Linacre House, Jordan Hill, Oxford 0X2 8DP, United Kingdom. Also available from www.amazon.com

  This book provides an understanding of each requirement of ISO 9001:2008 through explanations, examples, lists, tables and diagrams. Each requirement is covered by three basic questions 'What does it mean', 'Why is it important' and 'How is it demonstrated'. Chapters 15 and 16 of the book discuss Quality Policy and Quality Objectives respectively.

- International Trade Centre and International Organization for Standardization. ISO 9001 for Small Businesses – What to do: Advice from ISO/TC 176, ISBN 978-92-67-10516-1. Obtainable from ISO or ISO members (list at www.iso.org).

  Paragraphs 5.3 and 5.4.1 of this handbook deal with Quality Policy and Quality Objectives respectively.

REFERENCES

International Organization for Standardization. ISO 9001:2008, Quality management systems – Requirements. Obtainable from ISO or ISO members (list at www.iso.org).

International Trade Centre. ISO 9001:2008 Diagnostic Tool. www.intracen.org

34. What resources are required to implement an ISO 9001 quality management system?

ISO 9001 proposes that you should determine and provide resources for the implementation and maintenance of the quality management system (QMS), the continual improvement of the effectiveness of the QMS and the enhancement of customer satisfaction. The standard also states that it is the responsibility of your top management to ensure the availability of the required resources.

This section considers the resources needed to implement ISO 9001 throughout the main components of your business: human resources, infrastructure and work environment.

Human resources

Your staff should be competent to perform their work. They should have appropriate competence (i.e. education, training, skills and experience) for their particular duties. For example, the operators may need training on:

- How to adjust process parameters;
- How to calibrate a measuring instrument before use;
- Methods of assembling components, etc.

If you are a service company, your staff may also need to know how to use computers for processing customer inquiries or transactions, e.g. in a bank's front office or in a hotel room reservation process, in addition to knowing the steps of each process.

Some specific human resources should be available. These would include competent internal auditor(s), an effective management representative, persons with the ability to analyse data and information, knowledgeable persons able to determine the root causes of problems of product quality and system deficiencies as well as to take appropriate corrective actions.

Above all, you should be able to motivate your people to understand the importance of their activities for enhanced customer satisfaction.

Infrastructure

- Machine tools, hand tools, computer hardware, workplace, storage space, product handling equipment, measuring and testing instruments or equipment, etc. should be adequate to ensure product conformity.
- Support services such as uninterrupted supplies of electricity, water, fuel, steam, compressed air, as required, standby power supply and effluent treatment facilities should be provided.
- Equipment and facilities required for periodic maintenance should also be provided.
- Information sources (such as reference books and other publications, information databases on export, import and regulatory requirements) should be available. The required technology (e.g. software) for converting data and information into knowledge for use by the company should also be on hand.

Work environment

- Appropriate control of heat, humidity, light, air flow, noise, vibration, etc. at the work location should be carried out. In service companies, appropriate customer waiting areas and facilities should be provided. Proper sanitation and hygiene (e.g. for food, drink and pharmaceutical companies) should be maintained. Overall, the work environment should encourage productivity, creativity and the well-being of your people.

The units required of the above resources will depend on the nature of the product provided and the scope of the company's business operations. Implementing the ISO 9001 QMS does not necessarily always involve investing in additional infrastructure and in the work environment. In addition to adequacy of resources, you will need to re-examine processes, the roles and responsibilities of people, the analysis of measurement results and the actions taken to prevent the recurrence of quality-related problems. Sometimes when your own resources (competence and infrastructure) are not adequate, the standard also provides for outsourcing any process that may affect product conformity, provided necessary control on such outsourced processes is exercised at your discretion.

FOR MORE INFORMATION

- International Trade Centre and International Organization for Standardization. ISO 9001 for Small Businesses – What to do: Advice from ISO/TC 176, ISBN 978-92-67-10516-1. Obtainable from ISO or ISO members (list at www.iso.org).

  Paragraphs 6.1 to 6.4 of this handbook deal with resource management.

REFERENCES

Hoyle, David. ISO 9000 Quality Systems Handbook, 6th ed. 2009. ISBN 978-1-85617-684-2. It is a priced publication of Butterworth-Heinemann, Linacre House, Jordan Hill, Oxford 0X2 8DP, United Kingdom. Also available from www.amazon.com

International Organization for Standardization. ISO 9001:2008, Quality management systems – Requirements. Obtainable from ISO or ISO members (list at www.iso.org).

International Trade Centre. ISO 9001:2008 Diagnostic Tool. www.intracen.org

35. What are the false notions and problems encountered by SMEs in implementing ISO 9001?

Some false notions about ISO 9001

1. ISO 9001 is difficult to implement in small companies.

The standard is generic and can be used by all types and sizes of organizations. In fact, it may be easier for smaller companies to implement ISO 9001 as the line of command is short and responsibilities can be easily defined and communicated. The standard has been implemented by small companies, including even by a company run with a single employee. Defining a formal organizational structure is not necessary. If your company is not involved in design and development and manufactures to designs supplied by your client, your QMS will be exempt from the requirements for design and development. ITC and ISO have jointly published a handbook on ISO 9001 for use by small companies.

2. A great deal of expenditure is required to implement ISO 9001.

While there are costs, they will result in benefits to the company by preventing expensive failure costs in the future. The expenditure involved in establishing the QMS includes the costs of the following: training personnel in relation to the establishment of the system; development of documentation; closing gaps found in the system; and additional equipment, facilities, support services, etc. if found necessary. If you decide to obtain certification, then the certification fee will be another cost. With the rising competition among certification bodies, this fee is gradually falling.

3. It is essential to hire the services of a consultant to establish the ISO 9001 system.

Hiring a specialized service is necessary only if your staff do not have the skills to develop the QMS by themselves. A system developed by your staff will engender a stronger sense of ownership among them and will be cost effective. There are enough published materials available from the ISO website, national standards bodies, private publishers, United Nations organizations like ITC and UNIDO and in guide books published by industry associations, which you can use to understand and develop the system on your own. However, hiring the services of a good consultant (after due diligence) should be considered on the basis of a cost-benefit analysis.

4. It is necessary for the company to have its own trained and independent auditors to undertake internal audits.

If the company is small and it is not possible to have independent auditors from within the company, you can hire the services of competent external auditors for the periodic auditing of your QMS.

5. ISO 9001 requires too much paperwork.

Elaborate manuals, procedures and forms are developed by companies sometimes on the advice of their consultants. However, employees may get frustrated when they are asked to keep excessive records without much value addition to the process. Somehow an impression has been created that unless elaborate paperwork is done, it will not be possible to get certification. However, it is not necessary to document all processes. In many cases, flow charts may be sufficient. ISO 9001 requires only six mandatory documented procedures. These are: control of documents, control of records, internal audit, control of nonconforming product, corrective action and preventive action.

Also, the standard gives companies the flexibility to keep the documents (manual, procedures, records etc.) either in a printed version or in electronic form, or a combination of these.

Some challenges and suggested solutions in setting up and implementing ISO 9001

Challenges	Suggested solutions
Lack of information and training	
Difficulties in obtaining information and publications on ISO 9000 standards	The latest information on the ISO 9000 series of standards is available on the ISO website www.iso.org (click 'ISO 9000' on the home page of the site). Alternatively, you can study these documents or their national versions in the library of your country's bureau of standards (see question 29 for details).
Lack of understanding among company personnel of the requirements of the standard and their application to company processes.	This knowledge gap can be filled by self-study of the documents as detailed above, by attending short training courses on the subject or by hiring a competent consultant to impart knowledge to some of your employees.
High cost of training personnel in understanding, developing and implementing a quality management system.	In some countries such training is organized at nominal cost by trade or industry associations or chambers and bureau of standards. After your staff undergoes training, it will be good for your company to develop QMS on its own with need-based advice from a reputable consultant.
Inappropriate documentation	
Excessive procedures and records are created to maintain the system.	Procedures should be limited to what is required. The standard demands only one quality manual, six procedures and approximately 20 records. Additional procedures and records should be devised only if they add value to the system. It will be good to adopt your existing procedures, instructions, records, with modifications wherever required. All documentation on procedures and records could be stored in hard or electronic copies or a combination of both.
Lack of top management commitment	
People in the company are not fully convinced that the system can benefit them individually or as a company.	People will gradually get convinced of the value of the system once they start seeing results, e.g. achievement of set objectives or targets such as improved housekeeping, increased knowledge of the use of quality control tools, reduction in rejects, errors, customer returns, customer complaints, etc.
Difficulty in dealing with resistance to change, especially among middle managers who may be used to the ad hoc handling of problems and have a tendency to deviate from defined procedures.	This cannot be solved overnight. Top management should 'walk the talk', i.e. they should not allow deviations from set procedures or permit the release of materials with deviations. Under such an approach, the mid-level managers will start respecting system requirements.
Inadequate internal auditing	
Competent internal auditors are not available, and deficiencies in the system may therefore not be identified for corrective action.	Short training courses can be used to build the competence of internal auditors. Such training is provided by various training organizations, including some industry and trade associations or chambers.
Timely action on the deficiencies found during the monitoring of processes and product and those uncovered during the internal audit is not taken.	Management should encourage employees to highlight deviations in day-to-day monitoring of processes and product. The root causes of all discrepancies, deviations, nonconformities and customer complaints should be eliminated in such a way as to prevent recurrence of the problem in the future. If there is need for additional resources to take corrective actions, management should provide those resources on time.

Challenges	Suggested solutions
Over-emphasis on certification	
Companies are in a hurry to obtain certification and do not spend adequate time on implementing the system effectively.	Before you apply for certification, it is necessary first to ensure that your QMS system is being implemented effectively. This will require the system to be in place for at least three months and its effectiveness checked through an internal audit, followed by corrective actions on audit findings.
Organizations seek certification only because they want a certificate to bid for tenders or for other marketing reasons, etc.	Certification is not compulsory. Therefore a cost-benefit analysis of the need for certification should be carried out (see question 31 for details).

Source: S.C. Arora, India.

FOR MORE INFORMATION

- Hoyle, David. ISO 9000 Quality Systems Handbook, 6th ed. 2009. ISBN 978-1-85617-684-2. It is a priced publication of Butterworth-Heinemann, Linacre House, Jordan Hill, Oxford 0X2 8DP, United Kingdom. Also available from www.amazon.com.

  This book provides an understanding of each requirement of ISO 9001:2008 through explanations, examples, lists, tables and diagrams. Each requirement is covered by three basic questions: 'What does it mean', 'Why is it important' and 'How is it demonstrated'. Chapter 6 of the book deals with 'A flawed approach' and provides information on how to avoid mistakes in establishing a value-added QMS.

REFERENCES

International Trade Centre and International Organization for Standardization. ISO 9001 for Small Businesses – What to do: Advice from ISO/TC 176, ISBN 978-92-67-10516-1. Obtainable from ISO or ISO members (list at www.iso.org).

International Organization for Standardization. ISO 9001:2008, Quality management systems – Requirements. Obtainable from ISO or ISO members (list at www.iso.org).

International Trade Centre. ISO 9001:2008 Diagnostic Tool. www.intracen.org.

36. How do I ensure that my raw materials, purchased components and inputs from my outsourced processes are fit for use?

Materials, components and services

You may be doing an excellent job of controlling your own activities, but if your suppliers are not performing satisfactorily, you and your customers may be adversely affected. It is therefore important that your suppliers are reliable and exercise some form of quality control. You will need to:

- Identify which of the materials, components and services that you buy are critical for the quality of your final product or service.
- Define the specifications of the materials, components and services to be purchased.
- Establish criteria for the evaluation and selection of supplies and suppliers.
- Define procedures for accepting materials and services from your suppliers.

For the purchasing specifications, your first option should be to look for national or international standards rather than developing your own specifications; this will save you time and money. However, you should ensure that the standards you choose meet the requirements of your customers as well as your own. If there is no appropriate standard, you will have to set out your own purchasing specifications. These should cover technical characteristics, composition of raw materials, functional or performance characteristics, among other matters.

You have various options for selecting suppliers who can provide you with raw materials or components that comply with your purchasing specifications:

- *Your past suppliers.* You could choose your past suppliers on the basis of your experience with their ability to meet your requirements.
- *ISO 9001 registered firms.* You can identify potential suppliers from lists of firms certified to ISO 9001. This will provide you with an assurance of quality, as these suppliers will deliver consistently to your specifications.
- *Suppliers with certified products.* You can purchase products from suppliers that are licensed by third parties to use certification marks on their products, thus indicating their compliance with standards. This is possible if you are purchasing products which have been certified by a third party.
- *Supplier evaluation.* You could conduct an evaluation of new suppliers to assess their capability for meeting your requirements. To do this, you will have to define your criteria for evaluating and selecting suppliers.

You need to inform the suppliers you select about the specifications of the product or service you are purchasing and make the delivery deadline clear to them. In addition, you may include in your purchase order your acceptance procedures for the order. These may include submission of evidence of the quality management system used by the supplier, first piece approval of the product made by the supplier, approval of equipment used by the supplier, qualification of the personnel of the supplier, etc.

You also need to ensure that the product or service you receive from your supplier meets your requirements:

- You can rely on your supplier's quality assurance system and accept materials without further checks. However, for each lot of material, you may ask your supplier to send you the test data on the relevant batch of the material.
- Inspection and testing on a sampling or 100% basis can be carried out on receipt of the material.
- Inspection of suppliers' premises before the dispatch of materials from these premises.
- Engaging a third-party inspection agency to inspect suppliers' premises before they send the product to you.

Outsourced processes

You also have to be sure of the quality of the inputs that are managed by an external party on your behalf. Outsourced activities may be carried out on your premises or at an independent site. The following are examples of outsourced processes: getting the painting or electroplating of some of your components done by an outside body; obtaining information technology, housekeeping and training services from external agencies; having your machines and other equipment maintained by an external maintenance agency on your premises.

The reasons for outsourcing processes may be one of two. You may have the capacity for performing the activities yourself but do not want to divert your resources to doing them, or you do not have this capacity and therefore need the help of a reliable and competent external organization.

For all outsourced processes, you will have to define and implement your own control measures; these will include the evaluation of service providers and inspection or evaluation of the products and services received from them.

FOR MORE INFORMATION

- International Organization for Standardization. Introduction and support package: Guidance on 'Outsourced process'. Document No. ISO/TC 176/SC 2/N 630R3, issued in October 2008. Freely obtainable from ISO website: http://www.iso.org/iso/iso_catalogue/management_standards/quality_management/iso_9001_2008/guidance_on_the_documentation_requirements_of_iso_9001_2008.htm

  Provides guidance on the intent of ISO 9001:2008 clause 4.1, regarding the control of outsourced processes.

- International Trade Centre and International Organization for Standardization. ISO 9001 for Small Businesses – What to do: Advice from ISO/TC 176, ISBN 978-92-67-10516-1. Obtainable from ISO or ISO members (list at www.iso.org).

  Paragraph 7.4 of this handbook deals with the purchasing process, purchasing information and verification of purchased product.

REFERENCES

Hoyle, David. ISO 9000 Quality Systems Handbook, 6th ed. 2009. ISBN 978-1-85617-684-2. It is a priced publication of Butterworth-Heinemann, Linacre House, Jordan Hill, Oxford 0X2 8DP, United Kingdom. Also available from www.amazon.com.

International Organization for Standardization. ISO 9001:2008, Quality management systems – Requirements. Obtainable from ISO or ISO members (list at www.iso.org).

International Trade Centre. ISO 9001:2008 Diagnostic Tool. www.intracen.org

37. How do we publicize our achievements in quality management?

Possible ways of publicizing your achievements in quality management are detailed below.

Fulfilling promises made to the customer

It will not be wrong to say that in the marketplace customers are your best ambassadors. If customers are satisfied, they will tell others about their good experience with your product or service. However, it is also true, as the literature shows, that unhappy customers will spread news of their discontent even faster and wider. Furthermore, while most unhappy customers do not complain, they may leave you and do business elsewhere. It will not be correct to assume that customers are satisfied simply because they did not complain.

Some effective methods of satisfying customers are:

- Providing products and services to customers that meet their needs and expectations.
- Delivering the product or service within the agreed time.
- Providing the agreed post-delivery services to the customer without any delay.
- Responding quickly and effectively to customers' queries or complaints, if any.
- Providing the customer with free repair or product replacement services, if so warranted.

It is important to obtain regular formal or informal feedback from customers about their sense of satisfaction or dissatisfaction, as well as to take early action on any such feedback. Sometimes, a good suggestion from the customer may lead to improvements in your quality management system.

Organized publicity

This would include publicizing your achievements by:

- Sending publicity flyers or mailers to customers or prospective customers periodically.
- Highlighting your achievements in your publicity brochures and product literature. You may even quote verbatim the positive feedback received from your customers. A list of satisfied customers with their contact details may also be included in your brochure. Your prospective customers may want to check your credentials with satisfied customers. It is common now to display all this information on the company web page.
- Advertising in newspapers, industrial journals, magazines, periodicals of industry and trade associations, the yellow pages and in other print and electronic media; developing and updating your own website; using mass mailing to reach potential customers.
- Participation at trade fairs, making efforts to win national quality awards, etc.

Some industry or trade associations publish case studies of companies whose success can be attributed to implementing quality management systems or other quality improvement tools. This can be used as another source of publicity. Similarly, various organizations and industry associations organize seminars that give you the opportunity to present your own QMS-related case studies. All these opportunities for publicizing your success stories should be explored.

Certification of your quality management system by accredited certification bodies

Certification of your QMS by an accredited certification body generates confidence among your existing and potential customers and other interested parties that you are capable of supplying consistently conforming products or services.

Most certification bodies keep an updated list of certified companies and organizations and provide this list upon request to potential buyers or other interested parties. In some countries, a national register of ISO 9001 certified companies and organizations is maintained by a governmental or a non-governmental organization. These registers provide an authentic source of information to potential customers about the ability of a company to satisfy customers, and this may generate more business inquiries for you. If you are a certified company, then make sure that your name appears in such registers.

Although the certification of an ISO 9001 QMS gives an assurance to your customers that you can deliver a product and service that satisfies their needs, you may not use the logo of the certification body and that of the accreditation body on the product, product labels or product packaging or in any way that may be construed to mean that your product is certified. Indeed, it is not your product or service that is certified but your QMS, and no misleading information must be conveyed that leads the customer to think that the product is certified. However, you can use the logo of the certification body along with that of the accreditation body on your letterheads and other publicity materials to publicize your achievement of ISO 9001 certification. For this purpose, the conditions and guidelines of your certification body should be kept in mind.

FOR MORE INFORMATION

- International Organization for Standardization
  - Publicizing your ISO 9000 or ISO 14000 certification.
    http://www.simplyquality.org/publicity.pdf

    This leaflet aims to help ISO 9000 and ISO 14000 certificate holders to avoid the pitfalls of false, misleading or confusing claims in advertisements, promotional material and other means of letting the market know that they operate a quality management system which has been independently assessed and certified.
  - ISO Management Systems Magazine Database. http://www.iso.org/iso/iso-management-systems

    The electronic editions from 2001 to 2009 in both English and French of the ISO magazine 'ISO Management Systems' are available for consultation and downloading free of charge from the 'News and Media' section of the ISO website. The database provides a worldwide overview of ISO 9001, ISO 14001 and other global business standards developed by ISO and cites success stories of companies that have used these standards effectively.

REFERENCES

International Organization for Standardization

- Brochure on publicizing your ISO 9001:2008 or ISO 14001:2004 certification. Obtainable from ISO or ISO members (list at www.iso.org).
- ISO's logo is not for use.
  http://www.iso.org/iso/iso_catalogue/management_and_leadership_standards/certification/iso_s_logo_not_for_use.htm

B. ENVIRONMENTAL MANAGEMENT SYSTEMS

38. What is ISO 14001? Is it applicable to both the manufacturing and services sectors?

ISO 14000 family of standards

Organizations around the world as well as their stakeholders are becoming increasingly aware of the need for environmental protection. To enable organizations to manage environmental issues proactively, ISO has developed the ISO 14000 family of environmental management standards. Its two main standards are: 'ISO 14001:2004 Environmental management systems – Requirements with guidance for use' and 'ISO 14004:2004 Environmental management systems – General guidelines on principles, systems and support techniques'.

ISO technical committee TC-207, which is responsible for developing the ISO 14000 family, has since 1996 been developing standards in other areas as well, such as environmental labelling, life cycle assessment, greenhouse gas management and related activities, and carbon footprint of products.

ISO 14001:2004

ISO 14001 is the world's most recognized framework for environmental management systems (EMS). The overall aim of an EMS based upon ISO 14001 is to support environmental protection and the prevention of pollution in a balance with socio-economic needs.

ISO 14001 can be implemented by any type (public, private, manufacturing, service) and size (small, medium-sized or large) of organization. An EMS based upon ISO 14001 provides a framework to help you identify those aspects of your business activities that have significant impacts on the environment, to set objectives and targets to minimize those impacts, and to develop programmes to achieve targets and implement other operational control measures to ensure compliance with your environmental policy.

ISO 14001 does not establish a minimum level of environmental performance. Rather, it requires you to achieve the objectives for environmental performance that your management has set in your environmental policy. It also requires you to demonstrate a commitment to complying with the applicable environmental legislation and to the continual improvement of your environmental performance.

It will be possible for you to integrate your ISO 14001 EMS with your ISO 9001 QMS as they are compatible with each other.

The impact of the environmental performance of an organization goes beyond its customers and suppliers to a broader range of stakeholders – ordinary citizens, regulators, employees, insurance companies and shareholders. Everyone has an interest in the quality of the environment around them. Thus, demonstrating compliance with an environmental management system based on ISO 14001:2004 is a sound business decision.

Certification to ISO 14001 has been constantly increasing. By the end of December 2009, a total of 223 149 certificates had been issued to organizations in over 159 countries.

For further information on ISO 14001 and a diagram of the standards related to the environment, see question 17.

Applicability to the services sector

As has been said earlier, ISO 14001 is a set of generic environmental management system requirements that are applicable to all types and sizes of organization, and accommodate diverse geographical, cultural and social conditions. The system benefits both manufacturing and services industries, as all business activities have an impact on the environment.

Although the implementation of ISO 14001 is more popular in the manufacturing sector, it is equally applicable to the services industry. Public utility organizations like power-generating and power supply units, water supply agencies, waste collection and disposal agencies, domestic fuel and gas supply agencies, petrol stations dispensing petrol, diesel oil and gas to the public, and transport companies belong to the services sector. The implementation of ISO 14001 EMS will enable such entities to control their environmental aspects and minimize their environmental impact. For example, transport services could use less petrol, have more efficient and better tuned engines, and follow more efficient routes.

In addition to these public utility organizations, other services providers have made effective use of ISO 14001 EMS. Examples are hotels, construction agencies and general office services. A hotel can make substantial savings in power, fuel and water consumption by implementing ISO 14001. General office activities generate large quantities of waste such as computer monitors, printers, cartridges, telephones, cameras and other electronic devices (popularly called e-waste) which need to be safely disposed of. The implementation of ISO 14001 in offices can assist the organizations concerned in the handling, handling, recycling and disposal of e-waste.

FOR MORE INFORMATION

- Euromines. The ultimate SME implementation guide for QMS and EMS. 2005. http://www.euromines.org/publications_downloads/general.pdf

  This guide for the implementation of quality management systems (QMS) and environmental management systems (EMS) has been developed for small and medium-sized enterprises by Euromines.

- International Trade Centre. *Export Quality Management Bulletin* No. 78, An introduction to ISO 14000 – Environmental management systems. www.intracen.org/exporters/quality-management/Quality_publications_index

  This bulletin provides information on the ISO 14000 family of standards for environmental management systems and aims to help exporters implement such systems.

REFERENCES

International Organization for Standardization

- Environmental management – The ISO 14000 family of International Standards (brochure). http://www.iso.org/iso/theiso14000family_2009.pdf
- Survey of ISO 14001 certificates issued as on December 2009. http://www.iso.org/iso/survey2009.pdf.
- ISO Technical Committee ISO/TC 207 on Environmental Management. http://www.iso.org/iso/iso_technical_committee?commid=54808
- ISO 14001:2004 Environmental Management Systems – Requirements with guidance for use. Obtainable from ISO or ISO members (list at www.iso.org).
- ISO 14004:2004 Environmental Management Systems – General guidelines on principles, systems and support techniques. Obtainable from ISO or ISO members (list at www.iso.org).

39. Will implementation of ISO 14001 enable an organization to demonstrate compliance with environment-related legal requirements?

The use of ISO 14001 EMS is a good means of demonstrating compliance with legal environmental requirements. However, certification to the standard may not necessarily exempt you from inspection, audit and testing of effluent samples by your country's environmental regulatory authorities.

Although certification to ISO 14001 is voluntary, many foreign buyers prefer to trade with suppliers who can consistently demonstrate compliance with environmental requirements. Some buyers require their suppliers to obtain certification to ISO 14001. Furthermore, with the concept of sustainable development gathering momentum, many big retail chains and automobile manufacturers are moving towards greening their supply chain; in the process they are encouraging their suppliers to adopt clean and green technologies and to set up an ISO 14001 EMS.

The overall aim of ISO 14001 is to support environmental protection and the prevention of pollution. To achieve this broad objective you will need to develop and implement an environmental policy. This policy should provide for the following, among others:

- A commitment to continual improvement and the prevention of pollution.
- A commitment to comply with legal and other requirements related to the environmental aspects of your activities, products and services.

To demonstrate compliance with environmental legal requirements the following system elements of ISO 14001 will need to be implemented.

- As a first step, identify and obtain access to the environmental legal requirements applicable to your business activities and ensure that while setting up your EMS these legal requirements are kept in mind.
- Take the legal requirements into account while setting up your environmental objectives and targets.
- To achieve the above objectives and targets, set up environmental management programmes covering roles, responsibilities, resources, procedures and the time frame needed to achieve them.
- Your employees should be aware of the importance of conformity with your environmental policy (including the commitment to comply with legal requirements).
- Your employees should also be aware of the consequences of departures from specified requirements (including legal requirements).
- All operations that are associated with compliance with legal requirements should be planned and operational control procedures for the same should be followed by all concerned.
- Periodically evaluate compliance with applicable legal requirements.
- Identify any instances of non-compliance with legal requirements (or foreseeable non-compliance) and take prompt action to identify, implement and verify preventive and corrective action taken.
- Maintain records of compliance with legal requirements.
- While conducting periodic internal audits, assess issues related to legal compliance.
- Use information on changes to, or new, legal requirements when making modifications to your EMS.

FOR MORE INFORMATION

- International Institute for Environment and Development (IIED). Profiles of Tools and Tactics for Environmental Mainstreaming. No. 5. Environmental Management Systems (EMS). http://www.environmental-mainstreaming.org/documents/EM%20Profile%20No%205%20-%20EMS%20(6%20Oct%2009).pdf

  Explains environmental management systems (EMS), the issues they focus on, their main steps, and the pros and cons for such systems.

- International Organization for Standardization. ISO 14004:2004, Environmental management systems – General guidelines on principles, system and support techniques. Obtainable from ISO or ISO members (list at www.iso.org).

  This standard provides guidance on the establishment, implementation, maintenance and improvement of EMS and its coordination with other management systems.

REFERENCES

International Organization for Standardization. ISO 14001:2004, Environmental management systems – Requirements with guidance for use. Obtainable from ISO or ISO members (list at www.iso.org).

40. How does ISO 14001 help SMEs to increase the acceptability of their export products or services?

Every business actively, whether large, medium-sized or small, has the potential to cause environmental impacts right from the point of consumption of raw materials, natural resources and, energy, to the generation of waste during production, product distribution, product use by customers and finally product disposal. Thus the implementation of ISO 14001 EMS is equally relevant for SMEs and necessary for their business success. Implementation of ISO 14000 EMS can help SMEs in the ways discussed below to increase the market acceptability of their export products.

Export trade facilitator

Just as the ISO 9001 quality management system has become a facilitator for the export trade, so the development of a sound environmental management system can help SMEs to overcome trade barriers. With the increasing trend towards greening the supply chain, many large enterprises are now sourcing their products from suppliers who seriously demonstrate compliance with environmental requirements. Implementation of ISO 14001 EMS will thus help SMEs to be selected by the large retail chains, for example, as their suppliers. Wal-Mart, Tesco and Macy's examine compliance with environmental requirements when they evaluate potential suppliers. If such suppliers, in addition to meeting the buyers' minimum environmental performance requirements, can show that they are also implementing the ISO 14001 EMS and have been certified to it, they can expect to get preferential treatment.

Image booster

SMEs that implement ISO 14000 EMS are able to demonstrate responsible care of the environment to their stakeholders such as the ordinary citizen, shareholders, regulators, investors and insurance companies. This improved image will inspire confidence in both domestic and foreign buyers to use such SMEs as their preferred suppliers.

Competitive pricing

The aim of ISO 14001 EMS is the protection of the environment and prevention of pollution. This will require an organization to develop plans for and demonstrate conservation in the use of raw materials and resources like electricity, water and fuel. The implementation of these plans will enable SMEs to reduce their production costs and thus make them more price-competitive in both domestic and foreign markets.

For example, Hogarth, in her study of Milan Screw, an SME in Michigan, reported a cost savings of US$ 20,000 when the company designed a better oil removal system as a result of putting in place an ISO 14001 EMS. One company noted that, in addition to being able to recycle 94% of its waste, this also enabled the company to create a profit centre (Fielding, 1999). Another example is provided by the implementation of cleaner production by Ming Chi Computer, China which resulted in over US$ 1.8 million per year in savings from energy and water use and resource recycling (ITC, 2007).

FOR MORE INFORMATION

- International Organization for Standardization. ISO 14001 – The world's environmental management system standard. A concise video freely downloadable from ISO. http://www.iso.org/iso/pressrelease.htm?refid=Ref1061

  A film introducing ISO 14001 and its worldwide impact since it was launched in 1996. Available in English only. Run time: 5 min 7 sec.

- International Trade Centre and International Organization for Standardization. ISO 14001 Environmental Management Systems: An easy-to-use checklist for small business. Are you ready? 2011. ISBN 978-92-67-10531-4. Obtainable from ITC (http://www.intracen.org/about/e-shop/) and ISO (www.iso.org).

- ISO 14000 Environmental Management Systems Benefits. www.trst.com/iso1-frame.htm

  Information on the environmental benefits of ISO 14000 provided by Transformation Strategies on their website.

REFERENCES

Fielding, S. Going for the Green: ISO 14001 Delivers profits. *Industrial Management*. 1999. pp. 31-34.

International Trade Centre. *Export Quality Management Bulletin* No. 78, An introduction to ISO 14000 – Environmental management systems. www.intracen.org/exporters/quality-management/Quality_publications_index

Masero, Sonny. Eco-Competitiveness: Safeguarding Profitability and the World's Natural Resources. http://www.ca.com/~/media/Files/whitepapers/eco-competitiveness-safeguard-prof-nat-res-wp-us-en.pdf

Wal-Mart Sustainability Index. http://walmartstores.com/sustainability/9292.aspx

41. What are the costs and benefits of implementing ISO 14001?

The costs of implementing ISO 14001 and obtaining certification for it vary greatly. They depend on the size of the facility and the nature of the operation. They can be divided into the following three categories.

- Cost of establishing and implementing the EMS;
- Cost of maintaining the EMS;
- Cost of initial certification and cost associated with maintenance of certification.

The main cost items under each category are listed below. A discussion of the benefits of implementing ISO 14000 follows.

Cost of establishing and implementing the EMS

- Purchase of standards and subscription to publications to enable you to obtain up-to-date knowledge on the EMS standards and the applicable environmental regulations.
- Training of one or two company managers by an external trainer to enable them to understand the ISO 14001 EMS requirements.
- Assessing the current status of waste and pollutant generation and resource (water, fuel, electricity, raw materials, etc.) use in your company. At this stage, also list any policy or procedure relating to EMS which may already be in practice in your company. This activity is called an initial environmental review.
- As a result of 3. above, you may see that there is a need to revamp certain pollution abatement[5] equipment or install new ones. There may also be a need to make arrangements for the proper and safe storage of chemicals, fuels and hazardous wastes.
- Development of EMS-related documents (environmental policy and objectives, EMS manual, operational control procedures, system-related procedures).
- Creating awareness in all persons who have roles in, and responsibilities for, EMS-related activities and providing training where required.

Cost of maintaining the EMS

- Periodic testing of effluent.
- Periodic calibration of your testing equipment.
- Training some managers to perform periodic internal audits.
- Periodic reorientation, awareness generation and training activities for your employees to update them on new legislation and to ensure the continual improvement of your EMS.

Many training activities can be handled by the employees themselves after studying the ISO 14001:2004 standard and ISO 14004:2004, the guideline standard. One or two of these can be asked to undergo a short course on implementing ISO 14001 to supplement their knowledge. Alternatively, you could hire consultants or experts known in the field to carry out a training programme for your employees.

[5] Pollution abatement refers to the technology applied or measure taken to reduce pollution and/or its impacts on the environment. The most commonly used technologies are scrubbers, noise mufflers, filters, incinerators, waste-water treatment facilities and composting of wastes. United Nations Statistics Division, *Glossary of Environmental Statistics,* Sales number: 96.XVII.12.

Cost of initial certification and cost associated with maintenance of certification, payable to the certification body of your choice

- Registration or certification fee payable to the nominated certification body for a period of three years.
- Fee for two-stage certification audit by the auditors of the certification body.
- Fee for periodic surveillance audits by the auditors of the certification body.
- Travel, board and lodging of auditor(s) of the certification body for the above audits.

It may be added here that certification to ISO 14001 is not a mandatory step after the implementation of EMS. It is always a need-based decision which your management should take before incurring the above costs.

Benefits of implementing an ISO 14001 EMS

While there are several costs associated with implementing and maintaining an EMS, its many tangible and intangible benefits will offset these costs. The important benefits arising from implementing the EMS include the following:

- Enhanced public image leading to improved business opportunities, for both domestic and export trade.
- Many customers, including governmental procurement agencies, use ISO 14001 EMS as one of the criteria for evaluating their potential suppliers. The implementation of ISO 14001 EMS will give you an edge over other suppliers.
- Improved compliance with legislative and regulatory requirements will reduce penalties and remediation costs.
- EMS will help reduce incidents of release of uncontrolled pollutants and oil or chemical spills, for example, and thus cut expenses associated with their recovery.
- Cost savings can be obtained from recycling and reusing materials.
- One of the objectives of EMS is the reduction of waste and its possible reuse and recycling, which will result in lower disposal costs.
- Employees will have a safer work environment, thereby improving productivity, lowering the number of sick days and reducing insurable risks.

Here are some examples of the benefits that can be gained from an effective EMS.

In Singapore, SGS-Thomson has saved US$ 200,000 by improving the energy efficiency of its cooling plant. Another company, Sony Display Devices, has saved about US$ 7.5 million a year by eliminating raw material wastage. Baxter, which has obtained ISO 14001 certification, has disclosed savings and cost-avoidance of up to US$ 3.4 million by implementing an environmental management system.

A medium-sized manufacturer of precision fittings for the automotive and refrigeration industries identified inefficiencies in its oil recovery procedures in the course of the EMS implementation. By addressing the problem, the firm expects to realize more than US$ 20,000 per year in savings. Another manufacturer reported a 70% reduction in waste disposal costs as its ISO 14001 EMS was put into place.

Larger companies may not find it too difficult to implement the EMS – they have financial strength and economies of scale. However, many SMEs are likely to have problems in adopting environmental controls because of their lack of resources.

Some governments are therefore providing SMEs financial support for implementing EMS. For example, in Singapore, the government agency SPRING (Standards, Productivity and Innovation Board) has extended its Local Enterprise Technical Assistance Scheme to give financial assistance to SMEs wishing to implement EMS and gain certification to ISO 14001. In India, financial assistance is provided to SMEs for acquiring quality, environmental and food safety (HACCP) management systems.

FOR MORE INFORMATION

- Commission for Environmental Cooperation (USA). Successful Practices of Environmental Management Systems in Small and Medium-Size Enterprises: A North American perspective. http://www.cec.org/Storage/59/5200_EMS-Report_en.pdf

  Contains definitions of EMS and SME; discusses the effectiveness of environmental management systems in improving environmental performance, the benefits and characteristics of a successful EMS, and the drivers and barriers to EMS adoption by small and medium-sized businesses, among others.

- Environmental Management Systems (EMS). EMS case studies. http://www.p2pays.org/ref/19/18328/pdfs/nccaseall.pdf

  Presents case studies of private and public companies that applied ISO 14001.

- International Organization for Standardization
  - Environmental management – The ISO 14000 family of International Standards. This brochure is freely available from ISO. http://www.iso.org/iso/theiso14000family_2009.pdf
  - This brochure provides a basic introduction to the ISO 14000 family of standards, gives a concise idea of how they have evolved to provide comprehensive solutions to the range of environmental challenges facing business, government and society today and points out that the ISO 14000 standards result not only in environmental benefits but also in significant tangible economic gains.ISO 14001 – The world's environmental management system standard. Video. This video is freely available from ISO. http://www.iso.org/iso/pressrelease.htm?refid=Ref1061

    A concise film introducing ISO 14001 and the worldwide impact of the standard since it was launched in 1996. Available in English only. Run time: 5 min 7 sec.

  - ISO 14000 Environmental Management Systems Benefits. Information displayed by Transformation Strategies on their website www.trst.com/iso1-frame.htm
  - ISO 14004:2004, Environmental management systems – General guidelines on principles, systems and support techniques. Obtainable from ISO or ISO members (list at www.iso.org).

    This standard provides guidance on the establishment, implementation, maintenance and improvement of EMS and its coordination with other management systems. The Introduction section of the standard carries information on how the ISO 14001 EMS can help an organization to continually improve its environmental performance and derive economic benefits from it.

- International Trade Centre and International Organization for Standardization. ISO 14001 Environmental Management Systems: An easy-to-use checklist for small business. Are you ready? 2011. ISBN 978-92-67-10531-4. Obtainable from ITC (http://www.intracen.org/about/e-shop/) and ISO (www.iso.org).

- Shaheen, Rafi Khan and others. The Costs and Benefits of Compliance with International Environmental Standards. International Institute for Sustainable Development. 2002. http://www.iisd.org/tkn/pdf/tkn_pakistan_standards.pdf

  Study of the costs and benefits of complying with the ISO 14000 series.

REFERENCES

Development Commissioner (MSME), Ministry of Micro, Small & Medium Enterprises, Government of India. Quality Upgradation/Environment management for small scale sector through incentive for ISO 9000/ISO 14001/HACCP Certifications http://www.dcmsme.gov.in/schemes/sciso9000.htm

Environment International Ltd. Q & A: Environmental Management Systems and ISO 14000. http://www.eiltd.net/services/isoqa.shtml

Environmental Management Standards in Singapore. http://gsndev.org/archives/webs/sngs99/etc/Speech/vol20no6.html

International Trade Centre. *Export Quality Management Bulletin* No. 78, An introduction to ISO 14000 – Environmental management systems. www.intracen.org/exporters/quality-management/Quality_publications_index

United Nations Statistics Division. Environment Glossary. http://unstats.un.org/unsd/environmentgl/

C. FOOD SAFETY MANAGEMENT SYSTEMS

42. What is Hazard Analysis and Critical Control Points (HACCP) and why is it important for SMEs in the food sector?

Every person has the right to expect that the food he/she eats is safe and will not cause injury or illness. The hazards related to food safety are known as biological, chemical and physical hazards, which, if present in food, may cause injury or illness to the human being.

Hazard Analysis and Critical Control Points (HACCP) is defined as "a system, which identifies, evaluates and controls hazards which are significant for food safety" (FAO).

HACCP is a proactive concept. It helps to ensure that food is safe from harvest to consumption ('from farm to fork'). Each step involved in food production, i.e. purchasing, receiving, storage, processing, packaging, warehousing, distribution up to the point of consumption is subjected to hazard analysis and necessary controls are introduced. The premise is simple: if each step of the process is carried out correctly, the end product will be safe.

HACCP was first developed in 1960 in the early days of the space programme. NASA (National Aeronautics and Space Administration) wanted assurance that food taken on board space flights would not cause food-borne diseases. As a result of this requirement, the Pillsbury Company and the United States Army Natick Research Laboratories developed a process that would ensure production of safe food; the process was named HACCP.

In 1993, the Codex Alimentarius Commission (CAC) published guidelines for the application of the HACCP system. Later, in 1997, CAC incorporated HACCP into an appendix of the 'Recommended International Code of Practice General Principles of Food Hygiene (latest version: Rev.4-2003).

The HACCP system consists of seven principles, which give an outline of how to establish, implement and maintain a HACCP plan.

Seven principles of the HACCP system

1. Conduct a hazard analysis	Prepare a process flow diagram covering all steps from receipt of raw material to dispatch of finished product. Identify likely hazards at every process step. Describe the measures for control of hazards at each process step.
2. Determine the critical control points (CCPs)	Analyse each step by using the decision tree. Identify the steps (points) where control is critical for assuring the safety of the product.
3. Establish critical limits	Fix critical limit for control measures relating to each identified CCP (e.g. temperature, time, speed, pH, moisture content)
4. Establish a system to monitor control of the CCP	Decide on monitoring procedure, which should cover the nature of monitoring (observation, testing), monitoring frequency and responsibility for monitoring and recording monitoring results.
5. Establish corrective action to be taken when monitoring results indicate that a particular CCP is not under control.	Develop procedures for dealing with the deviation from critical limits when it occurs and how to bring the CCP back into control, including disposition of the affected product produced during deviation.
6. Establish procedures for verification to confirm that the HACCP system is working effectively.	Develop procedures for verification to confirm that the HACCP plan is working (e.g. periodic audit, random sampling and analysis, review of the HACCP system and its records)
7. Establish documentation on all procedures and records appropriate to the HACCP principles and their application.	Prepare and follow procedures and work instructions for each control measure, including those needed for maintaining hygiene conditions; keep records.

Source: S.C. Arora, India.

HACCP is not a stand-alone system. Good hygiene practices and other prerequisites for food processing as well as strong management commitment are also necessary. HACCP is not a substitute for these.

If your company produces a variety of food products, you should develop a separate HACCP plan for each product, abiding by the seven principles outlined above.

During the 1990s, HACCP was adopted by many countries (Australia, Denmark, Germany, India, Ireland, Netherlands, United States and others) in national standards specifying requirements for a food safety management system. It was also included in the regulations of the European Community dealing with 'Hygiene of foodstuffs'. The International Organization for Standardization (ISO) developed in 2005 an international standard, 'ISO 22000:2005 Food Safety Management Systems – Requirements for any organization in the food chain', which incorporates HACCP principles (see questions 44 and 45).

It is important for SMEs in the food processing business to use HACCP for two reasons. First, it brings internal benefits such as reduced risk of manufacturing and selling unsafe products, which will in turn generate greater consumer confidence in these products. Second, food regulatory authorities in many countries are adopting or are likely to adopt HACCP in their food regulations. By implementing HACCP, you will have greater chances of succeeding as an exporter to these countries (see question 46). For example, in the guidance document entitled 'Key questions related to import requirements and the new rules on food hygiene and official food control', issued by the European Commission's Directorate General, Health and Consumer Protection, EU has clarified that the new EU rules on food hygiene (effective 1 January 2006) confirm that all food businesses after primary production must put in place, implement and maintain a procedure based on HACCP principles. These rules are, however, more flexible than under the old system, as the HACCP-based procedures can be adapted to all situations (European Commission, 2006).

FOR MORE INFORMATION

- Asian Productivity Organization. Hazard Quality Enhancement in Food Processing Through HACCP (Analysis and Critical Control Point). 2004. http://www.apo-tokyo.org/00e-books/AG-14_HACCP/AG-14_HACCP.pdf

  Report of the APO Study Meeting on Quality Enhancement in Small and Medium Food Processing Enterprises through HACCP, held in India in 2002. APO stands for Asian Productivity Organization.

- Food and Agriculture Organization of the United Nations and World Health Organization. Assuring Food Safety and Quality: Guidelines for Strengthening National Food Control Systems.
  www.who.int/foodsafety/publications/capacity/en/Englsih_Guidelines_Food_control.pdf

  This document covers food safety, quality and consumer protection and highlights the specific issues of developing countries.

- International Trade Centre
  - *Export Quality Management Bulletin* No. 71, Introduction to HACCP.
    www.intracen.org/exporters/quality-management/Quality_publications_index.

    This bulletin provides information on what HACCP is, the HACCP principles; HACCP implementation, HACCP in international trade; gives an example of the use of the decision tree to identify critical control points; lists websites where information about HACCP can be obtained as well as published books and other documents on HACCP.
  - *Export Quality Management Bulletin* No. 85, An introduction to ISO 22000 – Food safety management. www.intracen.org/exporters/quality-management/Quality_publications_index

    Provides information on food safety, SPS measures, HACCP food safety basics, the ISO 22000 food safety management system (FSMS), benefits of FSMS, costs of FSMS, implementation and certification of FSMS, etc.

REFERENCES

Codex Alimentarius Commission. Recommended International Code of Practice General Principles of Food Hygiene (CAC/RCP 1-1969, Rev. 4-2003). Freely obtainable from www.codexalimentarius.org/standards/list-of-standards/en/

European Commission. Guidance document: Key questions related to import requirements and the new rules on food hygiene and on official food controls (Brussels, 5.1.2006). http://ec.europa.eu/food/international/trade/interpretation_imports.pdf

43. How is HACCP implemented?

Before a HACCP system is set up, it is necessary for the location, building, facilities, equipment of the food processing facility to be designed in accordance with basic hygiene principles. In addition, equipment maintenance, cleaning, pest control and waste management procedures should be in place; good personnel health and hygiene practices should also be present. These are commonly referred to as Good Manufacturing Practices (GMP) and Good Hygiene Practices (GHP) respectively.

The Good Manufacturing Practices are detailed in 'ISO/TS 22002-1:2009 – Prerequisite programmes on food safety', while the Good Hygiene Practices can be taken from 'Recommended International Code of Practice: General Principles of Food Hygiene', available at the Codex Alimentarius website.

Beyond designing your facility according to basic hygiene and manufacturing principles, the management of the food processing facility should also commit itself to supporting the development and implementation of the HACCP system. This can be done, for example, by nominating a HACCP coordinator, providing resources for HACCP implementation and periodically reviewing the development and implementation of the HACCP plan. Also, ongoing training of management and employees should be in place to enable them to acquire appropriate HACCP knowledge and skills.

The steps described below are recommended by the Codex General Principles of Food Hygiene for the development and implementation of a HACCP plan.

1. Assemble HACCP team (Pre-Step 1)

Appoint a multidisciplinary team with a HACCP coordinator. The team may comprise, for example, a food technologist, microbiologist and the supervisors of the following sectors: quality assurance, engineering, purchasing, production, maintenance. If necessary, external help can also be availed of.

At this stage, the scope (terms of reference) of the HACCP plan should be defined, i.e. the product or process lines for which the HACCP plan should be prepared. Then, the nature of the hazards (biological, chemical or physical or their combination) to be studied by the team should be determined.

2. Describe the product (Pre-Step 2)

Describe the product under study, e.g. its composition (ingredients), structure (liquid, powder or solid), processing condition (heat treatment, freezing, brining), packaging (bottled, packed or in bags), storage (ambient temperature, refrigeration, freezing), distribution (transport condition, e.g. ambient temperature, refrigeration), shelf life.

3. Identify intended use (Pre-Step 3)

Describe the expected use of the product by the end user or consumer such as consumption by an adult or by persons at high risk of food-borne illness (e.g. children, the elderly, patients in hospitals, pregnant women).

4. Construct the flow diagram (Pre-Step 4)

Prepare a detailed process flow diagram or diagrams showing each step in the operation from receipt of raw materials up to defined end use (receipt, storage, processing, storage, transport, end use). The flow charts should also indicate time and temperature requirements, product recycle or rework loops, equipment layout, personnel routes, water and water flow, waste flow.

5. On-site conformation of flow diagram (Pre-Step 5)

Observe actual operations during the normal working day, nightshift, weekend and confirm or amend the flow diagram.

6. List all potential hazards associated with each step, conduct a hazard analysis, and consider any measure to control hazards (Codex: Principle 1)

- List all potential hazards (identified in the scope) at each step of the process.
- Conduct a risk analysis of each hazard (probability of occurrence and its potential severity) to identify which hazards are of such a nature that their elimination or reduction to acceptable level is essential to the production of safe food.
- Describe the preventive measures (control measures) for each identified hazard (e.g. supplier control procedure, chilling, heating, screening, metal detection, personnel hygiene such as hand washing, headgear use, cleaning, maintenance).

7. Determine critical control points (CCP) (Principle 2)

- Apply the decision tree (as prescribed in the Codex General Principles of Food Hygiene) at each step (for each hazard) and identify the steps where control is critical for assuring the safety of food. These steps are called CCP.

8. Establish critical limits for each CCP (Principle 3)

- Specify the critical limit (control parameter that should be achieved to ensure that the product is safe, e.g. measurements of temperature, time, moisture level, pH, water activity (A_w), available chlorine and observation of sensory parameters such as visual appearance and texture, for each CCP. Critical limits are decided on the basis of a legal requirement, national or international standards or scientific data.

9. Establish a monitoring system for each CCP (Principle 4)

- Select an appropriate method for monitoring (e.g. observation, inspection, testing, measurement).
- Decide the frequency of monitoring, assign responsibility for monitoring activities and keep a record of monitoring results.

10. Establish corrective actions (Principle 5)

- Specify the action(s) to be taken to bring the process back to a state of being under control when the results monitored indicate a trend towards loss of control.
- Specify the disposition action to be taken on the product that has been produced when the CCP was out of control.
- Define the responsibility for corrective action and disposition action.
- Maintain a record of the action(s) taken.

11. Establish verification procedures (Principle 6)

- With a view to checking if the HACCP system is working satisfactorily, draw up the procedure for verification activity and designate responsibilities for it. Verification activities include review of the HACCP system and its records, internal and external auditing, random sampling, product testing, analysis of swabs.

12. Establish documentation and record keeping (Principle 7)

- Document and keep records efficiently, as required by the HACCP system. For example, hazard analysis, identified CCPs and their limits (including revisions, if any) should be documented. Examples of records are CCP monitoring records, records of deviation found and corrective action taken on them, verification records.

Third party certification of HACCP

As the Codex HACCP is a guidance document, direct certification to it is not possible. To fill this gap countries such as Australia, Denmark, Germany, India, Ireland, the Netherlands and the United States have developed national standards for food safety systems based on the Codex HACCP; certification against these standards is available.

As with other management systems, certification to HACCP is voluntary. If your management considers it a necessity, then an application for certification may be made to a certification body of your choice. The prerequisites for such certification include effective implementation of the system for at least three months, internal verification of the effectiveness of the system, followed by a management review.

FOR MORE INFORMATION

- International Organization for Standardization. ISO/TS 22002-1:2009. Prerequisite programmes on food safety – Part 1: Food manufacturing. Obtainable from ISO or ISO members (list at www.iso.org).

  Specifies requirements for establishing, implementing and maintaining prerequisite programmes (PRP) to assist in controlling food safety hazards.

- International Trade Centre

  – *Export Quality Management Bulletin* No. 71, Introduction to HACCP. www.intracen.org/exporters/quality-management/Quality_publications_index

    This Bulletin provides information on what HACCP is, the principles of HACCP, implementation of HACCP, HACCP and ISO 9000, HACCP in international trade, the use of the decision tree to identify critical control points. It also lists websites that provide information on HACCP as well as published books and other documents on HACCP.

  – *Export Quality Management Bulletin* No. 85, An introduction to ISO 22000 – Food safety management. www.intracen.org/exporters/quality-management/Quality_publications_index

    This Bulletin provides information on food safety, SPS measures, HACCP – the food safety basics, the ISO 22000 food safety management system (FSMS), benefits of FSMS, costs of FSMS, implementation and certification of FSMS.

- Technical Manual 38, HACCP: A Practical Guide, 2nd ed. A priced publication of Campden and Chorleywood Food Research Association, Chipping Campden Gloucestershire, GL55 6LD United Kingdom, website www.campden.co.uk, email pbs@campden.co.uk

  This manual describes the principles of HACCP and provides a practical guide for their application.

- World Health Organization. Strategies for Implementing HACCP in Small and/or Less Developed Businesses. 1999. Food Safety Programme, Avenue Appia 20, 1211 Geneva 27, Switzerland. http://www.who.int/foodsafety/publications/fs_management/en/haccp_smallbus.pdf

  This report presents the benefits of, and barriers to, implementing HACCP, gives advice on the development of sector-specific industry guides and provides guidelines for the application of the HACCP system to small and/or less developed businesses.

REFERENCES

Codex Alimentarius Commission. Recommended International Code of Practice General Principles of Food Hygiene (CAC/RCP 1-1969, Rev. 4-2003). Freely obtainable from www.codexalimentarius.org/standards/list-of-standards/en/

44. What is the difference between HACCP and ISO 22000?

The primary objective of both the Codex HACCP principles and the ISO 22000 food safety management system (FSMS) is to ensure that the food produced by an organization is safe for human consumption. The system elements of the Codex HACCP consist of seven principles (see question 42) and five pre-steps for developing and implementing a HACCP plan (see question 43). All these elements have since been included in ISO 22000 (published in 2005 as 'ISO 22000:2005 – Food safety management systems – Requirements for any organization in the food chain') and many more management system requirements have been added. The format of ISO 22000 is in line with the format of ISO 9001 ('Quality management system – Requirements'), thus making it compatible with other management systems.

The development of ISO 22000 was based on the assumption that the most effective food systems are designed, operated and continually improved within the framework of an organization's structured management system. ISO 22000 thus carries some management system requirements that are not explicitly stated in Codex HACCP. These include a food safety policy and related objectives, planning and documenting the food safety system, effective external and internal communication arrangements, the assignment of specific responsibilities to the food safety team leader, internal audits, management reviews, continual improvement and updating of FSMS. Briefly, the ISO 22000 requirements are a combination of the following four key elements:

- Interactive communications
- System management
- Prerequisite programmes
- HACCP principles.

The Codex HACCP uses the last element (the seven HACCP principles described in question 42) and also recommends that prerequisite programmes related to food hygiene (see question 43) should be in place before the development of a HACCP plan.

ISO 22000, backed by international consensus, harmonizes the requirements for systematically managing safety in food supply chains, and offers a unique solution for good practice on a worldwide basis. ISO cooperated closely with the Codex Alimentarius Commission in developing this standard. ISO 22000 makes extensive reference to the Codex hygiene recommendations for the development of prerequisite programmes for different sectors of the food industry. ISO 22000 in its Annex B provides a comparison of the various requirements of FSMS with those of Codex HACCP.

ISO 22000 is designed to allow all types of organizations within the food chain to implement a food safety management system. These include crop producers, feed producers, primary producers, food manufacturers, transport and storage operators, retailers, food service operators and caterers together with related organizations such as producers of the equipment, packaging materials, cleaning agents, additives and ingredients needed during food processing.

As CODEX HACCP is a guidance document, certification to it is not possible. To fill this gap many countries such as Australia, Denmark, Germany, India, Ireland and the United States have developed national standards on the basis of the Codex HACCP. The Netherlands also did so, and the standard is popularly referred to as the Dutch HACCP. Certification against these standards is possible. ISO 22000 has made it easier for organizations worldwide to implement the Codex HACCP system for food safety in a harmonized way, i.e. it does not vary with the country or food product or service concerned. ISO 22000 can be used for certification, and this may be acceptable as an alternative to certification against different national standards.

The table below compares ISO 22000 with the Codex HACCP.

Comparison of ISO 22000 and HACCP

ISO 22000	HACCP
A voluntary international standard developed by ISO with the participation by various stakeholders; its first version was published on 1 September 2005.	A guideline document developed by Codex Alimentarius Commission; the first version came out in 1997.
Has been adopted by many countries as their national standard and hard/soft copies can be purchased from ISO (www.iso.org) or from national standards bodies.	Generally adopted by national food regulatory authorities as part of their legislation on food safety. Freely downloadable from the Codex website (www.codexalimentarius.net)
Written in the format of a management system standard with auditable requirements; guidance for its use is separately published as ISO/TS 22004.	Written as a guideline in two parts: the HACCP seven principles and 12 steps for implementing the seven principles.
The standard can be used by organizations within the food chain – food producers, food manufacturers, transport and storage operators, retail and food service outlets. It can also be used by related organizations such as producers of equipment, packaging materials, cleaning agents, additives and ingredients, and service providers.	Can be applied throughout the food chain from primary production to final consumption of food.
The standard combines the following key elements to ensure food safety along the food chain: • Interactive communication • System management • Prerequisite programmes (PRPs) • HACCP principles	The Codex HACCP uses the seven HACCP principles and the 12 steps for implementing the principles. It also recommends that prerequisite programmes on food hygiene should be in place before the development of a HACCP plan.
The format of the standard has been aligned with ISO 9001 (QMS – Requirements) to enhance the compatibility of the two standards.	This is compatible with ISO 9001 to a limited extent – system management and interactive communications are not fully covered by the Codex HACCP.
Organizations can seek certification of their food safety management system or make a self-declaration of conformity to ISO 22000.	Being a guideline document, it cannot be directly used for certification. However, HACCP certification is possible against a national HACCP standard, for instance the Dutch or Danish HACCP.

Source: S.C Arora, India.

FOR MORE INFORMATION

- International Trade Centre. *Export Quality Management Bulletin* No. 85, An introduction to ISO 22000 – Food safety management. www.intracen.org/exporters/quality-management/Quality_publications_index

  This bulletin provides information on food safety, SPS measures, HACCP food safety basics, the ISO 22000 food safety management system (FSMS), the costs and benefits of FSMS, implementation and certification of FSMS.

REFERENCES

Codex Alimentarius Commission. Recommended International Code of Practice General Principles of Food Hygiene (CAC/RCP 1-1969, Rev. 4-2003). Freely obtainable from www.codexalimentarius.org/standards/list-of-standards/en/

International Organization for Standardization

- ISO 22000:2005. Food safety management systems – Requirements for any organization in the food chain. Obtainable from ISO or ISO members (list at www.iso.org).
- ISO Press Release: ISO 22000 for safe food supply chains. http://www.iso.org/iso/pressrelease.htm?refid=Ref966

45. What are the steps for implementing ISO 22000?

Before starting to implement the ISO 22000 food safety management system (FSMS), it is important for your top management to be fully committed to the development and implementation of the system. This includes providing resources (financial, infrastructural and competent human resources) for the development of the system.

The steps for implementing ISO 22000 are described below.

Step 1: Nomination of the food safety team (FST)

Your top management should appoint a competent food safety team with a team leader. Preferably the team should consist of a food technologist, microbiologist and the supervisors of the quality assurance, engineering, production and maintenance functions. One of the members of the team should have good knowledge of HACCP/FSMS. If the team members require additional training, this should be arranged by the team leader. The team will play a major role in the development of your food safety management system.

If you wish, you could also engage a food safety consultant to support your team, but in no way should this be regarded as an exercise in shifting responsibilities from the team to the consultant.

Step 2: Setting up prerequisite programmes (PRPs)

Depending upon the segment of the food chain in which you operate, you will need to set up the prerequisite programmes for maintaining a hygienic environment in your unit. These programmes include Good Hygienic Practice (GHP), Good Manufacturing Practice (GMP), Good Agricultural Practice (GAP), Good Distribution Practice (GDP) (see Annex C of ISO 22000:2005). If you find that your current PRPs are inadequate, you may have to devote additional financial resources and time to improving them. For example, you may need to improve your factory layout, floors, walls, ventilation system, lighting, drainage system and waste collection facilities.

Step 3: Development of the HACCP plan

Before you can develop your HACCP plan, you need to carry out a detailed hazard analysis of each step of the process (see question 42). This analysis will lead to the identification of critical control points (CCPs), the process step(s) on which exercising control will be essential to preventing or eliminating the hazards or reducing them to acceptable limits. A system for monitoring the CCPs and taking corrective action on the process should be set up for the products or processes. Control measures determined in the HACCP plan and operational PRPs should be validated prior to their implementation.

Step 4: Documentation

FSMS documentation includes the food safety policy and related objectives, documented procedures (for example, procedures for the control of documents, control of records, internal audit, handling of potentially unsafe products, control of nonconforming end product, corrective action and withdrawal of end product), HACCP plan(s), and certain records to demonstrate compliance with HACCP plans and the other requirements of your FSMS. The use of additional documents covering additional procedures and including process flow diagrams, specifications, methods of test, records, wherever required, should also be decided on and the documents developed by the team. A proper system of control of documents and control of records should be introduced.

Step 5: Training, awareness generation and implementation

All employees carrying out activities with an impact on food safety should be competent to do their jobs. Training on monitoring and taking corrective action should be provided to the employees who are responsible for these activities. In addition, your employees should be aware of the relevance and importance of their food safety activities. They should also understand the need for effective internal communication on food safety issues. After awareness generation and training as needed, system implementation can start and records should be maintained as evidence of the operating FSMS.

Step 6: Internal FSMS audit

The internal audit process determines how well your FSMS is working. Some of your employees should be trained to carry out internal auditing, including inter-functional audits. During the early period of FSMS implementation, the audits may be done more frequently; once the system stabilizes, the frequency of audit as prescribed in your internal audit procedure may be followed.

Step 7: Management review

The findings of internal audits, along with information on customer feedback and complaints, analysis of results of verification activities, lessons learned from emergency situations or accidents, if any, product withdrawals, if any, should be reviewed by your top management and decisions taken to improve the FSMS. A system for conducting such reviews on a periodic basis should be introduced.

Step 8: Certification

Certification to ISO 22000 is voluntary. If your top management considers it a necessity, then you may apply for certification to a certification body of your choice. The prerequisite for such certification is effective implementation of the system for at least three months, including one internal audit followed by a management review.

Action plan

A period of six to nine months is considered reasonable for fully developing and implementing the FSMS. An example of an action plan is given in the figure below.

ISO 22000 implementation action plan

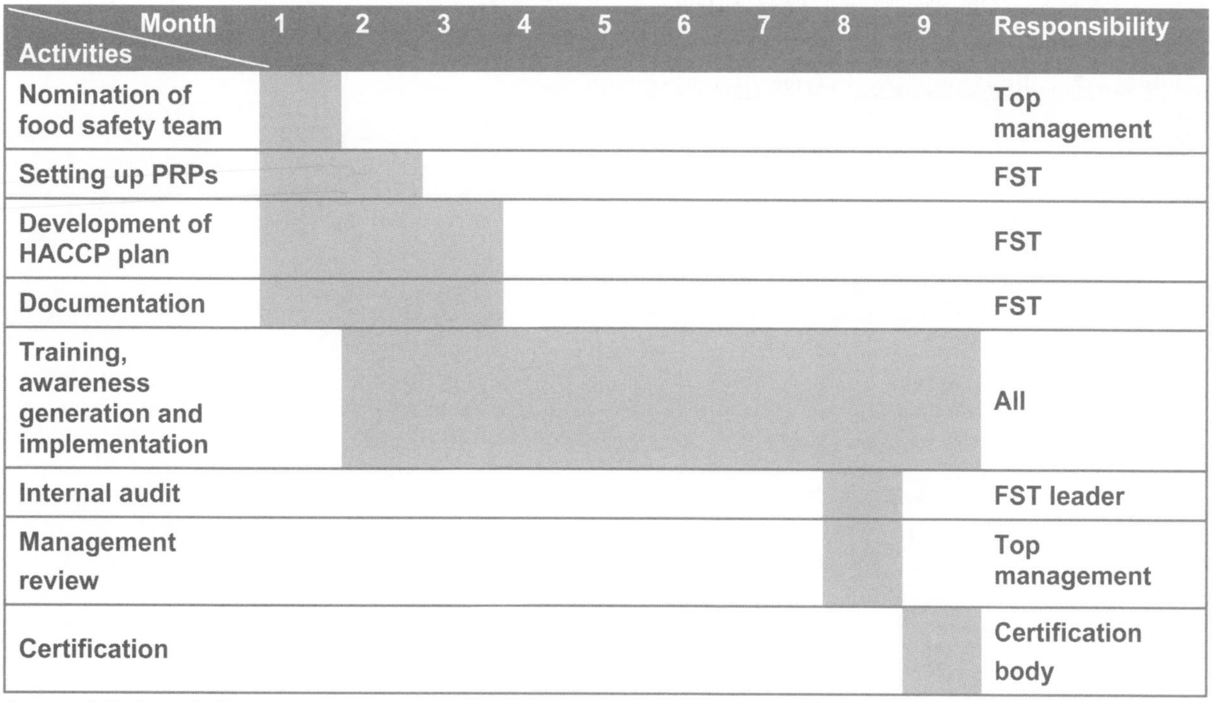

Activities / Month	1	2	3	4	5	6	7	8	9	Responsibility
Nomination of food safety team										Top management
Setting up PRPs										FST
Development of HACCP plan										FST
Documentation										FST
Training, awareness generation and implementation										All
Internal audit										FST leader
Management review										Top management
Certification										Certification body

Source: S.C. Arora, India.

FOR MORE INFORMATION

- Blanc, Didier. ISO 22000: From intent to implementation. In *ISO Management Systems*, May-June 2006, Special report. International Organization for Standardization. http://www.iso.org/iso/22000_implementation_ims_06_03.pdf

  How close is the intent of ISO 22000:2005 to its implementation by users? An expert who took part in its design and development has reviewed feedback from early users and gives some pointers to tackling the issues they raise.

- Færgemand, Jacob. The ISO 22000 series: Global standards for safe food supply chains. In ISO Management Systems. May-June 2006, Special report. International Organization for Standardization. http://www.iso.org/iso/iso22000_ims_08-3.pdf

  The launching in 2005 of the ISO 22000 series developed by ISO technical committee ISO/TC 34, Food Products, signalled the arrival of a truly global option for ensuring safe food supply chains. This article gives a technical overview of the different standards in the series and how they can be put to use.

- International Trade Centre. *Export Quality Management Bulletin* No. 85, An introduction to ISO 22000 – Food safety management. www.intracen.org/exporters/quality-management/Quality_publications_index

  This bulletin provides information on food safety, SPS measures, HACCP food safety basics, the ISO 22000 food safety management systems, the benefits and costs of FSMS, implementation and certification of FSMS.

- Smith, David, Rob Politowski and Christina Palmer. Managing Food Safety the 22000 Way. BSI Standards, 2007. ISBN 0580464059.

  This book provides user-friendly help in understanding and implementing a food safety management system to meet the requirements of the international standard ISO 22000:2005. It offers a simple methodology, together with extracts from the standard and clear explanations of the terms used. The book is also helpful for organizations wishing to integrate the ISO 22000 system with their other management system requirements.

REFERENCES

International Organization for Standardization

- ISO 22000:2005, Food safety management systems – Requirements for any organization in the food chain. Obtainable from ISO or ISO members (list at www.iso.org).
- ISO/TS 22004:2005, Food safety management systems – Guidance on the application of ISO 22000:2005. Obtainable from ISO or ISO members (list at www.iso.org).

International Organization for Standardization and International Trade Centre. ISO 22000 Food Safety Management Systems: An easy-to-use checklist for small business. Are you ready? 2007. ISBN 978-92-67-10435-5. Obtainable from ITC (http://www.intracen.org/about/e-shop/) and ISO (www.iso.org).

46. Will certification to HACCP/ISO 22000 enable an organization to demonstrate compliance with a country's legal food safety requirements?

Certification to HACCP/ISO 22000 is an established means of demonstrating compliance with, and effective implementation of, systems for ensuring food safety. However, regulatory authorities may not accept this certification unless it is specifically provided for in the regulations. In general, regulations prescribe a method of conformity assessment, and the enforcement agency will expect you to demonstrate compliance through that method. If a regulation states that certification will be an acceptable means of conformity assessment, then certification will assist you in meeting regulatory requirements as well.

Adoption of HACCP in national and regional regulations on food safety

As is widely known, the primary objective of regulatory requirements on food is to protect consumers from misleading labelling of food products and to ensure that the food is safe for human consumption.

The adoption of HACCP principles by the Codex Alimentarius Commission (CAC), which has 180 member governments, was a major step in promoting the use of HACCP (Hazard Analysis and Critical Control Points) in national and regional regulatory requirements for food safety. For example, Canada made HACCP mandatory in its fish processing industry in 1992, followed by the United States for seafood processing in 1995. The United States then required meat and poultry processing plants and producers of fruit and vegetable juices to have HACCP in place from January 1996. European Union rules on food hygiene (effective 1 January 2006, see European Commission, 2006 in the references section below) also state that all food businesses (i.e. dealing with food of animal origin, food of non-animal origin and food containing both processed ingredients of animal origin and ingredients of plant origin), after primary production, must put in place, implement and maintain a procedure based on the HACCP principles.

The WTO Agreement on Sanitary and Phytosanitary Measures also requires WTO Members to encourage the use of guidelines and recommendations established by the Codex Alimentarius Commission when framing their SPS measures. These measures relate to the protection of human or animal life from risks arising from additives, contaminants, toxins or disease-causing organisms in food. The implementation of the HACCP system as developed by CAC will also help you to overcome technical barriers to trade related to food safety.

Compliance with regulatory requirements during implementation of ISO 22000

By implementing the following steps, as required by ISO 22000, it will be possible for you to demonstrate to some extent compliance with statutory and regulatory requirements for food safety:

- When selecting and establishing prerequisite programmes (PRPs), your organization should consider the relevant statutory and regulatory requirements.
- Statutory and regulatory requirements should be identified in descriptions of specifications of raw materials, ingredients and product contact material.
- Statutory and regulatory requirements relating to the characteristics of the end product should also be identified.
- When determining acceptable levels of food safety hazards in your end product, you should take the statutory and regulatory requirements into account. These legal requirements should also be referred to when you determine the critical limits of critical control points.

Acceptance of ISO 22000 certification by retail chains

Food marketers, particularly retailers, are becoming increasingly interested in third-party auditing (certification) and are seeking to replace their own second-party audits of suppliers with the less costly solutions available through certification. By December 2009, a total of 13 881 certificates for ISO 22000 in 127 countries had been issued, according to a 2009 survey conducted by ISO. Your export customers may thus be the first to ask you whether or not you have a certified FSMS in place, as certification will assure them that you have met their national statutory and regulatory requirements.

FSSC 22000, a certification scheme for food safety systems, is based on ISO 22000:2005 and the Publicly Available Specification (PAS) for prerequisite programmes on food safety for food manufacturing (British Standard PAS 220:2008). FSSC stands for Food Safety System Certification and the scheme was developed by the Foundation for Food Safety Certification.

The scheme is applicable to manufacturers that process or manufacture animal products, perishable vegetable products, products with a long shelf life and other food ingredients like additives, vitamins and bio-cultures. It has been given full recognition by the Global Food Safety Initiative (GFSI). According to the Foundation for Food Safety Certification, the scheme is supported by the Confederation of the Food and Drink Industries of the European Union (CIAA).

FOR MORE INFORMATION

- Global Food Safety Initiative. GFSI Guidance Document. http://www.mygfsi.com/

  As of November 2010, GFSI has benchmarked (recognized) eight schemes for the food manufacturing sector (including the BRC Global Standards, Dutch HACCP and FSSC 22000), three for primary production (including GLOBALG.A.P.) and one for the primary and manufacturing sector.

- International Portal on Food Safety, Animal and Plant Health. www.ipfsaph.org

  Provides a single access point for authorized official international and national information across the sectors of food safety, and animal and plant health.

- International Trade Centre. *Export Quality Management Bulletin* No. 85, An introduction to ISO 22000 – Food safety management. www.intracen.org/exporters/quality-management/Quality_publications_index

  This bulletin provides information on food safety, SPS measures, HACCP food safety basics, the ISO 22000 food safety management system (FSMS), the cost and benefits of FSMS implementation and certification.

REFERENCES

European Commission. Guidance document: Key questions related to import requirements and the new rules on food hygiene and on official food controls. Health & Consumer Protection Directorate-General, Brussels, 5 January 2006. http://ec.europa.eu/food/international/trade/interpretation_imports.pdf

Foundation for Food Safety Certification. Founded in 2004 which developed FSSC 22000. http://www.fssc22000.com/en/

International Organization for Standardization

- ISO 22000:2005, Food safety management systems – Requirements for any organization in the food chain. Obtainable from ISO or ISO members (list at www.iso.org).
- Survey of ISO 22000 certificates issued as on December 2009. http://www.iso.org/iso/survey2009.pdf
- International Organization for Standardization and International Trade Centre. ISO 22000 Food Safety Management Systems: An easy-to-use checklist for small business. Are you ready? 2007. ISBN 978-92-67-10435-5. Obtainable from ITC (http://www.intracen.org/about/e-shop/) and ISO (www.iso.org).

47. What are the costs and benefits of obtaining certification to ISO 22000?

Setting up an ISO 22000 FSMS and having it certified have cost implications. The costs fall under the following categories.

- Cost of establishing and implementing the FSMS;
- Cost of maintaining the FSMS;
- Cost of initial certification and cost of maintaining the certification.

These costs can vary greatly, depending on the size of your facility, range of products, nature of your operation, existing infrastructure and facilities. The cost items and the benefits of implementing FSMS are described below.

Costs of establishing and implementing FSMS

- Cost of obtaining copies of the national and international standards and food legislation. You will also need the Codex guidelines on the general and specific principles of food hygiene, but these Codex documents are freely downloadable from the Codex website.
- Depending on the background of your multidisciplinary food safety team members and its leader, cost of training them on food safety hazards and related control measures, hazard analysis, development of the HACCP plan, method of developing FSMS documentation and their related control measures. The overall cost will include both the direct costs of training and the indirect cost of the time spent by your FST team in training.
- Depending on the nature of your product and the associated hazards, cost of making necessary alterations in the layout of your premises, floors, walls, ceilings, ventilation system, employees' facilities, waste disposal system, pest control system, water supply.
- Cost of introducing additional control measures to prevent, eliminate or reduce the hazards to an acceptable level. The direct costs involved may cover selection and acquisition of new processing equipment or technology; revamping temperature controls for storage (in freezers or cold storage) of raw materials and finished products; installing facilities for metal detection, packaging, heat treatment, freezing, brining, transport, personal hygiene, as needed; and the means for validating these control measures.
- Cost of developing FSMS documentation, e.g. documents on food safety policy and objectives, food safety procedures, prerequisite programmes, operational prerequisite programmes, HACCP plan.
- Cost of creating awareness in all persons who have roles and responsibilities for FSMS activities and cost of training when required.
- Cost of day-to-day monitoring activities, calibration of instruments, testing of raw materials and finished products, verification activities, product withdrawals, corrective actions.

Cost of maintaining the FSMS

- Cost of periodic reorientation, awareness generation and training of your employees to update them on new legislation and changes to your FSMS.
- Cost of training some of your managers to perform periodic internal audits.
- Cost of conducting periodic internal audits, corrective actions, continual improvement and management review of FSMS.

Cost of initial certification and cost associated with the maintenance of certification payable to the certification body you selected

- Registration or certification fee payable to the nominated certification body for a period of three years.
- Fee for a two-stage certification audit by the auditors of the certification body.
- Fee for periodic surveillance audits (at a frequency of every 6 to 12 months) by the auditors of the certification body.
- Travel, board and lodging of the auditor(s) of the certification body.

It may be added here that certification to ISO 22000 is not a mandatory step after the implementation of FSMS. The decision to have it is always a need-based decision, which your management should take before incurring the above costs.

Benefits

The implementation of ISO 22000 FSMS will provide both internal and external benefits, for example:

- Improved competence of employees through training and awareness generation, bringing about, among other benefits, clarity about their responsibilities and the designation of authority within FSMS.
- A defined system for obtaining information on emerging food safety hazards and control measures, and on applicable statutory and regulatory requirements.
- Cost savings from reduced instances of producing unsafe products, smaller number of customer complaints, low withdrawal levels of unsafe products from the supply chain.
- ISO 22000 compliance and its certification may generate opportunities for new business, including giving you a chance to become a preferred supplier of the big retail chains.
- Customers will have greater confidence in the food safety of products made by an ISO 22000 compliant or certified company.

FOR MORE INFORMATION

- Færgemand, Jacob. The ISO 22000 series: Global standards for safe food supply chains. In ISO Management Systems. May-June 2006, Special report. International Organization for Standardization. http://www.iso.org/iso/iso22000_ims_08-3.pdf

  The launching on 1 September 2005 of the ISO 22000 series, developed by ISO technical committee ISO/TC 34, Food Products, signaled the arrival of a truly global option for ensuring safe food supply chains. This article gives a technical overview of the different standards in the series and how they can be put to use.

- International Organization for Standardization and International Trade Centre. ISO 22000 Food Safety Management Systems: An easy-to-use checklist for small business. Are you ready? 2007. ISBN 978-92-67-10435-5. Obtainable from ITC (http://www.intracen.org/about/e-shop/) and ISO (www.iso.org).

  The checklist in this handbook is in 13 parts, each covering a particular aspect of ISO 22000, with a brief explanation of the relevant requirement and guidance on how to incorporate the requirement into a food safety management system geared to the needs of a particular enterprise. Question 1.5 provides information on how to adopt a FSMS.

- International Portal on Food Safety, Animal and Plant Health: www.ipfsaph.org

  Provides a single access point for authorized official international and national information across the sectors of food safety, and animal and plant health.

REFERENCES

International Organization for Standardization. ISO 22000:2005, Food safety management systems – Requirements for any organization in the food chain. Obtainable from ISO and ISO members (list at www.iso.org).

International Trade Centre. *Export Quality Management Bulletin* No. 85, An introduction to ISO 22000 – Food safety management. www.intracen.org/exporters/quality-management/Quality_publications_index

D. OTHER MANAGEMENT SYSTEMS

48. What are the requirements for complying with SA 8000 and what are its benefits for the export trade?

The rising concerns of customers in developed countries about inhumane working conditions in developing countries led to the creation in 1997 of the SA 8000 standard on social accountability. The purpose of developing this standard was to draw up a universal code of practice for labour conditions, so that consumers in developed countries could be confident that the goods they were buying – in particular clothes, toys, cosmetics and electronic goods – had been produced in accordance with good labour practices.

It has been estimated that 100 million children worldwide are in full-time labour (United States Department of Labor, 2010). The vast majority are in Africa, Asia and South America. Under the terms of SA 8000, companies must not support child labour. The standard also requires companies to ensure that none of their staff, or those working for their suppliers, is required to work more than 48 hours a week, or more than six days a week. Moreover, wages must be at least equal to legal or 'industry minimum' levels, and must be sufficient to leave the employee with some discretionary income.

SA 8000 is an initiative of Social Accountability International (SAI), an affiliate of the Council on Economic Priorities (a pioneer non-governmental organization dealing with corporate social responsibility). SA 8000 (its latest version was issued in 2008) is based on the international workplace norms of the International Labour Organization (ILO) Conventions, the Universal Declaration of Human Rights and the United Nations Convention on the Rights of the Child. The SA 8000 system has the following nine requirements:

1. *Child labour.* No workers under the age of 15 (unless the local minimum age law stipulates a higher age) should be employed. If the local law sets the minimum age at 14 years in accordance with developing-country exceptions under ILO Convention 138, the lower age will apply.

2. *Forced labour.* The company shall not engage in or support the use of forced labour (service that is extracted from any person under the menace of any penalty), nor shall personnel be required to lodge 'deposits' or identity papers upon commencing employment with the company.

3. *Health and safety.* The company shall provide a safe and healthy work environment; take steps to prevent injuries; give regular health and safety related training to workers; have a proper system for detecting threats to health and safety; provide access to toilets and potable water, etc.

4. *Freedom of association and right to collective bargaining.* The company should respect the worker's right to form and join trade unions and bargain collectively; where the law prohibits these freedoms, the company should facilitate parallel means of association and bargaining.

5. *Discrimination.* There should be no discrimination based on race, caste, origin, religion, disability, gender, sexual orientation, union or political affiliation, or age; there should be no sexual harassment.

6. *Discipline.* There should be no corporal punishment, mental or physical coercion or verbal abuse.

7. *Working hours.* The company should comply with the applicable law but, in any event, its employees should work no more than 48 hours per week with at least one day off for every seven-day period. Voluntary overtime is paid at a premium rate and should not exceed 12 hours per week on a regular basis. Overtime may be mandatory if this is part of a collective bargaining agreement.

8. *Compensation.* Wages paid for a standard work week must meet legal and industry standards and should be sufficient to meet the basic needs of workers and their families. There should be no disciplinary deductions.

9. *Management systems.* Facilities seeking to gain and maintain certification must go beyond simple compliance to integrate the standard into their management systems and practices.

Third-party certification to SA 8000, which is voluntary in nature, is being offered by certification bodies accredited and overseen by the Social Accountability Accreditation Services (SAAS). All types of industries can obtain SA 8000 certification.

According to the SAAS, as of 30 September 2010, a total of 2 330 facilities in 62 countries covering 66 industries have taken SA 8000 certification. The industrial sectors with the most certifications include apparel and textiles, building materials, agriculture, construction, chemicals, cosmetics, cleaning services and transportation in countries like Brazil, China, India and Italy.

The implementation of SA 8000 provides benefits to all stakeholders including workers, trade unions, businesses, consumers, investors. Workers become more aware of their labour rights; trade unions are better able to bargain collectively; businesses can attract and retain more skilled employees. The specific benefits to businesses in export trade include: enhanced company image and brand reputation, provision of assurance to buyers in developed countries that their suppliers have socially acceptable workplace practices; increased opportunities to join the socially responsible supply chain.

FOR MORE INFORMATION

- Center for International Private Enterprise/Social Accountability International. From Words to Action: A Business Case for Implementing Workplace Standards – Experiences from Key Emerging Markets.
  http://www.topkapiiplik.com.tr/Uploads/Userfiles/image/SA8000.pdf

  This publication presents several case studies. The case study on China focuses on capacity building, internalization and ownership of compliance programmes by workers and managers inside a garment factory. The India case looks at a world-renowned steel manufacturer, traces the usefulness of SA 8000 in managing contract workers and vendor companies that supply contract labour, even to a company with a long history of responsible labour practices. The Turkey study analyses the key drivers for, and results of, SA 8000 certification for the workers, managers and customers of a textile company.

- International Institute for Sustainable Development (IISD). http://www.iisd.org

  The IISD website offers useful information on sustainable development and provides case studies from different countries.

- Social Accountability International
  - From Principles to Practice: The Role of SA8000 in Implementing the UN Global Compact. 24 June 2010.
    http://www.sa-intl.org/index.cfm?fuseaction=Page.ViewPage&PageID=1012

    This publication shows how six participants in the UN Global Compact (UNGC) – companies of different sizes representing different sectors and corners of the world – use the SA 8000 workplace standard as a tool for implementing and reporting on commitments to the labour principles (Principles 3-6) of the Compact.

  - SAI and CIPE Case Study. 'From Words to Action: A Business Case for Implementing Workplace Standards'.
    http://www.sa-intl.org/index.cfm?fuseaction=Page.ViewPage&PageID=963

    These case studies look into different aspects of improving workplace conditions and analyse the benefits of doing so for workers and businesses.

- Stigzelius, Ingrid and Cecilia Mark-Herbert. Tailoring corporate responsibility to suppliers: Managing SA8000 in Indian garment manufacturing. Published in the *Scandinavian Journal of Management* 25, pp. 46/56, 2009.
  http://www2.ekon.slu.se/seminar/Stigzelius2.pdf

  This paper explores local management motives for implementing SA 8000 in Indian garment manufacturing. The impacts on business practices, in terms of obstacles and opportunities, are examined in a comparative case analysis, which demonstrates that suppliers need higher prices or long-term contracts as economic motivations for implementation. However, higher legal and social compliance may lead to business opportunities, such as a lower labour turnover and increased orders.

- United Nations Economic and Social Commission for Asia and the Pacific. Linking Sustainable Business and Export Promotion: Strategies for Exporters in Asia and the Pacific Region.
  http://www.unescap.org/tid/publication/chap5_2120.pdf

  This paper draws on the experience of several countries in the Asia and Pacific regions to suggest a simple three-step strategy for industry clusters to develop collective competence in responding effectively to the requirements of supply chains.

- Wang, Huimin. The Influence of SA 8000 Standard on the Export Trade of China. Department of Economics and Trade, Beijing Institute of Economic Management, Beijing 100102, China. Published in *Asian Social Science,* vol. 4, No. 1, January 2008. www.ccsenet.org/journal.html

  This article explores the influence of the SA 8000 standard on the export trade of China and how the Government of China should consider it as a means for helping enterprises to regulate and improve their management practices and become enterprises attractive to buyers abroad. The enterprises themselves should look at the standard in this way.

REFERENCES

Social Accountability Accreditation Services. Provides quarterly updated information on SA 8000 certified facility details and summary statistics. Website: http://www.saasaccreditation.org/certfacilitieslist.htm

Social Accountability International. SA 8000:2008 Standard on Social Accountability. 220 East 23rd Street, Suite 605, New York NY 10010. http://www.sa-intl.org

US Department of Labor. Report: Over 100 Million Worldwide Are Child Workers. 15 December 2010. Available at: http://www.voanews.com/english/news/Report-Over-100-Million-Worldwide-Are-Child-Workers-111970709.html

49. What is OHSAS 18001 and what is its relevance for the export trade?

OHSAS 18001 is a standard for establishing and practicing an occupational health and safety management system. It provides a framework for an organization to identify and control its health and safety risks, reduce its potential for accidents, ensure compliance with legislative requirements, and improve its overall health and safety performance.

OHSAS 18001 is not an ISO standard as it has not been developed by the International Organization for Standardization. It was formulated by three national standards bodies (those of Ireland, South Africa and the United Kingdom), 10 certification bodies and other stakeholders. The target was to address a gap where no third-party certifiable international standard existed. While developing this standard, in order to enhance its compatibility with other management system standards, due consideration was given to the provisions of ISO 9001, ISO 14001 and the guidelines for an occupational health and safety management system published by the International Labour Organization.

This standard can be used by all types (private, public, manufacturing, service) and size (small, medium-sized, large) of organizations. It can also accommodate diverse geographical, cultural and social conditions.

OHSAS 18001 only addresses occupational health and safety (OHS) issues at the workplace – for example, any physical location in which work-related activities are performed under the control of an organization. Health and safety at the workplace covers employees, individual contractors, customers and citizens. The standard does not deal with other health and safety areas such as the employees' well-being or wellness, product safety, property damage or environmental impact.

OHSAS 18001 covers the following key areas:

- Planning for OHS hazard identification, risk assessment and risk control;
- OHS management programmes;
- Organizational structure and responsibilities for OHS;
- Training, awareness and competence;
- Consultation and communication with stakeholders;
- Operational control on OHS;
- OHS-related emergency preparedness and response; and
- OHS performance measurement, monitoring and improvement.

As with any other management system standard, you will need to follow some steps for the implementation of OHSAS 18001:

- Develop an OHS policy and objectives;
- Carry out risk assessment to identify significant OHS hazards;
- Determine which of the OHS legal requirements are applicable to your type of business activities;
- Define OHS objectives and related programmes for implementing those objectives;
- Develop an OHS manual, operational control procedures and the other documents you need for the effective planning and control of OHS processes; this also covers the records to be maintained;
- Implement the system and monitor compliance and effectiveness through internal audits.

Once the system stabilizes and if you wish to obtain certification, you may select an accredited certification body from among those who provide OHSAS 18001 certification services. According to the BSI group, by the end of December 2009, a total of 54 357 certificates to OHSAS 18001 or its equivalent had been issued by various certification bodies. The process of certification is the same as that followed for other management systems such as ISO 9001, ISO 22000 and ISO 14001.

It may be added here that compliance with OHSAS 18001 does not exempt you from fulfilling legal obligations. However, it will enable you to demonstrate legal compliance in a systematic way.

By implementing OHSAS 18001, you will be able to provide assurance of safe work practices to foreign buyers who prefer to trade with suppliers that provide a safe working environment to their employees, for example.

FOR MORE INFORMATION

- A Practical Guide to Construction Site Safety Management. June 2005. Jointly developed by The Real Estate Developers Association of Hong Kong and the Hong Kong Construction Association.
  http://www.safetypartnering.com/smd/pdf/practical_guide.pdf

  A guidebook for interested parties, including contractors and subcontractors, on managing safety and health risks at construction sites and to meet the safety laws of Hong Kong (China).

- Chao, Chin-Jung and others. A Study for Safety and Health Management Problem of Semiconductor Industry in Taiwan. *Industrial Health* vol. 46. No. 6, 2008, pp. 575-581. http://www.jniosh.go.jp/en/indu_hel/pdf/IH_46_6_575.pdf.

  The study discusses and explores safety and health management in the semiconductor industry.

- European Commission. Safety and Health for New Workers (SHNW). Comparative analysis of the training experiences in labour prevention risks. http://www.leonardodavinci-projekte.org/prj/7278/prj/deliverable_1_vs6_101120.pdf

  An introduction to occupational health and safety (OHS), European directives and European strategies, and an exploration of the national OHS realities.

- International Labour Organization. Guidelines on Occupational Safety and Health Management Systems (ILO-OSH 2001). 2001.
  http://www.ilo.org/wcmsp5/groups/public/---ed_protect/---protrav/---safework/documents/publication/wcms_110496.pdf

  A four-page comprehensive guide to ILO-OSH 2001.

- International Register of Certified Auditors. Safety in numbers.
  http://www.irca.org/downloads/QW%20Jan%2007%20Safety%20in%20Numbers.pdf

  Comparison of the uptake of ISO 9001 and OHSAS 18001 in SMEs.

- OHSAS 18002:2007, Occupational health and safety management systems – Guidelines for the implementation of OHSAS 18001. The OHSAS Project Group Secretariat, c/o British Standards Institution. This standard can be purchased from BSI. E-mail: cservices@bsigroup.com, website: www.bsigroup.com.

  This standard can be adopted by any organization wishing to implement a formal procedure to reduce the risks associated with health and safety in the working environment for employees, customers and the general public.

REFERENCES

OHSAS 18001:2007, Occupational health and safety management systems – Requirements. The OHSAS Project Group Secretariat, c/o British Standards Institution This standard can be purchased from BSI. E-mail: cservices@bsigroup.com

50. What is WRAP and to which industry sectors does it apply?

In the late 1990s, the American Apparel and Footwear Association (AAFA) funded a three-year study to examine working conditions in factories making sewn products around the world. This study led to a programme which was later called WRAP (Worldwide Responsible Accredited Production).

The objective of WRAP is to promote and certify lawful, humane and ethical manufacturing in the sectors producing apparel, footwear and other sewn products. It also covers other labour-intensive industries such as the hotel and construction sectors and those producing jewellery, furniture, food, home furnishing, cutlery, glassware, carpets and rugs, lamps and other products throughout the world.

WRAP is also the registered trademark of the international, non-profit and independent organization that administers the certification programme.

WRAP principles

The 12 WRAP principles listed below are based on generally accepted international workplace standards, local laws and workplace regulations. They cover human resources management, health and safety, environmental practices, and legal compliance including compliance with import, export and customs regulations and security standards.

1. *Compliance with laws and workplace regulations.* Facilities will comply with laws and regulations in all locations where they conduct business.

2. *Prohibition of forced labour.* Facilities will not use involuntary or forced labor.

3. *Prohibition of child labour.* Facilities will not hire any employee under the age of 14 or under the minimum age established by law for employment, whichever is greater, or any employee whose employment would interfere with compulsory schooling.

4. *Prohibition of harassment or abuse.* Facilities will provide a work environment free of supervisory or co-worker harassment or abuse, and free of corporal punishment in any form.

5. *Compensation and benefits.* Facilities will pay at least the minimum total compensation required by local law, including all mandated wages, allowances and benefits.

6. *Hours of work.* Hours worked each day, and days worked each week, shall not exceed the limitations of the country's law. Facilities will provide at least one day off in every seven-day period, except as required to meet urgent business needs.

7. *Prohibition of discrimination.* Facilities will employ, pay, promote and terminate workers on the basis of their ability to do the job, rather than on the basis of personal characteristics or beliefs.

8. *Health and safety.* Facilities will provide a safe and healthy work environment. Where residential housing is provided for workers, it should be safe and healthy.

9. *Freedom of association and collective bargaining.* Facilities will recognize and respect the right of employees to exercise their lawful rights of free association and collective bargaining.

10. *Environment.* Facilities will comply with environmental rules, regulations and standards applicable to their operations, and will observe environmentally conscious practices in all locations where they operate.

11. *Customs compliance.* Facilities will comply with applicable customs laws, and in particular, will establish and maintain programmes to comply with customs laws on the illegal transshipment of finished products.

12. *Security.* Facilities will maintain security procedures to guard against the introduction of non-manifested cargo into outbound shipments (i.e. drugs, explosives, biohazards and other contraband).

WRAP certification

WRAP has adopted a management systems approach towards compliance. This requires senior management to adopt the WRAP principles in writing, assign the necessary staff to ensure that the required practices are implemented throughout the facility, and to put an internal audit system in place to provide an assurance of continuous compliance. Facilities must undergo a rigorous self-assessment and then be audited by an independent third-party monitoring company.

WRAP certifies facilities, not brands or businesses. Since 2006, it has provided a three-level facility certification programme. The 'Platinum' certificate is a two-year certificate awarded to a facility that has demonstrated full compliance with all WRAP principles for three consecutive years, and has successfully passed each audit with no corrective actions. The facility will be subject to an unannounced audit during its two-year certification. The 'Gold' certificate is a one-year certificate presented to a facility that has demonstrated full compliance with all WRAP principles. The 'Silver' certificate is a six-month certificate given to facilities that demonstrate substantial compliance with WRAP principles but has minor non-compliances in procedures or training that need to be addressed.

Over the years, WRAP certification has been in demand among purchasers in developed countries who want to have an assurance that facilities in developing countries are adopting ethical practices. In Bangladesh, over 140 facilities dealing with apparel and sewn products for export have obtained WRAP certification.

FOR MORE INFORMATION

- Das, Subatra. Case Studies on Social Compliance issues in the apparel sector of Bangladesh. http://silkwormmori.blogspot.com/2009/10/case-studies-on-social-compliance.html
- This deals with the issue of social accountability and the code of conduct to be observed in the apparel industry.Worldwide Responsible Accredited Production (WRAP). http://www.wrapcompliance.org/

  In addition to information on WRAP's purpose, principles and procedures, this site contains guidelines and forms for factories interested in becoming WRAP-certified and an application form for monitors seeking WRAP accreditation.

REFERENCES

WRAP Certification programme. Available free of cost from Worldwide Responsible Accredited Production. 2200 Wilson Boulevard Suite 601, Arlington, VA 22201, United States. http://www.wrapcompliance.org/

51. What are the other management system standards?

In addition to ISO management system standards such as ISO 9001 (see question 29), the sector-specific versions of ISO 9001 standards (question 30), ISO 14001 (question 38), ISO 22000 (question 44), and other management system standards such as the standards on occupational health and safety (question 49), social accountability (question 48) and WRAP (question 50), there are additional management system standards that you might also consider, depending on your type of business.

1. ISO standards

ISO/IEC 27000 series of standards

ISO's information security management systems (ISMS) is a systematic approach to managing sensitive company information so that it remains secure. It encompasses people, processes and information technology (IT) systems. It is becoming ever more important to establish a management system to prevent breaches in the security of records or data on electronic media (such as data on designs, banking transactions, stock trading).

The ISO/IEC 27000 series includes 'ISO/IEC 27001:2005 Information technology – Security techniques – Information security management systems – Requirements', which is a certifiable standard. The series provides good practical guidance on designing, implementing, auditing and certifying information security management systems to protect the confidentiality, integrity and availability of the information.

ISO/IEC 20000 international IT service management standard

This standard is published in two parts. 'ISO/IEC 20000-1:2005 Information technology – Service management – Part 1: Specification' is the formal specification and defines the requirements for an organization to deliver managed services of an acceptable quality for its customers. 'ISO/IEC 20000-2:2005 Information technology – Service management – Part 2: Code of practice' describes the best practices for service management processes within the scope of ISO/IEC 20000-1. The code of practice is of particular use to organizations preparing to be audited against ISO/IEC 20000 or planning service improvements.

The standard is applicable to any organization which makes use of IT services. The users covered include internal IT departments providing services to other parts of their companies and organizations that outsource their IT functions.

ISO 28000 series of standards on the security management systems of supply chains

The ISO 28000 series of international standards specifies the requirements for a security management system to ensure safety in the supply chain. The standards address potential security issues at all stages of the supply process; it thus targets threats such as terrorism, fraud and piracy.

'ISO 28001:2007 Security management systems for the supply chain – Best practices for implementing supply chain security, assessments and plans – Requirements' is a requirements and guidance standard that can be used for certification by organizations of all sizes involved in manufacturing, service, storage or transportation by air, rail, road and sea at any stage of the production or supply process. The standard could be applied to all ships, irrespective of size, type, purpose and whether operated internationally, domestically or within internal waters. The same can be said of all other transport segments in the supply chain.

ISO 50001 energy management systems

'ISO 5001:2011 Energy management systems – Requirements with guidance for use' was issued in 2011. Its purpose is to enable organizations of all types and sizes to establish the systems and processes necessary to improve energy performance, including energy efficiency, its use and consumption.

Implementation will lead to reductions in greenhouse gas emissions and other environmental impacts. It will also result in a fall in energy cost through the systematic management of energy. The term 'energy' in the standard covers electricity, fuels, steam, heat, compressed air, and other like media.

The standard has a high level of compatibility with ISO 9001 and ISO 14001.

2. Other important standards

Eco-Management and Audit Scheme (EMAS)

EMAS is the European Union's eco-management and audit scheme. The latest version of its enforcing regulation (EMAS III) is entitled 'Regulation (EC) No 1221/2009 of 25 November 2009 on the voluntary participation by organisation in a Community eco-management and audit scheme (EMAS)'.

The scheme is intended for companies and other organizations who wish to evaluate, manage and continuously improve their environmental performance. The system has been in operation since 1995. It incorporates an environmental management system in line with EN/ISO 14001. Organizations with an ISO 14001-certified EMS can progress towards EMAS registration by incorporating a number of additional elements.

EMAS III came into effect on 11 January 2010. This version improves the applicability of the scheme and strengthens EMAS's visibility and outreach. For instance, EMAS is strengthened by the introduction of environmental core indicators, against which environmental performance can be thoroughly documented.

Participation in EMAS is voluntary and extends to public or private organizations operating in the European Union and the European Economic Area (EEA) – Iceland, Liechtenstein and Norway. An increasing number of candidate countries are also implementing the scheme in preparation for their accession to EU. EMAS III makes registration to the scheme also possible for organizations and sites located outside EU and EEA.

International Safety Management (ISM) Code

The ISM Code, formulated by the International Maritime Organization (IMO) and made mandatory under the International Convention for the Safety of Life at Sea, provides an international standard for the safe management and operation of ships; it also covers the prevention of pollution.

The purpose of the ISM Code is:

- To ensure safety at sea;
- To prevent human injury or loss of life; and
- To avoid damage to the environment and to the ship.

In order to comply with the ISM Code, each ship class must have a working safety management system (SMS). The Code also imposes a mandatory planned maintenance system, according to which vessels must be maintained at specified intervals.

Each ISM-compliant ship is inspected regularly by a 'classification society' to check the effectiveness of its SMS. Once the classification society verifies that the SMS is working and effectively implemented, the ship is issued a safety management certificate. The American Bureau of Shipping is an example of a classification society.

Global Food Safety Initiative (GFSI)

The GFSI benchmarking process has been developed on the basis of internationally accepted food safety requirements, industry best practice and sound science, through a consensus-building process by key stakeholders in the food supply chain. The requirements can be found in the GFSI Guidance Document, which is freely available on their website.

GFSI is coordinated by the Consumer Goods Forum, the only independent global network for consumer goods retailers and manufacturers worldwide.

GFSI has benchmarked, as of November 2010, eight schemes for the manufacturing sector, including the BRC Global Standards, Dutch HACCP and FSSC 22000. It has also benchmarked three schemes for primary production (including GLOBALG.A.P.) and one for the primary sector. A brief description of three of the GFSI-benchmarked schemes is given below.

- **Foundation for Food Safety Certification: FSSC 22000**

  The FSSC scheme was developed by the Foundation for Food Safety Certification and is supported by FoodDrinkEurope.

  FSSC 22000 is a certification scheme for food safety systems based on the food safety management standard ISO 22000:2005 'Requirements for any organization in the food chain' and the publicly available specification (PAS) British Standard 'PAS 220:2008 for Prerequisite programmes on food safety for food manufacturing'. The latter standard is equivalent to ISO/TS 22002-1:2009. The scheme is applicable to manufacturers that process or manufacture animal products, perishable vegetal products, products with a long shelf life and other food ingredients like additives, vitamins and bio-cultures.

  The certification is accredited under the standard ISO/IEC 17021. Manufacturers that are already certified to ISO 22000 will only need an additional review against BS PAS 220 to meet the requirements of this certification scheme. The FSSC 22000 certification scheme has been given full recognition by the Global Food Safety Initiative.

- **GLOBALG.A.P.**

The GLOBALG.A.P. standard comes from EUREPGAP, a standard that was developed by the major European food retailers. GLOBALG.A.P. is a private sector body that sets voluntary standards for the certification of agricultural products, including fresh produce, livestock, fresh-cut flowers, etc. around the globe.

The private standard is primarily designed to reassure consumers that food is produced on farms that minimize the detrimental environmental impacts of their operations by reducing the use of chemical inputs and ensuring a responsible approach to worker health and safety, as well as animal welfare. GLOBALG.A.P. has established itself as a key reference for Good Agricultural Practices (GAP) in the global marketplace. GAP translates consumer requirements into agricultural production practices in a rapidly growing list of countries.

- **British Retail Consortium (BRC) Global Standards**

The BRC Global Standards comprise four technical standards that specify requirements to be met by an organization to enable the production, packaging, storage and distribution of safe food and consumer products. Originally developed in response to the needs of United Kingdom members of the British Retail Consortium, the BRC Global Standards have gained usage worldwide and are specified by a growing numbers of retailers and branded manufacturers in the European Union, North America and other regions.

Certification by accredited certification bodies is available for the above ISO and private standards. Further details of the schemes can be obtained direct from the website of the certification bodies concerned.

FOR MORE INFORMATION

- International Organization for Standardization. International standards and 'private standards'. A freely downloadable brochure. http://www.iso.org/iso/private_standards.pdf

  The brochure clarifies the distinctions between international standards of the type developed by the ISO system, using well-described and accepted principles and disciplines, and private standards developed by industry consortia and other groupings.

- The Consumer Goods Forum. www.consumergoodforum.com

  The Consumer Goods Forum (CGF) is a global, parity-based industry network, driven by its members. It brings together the CEOs and senior management of over 650 retailers, manufacturers, service providers and other stakeholders across 70 countries and reflects the diversity of the industry in geography, size, product category and format.

REFERENCES

British Retail Consortium. Global Standards. www.brc.org.uk

Eco-Management and Audit Scheme. http://ec.europa.eu/environment/emas/about/summary_en.htm

FSSC 22000. http://www.fssc22000.com/en/index.php

GLOBALG.A.P. http://www.globalgap.org

GFSI Guidance Document. http://www.mygfsi.com/

International Organization for Standardization

- ISO 50001: Energy management progresses to Draft International Standard. Obtainable from ISO or ISO members (list at www.iso.org).
- ISO 28001:2007, Security management systems for the supply chain – Best practices for implementing supply chain security, assessments and plans – Requirements and guidance. Obtainable from ISO or ISO members (list at www.iso.org).
- ISO/TS 22002-1:2009, Prerequisite programmes on food safety – Part 1: Food manufacturing. Obtainable from ISO or ISO members (list at www.iso.org).

International Organization for Standardization and International Electrotechnical Commission

- ISO/IEC 27001:2005, Information technology – Security techniques – Information security management systems – Requirements. Obtainable from ISO or ISO members (list at www.iso.org) and from the IEC or IEC National Committees (list at www.iec.ch).
- ISO/IEC 20000 – 1: Information technology – Service management – Part 1: Specification. Obtainable from ISO or ISO members (list at www.iso.org) and from the IEC or IEC National Committees (list at www.iec.ch).
- ISO/IEC 20000 – 2: Information technology – Service management – Part 2: Code of practice. Obtainable from ISO or ISO members (list at www.iso.org) and from the IEC or IEC National Committees (list at www.iec.ch).

International Safety Management (ISM) Code. www.ismcode.net

E. IMPLEMENTING MANAGEMENT SYSTEMS

52. What factors should I consider when choosing a management system standard for my company?

Your criteria for selecting a management system standard will depend upon the following.

- Do you need a generic system focusing on a management area or a sector-specific system?
- If you are aiming at a generic system, what area do you want to focus on: quality, the environment, information security, or a combination of these?
- If you need a sector-specific system, in which field do you operate: automotive parts, medical devices, software development?

Table A below provides details of generic system standards developed by both ISO and the private sector. Table B gives similar information on sector-specific systems.

Table A
Generic management system standards

Purpose of implementation	Standard	Reference
To obtain customer satisfaction by consistently providing conforming products or services	ISO 9001	See question 29
To ensure the security of your company's valued information and create confidence among customers in the security of the information they provide	ISO 27001	See question 51
To demonstrate to your stakeholders that your company is environmentally responsible	ISO14001	See question 38
To provide a safe workplace to your employees by managing occupational health and safety risks at the workplace	OHSAS 18001	See question 49
To ensure your employees' welfare and demonstrate compliance with social accountability policies, procedures and practices to interested parties.	SA 8000	See question 48
To improve energy performance, including energy efficiency, energy use and consumption	ISO 50001	See question 51

Table B
Sector-specific management system standards

Field: Quality management		
Purpose of implementation	**Standard**	**Reference**
To become a reliable supplier of automotive production materials, parts and services meeting OEM requirements	ISO/TS16949	See question 30
To become a reliable supplier of equipment and materials needed by the petrochemical, oil and gas industry supply chain	ISO/TS 29001	See question 30

To become a reliable supplier to companies involved in the design, production, installation and servicing of medical devices	ISO 13485	See question 30
To become a reliable supplier in the aviation, space and defence industry supply chain.	AS 9100	See question 30
To demonstrate your ability to supply products or services to telecommunications service providers and their suppliers	TL 9000	See question 30
To become a reliable computer software development and service supplier	TickIT	See question 30
To become a reliable provider of IT services either within your own organization or to external organizations obtaining outsourced services from you.	ISO/IEC 20000	See question 51
Field: Supply chain security management		
To reduce risks to people and cargo within the supply chain	ISO 28001	See question 51
Field: Environmental management		
To evaluate, manage and continuously improve your environmental performance either within the European Union or outside it	EMAS and Regulation (EC) No. 1221/2009 (EMAS III)	See question 51
Field: Work place safety		
To promote lawful, humane and ethical manufacturing in the apparel, footwear and sewing industries as well as in other labour-intensive sectors such as the hotel and construction industries and the manufacturing sectors for jewellery, furniture, food, home furnishing, cutlery, glassware, carpets and rugs, lamps.	WRAP	See question 50
To ensure safety at sea, to prevent human injury or loss of life and to avoid damage to the environment and to your ship.	ISM Code	See question 51
Field: Food safety		
To ensure that the food your company processes is safe for human consumption	HACCP-based food safety system	See question 42
To ensure the safety of various food items, i.e. those manufactured from animal products, perishable vegetal products, products with a long shelf life and food ingredients like additives, vitamins and bio-cultures.	FSSC 22000 (a combination of ISO 22000 and BS PAS 220)	See question 51
To ensure the production, packaging, storage and distribution of safe food and consumer products	BRC Global Standards	See question 51
To reassure consumers that food is produced on farms that minimize the detrimental environmental impacts of farming operations by reducing the use of chemical inputs and that apply a responsible approach to worker health and safety as well as animal welfare.	GLOBALG.A.P.	See question 51

Source: S.C. Arora, India.

If you wish to have a management system that integrates several management areas, such as quality assurance, environmental safety and information security, you may select the appropriate generic systems listed in table A. If you want an integrated but sector-specific system, you may use several systems listed in table B. You could, for example, use both the ISO 22000 food safety system and the BRC Global Standards. A combination of generic and sector-specific systems is also possible. For instance, a manufacturer of automotive parts may integrate ISO/TS 16949 with the ISO 14000 environmental management system (see question 54).

FOR MORE INFORMATION

- Chartered Quality Institute (CQI). Management system standards.
  http://www.thecqi.org/Knowledge-Hub/Knowledge-portal/Compliance-and-organisations/Management-system-standards/

  Briefly explains what management system standards are and how they have evolved over time.

REFERENCES

Standards Australia International (SAI). www.standards.com.au

British Standards Institution (BSI). www.bsigroup.com

DNV Certification services. www.dnv.com

53. What is the purpose of internal audits of management systems and how are they conducted?

Once you have established a management system, it will be necessary for you to introduce measures that will inform your management whether the system is being effectively implemented. Installing any system without testing its functioning could merely be a waste of time and effort.

The internal audit is one such measure. It is an important component of most management system standards (ISO 9001, ISO 14001, ISO 22000, ISO 27001, OHSAS 18001 and others). Audits provide evidence in areas requiring attention to reduce, eliminate and, most importantly, to prevent non-conformities in the system.

Internal audits are carried out for one or more of following purposes:

- To determine the extent of the conformity of the management system with the defined audit criteria;
- To determine the effectiveness of the implemented system in meeting specified objectives; and
- To provide the auditee with an opportunity to improve its management system.

You should not use audits in a way that results in transferring the responsibility for detecting and correcting process deviations from the operating staff to the auditors.

The process of internal audit typically comprises the seven steps shown in the figure below.

Steps of an internal audit

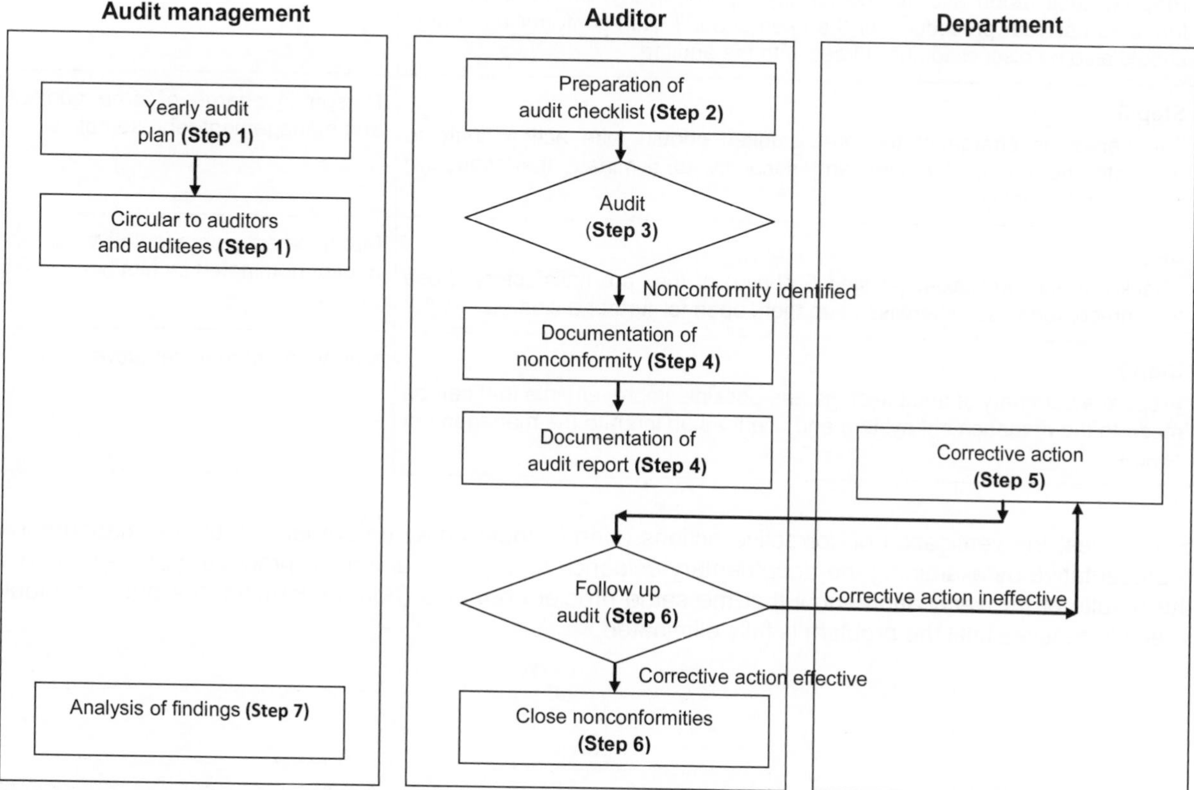

Source: S.C. Arora, India.

The management representative or any other manager can be made responsible for the internal audit function. The typical tasks include: preparing annual audit programme, assigning trained auditors to various processes for auditing; ensuring each process owner takes timely corrective action on the audit findings, using audit results to improve the management system wherever possible. Most organizations identify and train their employees to do inter-functional audits as a part-time activity. In a small company where employees carry out multiple activities, it may not always be possible to find an independent person. If this is the case, you can hire management system consultants who provide audit services. The steps involved in the audit process shown in the figure above are briefly explained below.

Step	Responsibility
Step 1 Prepare the annual audit programme. (The frequency of audit could be increased for business processes and reduced for support processes.) Ensure the availability of trained auditors and take steps to guarantee their independence during their auditing work.	Management representative
Step 2 Study processes to be audited, their related documents and previous audit findings. Prepare a checklist of the requirements to be examined during the audit.	Auditor
Step 3 Conduct the audit on the planned date and obtain evidence by asking questions of the people who carry out the activities, observing activities, checking records and other documents. Also look for the results of the processes, e.g. whether targets fixed for each objective are achieved or not.	Auditor
Step 4 Prepare audit report and non-conformity reports, if any, on the prescribed forms as per your procedure for the internal audit. Non-conformities, if any, should also be discussed and agreed with the auditee.	Auditor
Step 5 The person in charge of the area audited should take action firstly to eliminate the non-conformities and secondly to eliminate their cause(s) without undue delay.	Person in charge of area audited and management representative
Step 6 Check the action(s) taken (at step 5 above). If they are satisfactory, close the non-conformities; otherwise keep them open for further action.	Management representative or an auditor nominated by him/her.
Step 7 Prepare a summary of audit findings and possible improvements that can be made to the management system and use it as an input to the management review	Management representative

Sometimes, the verification of corrective actions (step 6 above) may be carried out by the management representative by examining the documentary evidence such as an amended procedure or instruction. If the results of the verification show that the same problem remains (non-conformity), the auditee should seek alternatives until the problem is fully eliminated.

FOR MORE INFORMATION

- Chartered Quality Institute (CQI). Surviving internal auditing.
  http://www.thecqi.org/Knowledge-Hub/Resources/The-Quality-Survival-Guide/Surviving-Internal-Auditing/

  Good explanation on the process of internal auditing: purpose, steps, coverage, etc.

- International Trade Centre and International Organization for Standardization. ISO 9001 for Small Businesses – What to do: Advice from ISO/TC 176, ISBN 978-92-67-10516-1. Obtainable from ISO or ISO members (list at www.iso.org).

  This handbook gives guidance to small organizations on developing and implementing a quality management system based upon ISO 9001:2008. It offers some practical advice on different options, should you wish to introduce a quality management system into your organization, or update an existing one. Para 8.2.2 of this handbook deals with internal audit.

REFERENCES

International Trade Centre. ISO 9001:2008 Diagnostic Tool. www.intracen.org

54. Can I combine various management systems into one integrated system and how should I proceed?

ISO has been developing international standards for management systems since 1987. The earliest was the ISO 9000 family on quality management systems (now in its fourth edition, published in 2008). This was followed by ISO 14000 on environmental management systems (its second edition came out in 2004), ISO 22000 on food safety management systems (issued in 2005) and ISO/IEC 27001 on information security (2005), among others. Another, but non-ISO, management system is OHSAS 18001 on occupational health and safety (in its second edition, published in 2007). Organizations started implementing these systems as soon as the standards came out, creating a multiplicity of systems within them.

If your company is planning to implement these systems, it has two options. The first is to implement each system separately. In that case, you might consider adopting the following sequence: ISO 9001, ISO 14001, OHSAS 18001, ISO/IEC 27001. If you are in the food processing industry, then you might start with HACCP/ISO 22000 and then follow the above sequence. Each of these systems has a specific purpose (see question 52).

But if you wish to have an integrated system consisting of more than one scheme, you could do this as well. You could, for instance, combine your existing systems with new ones. Or, you could create an integrated system right from the beginning if you wish to start with more than one scheme.

ISO 9001, ISO 22000 and ISO 27001 have similar formats, as do ISO 14001 and OHSAS 18001. All these standards have the following common features:

- For all concerned, including the management representative, defining responsibilities and designating authorities;
- Resource management;
- Control of documents;
- Control of records;
- Internal audit;
- Corrective action;
- Preventive action;
- Continual improvement of the system; and
- Periodic review of the system by top management.

As the system is integrated, you will standardize the above procedures, bringing about a reduction in the multiplicity of documents and reducing the time and resources required to carry the related activities out.

The methodology for developing an integrated management system will include:

- Nominating a multidisciplinary team and a team leader to carry out the development activities for the integrated management system.
- Developing a good understanding of the content and the intent of the standards to be integrated.
- Determining the processes to be included in the integrated system.
- Carrying out risk assessment of activities whose outcomes have an impact on customers, end users, employees, the environment and information security.
- Developing controls and a monitoring mechanism for all operations with significant issues.

- Determining the documentation structure and preparing a plan for developing documents. These should include statements of policy and objectives, manuals, control plans, documents setting out operational controls, common procedures, instructions. The format of these documents should also be decided on.
- Training all employees concerned on their roles and responsibilities in the integrated management system. Some senior persons should also be trained to conduct the periodic system audits.
- Monitoring deviations and departures from specified requirements. Whenever nonconformities are brought out by customers, employees, internal auditors and other stakeholders, initiate corrective actions.

If your management decides to obtain certification, then you may select an appropriate certification body that can offer you an auditing service for an integrated management system.

To understand the integration of individual processes, refer to the relevant ISO standards, as each standard has a correspondence to a greater or lesser degree with other standards. For example, two tables in Annex A of ISO 9001 show its correspondence with ISO 14001 as well the correspondence of ISO 14001 with ISO 9001. OHSAS 18001 gives a comparison of its provisions with those of ISO 9001 and ISO 14001, as does ISO 22000 with ISO 9001. ISO 27001 also details its similarities with ISO 9001 and ISO 14001 in its Annex C.

Some of the cost reductions that can be achieved through integration arise from:

- The reduced time and effort spent by senior management on giving directions and reviewing the system.
- Optimal utilization of resources (e.g. the appointment of joint management representatives, the use of common processes for controlling documents, internal auditing, management reviews).
- The reduced time and effort devoted to root cause analysis of failures and to taking corrective actions.

The cost of conducting audits by certification bodies could also fall as these bodies may be able to conduct joint audits of the systems.

FOR MORE INFORMATION

- British Standards Institution (BSI). PAS 99 Integrated Management: www.bsigroup.com or http://www.bsigroup.com/en/Assessment-and-certification-services/management-systems/Standards-and-Schemes/PAS-99/

  PAS 99 is the integrated management system specification based on the six common requirements of ISO Guide 72 (a guide for standards writers). It may help you to align your processes and procedures into one holistic structure which will enable you to run your operations more effectively.

- International Organization for Standardization. The integrated use of management system standards. ISBN 978-92-67-10473-7. Obtainable from ISO or ISO members ((list at www.iso.org).

  This book provides organizations with guidance on how to integrate the requirements of multiple ISO or non-ISO management standards with their current management system. It does not give preference to any management system and is not intended to be a normative document.

- Spilka, M., A. Kania and R. Nowosielski. Integration of management systems on the chosen example. *Journal of Achievements in Materials and Manufacturing Engineering*, vol. 35, issue 2, August 2009. http://www.journalamme.org/papers_vol35_2/35213.pdf

  This paper presents the effects of integrated management systems. Integration improves an organization's image and increases its working efficiency.

- Zaffora-Reeder, Scot and Doug Stoddart. Integrated Systems for Quality, Occupational Health & Safety, and Environmental Management (One Company's Approach). Published by ASQ. http://section206.asqquality.org/Meetings%202009/Fall%20Conference/Integrated%20Systems.pdf

  PowerPoint with a good visual presentation on the integrated implementation of ISO 14001 and OHSAS 18001.

REFERENCES

International Organization for Standardization

- ISO 9001:2008, Quality management systems – Requirements. Obtainable from ISO or ISO members (list at www.iso.org).
- ISO 14001:2004, Environmental management systems – Requirements with guidance for use. Obtainable from ISO or ISO members (list at www.iso.org).
- ISO 22000:2005, Food safety management systems – Requirements for any organization in the food chain. Obtainable from ISO or ISO members (list at www.iso.org).

International Organization for Standardization and International Electrotechnical Commission. ISO/IEC 27001:2005, Information technology – Security techniques – Information security management systems – Requirements. Obtainable from ISO or ISO members (list at www.iso.org) and from IEC or IEC National Committees (list at www.iech.ch).

OHSAS 18001:2007, Occupational health and safety management systems – Requirements. The OHSAS Project Group Secretariat, c/o British Standards Institution This standard can be purchased from BSI. E-mail: cservices@bsigroup.com

CONFORMITY ASSESSMENT

A. CONCEPT OF CONFORMITY ASSESSMENT

55. What is conformity assessment?

Conformity assessment is a collective term covering the many elements required to demonstrate that a product or a service complies with stated technical and other requirements. In general, testing, inspection and certification are considered the core conformity assessment services (see questions 59, 65, 68, and 69) and they are used either individually or collectively as circumstances demand.

Testing, inspection and certification are supported by metrology and calibration to ensure the validity of measurements (see question 79), and by accreditation to ensure the technical competency of the conformity assessment service providers (see question 88).

Conformity assessment can be performed on products, services, processes, systems and even persons. The whole system is shown graphically in the figure below.

Conformity assessment system

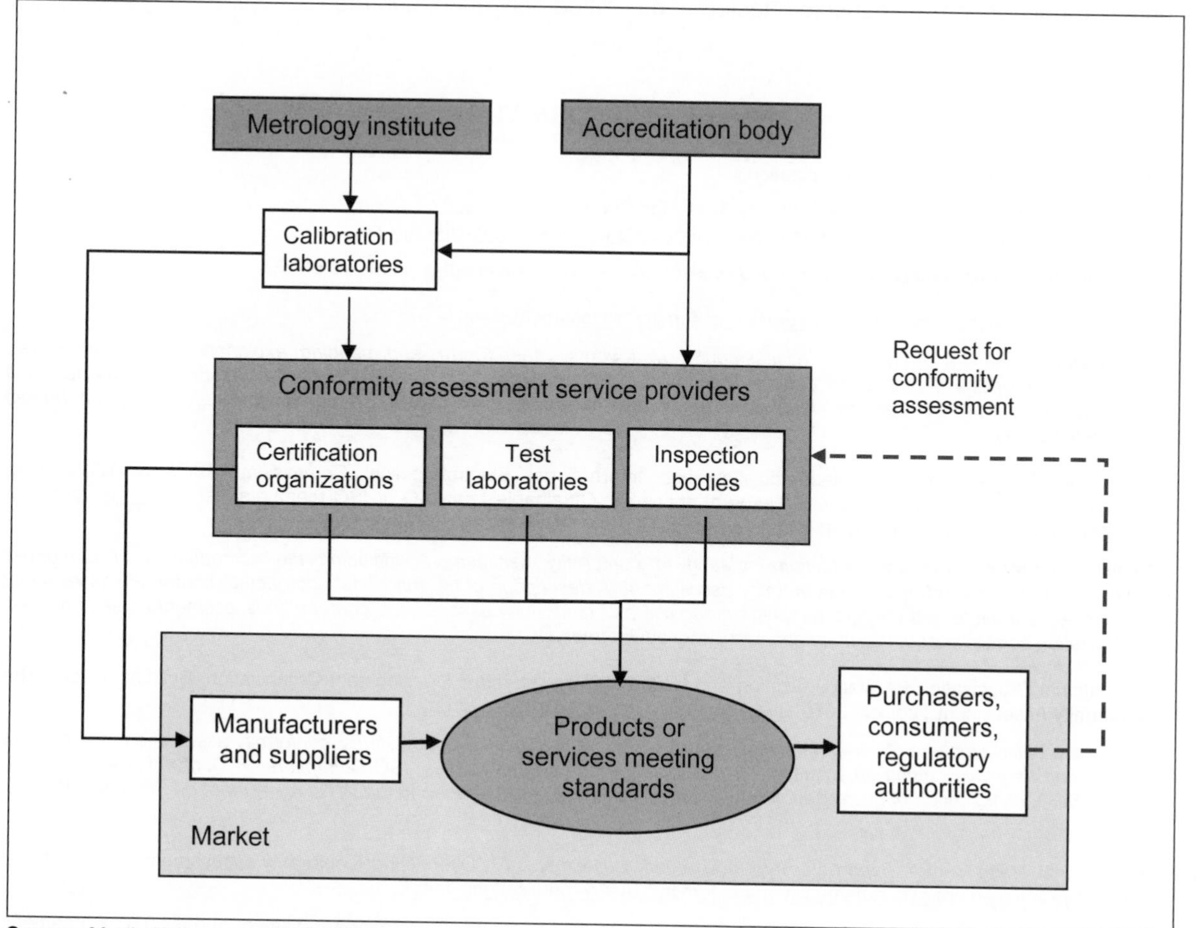

Source: Martin Kellermann, South Africa.

Conformity assessment services can be provided by the manufacturer – in which case it is considered first-party conformity assessment or a supplier's declaration of conformity (see question 57). They can also be conducted by the purchaser, i.e. the second party. This is an expensive option for the purchaser, so second-party assessment is generally encountered only among major purchasers operating their own inspection and testing infrastructures. Much more acceptable, though, especially for SMEs in developing economies, is the provision of conformity assessment services by an organization that is independent of both the supplier and the purchaser. Such an organization would be a third-party conformity assessment body.

Third-party conformity assessment can be provided by either public or private organizations. The main issues are that they should be able to demonstrate their technical competency through internationally accepted accreditation and that their test reports (see question 60) and certificates are recognized in your export markets (see question 70 on selecting a certification body). The fact that a conformity assessment service provider is a government body, i.e. the national standards body or government laboratory, does not lead to automatic acceptance of their test reports or certificates. Furthermore, sometimes the market or regulatory authorities abroad may not accept their test reports and certificates even though they are accredited. This situation is getting better with time.

In developing countries, inspection, testing and certification services are frequently provided only by the national standards body and government laboratories. There are many private inspection bodies, testing laboratories and certification bodies that operate in the marketplace. Some of these are extremely successful, large multinational organizations with offices in more than 100 countries.

Choosing your conformity assessment service provider is therefore not all that easy (see question 70). The proximity of the service provider, its local level of service, its acceptance in the target market and the price of its services are all issues that have to be carefully considered. The ultimate goal is to have your produce, product or service inspected, tested and certified only once, and then accepted everywhere.

FOR MORE INFORMATION

- International Organization for Standardization
  - Conformity Assessment. Presentation by Sean Mac Curtain. October 2007. http://www.ghtf.org/meetings/conferences/11thconference/D/04MAC-CURTAIN.pdf

    This is a Power Point presentation that discusses conformity assessment and the role of ISO.
  - Conformity Assessment. www.iso.org/iso/conformity_assessment

    Detailed overview of conformity assessment, how it works, various terms and meaning; explanations are given to help both companies beginning to explore the possibility of obtaining certification for themselves or their products and customers who are seeking clarification of the various certification claims they encounter. Information on related publications.
- International Organization for Standardization and International Electrotechnical Commission. ISO/IEC 17000:2004, Conformity assessment: Vocabulary and general principles. Obtainable from ISO or ISO members (list at www.iso.org) and from IEC or IEC National Committees (list at www.iech.ch).

  Specifies general terms and definitions relating to conformity assessment, including the accreditation of conformity assessment bodies and the use of conformity assessment. A description of the functional approach to conformity assessment is included as a further aid to understanding among users of conformity assessment, conformity assessment bodies and their accreditation bodies, in both voluntary and regulatory environments.
- International Organization for Standardization and United Nations Industrial Development Organization. Building Trust – The Conformity Assessment Toolbox. 2010. www.iso.org/iso/casco_building-trust.pdf

  Covers the basic concepts of conformity assessment, techniques, schemes and systems; conformity assessment bodies; how UNIDO can help with setting up a quality infrastructure; includes case studies; ISO Committee on Conformity Assessment, ISO/CASCO; coordination of accreditation bodies; and conformity assessment and the WTO Agreement on Technical Barriers to Trade.
- International Trade Centre. *Export Quality Management Bulletin* No. 77, Overview of conformity assessment in international trade. www.intracen.org/exporters/quality-management/Quality_publications_index
- United States Agency for International Development. Standards, Metrology, Conformity Assessment and the TBT Agreement: A Desk Top Reference Handbook. http://pdf.usaid.gov/pdf_docs/PNADP635.pdf

  Detailed presentations on the above topics. Excellent source to deepen understanding of metrology and conformity assessment.

56. What type of conformity assessment is required to prove compliance with technical requirements?

The functional approach to conformity assessment as defined in ISO/IEC 17000 is a useful way of approaching this question. It is based on three functions to demonstrate that technical requirements are fulfilled:

- Selection;
- Determination; and
- Review and attestation.

Functional approach to conformity assessment

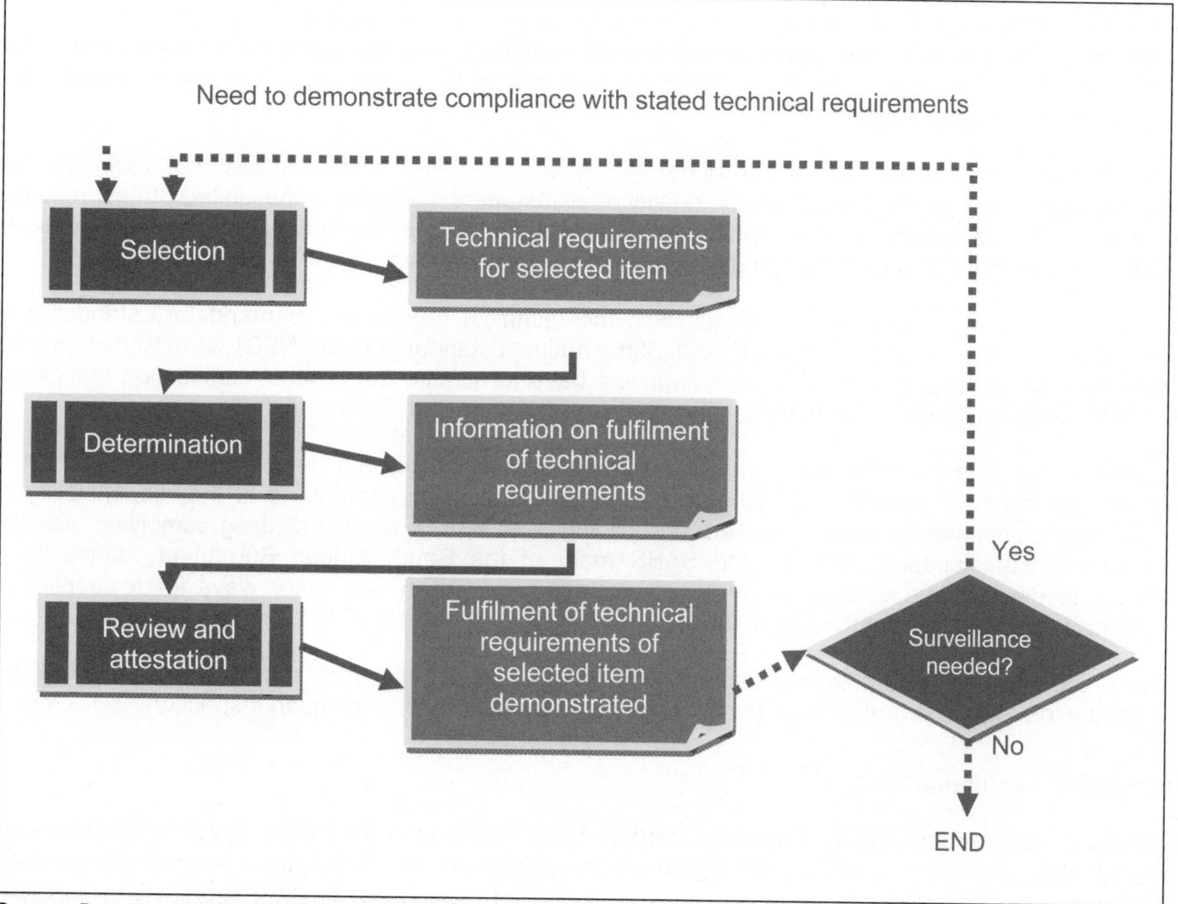

Source: Based on ISO/IEC 17000.

Many types and combinations of conformity assessment may be required to prove compliance with technical requirements. The challenge is to determine which ones.

Under the functional approach (as shown in the figure above) we select which technical requirements need to be demonstrated, then determine by inspection, testing, auditing and other means whether the technical requirements have been met, review the results to establish whether the stated requirements have been fulfilled, and attest (e.g. certify) that the requirements have been met.

This process can be used whether the technical requirements are demanded by technical regulations and SPS measures (see questions 18 and 19) or in contractual obligations imposed by a specific purchaser (see question 22), or whether compliance is needed simply to enhance the supplier's competitiveness.

In the case of technical regulations and SPS measures, conformity assessment may have to be undertaken by very specific inspection bodies, laboratories or certification organizations designated by the authorities such as the 'notified bodies' in the European Union. In some countries, assurance of compliance with technical regulations and SPS measures can be provided by an accredited organization, in others only by government organizations. In certain cases, a supplier's declaration of conformity (SDoC) suffices. The spectrum is extremely wide-ranging. A few examples are provided in the paragraphs below and in the succeeding sections of this guide.

Further details are given below about the type of conformity required to demonstrate compliance against technical regulations, purchasers' requirements and market requirements.

Technical regulations

Under the EU New Directives, the type of conformity assessment required for any pertinent product is specified very clearly. Basically, eight combinations of conformity assessment are legally available to the developers of the Directives. The New Directives and their eight conformity assessment modules are discussed in more detail in question 58.

A similar situation prevails with some technical regulations in the United States. For example, the Fastener Quality Act, which determines the quality of all fasteners marketed in the United States, requires the testing of the fasteners by an accredited laboratory acceptable to the National Institute of Standards and Technology (NIST) against the standards listed in the Fastener Act.

For most developing countries, compliance with the technical regulations or mandatory standards is demonstrated by the product certification mark of the national standards body (NSB), as in Kenya and the United Republic of Tanzania. In this case, suppliers have to acquire the product certification mark from the NSB in order to demonstrate compliance with the stated technical requirements.

In some economies, the NSB mark confers evidence of compliance with mandatory standards on the product, but the NSB mark is not mandatory. In South Africa, for example, it is the responsibility of construction companies to provide workers on building sites with protective clothing complying with the relevant national standards. Holding the SABS mark of the South African Bureau of Standards is sufficient to demonstrate compliance with safety procedures. There are other ways for a supplier to demonstrate compliance, but the use of the NSB mark is often the easiest.

In some countries the conformity assessment requirements are not as clearly stated. Compliance may be decided by the regulatory authority or even by the inspector on duty during import inspection.

Purchasers' requirements

Purchasers' requirements are the easiest to identify, as purchasers normally know exactly what they want and state their requirements clearly. But whether the supplier can provide products that can demonstrate compliance is another issue.

The process for determining conformity is transparent and can involve design approval, pre-delivery testing of samples, and continuous surveillance testing and certification during the whole delivery period. International standards, national standards, private standards, any one of these or a combination may be stipulated by the purchaser in the contract.

In some cases, a product certification mark may be given preference by the purchaser. Examples of such marks are the UL marks of United Laboratories for certain goods destined for the United States, the CSA mark for Canada, or the IEC marks in many economies (see question 73). The supplier therefore needs to identify and thoroughly understand the specifications or contractual obligations imposed by the purchaser.

Market requirements

For some markets, it may be important to have a product certification mark in order to convince consumers that the product is of good quality (see question 68). This is especially the case if the brand is still unknown in the marketplace. The NSB mark of the importing country may be the one that is known and accepted, whereas the NSB mark of the exporting country may be unknown. In this case, the supplier will have to obtain a licence to use the NSB mark of the importing country. This means, however, that the supplier will have to obtain the NSB mark for every country that he chooses to deal with. Hence, this is a decision that should not be made lightly.

In the more developed markets, environmental and social certification may also be important to penetrate the market (see question 17). In this case, the various markets may all accept the same certification, which would be more cost effective for suppliers. Since there are many types of certifications, the choice would ultimately be decided by the supplier.

FOR MORE INFORMATION

- International Organization for Standardization and United Nations Industrial Development Organization. Building Trust – The Conformity Assessment Toolbox. 2010. www.iso.org/iso/casco_building-trust.pdf

  Covers basic concepts of conformity assessment, techniques, schemes and systems; conformity assessment bodies; how UNIDO can help with setting up a quality infrastructure; case studies; the ISO Committee on Conformity Assessment, ISO/CASCO; coordination of accreditation bodies; and conformity assessment and the WTO Agreement on Technical Barriers to Trade.

REFERENCES

CSA Marks. www.csa-international.org

European Commission. European standards: List of references of harmonized standards. New Approach directives. http://ec.europa.eu/enterprise/policies/european-standards/documents/harmonised-standards-legislation/list-references/

Fastener Quality Act. www.nist.gov/pml/wmd/metric/fqa.cfm

International Organization for Standardization and International Electrotechnical Commission. ISO/IEC 17000:2004, Conformity assessment – Vocabulary and general principles. Obtainable from ISO or ISO members (list at www.iso.org).

SABS Mark Scheme. www.sabs.co.za/index.php?page=certsabsmarkscheme

57. What is a supplier's declaration of conformity (SDoC)?

This section defines the supplier's declaration of conformity (SDoC), shows its main typical contents, discusses when this declaration of conformity is applicable, and illustrates with some examples where an SDoC is accepted.

Supplier's declaration of conformity

When a supplier declares that a product, service, process, body or management system meets the stated technical requirements without second or third-party involvement, one speaks of a supplier's declaration of conformity (SDoC). The expression 'self-certification' is also heard, but this terminology should be avoided as it only leads to confusion – 'certification' is to be used only if a third party is involved. This is so even if a supplier uses the services of an outside laboratory, but issues the declaration of conformity on its own responsibility. Developing countries may be at a disadvantage to some extent, as the market may readily accept the SDoC only from major and well-known manufacturers.

An SDoC is the most cost effective approach to demonstrating conformity, as it does not require third-party inspection, testing and certification. The major cost saving, however, is associated with the sales losses due to the time needed for third-party approvals.

It has been shown in studies by the Organisation for Economic Co-operation and Development (OECD – see 'For More Information') that the use of SDoC instead of third-party conformity assessment regimes leads to an increase in trade. It is therefore no surprise that major industry groupings such as the information technology industry or the automotive industry are advocating the use of an SDoC wherever they can. The international standard ISO/IEC 17050 Parts 1 and 2 details the requirements for an SDoC. The standard has been adopted by the European Union and many national standards bodies.

Contents of an SDoC

According to ISO/IEC 17050 (see References for the full title), an SDoC should contain at least the following information:

- The name and address of the supplier;
- The identification of the product, process or service;
- The conformity statement;
- The referenced normative documents (standards, technical regulations, etc.);
- The date and place of issue of the declaration; and
- The authorized signatory(ies) on behalf of the supplier.

Where an SDoC is accepted to demonstrate compliance in technical regulations, its contents could be indicated in these regulations. If this is the case, the contents may differ from the ISO/IEC 17050 list, and the regulation list has to be followed scrupulously.

When is an SDoC applicable?

An SDoC is generally acceptable if any or a group of the following are in place:

- The market demands or allows it;
- The risks associated with non-compliance are generally low;
- The penalties for non-compliance are effective deterrents;
- Options for efficient recourse in the event of non-compliance exist; and
- The industry sector to which it applies is highly dynamic, responsible and has a history of compliance.

In the case of technical regulations, an SDoC is acceptable only if the regulation or measure specifically allows it. Otherwise, the third-party conformity assessment requirements of the regulation or measure have to be fully complied with. Some examples of an acceptable SDoC for regulatory purposes are shown in the table below.

Acceptable SDoC for regulatory purposes

Country/area	Year	Product category
Australia/New Zealand	Late 1990s	Telecommunication equipment, computers and computer peripherals
Brazil	2001-2006	Disposable cigarette lighters, installation systems for vehicle natural gas, steel profile for power transmission
Canada	1950s	Broadcast equipment
	1971	Motor vehicles and components
	1990s	Low-risk radio equipment
	2002	Telecommunication terminal equipment
EU	1990	Toys
	1992	Personal protective equipment
	1993	Medical products (Class I)
	1993	Machinery
	1996	Electrical/electronic products
	1996	Recreational craft
	1996	Equipment for use in potentially explosive atmospheres
	2000	Radio and telecommunication terminal equipment
Japan	2004	Certain radio and telecommunication terminal equipment
Republic of Korea	2003	Automotive sector
	2007	Certain low-risk consumer products (47 items)
Chinese Taipei	2002	19 items, mainly parts or accessories for IT products such as electronic calculators, hard disk drives, storage units and power supplies
United States	1966	Motor vehicles and motor vehicle components
	1999	Computers and computer peripherals
	2003	Telecommunication terminal equipment

Source: Organisation for Economic Co-operation and Development.

REFERENCES

Fliess, B., F. Gonzales and R. Schonfeld. Technical Barriers to Trade: Evaluating the Trade Effects of Supplier's Declaration of Conformity. *OECD Trade Policy Working Papers,* No. 78. OECD Publishing, 2008. www.oecd.org/dataoecd/57/3/41481368.pdf

International Organization for Standardization and International Electrotechnical Commission

- ISO/IEC 17050-1:2004, Conformity assessment – Supplier's declaration of conformity – Part 1: General requirements, ISO/IEC, 2004. Obtainable from ISO or ISO members (list at www.iso.org) and from IEC or IEC National Committees (www.iec.org).
- ISO/IEC 17050-2:2004, Conformity assessment – Supplier's declaration of conformity – Part 2: Supporting documentation, ISO/IEC, 2004. Obtainable from ISO or ISO members (list at www.iso.org) and from IEC or IEC National Committees (list at www.iec.ch).

58. What is CE marking and how does it help exports?

This section discusses the principles underlining the CE marking, some compliance issues to be taken into consideration, the modules involved in the CE marking regulation and the combination of modules required for some key industries.

Principles

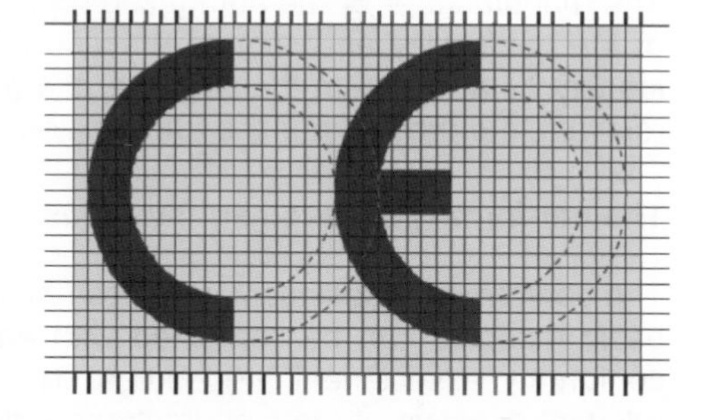

The CE marking is a regulatory device that EU uses to identify products that meet all the requirements of a specific EU New Directive (i.e. EU technical regulation – see question 18). It is neither the EU nor any third-party conformity assessment service provider that does the marking, but the manufacturer or supplier. Thus the manufacturer or supplier takes full responsibility for the integrity of the product. All of this is based on the New Directive principles published in 1985:

- Legislative harmonization is limited to essential requirements that products placed on the EU market must meet;
- The technical specifications of products meeting the essential requirements set out in the directives are laid down in harmonized standards (EN);
- Application of the harmonized standards remains voluntary, and the manufacturer may apply other technical specifications to meet the essential requirements; and
- Products manufactured in compliance with the harmonized standards benefit from a presumption of conformity with the corresponding essential requirements.

In support of the New Directive principles, EU also developed in 1989 the Global Approach for testing and certification to demonstrate compliance with the Directives. The Global Approach lists eight different conformity assessment modules, one or more of which must be selected by the relevant New Directive. In addition to these modules, the rules for affixing the CE marking are clearly defined.

Compliance issues

This is a system common to the whole of the Union. Once your product complies with the essential requirements, and this compliance is successfully demonstrated by the appropriate conformity assessment module, then you can apply the CE marking and the product can be marketed in the entire EU. This is a great advantage, but there are a few issues you should consider carefully:

- Identify the specific New Directive your product falls under. All the New Directives are listed on the EU website. Links are given in the 'For more information' section below.
- Identify the relevant EN Standard from the official list at: http://ec.europa.eu/enterprise/policies/european-standards/documents/harmonised-standards-legislation/list-references/

Although you may use standards other than the harmonized EN standards, it is usually much easier to use them, as compliance with the listed EN standards confers a presumption of conformity with the essential requirements of the relevant New Directive.

Identify the required conformity assessment module and if it involves third-party laboratories or certification organizations, then you must obtain the services of a 'notified body'. These are conformity assessment service providers that have been found competent by their government and notified accordingly to the European Commission. All the notified bodies are resident in the European Union.

The list of notified bodies can be found on the NANDO (New Approach Notified and Designated Organisations) webpage of the European Union. There is also a list of countries and their conformity assessment service providers covered by multilateral recognition agreements (MRAs) between the European Community and countries outside EU.

As a manufacturer outside EU, you must appoint an authorized representative resident in EU, who will be addressed by the authorities in lieu of you for any queries or problems with the product.

The manufacturer has to compile and maintain a technical file on the product to provide information on the design, manufacture and operation of the product, as well as to demonstrate compliance with the relevant directive. This file has to be maintained up to 10 years after the manufacturer has ceased to market the specific product.

The manufacturer or the authorized representative must compile an EC declaration of conformity as part of the conformity assessment procedure of the New Directive. The EC declaration of conformity must identify as a minimum the directive, the manufacturer, the authorized representative, the notified body if relevant, the product and the harmonized standard.

The conformity assessment modules

The conformity assessment modules relate to the design phase, the production phase, or both. The eight basic modules can be combined with each other in a variety of ways in order to establish complete conformity assessment procedures. The actual module or modules to be used are identified in the relevant directive. If the manufacturer is given a choice, then the criteria governing the choices are listed as well. A simplified diagram of the eight modules is shown below as an illustration – actual directives provide the necessary detail for implementation.

EU New Directives: conformity assessment modules

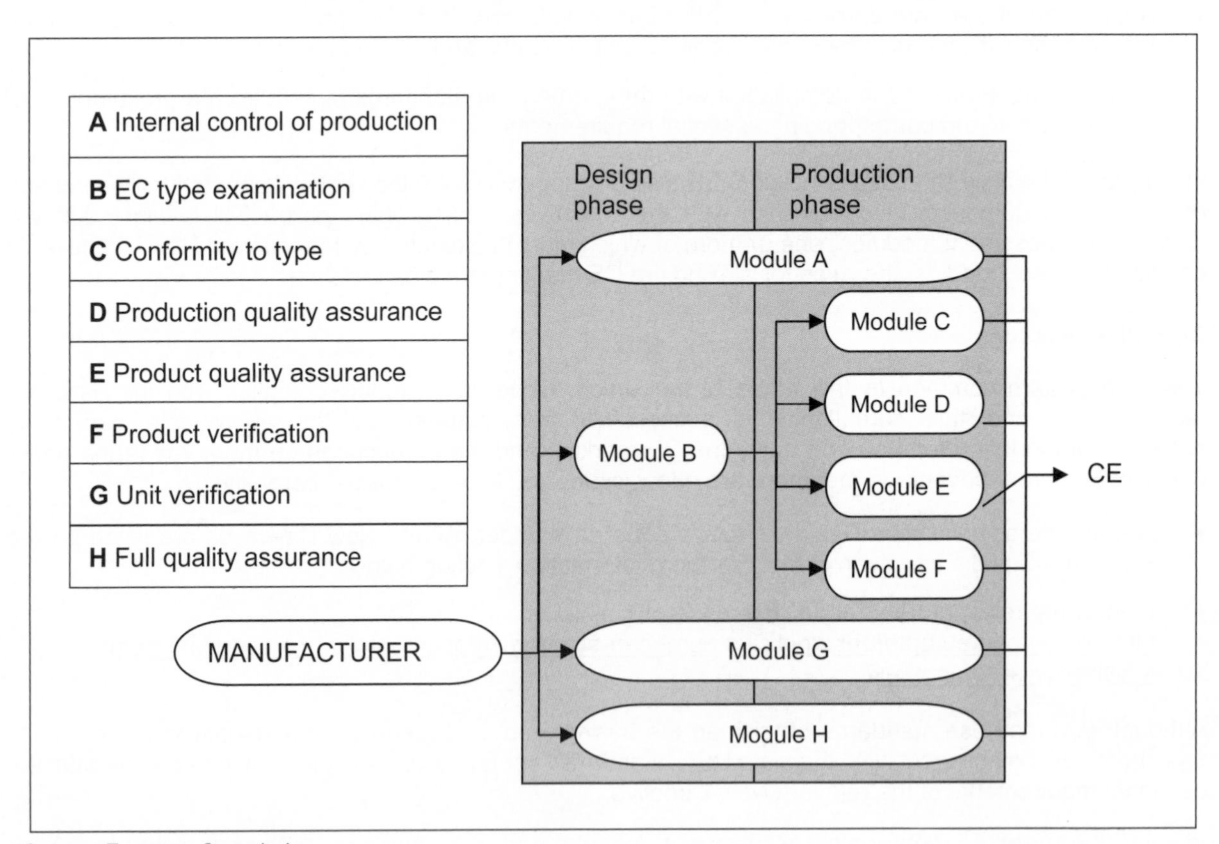

Source: European Commission.

Module A is used if the products are of a low risk type or the manufacturing sector has a very good reputation for compliance. The manufacturer conducts the testing and evaluation, a third party is not involved, except under the variant Modules Aa1 and Aa2. In its most basic form, Module A can be considered a manufacturer's declaration of conformity (see question 57). For Module B a notified body is required, as is the case for Modules C to H. Module B is always combined with any one of the Modules C to F. Typical modules are shown in brackets next to product names in the next paragraph.

Products

Products for which New Directives have been published and for which the CE marking is mandatory include low voltage equipment (A); simple pressure vessels (A+, B, Cbis2, F); toys (A); construction products, electromagnetic compatibility (A, B, C); machinery (B,A); personal protective equipment (A, B, Cbis2, D); non-automatic weighing instruments (B, D, F, G); active implantable medical devices (B, D, F, Hbis); gas appliances (B, C, D, F, G); hot water boilers (B, Cbis2, D, E); civil explosives (B, Cbis2, D, E, F, G); medical devices (A to F); potentially explosive atmospheres (A, A+, B, Cbis1, D, E, F); recreational craft (A to H); lifts (A to G); refrigeration appliances (A); pressure equipment (A to G); telecommunication equipment (B, Cbis2, D, H); in vitro diagnostic medical devices (A to H); radio and telecommunication terminal equipment (A, Aa+, H). New Directives have also been published for packaging and packaging waste, high-speed rail systems and marine equipment, but the CE marking is not generally required for these.

FOR MORE INFORMATION

- BSI technical handbooks. http://shop.bsigroup.com/en/Browse-by-Sector/Manufacturing/Technical-handbooks

  Technical publications on electrical equipment, machinery, automotive equipment, pressure vessels, personal protective equipment and construction products and applicable international regulations and approval requirements, CE marking, directives and other legislative requirements.

- European Commission. Guide to the implementation of directives based on the New Approach and the Global Approach. 2008. Available in the 11 EU official languages.
  http://ec.europa.eu/enterprise/policies/single-market-goods/files/blue-guide/guidepublic_en.pdf

  Provides a clear and complete overview of the New Directives and Global Approach system.

- European Commission, Enterprise and Industry. CE marking.
  http://ec.europa.eu/enterprise/policies/single-market-goods/cemarking/index_en.htm

  Information on how the process of affixing the CE marking on a product works. This website leads a manufacturer through the process of affixing the CE marking to his specific product, by clearly illustrating the key steps to undertake from the beginning to the trading of the product.

- European Commission/EFTA/CEN/CENELEC/ETSI . New Approach Standardisation in the Internal Market.
  www.newapproach.org/

  Provides access to information on directives and standards and routes into the standardization process, irrespective of which of the three European standards organizations is responsible for the standards applicable to the products; offers search facility by keywords.

REFERENCES

European Commission

- European standards: List of references of harmonized standards. New Approach directives.
  http://ec.europa.eu/enterprise/policies/european-standards/documents/harmonised-standards-legislation/list-references/
- NANDO (New Approach Notified and Designated Organisations). http://ec.europa.eu/enterprise/newapproach/nando/

B. TESTING

59. What is testing and why is it important in international trade?

For the purposes of this book, the definitions of 'test' and testing' given in 'ISO/IEC 17000:2004 Conformity assessment – Vocabulary and general principles', published jointly by ISO and IEC, are regarded as definitive. Testing is defined as a 'technical operation that consists of determination of one or more characteristics of an object of conformity according to a procedure'. Typical tests involve measurement of dimensions and determination of chemical composition, microbiological purity and strength or other physical characteristics of materials or structures such as freedom from defects.

The results of testing often provide sufficient information to permit a competent person to draw a conclusion as to whether or not a product or service meets requirements specified by regulatory authorities, buyers or other users. In other cases, such as in-service inspection of elevators and motor vehicles, inspection (see question 65) alone may be sufficient. It is important to recognize that the boundaries between testing and inspection are quite blurred as there is some overlap; the same activity may be labelled as being in either field.

The broad field is called 'conformity assessment', comprising testing, inspection and certification. While testing and inspection are very common means of determining conformity, in some cases, testing or inspection alone is regarded as insufficient by either the regulator or the customer. In some product sectors, certification by a third-party is also required.

This is the case in product sectors where products may be of relatively low volume and high risk. Examples are implantable medical devices and electrical equipment for use in explosive environments. Such certification of products is always underpinned by testing and/or inspection. Certification against systems standards (e.g. ISO 9001, ISO 14001) is available for any service or manufacturing activity and does not involve testing to the same extent as where full technical conformance is required to be demonstrated.

Testing is most often conducted in a laboratory, either before dispatch or upon delivery to the customer. However, in many cases it may be performed in the field or on-site following delivery or installation. This is true of large or complex machinery and welded pipelines and rail tracks.

Standards and conformity assessment have been recognized as trade barriers for many years and were first addressed internationally during the Tokyo Round of the GATT negotiations in the early 1970s. The result was the development of the GATT Standards Code of 1979 – the precursor of the WTO TBT Agreement. Bodies with trade policy interests, such as WTO, the European Commission and the Asia-Pacific Economic Cooperation forum (APEC), have continued to acknowledge that the lack of acceptance or recognition of foreign test results remains one of the most serious impediments to free trade.

Regulatory authorities and commercial buyers of foreign products frequently require testing at the point of import or delivery by their own designated laboratories even when adequate testing has been performed in the country of manufacture. These practices have led to the development of mutual recognition agreements and arrangements, discussed further in question 91, to minimize their impact.

Such policies are regarded as technical barriers to trade because they add cost through duplication and delays. If the testing carried out at the point of manufacture is performed competently and in accordance with the requirements of the customer or of the import market, then there is no technical reason for the product to be retested unless conditions during transit may cause the product to deteriorate.

A prudent manufacturer will always ensure that a non-conforming product is not shipped and will have had the product designed and tested to comply with the requirements of the foreign market prior to shipment. Any delay in entry into the foreign market reduces the product's competitive advantages by increasing costs (for instance, for retesting) and delaying payment, to the benefit of competitors and domestic suppliers. If testing in the exporting country is carried out competently, this greatly reduces the need for any retesting prior to release on to the importing market.

Not all testing is conformity assessment and a substantial amount of testing is concerned with data collection rather than simply product compliance. Some of this may relate to matters such as environmental measurements that may not be associated with a particular product but which may still have trade implications.

As manufactured goods become more technically sophisticated and market demands grow more stringent, testing will become an increasingly important part of trade protocols. The move to freer trade will call for greater recognition of testing carried out in the country of origin, but this can happen only if end users can have confidence in the competence of the laboratories conducting the tests in the first place. The ultimate objective is to have your product tested and certified once, and then accepted everywhere (see question 91).

REFERENCES

International Organization for Standardization and International Electrotechnical Commission. ISO/IEC 17000:2004, Conformity assessment – Vocabulary and general principles. Obtainable from ISO or ISO members (list at www.iso.org) and from IEC or IEC National Committees (list at www.iec.ch).

60. How do I ensure that the test report for my product is accepted overseas?

There is no single system, covering all products and sectors, to ensure that test reports from an exporting country will be accepted in the importing market. It is also true to say that for some markets different rules apply within particular sectors depending on product types and the policies of individual regulators, who may have high levels of independence in the way they operate their particular sectors (a vertical system). This may be contrasted with a horizontal system in which all regulators operate within general rules as in the EU Global Approach.

This occurs, for instance, in markets like the United States and Japan, where there are very vertical systems of regulation. The US Food and Drug Administration (USFDA), US Department of Agriculture (USDA) and the Federal Communications Commission (FCC) all have different attitudes to recognition of foreign testing laboratories. USFDA requires that it may provide direct supervision of all manufacturers, wherever they are located, while the FCC will accept results from foreign laboratories accredited by particular accreditation bodies. Rather than rely on accreditation, Japanese authorities often demand specific endorsement from the government of the exporting country before they recognize a foreign laboratory's test data.

It is therefore the responsibility of the exporter, manufacturer or importing agent to ensure that the rules of the market for the particular product have been satisfied.

Any recognition of a test report, whether it is domestic or foreign, requires its acceptance by all regulatory authorities having an interest in the product and by the buyer in the intended market. Commercial buyers, large retail chains for instance, may have quality requirements beyond the safety demands of the regulator, so both interests need to be accommodated. Clearly, without regulator acceptance, no product can be sold to anyone, but the demands of the commercial market must also be considered.

The general principles laid down in the WTO Agreement on Technical Barriers to Trade (the TBT Agreement), state that technical barriers are to be avoided and that Members are strongly encouraged to accept conformity assessment performed in the country of origin. These principles recognize, however, that, with certain provisions, countries are entitled to determine their own levels of protection and to be assured of the competence of foreign bodies providing conformity assessment reports. While the TBT Agreement mentions the application of mutual recognition agreements (MRAs), based on accreditation, as suitable tools for giving confidence in competence, it also permits the development of other confidence-building measures such as exchanges of experts and testing intercomparisons over extended periods of time. Question 91 addresses MRAs in more detail.

Recognition or otherwise of accreditation is the prerogative of the importing country, and not of the exporting country.

With respect to MRAs, the TBT Agreement refers to government actions and policies. This means that MRAs may be negotiated between two or more governments, which one expects then to become binding on the participating governments. Two well-known examples of MRAs are those of the International Laboratory Accreditation Cooperation (ILAC) and the International Accreditation Forum (IAF). However, they are in the private sector and governments are free to recognize such agreements or not, as they see fit. Similarly, the private commercial sector is not bound by such agreements and individual users must decide for themselves whether or not such agreements provide them with adequate confidence in the conformity assessment activities of the parties involved. ILAC and IAF are aware of these factors and pay much attention to the degree of recognition afforded to their MRAs and to addressing any potential weaknesses in them.

In summary, while WTO urges Members to accept testing performed in the country of export, there is a wide range of mechanisms that are used in different jurisdictions. These require that the testing laboratory providing the data be:

- Operated by the regulatory authority of the importing country;
- One with a good reputation established with the accepting authority;
- Recognized by the regulatory body;

- Accredited by the national body of the importing country;
- Recognized by one of the partners under a government-to-government MRA; or
- Accredited by a body within the ILAC Arrangement.

In today's trading environment, accreditation is the most widely used tool for establishing and maintaining confidence in the competence of conformity assessment bodies, but it is the responsibility of the exporter to understand the rules of the importing market. For an insight into the practical application of ISO/IEC 17025 to seafood and other fishery products in the European Union, **see** link in For more information.

FOR MORE INFORMATION

- European Commission, Directorate General for Health & Consumers. EU import conditions for seafood and other fishery products. http://ec.europa.eu/food/international/trade/im_cond_fish_en.pdf

  In the European Union, accreditation to ISO/IEC 17025 is needed for fishery products. For an analytical result of fishery products to have 'official' validity, it must come from a laboratory accredited for the parameters to be analysed.

- International Laboratory Accreditation Cooperation. Success stories from ILAC Signatories. Marketing & Communications Committee (MCC). http://www.ilac.org/successstories.html

  ILAC MCC has been asking its members to provide 'good news' stories that emphasize the benefits accreditation and the ILAC Arrangement have brought to a variety of stakeholders. A collection of good news stories is available on the ILAC website.

- International Organization for Standardization and International Electrotechnical Commission. ISO/IEC 17025:2005, General requirements for the competence of testing and calibration laboratories. Obtainable from ISO or ISO members (list at www.iso.org) and from IEC or IEC National Committees (list at www.iec.ch).

  ISO/IEC 17025:2005 specifies the general requirements for competence to carry out tests and/or calibrations, including sampling. It covers testing and calibration performed using standard methods, non-standard methods and laboratory-developed methods.

- United Nations Industrial Development Organization. Complying with ISO 17025: A practical guidebook for meeting the requirements of laboratory accreditation schemes based on ISO 17025:2005 or equivalent national standards. http://www.unido.org/fileadmin/user_media/Publications/Pub_free/Complying_with_ISO_17025_A_practical_guidebook.pdf

  A guidebook on how to meet the requirements of laboratory accreditation schemes based on ISO 17025:2005 or equivalent national standards.

REFERENCES

World Trade Organization. Agreement on Technical Barriers to Trade. http://www.wto.org/english/tratop_e/tbt_e/tbt_e.htm

61. Why is proficiency testing important and where can I find proficiency testing providers?

Proficiency testing (PT) is a set of organized programmes for practical testing comparisons between laboratories that provides an objective method for judging the actual performance of individual laboratories within a group of laboratories and gives a confirmation of competence. Some laboratory recognition or approval schemes rely entirely on this form of assessment but it is more common to find proficiency testing being used to support other laboratory assessments such as accreditation and peer assessment. In all circumstances, a consistent successful participation in professionally managed PT programmes is necessary to maintain a recognition status in all approval schemes.

It is important to acknowledge that participation in a single PT programme is of very limited value as it provides only a 'snapshot' of a laboratory's performance and a successful result may have been only a matter of chance. Similarly, an unsatisfactory outcome may equally be a matter of a simple error that inevitably occurs in all laboratories from time to time, but that does not mean that that the laboratory is not competent. The important issues are consistent performance over an extended period and the use of proficiency testing data by the laboratory as a tool for improving management systems and the technical performance of personnel.

Approval programmes based on proficiency testing alone demand frequent participation and rigorous analysis of results along with immediate attention to corrective actions. They are very expensive to operate and for some areas of testing they are virtually impossible to maintain. Some calibration and other non-destructive proficiency testing programmes require extremely long time frames to complete and have limited value as approval programmes. For these reasons, accreditation systems, which are based on some form of peer review in accordance with ISO/IEC 17011:2004 and ISO/IEC 17025:2005 (see References for the titles of these standards), use proficiency testing as an essential element of their surveillance arrangements, but they are not sufficient for accreditation or recognition per se.

Many forms of proficiency testing have been developed, since testing and measurement are used as a basis for acceptance of goods. Traditionally, programmes were operated by one of the parties to the sale, either the buyer or the seller, but in recent years there has been a substantial growth in proficiency testing as a third-party activity, with providers focused on the provision of such services on a commercial basis. Standards such as ISO/IEC 17043:2010 have been developed to enhance the reliability of such programmes, while accreditation systems have been initiated to add credibility to the competence of the providers.

The tools for proficiency testing (interlaboratory comparison tools) are also used in method validation and studies related to the development of standard test methods such as assessing the robustness of a particular method. The same tools are utilized by reference material producers when using an interlaboratory comparison involving a number of competent laboratories to assign values and associated uncertainties to certified reference materials.

The International Committee for Weights and Measures (CIPM) also employs a specialized form of interlaboratory comparison (Key Comparisons) to monitor the calibration and measurement capabilities of national measurement laboratories (see question 79). PT programmes themselves are sometimes used in this context and they not infrequently reveal challenges associated with the application of some standards and traditional methods. This factor alone adds substantial value to proficiency testing regimes.

Any Internet search for proficiency testing providers will yield many hundreds of responses. Some providers specialize in narrow fields, such as medical testing, waters and foods, while others offer programmes across a number of fields. The most comprehensive source of information on PT programmes is the database of the European Proficiency Testing Information System (EPTIS, link provided below), which cross-references the sites of over a thousand PT providers worldwide.

International proficiency testing programmes offer a wide range of materials and competently run programmes. However, international air transport rules and many national customs and quarantine regulations inhibit complete reliance on PT programmes from foreign sources, particularly where materials may be associated with hazards such as toxicity or flammability. Where possible, it is desirable to have a national capability to provide some proficiency testing, especially in those technical areas where there is significant domestic usage or production. ISO/DTR 11773 provides information on the global distribution of reference materials.

In recent years, with the greatly enlarged demand for proficiency testing, there has been some concern about the competence of PT providers and the desirability of having some form of accreditation system for them. Some ILAC members now offer such a service which provides greater transparency and fairness.

FOR MORE INFORMATION

- European Proficiency Testing Information System (EPTIS). www.eptis.bam.de

  EPTIS is a cooperation of 39 partner organizations from all continents. Most of these are national metrology institutes, testing institutes or accreditation bodies. The EPTIS database contains a list of proficiency testing schemes (PT schemes) operated in Europe, the Americas and in Australia, both accredited and non-accredited. The information contained in the database is based on self-declarations from the proficiency testing providers.

- International Laboratory Accreditation Cooperation Benefits for Laboratories Participating in Proficiency Testing Programs. 2008. http://www.ilac.org/documents/ILAC_PT_Brochure.pdf

  Didactic brochure that discusses the confirmation of competent performance, how to identify testing or measurement problems, and how to compare methods and procedures, among others.

- The American Association for Laboratory Accreditation. R302 – General Requirements: Accreditation of ISO/IEC 17043 Proficiency Testing Providers. 2011. http://www.a2la.org/requirements/PT_PROVIDERS_ACCREDITATION_REQUIREMENTS.pdf

  This document sets forth the general requirements for the A2LA (American Association for Laboratory Accreditation) accreditation of proficiency testing providers. The A2LA is a non-profit, non-governmental public service membership organization dedicated to operating a nationwide broad spectrum accreditation system.

REFERENCES

International Organization for Standardization

- ISO Guide 35:2006, Reference materials – General and statistical principles for certification. Obtainable from ISO or ISO members (list at www.iso.org).
- ISO/DTR 11773, Global Distribution of Reference Materials. Obtainable from ISO or ISO members (list at www.iso.org).

International Organization for Standardization and International Electrotechnical Commission

- ISO/IEC 17025:2005, General requirements for the competence of testing and calibration laboratories. Obtainable from ISO or ISO members (list at www.iso.org) and from IEC or IEC National Committees (list at www.iec.ch).
- ISO/IEC 17011:2004, Conformity assessment – General requirements for accreditation bodies accrediting conformity assessment bodies. Obtainable from ISO or ISO members (list at www.iso.org), and from IEC or IEC National Committees (list at www.iec.ch).
- ISO/IEC 17043:2010, Conformity assessment – General requirements for proficiency testing. Obtainable from ISO or ISO members (list at www.iso.org), and from IEC or IEC National Committees (list at www.iec.ch).

62. Should I set up my own testing laboratory or use external laboratories?

Fundamentally, this is a financial decision. For most products, access to a competent laboratory is essential for testing for control of the manufacturing process and for the final acceptance tests prior to release on to the market. Laboratories are expensive to establish and maintain, even at the most rudimentary level. Generally, the more sophisticated the tests required, the greater the capital costs and the higher the staffing and maintenance costs.

Anyone considering the question therefore must address a number of issues, as detailed below, and balance the costs and benefits.

The first consideration is the likely volume of testing that will be required. Is it envisaged that there will be any component of product development? This may provide added motivation to establish facilities. What is the inherent variability in the product and processes and does this mean that immediate access to laboratory facilities is necessary? What is the mandatory level of testing for acceptance purposes?

When considering possible outsourcing of laboratory activities, a common practice is to maintain some testing capacity in-house while engaging the services of more specialized facilities for tests where it is judged that it is not worthwhile to develop an in-house capability. An example is the determination of very low levels of residues in fish products. This also raises the question of convenience of access to suitable external facilities.

Where there are groups of smaller producers in near proximity, it is not uncommon that a commercial laboratory, offering comprehensive services to all, may be established by one of the international companies or as a local initiative.

In addition to the direct costs of testing, other considerations include the potential costs that may arise because of inadequate testing. What are the risks and costs of product failure? What are the safety issues associated with the manufacturing process and the use of the product in the field? What are the likely costs of product rejection on attempted entry to a market and associated recalls, reworking of product or destroying that which is non-redeemable, etc.?

Another element for consideration, particularly for developing countries, has to do with any difficulties associated with access to maintenance, consumables and other necessary technical support for testing equipment. Where such difficulties are insurmountable and if the particular tests are required, then outsourcing to an external laboratory is the only practical way to have those tests carried out.

There are advantages in having immediate access to in-house testing facilities, particularly where time is important in monitoring the production process, but also in developing a deeper understanding of the product and its behaviour during manufacture.

FOR MORE INFORMATION

- Labnetwork. Key Functions and Test Methods.
  http://www.labnetwork.org/en/component/content/article/37-textile-and-leather/128-key-functions-and-test-methods

  Presents a discussion on dimensional and density measurements, quality control samples, mechanical properties, and product suitability, among others.

63. Why should I have my testing and measuring equipment calibrated and at what intervals?

This question raises a number of concepts that may be unfamiliar to the general reader. The essential purposes of calibration are consistency, reliability and confidence in testing and measurement (see question 87). All interested parties are entitled to trust the integrity of the test and measurement data that they use for whatever purpose. Calibration at the appropriate level is therefore a prerequisite.

Calibration is concerned with giving confidence that the measurements bear a known relationship to fundamental standards – the kilogram, volt, metre, etc. (see question 84). The more accurate the required measurement, the more certain (less uncertainty) must be this relationship between the instrument used for testing and the standard.

Traceable calibration is recognized as the pathway between the measurement and the standard from which it is derived and is described as a documented, unbroken chain of competent intercomparisons between the measuring instrument with other devices of increasingly higher level of accuracy leading back to the fundamental standard. In some cases it is not feasible to demonstrate traceability to units of the International System of Units or SI units (e.g. the pH meter). In these cases, an internationally agreed (and stated) reference is acceptable.

It is also important to recognize that much complex instrumentation is calibrated directly against reference materials, whose provenance satisfies the same principles of linkage to fundamental quantities. However, with the current state of the art reference materials, the reference values may be consensus values rather than absolute values. This reality is reflected in the statement of uncertainty for the value.

All equipment must be calibrated before being put into service, even instruments of low accuracy. It is important to understand that while the accuracy of calibration should only be at the level required for particular tests, all instruments must be checked against a higher level device to ensure that the instrument or system is fit for its intended purposes.

Calibration is dealt with in more detail in the chapter on metrology, but for the purposes of this section, suffice it to say that it is a process of comparing an instrument with another of higher known accuracy and that process continues up the chain to the standard. For most measurement situations, it is necessary to know the range of the probable level of difference of the instrument from the standard at various points – the so-called uncertainty of the measurement. Knowing the relationship with the 'true value' and the uncertainty associated with the measurement, it is possible to estimate corrections to the measurement obtained.

In some tests, however, it is only necessary to know that the instrument is within a specified difference across the operating range. Equipment may be graded 'class A', 'class B', etc. Strictly speaking, this process is called verification but is often referred to as calibration. When using instruments checked in this way, no corrections may be applied and the data produced is accepted at the values given directly from the test. This is the general approach taken in trade measurement.

The performance of measuring and test equipment may change with time, depending on the environment to which it is exposed, wear and tear, overload or because of improper use. This applies to all measuring equipment, not just complex instruments that might be expected to change with time. The accuracy of the measurement given by the equipment needs therefore to be checked from time to time. The period between successive calibrations is called a calibration interval and every calibration after the first is called a recalibration.

Calibration intervals are usually recommended by the manufacturer of the measuring or test equipment, and these should be observed unless circumstances indicate otherwise. The performance of an instrument depends on the care with which it is handled and its use. Operators must always be alert to unusual readings that might indicate some deterioration of the device. In this event, the device should then be withdrawn from service and immediately recalibrated. Recalibration is certainly necessary if the instrument is overloaded in any way, or after the equipment has been exposed to shock, vibration, improper electrical supply or other instances of mishandling. Corrective action is the responsibility of the user of the instrument.

Where the instrument is used within a facility accredited by an external accreditation body, that body may impose mandatory maximum recalibration intervals less than those recommended by the manufacturer. These requirements will take precedence over the manufacturer's recommendations. Even in this situation, however, remember that these are only maximum intervals and the responsibility lies with the user to ensure that the equipment is properly managed and maintained, including adequate calibration, depending on the operational conditions outlined above. The equipment that is in constant use may need unusually short recalibration intervals and may also need spot checking on a daily basis (see question 82).

FOR MORE INFORMATION

- Accredited calibration laboratories are listed by national accreditation bodies. ILAC and regional accreditation organizations maintain websites with links to their members that are national accreditation bodies:
  - Asia Pacific Laboratory Accreditation Cooperation (APLAC). www.aplac.org/membership.html
  - European co-operation for Accreditation (EA). www.european-accreditation.org/content/ea/members.htm
  - InterAmerican Accreditation Cooperation (IAAC). www.iaac.org.mx/English/Members.php
  - International Laboratory Accreditation Cooperation (ILAC). www.ilac.org/documents/mra_signatories.pdf
  - Southern African Development Community Accreditation (SADCA). www.sadca.org/documents/SADCA%20contact%20details-English.pdf
- International Laboratory Accreditation Cooperation and International Organization of Legal Metrology. Guidelines for the determination of calibration intervals of measuring instruments. ILAC-G24/OIML D 10) 2007. www.ilac.org/guidanceseries.html or www.oiml.org/publications/D/D010-e07.pdf

  This document identifies and describes the methods that are available and known for the evaluation of calibration intervals. It is intended for use by calibration laboratories. Normal users of instruments should rely on the recommendations of the manufacturers; however, the document contains information of general interest and may be consulted for a better understanding of the requirements.
- International Organization for Standardization. ISO 10012:2003, Measurement management systems – Requirements for measurement processes and measuring equipment. Obtainable from ISO or ISO members (list at www.iso.org).

  This standard provides guidance for the management of measurement processes and actions necessary to demonstrate compliance of the measuring equipment used with metrological requirements.

64. What is metrological traceability and how can I demonstrate it?

Traceability is an unbroken and documented chain of calibration linking the working instrument to the fundamental measurement standard. Such a chain may be quite long, and the consequence is that uncertainty increases along the way, even though the measuring instrument may still be fit for its intended use.

The fundamental or primary standards are the direct realizations of the International System of Units (SI). In the case of the kilogram it is an artifact in the custody of the International Bureau of Weights and Measures (BIPM) in Paris (see question 84). All other standards are derived by scientific experiments within a limited number of national and other top-level institutions using similar techniques and inter-comparing results among participating laboratories. At this level, there must be strong agreement between laboratories on the actual value before the techniques are adopted as suitable for defining a particular quantity. Such laboratories are constantly searching for better and better realizations of the SI unit and it is only when the international community, through the International Committee for Weights and Measures (CIPM), is satisfied that the new methodologies do indeed produce a more refined standard that it is accepted (see question 91).

Secondary standards are devices that are compared directly with primary standards. They are both very accurate and have very low uncertainties of measurement. For many countries, secondary standards provide the national standard.

Working standards are one level further removed from the primary standard and are directly compared with secondary standards. Working standards are entirely satisfactory for national standards in countries that do not have a sophisticated manufacturing capability. They are entirely acceptable for many industrial and commercial situations. High-level calibration laboratories will also maintain secondary or working standards as their reference standards.

A laboratory seeking calibration of its equipment will normally approach either a specialist calibration laboratory or its national metrology institute or perhaps a foreign calibration service. It will need to ensure that the laboratory providing such services is able to provide calibration at the appropriate range of measurement and at the necessary accuracy and uncertainty of measurement.

Professional calibration laboratories will provide their services at various levels of accuracy depending on the intended use of the equipment. They advertise their services on the basis of available physical quantities, ranges of measurement offered and least uncertainty for each quantity and within each range. For instance, capabilities in regard to the calibration of pressure and vacuum measuring devises may be expressed in the following way:

Calibration to the requirements of AS 1349, ASME B40.1, BS 1780, EN 837-1
and similar standards

Pressure gauges (including test gauges)

From 0 to 70 MPa in air or liquid
with uncertainties of measurement of:
0.02% of reading or 1.4 kPa (whichever is the greater)

Vacuum gauges (Bourdon gauge)

From -95 to 0 kPa
with least uncertainties of measurement of:
0.02 kPa

Note: kPa = kilopascal; MPa = megapascal (a million Pascals)

The increasing international awareness of traceability has led accreditation bodies to pay particular attention to the concept. They have rules and policies for themselves, for accredited calibration laboratories and for accredited laboratories using those services to ensure greater transparency of the process and to enhance their own credibility. Using accredited calibration services is therefore a clear and well-accepted demonstration of traceability.

If, however, non-accredited calibration services are used, it is the responsibility of the user to satisfy himself that there is appropriate traceability. This will require discussion with the calibration service and an examination of its records and other evidence to provide a reasonable level of confidence in any claimed traceability.

FOR MORE INFORMATION

- EURACHEM/Cooperation on International Traceability in Analytical Chemistry. Quantifying Uncertainty in Analytical Measurement. 2nd ed. EURACHEM/CITAC Guide CG 4. http://www.eurachem.org/guides/pdf/QUAM2000-1.pdf

  This guide explicitly provides for the use of validation and related data in the construction of uncertainty estimates in full compliance with formal ISO Guide principles. The second edition of the guide is freely available and the third edition is under development.

- EURAMET. Metrology – In Short. 3rd ed. July 2008. www.euramet.org/. Contact: secretariat@euramet.org

  This booklet contains a comprehensive overview on metrology. It explains important terms, describes international and regional organizations and gives relevant links; it also provides examples of the impact of measurements.

- International Bureau of Weights and Measures (BIPM). The International System of Units (SI). 8th ed. 2006. http://www.bipm.org/utils/common/pdf/si_brochure_8_en.pdf

  Brochure on SI units, writing unit symbols and names, and units outside the SI, among others. Available in several languages.

- European co-operation for Accreditation. Traceability of Measuring and Test Equipment to National Standards. EAL-G12. November 1995. http://www.european-accreditation.org/n1/doc/ea-4-07.pdf. Contact: secretariat@european-accreditation.org

  This publication guides organizations on how to comply with traceability requirements in relevant standards, such as those in the EN ISO 9000 and EN 45000 series.

- International Laboratory Accreditation Cooperation. ILAC Policy on Traceability of Measurement Results. ILAC-P10:2002. http://www.ilac.org/documents/ILAC_P10_2002_ILAC_Policy_on_Traceability_of_Measurement_Result.pdf

  Defines the concept of traceability and measurement results for ILAC.

- International Organization for Standardization. ISO/REMCO for reference materials. http://www.iso.org/iso/remco_2009.pdf

  This booklet can be downloaded from the ISO website for free.

- International Organization for Standardization and International Electrotechnical Commission. ISO/IEC Guide 98-3:2008, Uncertainty of measurement – Part 3: Guide to the expression of uncertainty in measurement (GUM:1995). Obtainable from ISO or ISO members (list at www.iso.org) and from IEC or IEC National Committees (list at www.iec.ch).

- Laboratory Accreditation Bureau. www.l-a-b.com/content/measurement-uncertainty

  Good reference for uncertainty. Look for the answers to the questions: 'What is to be considered in an uncertainty of measurement budget?' and 'How is uncertainty applied to a measurement when making a statement of compliance according to ILAC G8?'

  If you want to know what a provider of a measurement result or value of a standard must document to claim traceability, you will find information on this web page.

C. INSPECTION

65. What are the various types of inspection?

By some definitions, inspection covers all other forms of conformity assessment and it can be considered its oldest form. However, the modern practice is to define inspection more narrowly. Even in this case, however, its scope varies greatly with administrative systems and cultural traditions.

There are numerous definitions of inspection, but all of them include the concepts of information gathering (testing, measuring), observation (of conditions) and forming judgements on suitability for use or compliance with requirements. As judgement is an essential element of the process, inspection is therefore prone to some variability of outcome. For this reason, it is crucial that inspectors be thoroughly trained for the sectors in which they are expected to work.

Inspection is not limited to its application to manufacturing processes and products. It can also be used in diverse activities such as design verification, installation and commissioning of equipment, in-service monitoring, regulatory affairs, financial auditing and failure investigation.

The table below is indicative only of the various interests of organizations that make use of common types of inspection services.

Inspection in trade

Inspection \ User	Manufacturer	Customer	Regulator	Traders
Process control	X			
Compliance in relation to safety and other regulatory issues	X	X	X	X
Design verification		X	X	
Installation of major plant		X	X	
Commission of major plant		X	X	
Maintenance		X	X	
Quantity	X			X
Quality	X	X		X

Source: John Gilmour, Australia.

In many societies, inspection is always and exclusively used in the context of regulatory control, while in others it may also cover commercial supervision by third-party bodies and in-house production control by the manufacturer itself.

In the regulatory sense, inspection may cover mandatory product compliance with technical regulations prior to being made available in the market. In some societies, most notably those belonging to the former Soviet Union, there may be several thousand products that require mandatory approval before release to the market. This practice normally focuses on domestic products but may also apply to imported products in some sectors. While called inspection, such activities are often largely testing leading to a certificate of compliance.

Inspection also includes both pre- and post-market surveillance activities and regular examination of installations for safety purposes. Inspection of this type is applied to common products like motor vehicles, cranes and lifting gear, boilers and pressure vessels, and electrical installations. Probably the most common form of regulatory inspection takes place in the area of food safety and food outlet hygiene. Some inspection activities are associated with excise and taxation supervision.

In the manufacturing sector, inspection, including testing and gauging or measurement, is an essential tool for production control. It may extend to physical examination of in-process product to assess its fitness (e.g. cleanliness) to proceed to the next step. Inspection departments may also be responsible for calibration of process control instrumentation and will carry out any final inspection prior to dispatch to the customer.

Inspection is used in the services sector as well, to establish conformity with performance and service delivery specifications. This can include checks for process readiness or compliance with service procedures and specifications, including timeliness and fulfilment of other critical service characteristics.

In the manufacture of complex products or assemblies or if a non-conforming product may have catastrophic consequences for the customer, it is not uncommon for the customer either to participate in the multi-production inspection process or to engage a third-party inspection body to represent its interests. In all such cases, as in aircraft manufacture and shipbuilding, the customer will pay great attention to the inspection systems adopted by the manufacturer and the management of those systems.

Pre-shipment inspection is usually performed by the manufacturer but, where the product is being exported, additional inspection may be required at the point of shipping. 'Cargo superintending' is the term often applied to this activity. It involves not only inspection of the product but also of its packaging, handling, quantity and documentation. The cargo superintending company acts as the customer's agent.

When countries have products which they have designated as being of particularly high value but which are prone to damage during transportation or when they wish to bolster or protect an image in the market, governments themselves may impose an inspection prior to shipment. This was a key strategy of Japan for a number of products such as quality optical equipment. Australia also requires export certification for a range of perishable food products.

Finally, the customer may impose additional inspection at the point of receipt.

A number of countries impose import inspection for the purpose of ensuring freedom from disease, rather than because of any concern over quality. Such regimes are most rigorous for countries that are generally free of animal and plant diseases such as Australia and New Zealand but may also be imposed as an emergency measure where outbreaks of human diseases occur. Importing countries may designate private organizations as their agents to conduct pre-export inspection or approve import consignments in relation to official requirements.

While inspection may be the oldest form of conformity assessment, it has been the last to be internationally standardized. The pervasive use of inspection throughout all industries led the European Union to introduce a common standard (EN 45004 General Criteria for the Operation of Various Types of Bodies Performing Inspection) when it created the single market. This initiative was followed by the international community when it adopted EN 45004 as ISO/IEC 17020:1998, which carries the same title and is identical with the EN. This standard is now used by accreditation bodies to accredit inspection bodies in a number of countries.

The standard defines types of inspection bodies on the basis of formal separation from possible sources of influence:

- Type A bodies are those not directly linked to an organization involved with the design, manufacture, use or maintenance of items under inspection;
- Type B bodies may form part of a user or supplier organization but must be identifiably separate from the parent;
- Type C bodies are similar to type B but are not required to be identifiably separate from the parent.

The major uptake of the standard by inspection bodies has been in the commercial sector. Regulatory inspection services have tended to maintain their traditional systems.

In most developed economies, commercial inspection activities have an impact across all sectors, and are generally concerned with safety, customer satisfaction and the quality of manufactured products. There is also a trend for governments, and their regulators, and other large procurement agencies to outsource inspection functions to commercial inspection bodies.

FOR MORE INFORMATION

- Anjoran, Renaud. Quality Inspection Tips. Practical Advice for Importers Sourcing in Asia. February 2010. http://www.qualityinspection.org/quality-inspection-services/

  Gives an interesting diagram on the four types of quality inspection services: pre-production inspection, inspection during production, final random inspection, and container loading inspection. A click on the name of each service will take the reader to further information on the service.

- FAO/WHO. Codex Alimentarius – Food Import and Export Inspection and Certification Systems. Combined Texts. 2005. ISBN 92-5-105321-9. ftp://ftp.fao.org/docrep/fao/008/y6396e/y6396e00.pdf

  Following the FAO/WHO Conference on Food Standards, Chemicals in Food and Food Trade in March 1991, the Codex Alimentarius Commission undertook the development of guidance documents for governments and other interested parties on food import and export inspection and certification systems. This guide includes texts up to 2004.

- International Accreditation Forum and International Laboratory Accreditation Cooperation. Guidance on the Application of ISO/IEC 17020. 2004. IAF/ILAC-A4:2004. www.ilac.org/ilaciafjoint.html

  This guidance document forms the basis of mutual recognition arrangements between accreditation bodies and is considered necessary for the consistent application of ISO/IEC 17020.

- International Labour Organization. Using Inspection Checklists for Quality Control. http://www.ilofip.org/GPGs/Using%20Inspection%20Checklists.pdf

  This 'Good Practice Guide' focuses on the use of inspection checklists for quality control.

- Observations on the Use and Usefulness of Pre-Shipment Inspection Services. Mark Dutz. World Bank Discussion Paper No. 278. The World Bank, Washington, D.C. 1998. http://siteresources.worldbank.org/INTRANETTRADE/Resources/Dutz.pdf

  The paper reviews available evidence of the effectiveness of pre-shipment inspection (PSI) services in three areas: disbursement verification, revenue collection and trade facilitation.

- Sakthivel, K. Various Methods of Inspection Systems for Apparels. Fibre2fashion. http://www.fibre2fashion.com/industry-article/printarticle.asp?article_id=1483&page=1

  An example of quality inspection applied to the garment industry.

REFERENCES

International Organization for Standardization and International Electrotechnical Commission. ISO/IEC 17020:1998, General criteria for the operation of various types of bodies performing inspection. Obtainable from ISO or ISO members (list at www.iso.org) and from IEC or IEC National Committees (list at www.iec.ch).

66. How does inspection relate to other forms of conformity assessment and what is its place in international trade?

In technical terms, activities commonly referred to as inspection range from what might otherwise be labelled 'testing' through to 'certification'. At the technical end of the spectrum, inspection bodies will undertake **tests** that might otherwise be conducted in a formal laboratory environment and inspection is an integral part of all product certification programmes. In its simplest form, inspection consists of visual examination, which may, however, demand great knowledge, skill and experience on the part of the inspector. In this form, inspection may be the sole tool for certification.

As discussed in Question 65, inspection includes many elements of other forms of conformity assessment but is distinguished by the degree of subjectivity and judgement inherent in many situations. 'Is this article fit for purpose? Is it safe?' are questions that may require both objective data (test results) and the judgement of a knowledgeable and experienced inspector. Such questions may also form part of the decision-making process on whether or not to issue a certificate of compliance for batches of product or for individual products or installations.

Because inspection has very strong traditions in some countries and in some industry sectors, there are differences of opinion as to the types of documents that should be called 'certificates' and those that should not and when the preferred title of such documents should be 'report'. Unfortunately, such subtleties are not always recognized by legislation and the authorities. This answer to question 66 attempts to take the pragmatic view, recognizing the variation that exists.

ILAC and IAF have jointly published a guidance document (A4 2004) which addresses these overlaps between the three conformity assessment elements.

In the context of trade, inspection is used to control and monitor not only the quality and technical aspects of the import and export products, but also quantity, packaging, handling and logistics.

For non-perishable goods, import inspection may simply involve checking documentation to ensure that the goods as dispatched match those received in both quantity and condition. In this situation inspection will normally be a purely visual examination without recourse to retesting.

Perishable materials are subject to much more rigorous inspection at the point of import as importing authorities and customers need to be assured that the goods were properly transported from the point of manufacture or production and that the goods being received are in a condition fit for sale. This may entail some selective re-examination of the product's biological condition. Again, the final inspection is a combination of observation and measurement.

Some countries have very stringent quarantine requirements, as permitted by the WTO SPS Agreement, and certain classes of products are always subject to very thorough inspection at the point of import where the emphasis is on freedom from pests and diseases that may cause serious problems for agriculture in the importing country. Most often this will be a visual examination for signs of infestations by insects or plant diseases such as moulds and fungi.

FOR MORE INFORMATION

- International Organization for Standardization and United Nations Industrial Development Organization National Standards Bodies in Developing Countries. http://www.iso.org/iso/fast_forward.pdf

  Covers the main principles of standardization at national, regional and international levels and illustrates the structural elements from which it is necessary to choose in order to manage the process at a national level. Figure 1 (page 11) has an interesting perspective on how metrology, accreditation, conformity assessment, standardization and an efficient trading system are interconnected.

REFERENCES

International Accreditation Forum and International Laboratory Accreditation Cooperation. Guidance on the Application of ISO/IEC 17020. 2004. IAF/ILAC-A4:2004. www.ilac.org/ilaciafjoint.html

67. How do I obtain approval to export products subject to SPS measures?

The basic rule is that goods can be exported if they meet the official requirements, including SPS requirements, of the importing country. It is the responsibility of the exporter to ensure that the goods conform to the relevant requirements, and typically there is no need for intervention by the authorities of the exporting country. Most goods do not require 'approval' to be exported. The importing country may check the goods on arrival to verify that they conform with local food standards, or are free of pests and diseases, before allowing entry. These checks are not usually referred to as 'approval' procedures.

However, in some instances, importing countries impose requirements for the inspection of goods in the country of origin as a condition for entry into their markets. For instance, importing countries may specify that commodities like fresh meat and seafood must be inspected and certified by competent official bodies in the exporting country as a condition for entry into the import market. The protocols for such inspection – as is the case for fresh meat destined for the EU and United States markets – may be extremely detailed and their implementation may be subject to verification by relevant bodies in the importing country. Often the rules for pre-export inspection will include a requirement for registration of export establishments (e.g. abattoirs and fish-processing plants) from which products will be eligible for export.

In another instance, importing countries may require shipments of fresh fruit and vegetables to be accompanied by a phytosanitary certificate issued by the authorities of the exporting country. The certificate should attest that the products have been fumigated or inspected, thus ensuring that there are no quarantine pests present.

Information on such requirements can be obtained from the competent authority in the exporting country. It can also be sought from the local mission of the importing country, or from appropriate authorities in the importing country. An export promotion agency may also be able to assist.

Importing countries may ask private organizations to conduct on their behalf pre-export inspection or approval of import consignments in relation to official requirements. For example, a certificate may be required from an independent body (a 'third-party certifier') stating that a consignment of food meets the food standards of the importing country. In this case, exporters should approach the certifying agent to obtain information on the specific requirements that are applicable. Typically, a fee will be levied for the inspection and certification services provided by third-party certifiers.

Under the Food Safety Modernization Act 2011, the Food and Drug Administration of the United States has the authority to require certification by an accredited third-party auditor for imported foods and the facilities they come from, depending on type, history or region. Third parties may be foreign governments or private auditors who meet accreditation requirements.

Some countries, such as Australia, operate import control regimes under which, for certain kinds of goods such as fresh fruits and vegetables, importation is prohibited unless the importing country authorities have set specific conditions for allowing imports on the basis of a risk analysis. In such situations, it will be necessary for the government of the exporting country to request the authorities of the importing country to establish the specific conditions under which market access can occur.

The operation of official approval procedures is subject to the provisions of Annex C of the SPS Agreement. In brief, the provisions require that control, inspection and approval procedures should be transparent, efficient and not unduly onerous. Since the conduct of a risk analysis by an importing country may mean that the authorities of the exporting country have to collect and supply a great deal of scientific and other data to their counterparts in the importing country, official market access requests can use up significant resources. Such requests should therefore be justified by the likely volume of export trade should a successful outcome be attained.

FOR MORE INFORMATION

- Bathan, Bates and Flordeliza Lantican. Economic Impact of Sanitary and Phytosanitary Measures on Philippine Pineapple Exports. *Journal of ISSAAS* vol. 15, No. 1, 2009, pp. 126-143. http://www.issaas.org/journal/v15/01/journal-issaas-v15n1-bathan-lantican.pdf

  This paper examines the economic impact of sanitary and phytosanitary measures on Philippine pineapple exports under the WTO SPS Agreement and in the face of the requirements of importing countries.

- Ministry of Agriculture, Government of India. Standard Operating Procedures for Export Inspection and Phytosanitary Certification of Plants/ Plant Products & other Regulated Articles. December 2007. http://plantquarantineindia.org/pdffiles/SOP-Export%20Inspection.pdf

  Provides guidance for the operation of a national export certification system in India and prescribes standard operating procedures for a valid and credible phytosanitary certification procedure for export consignments of plants and plant products and other regulated articles. The objective is to meet the phytosanitary requirements of importing countries while fulfilling the international obligations enshrined in the International Plant Protection Convention and WTO SPS Agreement.

- Neeliah, Shalini and others. Sanitary and phytosanitary issues for fishery exports to the European Union: A Mauritian insight. February 2011. http://www.academicjournals.org/jdae/PDF/Pdf2011/Feb/Neeliah%20et%20al.pdf

  Paper discusses the effect of SPS measures on the agro-food trade of Mauritius. The paper argues that the country should adopt not only a reactive but also an increasingly proactive stance to secure its market, to tap emerging ones and to safeguard its image as a safe fish exporter.

- Strickland, Ella. EU Sanitary and Phytosanitary Standards. Uganda. 2010. http://trade.ec.europa.eu/doclib/docs/2010/december/tradoc_147162.pdf

  PowerPoint presentation discussing the EU market and the implications of SPS measures for developing countries.

- Will, Margret and Doris Guenther. Food Quality and Safety Standards. As required by EU law and the Private Industry. A Practitioner's Reference Book. 2nd ed. GTZ. 2007. http://www2.gtz.de/dokumente/bib/07-0800.pdf

  Reference book for food quality management systems; discusses legislative and industry market requirements in the European Union for selected product groups such as fresh and processed fruits and vegetables.

REFERENCES

SPS: The Sanitary and Phytosanitary Export Database. http://madb.europa.eu/madb_barriers/indexPubli_sps.htm

US Food and Drug Administration. The New FDA Food Safety Modernization Act (FSMA). http://www.fda.gov/food/foodsafety/fsma/default.htm

World Trade Organization. Sanitary and Phytosanitary Agreement – Annex C. http://www.wto.org/english/tratop_e/sps_e/spsagr_e.htm

D. CERTIFICATION

68. What is product certification and how can it be obtained?

Product certification basics

Product certification is the mechanism whereby a certification organization attests that products, either a batch or the continuous production thereof, have been inspected and tested by it and that the products collectively comply with specified requirements, usually contained in a standard (see question 13). The attestation by the certification organization is in the form of a certificate supported by a product certification mark that the manufacturer or producer affixes on the product after being licensed to do so. The certification organization therefore provides an assurance about the quality of the product.

Product certification services are offered by many certification organizations, in both public and private domains, at the national and international levels. In developing economies, national standards bodies frequently provide the only product certification with any market relevance. In developed economies, private certification bodies are often more important from a market perspective. Product certification is mostly accepted only in the home market of the certification organization, but a few operate successfully at the regional or even at the international level.

Typical examples of product certification marks are the BSI Kitemark (general products – United Kingdom), the SABS mark (general products – South Africa), the GS mark (product safety – Germany), the VDE mark (electrical and electronic equipment – Germany), the UL mark (product safety – United States), the ASME mark (pressure vessels – United States), the CSA mark (general products – Canada), KEMA (electrical equipment – the Netherlands) and AGMARK (agricultural products – India). There are many, many more. It should be noted that the CE mark is not a product certification mark but a regulatory device of the European Union (see question 58).

Processes can be certified as complying with stated requirements and in accordance with the definition of 'product'. Such process certification is also considered product certification. An example is the certification of 'good agricultural practices' or GAP.

The process of product certification

The process will always include an assessment of the product, whether sampled at the factory, from the batch or from the marketplace. It may include an audit of the manufacturing processes initially or on a continuous basis, or it may just be based on surveillance testing in the market. Compliance with management systems such as ISO 9001 (see question 69) or HACCP may be required (see question 46). Once compliance has been demonstrated, the manufacturer may be licensed to affix the product certification mark of the certification organization on the product or on the packaging or both, thereby denoting compliance with the standard. The table below broadly illustrates the different types of product certification as defined in ISO/IEC Guide 67.

System (ISO/IEC Guide 67)	Description
System 1a and 1b	Batch inspection
System 2	Surveillance testing on the open market
System 3	Testing of products in the factory
System 4	Type testing plus production control
System 5	Type testing plus quality assurance including market surveillance
System 6	Services

Some certificates are valid for a specific period (typically a year), after which the certification organization will conduct a review and reissue the certificate. Others have no time limit – as long as the manufacturer meets the requirements and pays the annual fees, the certificate stays valid.

Obviously, the manufacturer has to pay for the certification process. Payments will cover the testing of the product (initial and control tests after licensing), the initial and surveillance audits of the manufacturing process, clearance of any non-conformances found during the audits, the annual licence fee, etc. The licence fee may be a flat fee, but it is more commonly related to the number of units produced with the mark. It is very difficult to provide information on the typical pricing of product certification, and manufacturers are urged to obtain up-to-date information from the relevant certification body. A rule of thumb that has proven useful is that the total cost of product certification would typically add 1% to 2.5% to the factory cost of the product.

Product certification process

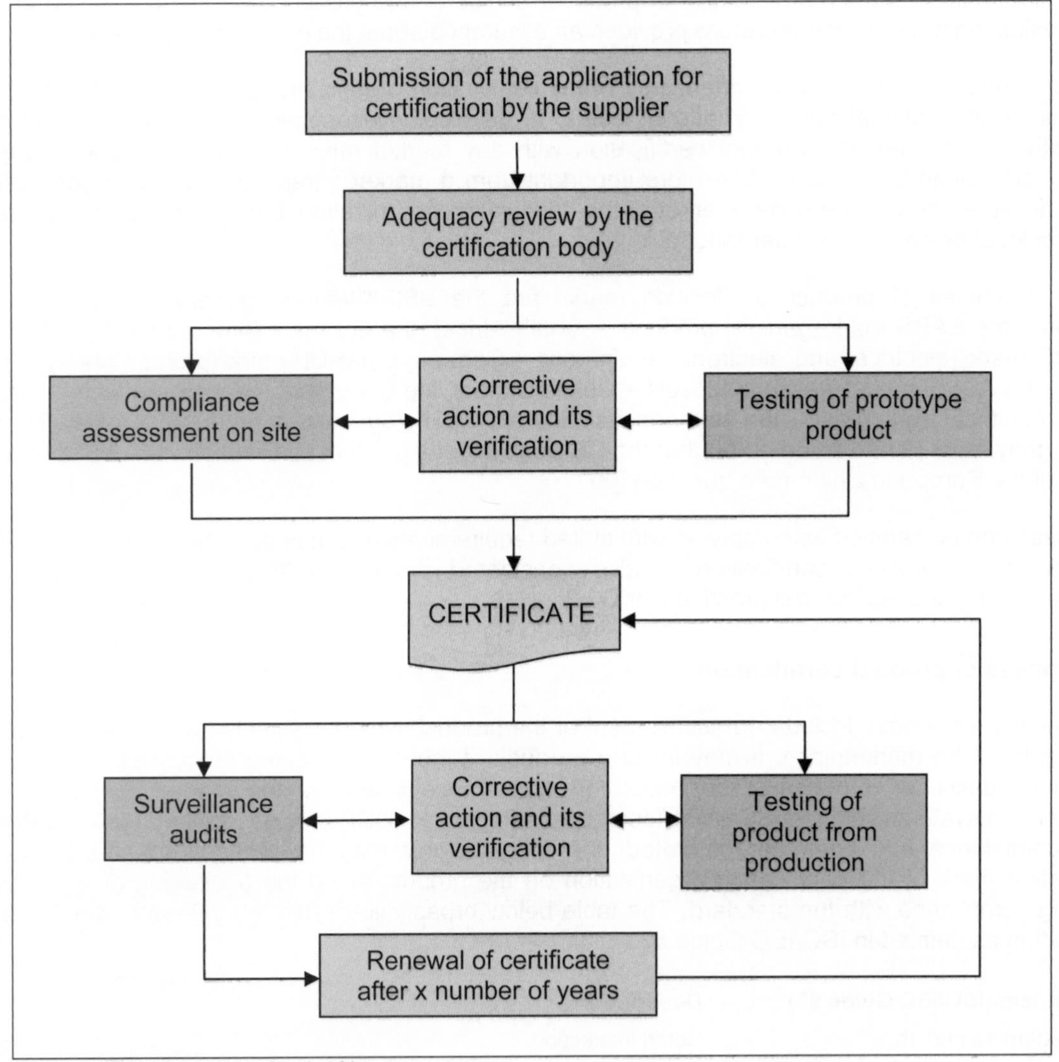

Source: Martin Kellermann, South Africa.

Value of product certification

Why would you need product certification? Some of the reasons may include:

- The manufacturer wants to build its reputation, expand its market share, gain access to new markets, improve competitiveness, or promote new products.

- The purchaser (e.g. individual, stockist, manufacturer, public procurement organization, importer, supplier, employer) wishes to have an independent guarantee of the quality of the product purchased.
- In some countries, product certification marks are considered evidence that the product meets technical regulations or mandatory standards. The CSA mark (electronic products – Canada), the ASME mark (pressure vessels – United States), the BIS mark (LPG cylinders – India), the TBS mark (compulsory standards – United Republic of Tanzania) are typical examples.

FOR MORE INFORMATION

- Agricultural Marketing Information Network (AGMARK) India. www.agmarknet.nic.in/

  Provides information on AGMARK's quality grading and certification for export and the domestic trade, as well as at the farm level grading.
- American Society of Mechanical Engineers (ASME), United States. www.asme.org
- BSI Kitemark, United Kingdom. www.bsigroup.com

  The Kitemark is that of BSI, a non-profit, private organization that is involved in the development of private, national and international standards, the assessment and certification of management systems and medical devices, the testing and certification of products and services, the provision of governance, risk and compliance solutions, and training services.
- Bureau of Indian Standards (BIS). www.bis.org.in/
- Canadian Standards Association (CSA). www.csa-international.org
- Geprüfte Sicherheit (GS) Mark, Germany. http://www.tuv.com/uk/en/tuev_rheinland_gs_mark.html

  The Geprüfte Sicherheit ('Tested Safety') or GS mark is a voluntary certification mark for technical equipment. It indicates that the equipment meets German and, if available, European safety requirements for such devices. The main difference between the GS and CE marks is that compliance with European safety requirements has been tested and inspected by a State-approved (but independent) body. Several certification bodies, such as TUV, offer the GS mark.
- International Organization for Standardization and United Nations Industrial Development Organization. Building Trust – The Conformity Assessment Toolbox. Geneva, 2009. www.iso.org/iso/casco_building-trust.pdf

  Extensive and in-depth overview of all the various types of conformity assessment systems that are available, their advantages, risks and acceptability in the marketplace.
- KEMA, Netherlands. www.kema.comSouth African Bureau of Standards (SABS). www.sabs.co.za/index.php?page=certcprocess
- Tanzania Bureau of Standards (TBS). http://www.tbstz.org/
- Underwriters Laboratories Inc. (UL), United States. www.ul.com
- Verband der Elektrotechnik Elektronik Informationstechnik (VDE), Germany. www.vde.com

REFERENCES

International Organization for Standardization and International Electrotechnical Commission. ISO/IEC Guide 67:2004, Conformity assessment – Fundamentals of product certification. Geneva. 2004. Obtainable from ISO or ISO members (list at: www.iso.org) and IEC or IEC National Committees (www.iec.ch).

69. What is management system certification?

Management system certification basics

In product certification, the product is attested (see question 68). Management system certification deals with the processes and procedures of the manufacturer, producer, supplier or service provider. The management system can be assessed against the requirements of the relevant standards and, if found to conform, certified by a certification body.

These two certification systems therefore have one fundamental difference. In product certification, the quality of the product is attested as conforming to a specific standard; it is normally a supplier-consumer issue. Management system certification is usually a business-to-business requirement and the product standard could vary from customer to customer. It is only the ability of the manufacturer to comply with customer requirements that is assessed and not the product quality itself.

The best known management certification system is based on ISO 9001, for which more than a million certificates have been issued worldwide since its introduction in the late 1980s. A number of other ISO and international standards are used for management system certification, as well as a growing number of private standards (see questions 14 and 52). Some are important in specific sectors of the economy; others are more general in their application.

Some of the more important management certification systems are shown in the table below. The list is not exhaustive, and suppliers will need to determine which one is important for their sector and for the envisaged or actual target markets.

Level	Sector	Standard
International standards	Medical devices	ISO 13485:2003
	Automotive	ISO/TS 16949:2009
	Food safety	HACCP ISO 22000:2005
	Information security	ISO/IEC 27001:2008
	IT service management	ISO/IEC 20000
	Supply chain security	ISO 28000:2007
	Petroleum and gas	ISO 29001:2003
Private standards	Aerospace	AS 9100
	Food safety and horticulture	British Retail Consortium GLOBALG.A.P. FSSC 22000
	Social accountability	SA 8000
	Telecommunications	TL 9000
	Occupational health and safety	OHSAS 18001

Most of the standards are clear and a single management certification system is operated worldwide. Exceptions occur in the food and horticultural sector, where there are a number of standards being used. HACCP is the original, and one which has been set as a regulatory requirement by a large number of countries and areas, including the European Union, Canada, South Africa and the United States. Subsequently, retail organizations in Europe and the United Kingdom developed their extended versions of food safety in GLOBALG.A.P. and BRC respectively. ISO 22000 has been published to harmonize the requirements of food safety management systems (see question 44) with ISO 9001. However, in view of the fact that certain elements of food safety needed to be emphasized, a new private standard, FSSC 22000, has been developed (see question 51).

The certification process

The certification process is harmonized in the international standard ISO/IEC 17021 (see also question 75). It provides for a two-stage process. The stage 1 audit by the certification body includes a document review and provides a focus for planning the stage 2 audit. For most management systems, it is recommended that at least part of the stage 1 audit be carried out at the client's premises. Once the stage 2 audit has been successfully completed and all the non-conformities have been rectified and verified as such, the certificate is issued, valid for three years. During the three years of validity, surveillance audits are conducted, usually once a year. After three years, the certification body has to re-evaluate the performance of the organization. If the system is in full compliance, another certificate of three years is granted.

Why get certified?

Management system certification, especially to ISO 9001, is seen as the minimum that you have to demonstrate compliance with in order to gain market acceptance, i.e. it opens the door for further trade negotiations. Certification to ISO 9001 does not guarantee any business, but without it you may have a hard time convincing potential customers that you can deliver products of suitable quality.

This situation is helped by the fact that international organizations such as the International Accreditation Forum (IAF) have a meaningful oversight over the accreditation system for certification organizations, leading to universal acceptance of certificates in the marketplace and increasingly by regulatory authorities (see question 87). This is good news for the certified organization, because it means that the management system is audited once, certified once and accepted everywhere.

Some of the other management certification systems are an absolute necessity if you wish to be competitive in sophisticated markets. Typical examples are the EU food and horticulture sectors where GLOBALG.A.P. and BRC certification is imperative if you wish to supply the major retail groups. HACCP certification will help you to demonstrate compliance with the food safety regulations of quite a number of countries. Another good example is certification to ISO/TS 16949 in the automotive sector if you need to supply original equipment manufacturers in the western world with automotive parts.

The implementation of management systems such as ISO 9001 does encourage improved control of the manufacturing and other processes. This leads to better brand recognition, diminished customer returns, minimized warranty costs, increased productivity and lower overall production costs. In addition to the market forces or regulatory regimes requiring management certification, some suppliers therefore see certification as the final prize for implementing the disciplines that lead to all the benefits listed above. Such suppliers frequently have the best approach to management systems and gain the most out of them, because they do it out of conviction and not because they are forced into it.

Cost of certification

Management system certification is a big business worldwide. It therefore attracts all sorts of organizations providing certification services – from the very cheap and not so good, to the very expensive and highly professional organizations. The only certification that you should consider is one from certification bodies accredited by a member of a recognized multilateral arrangement of mutual recognition. Certification organizations that are not accredited may provide cheaper service, but they frequently also follow questionable business practices such as providing a consultancy service to develop your management or quality documentation, implement the system and certify you all within a very short time. Such certification may not be accepted by the purchasers.

The best way is to obtain a quote from a couple of reputable certification organizations operating in your market (see also question 71 on selecting a certification body). Most certification organizations will charge an application fee, a fee for the adequacy audit, and a fairly expensive fee for the compliance assessment on site, as this would involve a number of auditors and specialists who will have to spend time at your premises. The same applies to the verification of non-conformities. Once you are certified, you will have to pay an annual certification fee that normally covers the surveillance audit activities. The recertification exercise after three years will be priced on its own.

Some certification organizations such as national standards bodies have special programmes for SMEs in place – inquire from the one in your vicinity. In some countries, the government provides incentives for SMEs to get certified and will pay back a percentage of the certification fees once you have achieved certification and an additional pay-back should you retain the certification for a period of three years. SMEs should also make inquiries with their trade ministry. Sometimes these schemes are operated by the trade promotion organization on behalf of the government.

FOR MORE INFORMATION

- International Organization for Standardization. The integrated use of management system standards. 1st ed. 2008. www.iso.org/iso/publications_and_e-products/management_standards_publications.htm

  Provides organizations with guidance on how to integrate requirements of multiple ISO or non-ISO management system standards with their organization's management system.

- International Organization for Standardization and United Nations Industrial Development Organization. Building trust – The Conformity Assessment Toolbox. Geneva, 2009. The handbook can also be downloaded as a PDF file free of charge from the ISO (www.iso.org) and UNIDO (www.unido.org) Websites.

  Extensive and in-depth overview of all the various types of conformity assessment systems that are available, their advantages, risks and acceptability in the marketplace.

REFERENCES

BRC Global Standards. www.brcglobalstandards.com/

GLOBALG.A.P. www.globalgap.org

ISO/TS 16949: 2009. Quality management systems – Particular requirements for the application of ISO 9001:2008 for automotive production and relevant service part organizations. Obtainable from ISO or ISO members (list at www.iso.org).

70. What are the criteria for selecting product certification bodies?

Selecting the most appropriate certification body should ensure a valuable long-term partnership. A structured approach to the selection process is therefore crucial. Some of the key questions that may help you in the selection process are discussed below. See also question 71 on the selection of system certification bodies, as many of the criteria will be very similar.

Is the certification body accredited?

Two questions that you need to ask right in the beginning are:

- Is the certification body accredited for the standard to which you want certification, and if so, by which accreditation body?
- Is that accreditation body a signatory to a multilateral recognition arrangement (MLA) managed by a body like the International Accreditation Forum (IAF)?
- Does the certification body have the accredited scope which covers your company's products?

In general, for product certification (see question 68), the certification body should be accredited by an accreditation body that is a signatory of the relevant IAF MLA. It should also be accredited with the appropriate scope for your products to ISO/IEC Guide 65 (to be replaced by ISO/IEC 17065 in the course of 2012).

However, there are product certification schemes, especially those with a more international feature, for which the product certification bodies are approved or recognized by the international bodies controlling those schemes, for example:

- Various IEC conformity assessment schemes, such as the IECEE CB, IEC_X and IECQ schemes (see question 73).
- The OIML Basic Certificate Scheme (see question 73).

The list and contact details of the recognized product certification bodies for these schemes are available on the websites of the controlling international bodies. The modalities vary from scheme to scheme, and it would be prudent to determine what they are before starting a project to comply with their requirements.

Does the market recognize product certification marks?

Some product certification marks have gained a predominant position and the products carrying them are recognized as good value for money or as high-quality products by purchasers in many markets. This is especially true in the home markets of the major product certification bodies in developed and developing countries, less so in markets abroad. It is therefore important to obtain relevant information in this regard (see also questions 72 and 74).

Some product certification marks have gained market acceptance in much broader markets. This information can be invaluable in gaining market share where the market does not yet recognize the brand names of foreign products, especially if the manufacturer is unknown or is a new entrant to the market.

Do regulatory authorities recognize product certification marks?

If the product you wish to market falls within the scope of a technical regulation, and you need certification for your product or process, then you must ensure that the product certification provided by your certification body of choice is acceptable to the regulatory authorities in the target market. There are various ways that this is organized in different markets and by different authorities:

- The certification body needs to be accredited.
- The certification body needs to be accredited and recognized, designated or notified by the authorities, e.g. the 'notified bodies' for the EU New Directives (see question 56).

- The certification body has to be a participating member of an international certification scheme, such as some of the IEC and OIML schemes (see question 73).
- The certification body has to be specifically designated by the relevant regulatory authorities. These authorities accept product certification only from national product certification bodies identified in regulations or other legislation.
- Any 'reputable' certification body will be accepted.

How much will it cost?

Product certification schemes vary tremendously in how they are financed. In some cases, there is an annual fee based on the actual production that will carry the product certification mark; this fee covers all surveillance and post-award testing activities. In others, these are to be paid for separately. Some have a base charge independent of production combined with a fee calculated from production figures. You should familiarize yourself with all the costs, and always ask about auditor rates, application fees, expense policy (e.g. travel and per diem), surveillance audit fees, testing charges, certification charges, follow-up audit charges to clear non-conformities, and recertification charges.

FOR MORE INFORMATION

- International Electrotechnical Commission. http://www.iec.ch/conformity/systems

  The website explains the major principles of the IEC Conformity Assessment Systems, namely openness, transparency and obligatory mutual recognition. It contains details about policies, procedures, peer evaluation, governance of the schemes and the participating country responsibilities.

- International Organization for Standardization. ISO and conformity assessment, 2005. www.iso.org/iso/casco_2005-en.pdf

  A four-page introduction to the benefits of conformity assessment for suppliers, consumers and regulators, and for trade in general.

REFERENCES

International Organization for Standardization and International Electrotechnical Commission

- ISO/IEC Guide 65: 1996, General requirements for bodies operating product certification systems. Obtainable from ISO or ISO members (list at www.iso.org) and from IEC or IEC National Committees (list at www.iec.ch).
- ISO/IEC DIS 17065. Conformity assessment – Requirements for bodies certifying products, processes and services. Obtainable from ISO or ISO members (list at www.iso.org) and from IEC or IEC National Committees (list at www.iec.ch).

International Organization of Legal Metrology. OIML Certificate System for Measuring Instruments. http://www.oiml.org/certificates/

71. What are the criteria for selecting management system certification bodies?

Selecting the most appropriate management system certification body should ensure a valuable long-term partnership. A structured approach to the selection process is therefore crucial. Some of the key questions that may help you in the selection process are given below. See also question 70 on the selection of product certification bodies, as many of the criteria will be of similar nature.

Is the certification body accredited?

Three questions that you need to ask upfront are:

- Is the certification body accredited for the public or private standard to which you want certification, and if so, by which accreditation body?
- Is that accreditation body a signatory to a multilateral recognition arrangement (MLA) managed by a body like the International Accreditation Forum (IAF)?
- Does the certification body have the accredited scope which covers your company's systems or processes?

Certification bodies providing management system certification (see question 69) should be accredited to ISO/IEC 17021 by an accreditation body that is a signatory of the relevant IAF MLA (see question 91). Their scope of accreditation should include the standard for which you wish to obtain certification, e.g. ISO 9001, ISO 14001, ISO 22000, HACCP, GMP. You should also check in the case of ISO 9001, for example, whether their scope of accreditation includes your business sector, e.g. agriculture and fishing, food products and beverages, textiles and textile products, pulp and paper products, manufacturing, transport and storage.

For certification schemes based on various sector-specific or private standards, the certification body has to be specifically accredited or recognized, for example:

- For the GLOBALG.A.P. and BRC standards, a certification body accredited by GLOBALG.A.P. and BRC for the scope of your operations, e.g. food products, transport and storage or horticulture.
- For the automotive industry (ISO/TS 16949), a certification body under contract to the International Automotive Task Force (IATF).

The list of certification bodies accredited or contracted to these controlling bodies can be found on their respective websites.

Does the market recognize the certification body?

If the certification body has well-known names in its list of certified organizations, this could be a good indicator. A certification body that has confidence in its operations will not object to putting you in touch with a selection of its clients for some feedback on its performance. If the certification body is also operating in a number of countries, this could be an added advantage, especially if you are paying attention to its standing in the export markets of interest to you. The preferences of the major purchasers should also not be overlooked.

Can the certification body provide an integrated service?

Your certification needs may be manifold, either now or in the future. Some certification bodies can provide an integrated certification service, i.e. a system that integrates quality management certification with certification on environmental management and/or health and safety and/or risk management, and even product certification. If this is a desired feature for your operation, it can lead to more cost-effective and efficient audits.

Is the certification body sensitive to the needs of SMEs?

It is important for the certification body to recognize the particular constraints and operating practices that are unique to SMEs and to take these into account.

Making the choice

When choosing a certification body, you should consider the following factors: competence, market acceptance, reputation and cost. You should also choose an organization that is willing to work in partnership with you. After choosing the certification body, make an effort to provide the other candidates with some feedback. Most will appreciate and learn from your feedback.

How much will it cost?

Costs may vary widely, especially because of the competition among the many certification bodies. To ensure that you are getting a cost-effective service means evaluating a number of parameters and not necessarily going for the cheapest initial quote. You should be aware of hidden costs, and always ask about auditor rates, application fees, expense policy (e.g. travel and per diem), surveillance audit fees, testing charges, certification charges, follow-up audit charges to clear non-conformities, and recertification charges.

Reputable certification bodies are normally straightforward about their charges, and you should be able to obtain a detailed, upfront estimate of their charges which should be based on the complexity and extent of your operation. This means that you may be required to complete a comprehensive set of questions in order to receive a formal quote. This is necessary so that the certification body can get a good estimate of your operations without necessarily visiting your premises. Many certification bodies will also send a representative to your site.

A reputable certification body will not be afraid to turn down work if it is outside its area of competence or scope of accreditation. It may even recommend a more appropriate body for your needs. Alternatively, it may be able to give you an estimate of how long it will take to extend its accreditation scope accordingly.

FOR MORE INFORMATION

- International Automotive Task Force (IATF). www.iatfglobaloversight.org

  Information on IATF, its oversight offices, contracted certification bodies, sanctioned auditor training, sanctioned interpretations of ISO/TS 16949 and OEM customer-specific requirements.

- International Organization for Standardization. ISO and conformity assessment, 2005. www.iso.org/iso/casco_2005-en.pdf

  A four-page introduction to the benefits of conformity assessment for suppliers, consumers and regulators, and for trade in general.

72. Will my certification be accepted in another country?

In general, the acceptance of product certification is still limited to the country of residence of the certification organization, although some schemes have begun to expand regionally and even internationally. For management certification schemes, a more favorable scenario is in place – ISO 9001 and ISO 14001 certificates from accredited certification bodies are widely accepted, for example. The situation is also quite different for products falling within the scope of technical regulations or SPS measures. A few pointers are provided below, but you must be aware that you must determine from the market you are interested in whether your certification is acknowledged or not.

Mutual recognition agreements (MRA)

During negotiations between countries and/or trading blocks, recognition arrangements or agreements on the mutual acceptance of certification systems, especially for regulatory purposes, may have been signed between the negotiating parties. Two examples are the mutual recognition of product certification marks of the Partner States of the East African Community and the WP 29 World Forum for Harmonization of Vehicle Regulations of the United Nations Economic Commission for Europe (UNECE).

Cooperative (voluntary) arrangements

Domestic and foreign certification bodies may enter into voluntary recognition arrangements. They could include arrangements between accreditation bodies, individual laboratories and inspection bodies. Such arrangements have been around for years, and have been developed for the commercial advantage of the participants. Governments and regulatory authorities have recognized some of these arrangements in the regulatory domain from time to time as the basis for accepting test results and certification activities in the mandatory sector.

An example is the International Electrotechnical Commission's system for conformity testing and certification of electrical and electronic equipment. The IEC manages three of these systems, namely the IEC CB scheme for mutual acceptance of test reports and certificates dealing with the safety of electrical and electronic components; the IECEE scheme for electrical equipment; and the IEC_X scheme for equipment to be used in explosive environments. This is a multilateral agreement between certification organizations and participating countries. A manufacturer using an IEC CB scheme test report, for example, may be able to obtain product certification in most other countries that are members of the scheme (see question 73 for details).

Another example is the OIML scheme for the testing of measuring equipment. A test report from an OIML-approved laboratory may be accepted by the legal metrology authorities in the other countries that are participating in the scheme (see question 73).

Accreditation

Accreditation bodies have been working towards the universal acceptance of test reports and certificates from accredited organizations for years. This has resulted in global networks overseen by IAF (management systems) and ILAC (laboratories). These two international organizations have established and managed multilateral recognition arrangements for the sectors they represent (see question 91), whereby each participant undertakes to recognize the certificates issued by another party in the system as being equal to one issued by itself, even in the regulatory domain.

This is generally the case in Europe, Australia, New Zealand and South Africa. In contrast, in China, India and the United States, this is not yet fully implemented and designated laboratories and certification bodies are still very much the norm. For products outside the regulatory domain, on the other hand, acceptance of test results and certificates from internationally accredited service providers is increasing in most countries.

Government designation

Governments or regulatory authorities may designate laboratories and certification organizations they trust, including bodies outside their territories, to undertake testing and certification in relation to technical regulations and SPS measures. The European Union, for example, has designated the testing laboratories of the South African Bureau of Standards to undertake the necessary testing of fish products from the region destined for the European market.

Designation was the norm a few decades ago, and it was especially government laboratories that were considered competent by virtue of their position. This situation is slowly changing, and accreditation is being required more and more as it is acknowledged that competency has to be earned, not conferred by legislation.

Unilateral recognition

A government or regulatory authority may unilaterally recognize the results of foreign conformity assessment organizations. The conformity assessment body may be accredited internationally, or it may demonstrate its competence through other means, even through a long-standing tradition of providing trustworthy results. This is frequently the case in developing economies, where the regulatory authorities will readily recognize test results and certificates from well-known or government laboratories and certification bodies from abroad.

FOR MORE INFORMATION

- IECEE, IEC_X and CB. www.iec.ch

  Information on IEC, its activities, conformity assessment, standards development. Details of the IEC schemes, which are based on the principles of mutual recognition and reciprocal acceptance of test results by its members for obtaining certification or approval at the national level, are provided. IECx has solutions for equipment in refueling operations, and CB is applicable to electrical and electronic devices.

- OIML Certificate System for Measuring Instruments. www.oiml.org/certificates

  Provides information on OIML, publications, technical structures, OIML systems, national regulations, meetings, seminars, and events. Details of the OIML certificate system are set out on this web page and the others following it. Lists instrument categories, issuing authorities and recipients.

REFERENCES

Permanent Tripartite Commission for East African Co-operation. http://www.africa-union.org/root/au/recs/eac.htm

World Forum for Harmonization of Vehicle Regulations.
http://live.unece.org/trans/main/wp29/meeting_docs_wp29.html?expandable=0&subexpandable=99

World Trade Organization. Second Triennial Review of the TBT Agreement. Annex 5.
http://www.wto.org/english/tratop_e/tbt_e/tbt_work_docs_e.htm

73. Are there international certification systems for products?

There are international certification systems for products. Some of these are described below.

Multinational certification bodies

Certification has become a big business, with more than a million ISO 9001 certificates issued by 2010. It is therefore inevitable that multinational inspection and certification organizations have become involved, providing inspection, testing and certification services on a worldwide basis, many of them operating in more than 100 countries. Typical examples in the manufacturing sector are organizations that have undertaken shipping inspections for many years, such as SGS, BVQI, DNV and Lloyds. There are also organizations that have expanded their business from their original national base into the international arena, such as some of the TÜV and UL organizations.

In the food and horticulture domains, the GLOBALG.A.P. certification is internationally recognized owing to the vast amounts of food EU imports from all over the world (see questions 14 and 15). Other types of certification that are important from an international trade perspective are FairTrade, SA 8000 and FSC (see question 17).

The certification organizations operate on business principles, are privately owned and managed, and are frequently accredited for the services they are offering. They do provide a useful inspection, testing and certification service for both the market and the regulatory domains. Many of them are also 'notified bodies' in the European Union, hence able to provide a comprehensive service tailored to what the client wants or needs. They are a choice that cannot be ignored, but they may be more expensive.

International Electrotechnical Commission (IEC)

IEC operates a number of international certification schemes for various types of products. Here is a broad overview of these schemes.

- The IECEE CB scheme targets electrical equipment primarily intended for use in homes, offices, workshops, healthcare facilities and similar locations.
- The IECEx scheme covers equipment to be used in potentially explosive atmospheres such as found in oil refineries, coal mines, chemical plants, gas installations, grain handling and storage and the like.
- The IECQ programme assesses electronic components against quality requirements and certifies their conformity to standards. It covers electronic components and related materials and processes, manufacturers and distributors, specialist contractors, testing laboratories and the process management of hazardous substances.

The schemes are based on the principle of mutual recognition (reciprocal acceptance) by IEC members of test results and factory audits carried out for the purpose of obtaining certification or approval at the national level. Products or facilities are inspected, tested and audited under the auspices of a member of the relevant IEC scheme, referred to as a national certification body or NCB. The list of recognized NCBs is posted on the schemes' websites.

Under the schemes, NCBs designate laboratories to be used. You can then take the test and audit results to another country, and the NCB in that country will issue the certification in that country as required by the marketplace or the regulatory authorities.

The IECEx scheme enables you to gain a licence to affix the IECEx conformity mark on your products, which is recognized by the other countries that are members of the scheme as evidence that the product meets relevant IEC standards. Equipment used in explosive atmospheres is subject to technical regulation in most countries, and these regulations are frequently based on IEC standards. Hence, these schemes may provide a cost-effective means for meeting regulatory requirements and satisfying market preferences in a growing number of economies.

International Organization of Legal Metrology (OIML)

The OIML operates two international schemes: the OIML Basic Certificate System and the OIML Mutual Acceptance Arrangement or MAA.

The OIML Basic Certificate System for Measuring Instruments enables manufacturers to obtain an OIML Basic Certificate and an OIML Basic Evaluation Report indicating that a given instrument type complies with the requirements of the relevant OIML international recommendation. Certificates are issued by OIML Member States that have established one or several issuing authorities responsible for processing applications from manufacturers wishing to have their instrument types certified.

The certificates are accepted by national metrology services on a voluntary basis, and under the mutual recognition of test results developed between OIML Members. The OIML Basic Certificate System simplifies the type approval process for manufacturers and metrology authorities by eliminating expensive duplication of application and test procedures.

In addition to the OIML Basic Certificate System, OIML has developed a mutual acceptance arrangement (MAA). The System uses the MAA as an additional tool for increasing mutual confidence throughout the System. At the time of this writing, it was still a voluntary system with the following features:

- To increase confidence in testing laboratories involved in type testing, these laboratories are evaluated on the basis of the international standard ISO/IEC 17025. The evaluation may be carried out either by accreditation or by peer assessment.
- It provides assistance to Member States who do not yet have their own test facilities and makes it possible for legal national metrology bodies to rely on the facilities and competences of other countries' bodies.
- It makes it possible for interested parties to take into account (in a Declaration of Mutual Confidence, or DoMC) the additional requirements imposed by various countries beyond those stipulated by the OIML Recommendations.

The aim of the MAA is for the participants to accept and use MAA evaluation reports validated by an OIML MAA certificate of conformity. To this end, MAA participants are either issuing participants or utilizing participants. For manufacturers, the MAA helps avoid duplication of tests for type approval in different countries and makes them aware, at the beginning of the evaluation process, of the additional requirements imposed in the various countries in which they will apply for type approval.

Global harmonization of automobile standards

The World Forum for Harmonization of Vehicle Regulations of the United Nations Economic Commission for Europe (UNECE WP 29) currently has the leading role in the global harmonization of automotive regulation. It is responsible for the implementation of two major agreements reached by the participating countries, known in short as the 1958 Agreement and the 1998 Global Agreement.

The UNECE 1958 Agreement provides for the mutual recognition of governmental certifications based on the ECE Regulations (approximately 120 at the time of this writing), while the purpose of the 1998 Global Agreement is to harmonize the regulations. Mutual recognition is excluded from the 1998 Global Agreement. The ECE Regulations under the 1958 Agreement and the Global Technical Regulations (GTR) under the 1998 Global Agreement are both discussed at WP 29.

The mutual recognition of approvals provided under the 1958 Agreement aims to facilitate the international trade in vehicles and their components. If a component type is approved according to a UNECE Regulation by any of the contracting parties to the 1958 Agreement, all other contracting parties who have signed the Regulation will recognize this approval. This avoids repetitive testing and approval of components in the various countries to which the components are exported. It also helps to reduce the time and resources devoted to design, manufacture and approval, as well as the entering into service of vehicles and their components.

Around 50 countries are contracting parties to the 1958 Agreement, and approved products are typically marked with a big E in a circle also containing the number assigned under the Agreement to the approving country.

REFERENCES

IECEE CB. www.iecee.ch

$IECE_X$. www.iecex.ch

IECQ. www.iecq.org

United Nations Economic Commission for Europe (UNECE). WP.29 – How it Works – How to Join it. http://www.unece.org/ar/trans/main/wp29/publications/other_vehicles.html

74. Where can I get information about certification bodies operating in various countries?

There are many sources of information on certification bodies that you can access. They include the certification bodies themselves, national accreditation bodies, your clients' preferences, and the authorities especially in as far as regulations are concerned. You should also not neglect to use the services of your national trade promotion organization to collect information about certification bodies.

Certification bodies and laboratories

Certification is big business, and there are many certification bodies operating in the marketplace. Hence, most certification bodies have to advertise their presence and their services quite extensively. Almost all of them, but especially those in private industry, will maintain fairly extensive websites. If you access the websites of multinational certification bodies such as SGS, DNV, TÜV, BVQI, and others, you can quickly obtain information on whether they operate in the market that you are interested in.

In many developing economies, national standards bodies frequently provide certification services, and the advantage of using them is that they are often less expensive than private certification bodies. They are also often more accessible to the SME sector. It would be useful to contact them as well, even though their websites may not always be up-to-date or as complete as those of private certification bodies (see question 70 on selecting a product certification body).

The names of certification bodies or laboratories (sometimes called 'contracting parties' or 'bodies') that participate in international schemes such as those managed by the IEC, OIML and WP 29 (see question 73) can be found on the websites of these organizations. The same applies to the certification bodies that have been approved for standards such as GLOBALG.A.P., BRC, FSC and SA 8000.

Accreditation bodies

Every national accreditation body has to maintain a list of organizations that it accredits. These may be testing and calibration laboratories, or inspection and certification bodies. These lists are almost always available on the Internet. In order to identify the national accreditation bodies that are either already signatories to the IAF Multilateral Recognition Arrangement (see question 91) or are just IAF members, refer to the IAF website. It will provide the link to the accreditation body in the country that you are interested in. You can get a link to the accreditation organizations involved in laboratory accreditation on the ILAC website.

Your client

If you are marketing your product or service directly to a client in a foreign market, you may find that this client has a preferred certification body. You will have to respect this preference if you want to develop a positive relationship with him and be successful in your marketing endeavour. Even if the client does not have an exclusive preference for a specific certification body, he may be able to tell you which certification bodies have the better reputation in his market and for the specific product or service you are wishing to export.

Regulatory authorities

If the product or service you wish to export falls within the scope of a technical regulation or SPS measure, then you should obtain information about the preferred or even designated certification bodies from the relevant authorities in the export market. Your national enquiry points for TBT and SPS (see question 23) should be able to help you find this information.

Trade promotion organizations

In general, TPOs gather all sorts of information about current or potential export markets to support the export industry. They are also helpful in putting suppliers and importers in touch with each other for the purpose of concluding business deals. TPOs therefore frequently know which certification bodies operate in foreign markets and which ones have a good market reputation. If not, they have an extensive network available that could be used to obtain the appropriate information.

FOR MORE INFORMATION

- International Trade Centre
  - Products Map. www.intracen.org/about/product-map/

    Web-based portal on 72 industries, gathering international market research and business development information on each. Overall, 5,300 products (at the HS six-digit level) traded by over 180 countries are referenced.
  - Standards Map. www.standardsmap.org.

    A web-based interactive tool that allows users to review information on over 30 voluntary standards covering more than 40 product groups.
  - World Directory of Trade Promotion Organizations. 2010. www.intracen.org/tpo

    An online directory of TPOs and trade support institutions.
- World Trade Organization
  - Technical barriers to Trade, national enquiry points. http://www.wto.org/english/tratop_e/tbt_e/tbt_enquiry_points_e.htm.

    Lists names and contact details of enquiry points and provides additional information.
  - Sanitary and Phytosanitary Measures, National enquiry points. www.wto.org/english/tratop_e/sps_e/sps_e.htm.

    A database of WTO information on SPS notifications, concerns raised, documents available, enquiry points, etc.

REFERENCES

International Accreditation Forum (IAF). www.iaf.nu.

International Laboratory Accreditation Cooperation (ILAC). www.ilac.org

75. What activities are undertaken by certification bodies before and after the grant of a management system certification?

Whereas there may have been differences in the approach and processes of certification bodies in the past, nowadays most certification bodies follow the process listed in ISO/IEC 17021, the international standard for their accreditation. This is good news for any supplier that is planning to be certified, as it brings about clarity and harmonizes practices across certification bodies. The process is shown graphically in the figure below.

Application stage

Once you have decided to obtain certification and have made a choice of the certification body (see question 71), you have to apply formally for certification. The application forms have to be completed and you have to provide a large amount of information about your company and its operations to enable the certification body to determine the scope of the certification activities and to appoint the team leader for the audit process.

The initial certification audit consists of a two-stage audit as described below.

Stage 1 audit

At this stage, you need to supply all your relevant management and quality documentation. The certification body determines on the basis of this documentation whether you are ready to undergo the stage 2 or compliance audit. If the certification body finds that you are not yet ready for the compliance audit, it will inform you accordingly and stop the process. If the finding is that you are ready, but that a few non-conformities have to be rectified before the compliance audit can take place, the certification body will provide you with a report.

After you have rectified the non-conformities and informed the certification body, and it concurs with your actions, a compliance audit is arranged.

Management system certification process

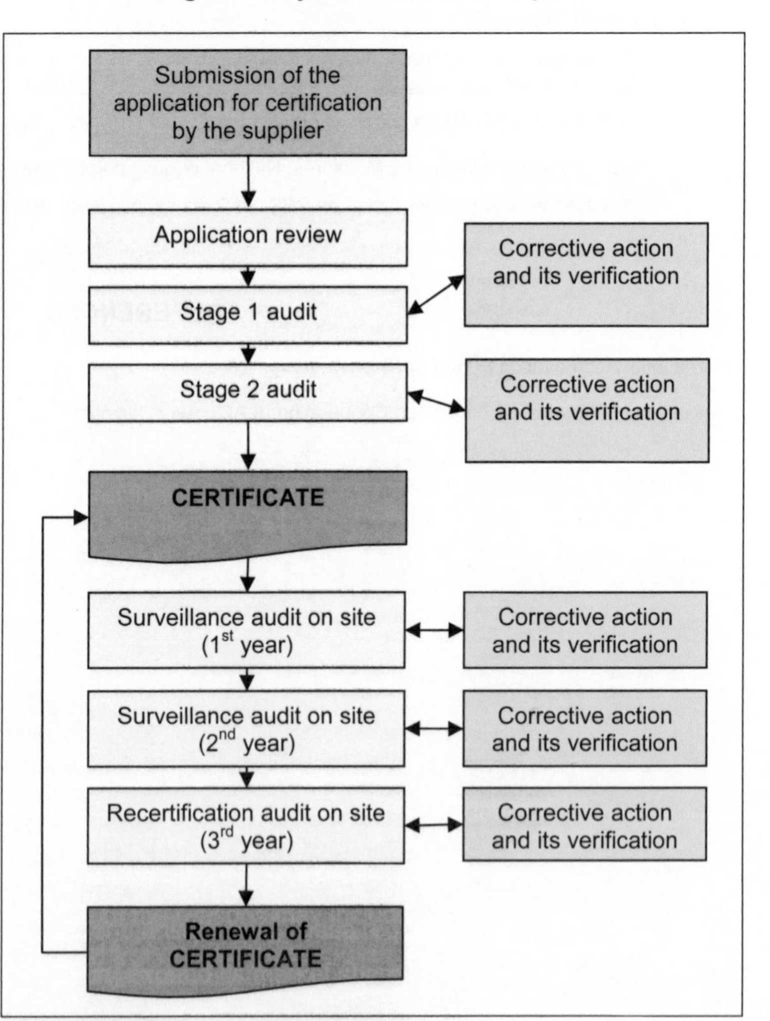

Source: Martin Kellermann, South Africa.

Stage 2 audit

The team leader will assemble a team of auditors and experts concomitant with your scope of activities, the complexities and size of your operations, and will conduct the stage 2 audit to evaluate the implementation and effectiveness of your management system at your premises at a mutually agreed time. After the opening meeting, each auditor or expert will audit a specific area of your operations. He/she will assess whether the contents of the documentation provided is consistent with the activities of your company as well as the standard against which your business is being audited. You have to ensure that you have a representative accompanying every auditor or expert, to take notes and to sign off any non-conformity that is found.

At the end of the stage 2 audit, the team leader will hold a closing meeting, during which he/she will present their overall findings and the list of non-conformities (if any). The team may find that you comply with the requirements of the standard (e.g. ISO 9001, ISO 14001) and will recommend to the certification committee of the certification body that you should be certified.

It is much more likely, though, that the team will find that there are still some non-conformities that have to be dealt with before they can recommend you for certification. In this case, they will agree with you a time schedule and the modalities for rectifying the non-conformities. They may wish to witness the new procedures, or if the non-conformities are of a minor nature, would be happy for you to send them evidence that these non-conformities have been fixed. Once all the non-conformities have been successfully cleared within the given time period, typically three months, the team leader will forward your certification recommendation for review and decision by the authorized persons or committee.

Certification

The decision-making process is totally independent of the auditing process. Authorized persons or a committee which was not involved in the audit will review the audit report and the clearance report of the nonconformities and make a decision regarding certification. The decision will be followed by the issue of certification documents which usually take the form of a certificate with or without annexes detailing the scope of certification and locations covered by the certificate.

Surveillance audits

After certification, the certification organization will conduct a surveillance audit usually once a year. This is to ensure that your system is firmly established and still functioning in accordance with the standard and your documentation. These audits will not normally be as extensive as the initial certification audit. There are a few areas, however, that will always be included in the surveillance audit, such as internal audits and management reviews as well as your non-conformity system. Obviously, any non-conformity that is raised during the surveillance audits has to be dealt with efficiently within an agreed time frame, otherwise you may lose your certification.

Recertification audit

In the third year of certification, a recertification audit will be conducted, similar to the original compliance audit. If this is negotiated successfully, your company will be recertified for another three-year period, and the whole cycle repeats itself.

FOR MORE INFORMATION

- International Organization for Standardization and International Electrotechnical Commission.
  - ISO/IEC 17021:2011, Conformity assessment – Requirements for bodies providing audit and certification of management systems. Obtainable from ISO or ISO members (list at www.iso.org) and IEC or IEC National Committees (www.iec.ch).

    Principles and requirements for the competence, consistency and impartiality of the audit and certification of management systems of all types (e.g. quality management systems or environmental management systems) and for bodies providing these activities.
  - ISO/IEC 17011:2004, Conformity assessment – General requirements for accreditation bodies accrediting conformity assessment bodies. Obtainable from ISO or ISO members (list at www.iso.org) and IEC or IEC National Committees (www.iec.ch).

    General requirements for accreditation bodies assessing and accrediting conformity assessment bodies (CABs); also appropriate as a requirements document for the peer evaluation process for mutual recognition arrangements between accreditation bodies.

76. Can certification to private standards guarantee market access?

First, it is important to clarify that no certification, whether private or offered by a government certification organization, will guarantee by itself any type of sales. A successful sale will depend on many issues, including such aspects as price, delivery, support service, product design and product quality.

Also, you should keep in mind that products and services have to comply with technical regulations and SPS measures by law (see questions 18 and 19). Without compliance with these requirements, there is no market access. If the certification to private standards does not include regulatory requirements, it cannot guarantee anything. In any case, it is your responsibility to comply with mandatory requirements; no certification body will ever accept this responsibility.

But what certification may do is to open doors and give you access to the market for you to start sales negotiations. This is the case with certifications to private standards such as GLOBALG.A.P., BRC, WRAP, SA 8000 and FSC. Purchasers need some assurance that you are a producer or manufacturer of integrity, especially if you are based in a developing economy far away from the targeted marketplace. You can look at it as a sort of pre-contract approval process without which you do not even get to open the door for further discussions.

See also question 70 on the selection of certification bodies, and question 72 on the acceptance of certification in foreign markets for additional information.

FOR MORE INFORMATION

- International Trade Centre
  - Market Access, Transparency and Fairness in Global Trade: Export Impact for Good. 2010. ISBN 9789291373871.

    Presents a detailed and in-depth analysis of the outcomes and impact of the Fairtrade voluntary standards on producers and exporters in developing countries; deals with the producer's perspective on facilitating market access or facing a new market barrier.
  - Standards Map. www.standardsmap.org

    Standards Map is the web-based portal of ITC's Trade for Sustainable Development (T4SD) programme and a partnership-based effort to enhance transparency in voluntary standards and to increase opportunities for sustainable production and trade.

77. How do I obtain certification to private standards like WRAP, Fairtrade, SA 8000, GLOBALG.A.P., and what are the costs involved?

The certification process for private standards is in essence no different from the certification processes described in questions 68, 69, 71, and 72, but the choice of certification organization is very specific. A few examples of certification to private standards are given below. For information on social, environmental, and ethical standards, see also question 17.

Worldwide Responsible Accredited Production (WRAP)

The Worldwide Responsible Accredited Production (WRAP) is an independent, non-profit organization dedicated to the certification of lawful, humane and ethical manufacturing throughout the world. A fair number of clothing, apparel and footwear associations from various countries are participating members of WRAP.

The WRAP principles are based on generally accepted international workplace standards, local laws and workplace regulations which encompass human resources management, health and safety, environmental practices and legal compliance, including compliance with import/export regulations and security standards.

WRAP has adopted a management systems approach toward compliance. This means that senior management has to adopt the WRAP principles in writing, assign the necessary staff to ensure that the required practices are implemented throughout the facility, and make sure that an internal audit system is in place for continuous compliance. Facilities seeking certification must undergo extensive self-assessment and then be audited by an independent third-party monitoring company. More information on WRAP certification (procedures, application for certification, fees, application form for monitors seeking WRAP accreditation) is available on the WRAP website.

FAIRTRADE

The FAIRTRADE certification mark is a product label controlled by the holding company Fairtrade International (FLO) representing 25 organizations worldwide. The mark is mainly intended for use on the packaging of products. FLO works through FLO-CERT GmbH, an independent certification company registered in Germany and accredited by Deutsche Akkreditierungsstelle (DAkkS, the German Accreditation Body).

Applying for the use of the FAIRTRADE mark is a two-stage process. First, the applicant has to be audited by FLO-CERT to determine whether it complies with the requirements of the relevant Fairtrade standards. This can take anything from four days for a small producer organization to four to six weeks for the largest cooperatives. Once compliance has been determined, the applicant can apply for a licence to use the FAIRTRADE mark from either a Fairtrade initiative in the applicant's country (Fairtrade initiatives are present in Europe, North America, Australia, Japan and New Zealand, a total of 23 countries) or, if there is no Fairtrade initiative in the applicant's country, directly from FLO. Once certified, the operator will be audited annually as part of a three-year cycle of recertification. Detailed information on FLO can be found on its website; contact details and certification application procedures can be accessed from the FLO-CERT website.

SA 8000

SA 8000 certification is controlled worldwide by Social Accountability Accreditation Services (SAAS). In order to be certified, SAAS recommends that facilities contact at least three SAAS accredited certification bodies and ask them to bid for certification services. Auditors from the selected certification body visit facilities, assess corporate practice on a wide range of issues and evaluate the state of a company's management systems to ascertain whether ongoing practices are acceptable from the perspective of the SA 8000 standard. Certified facilities can display the SA 8000 certificate, but individual products cannot be so labelled as the certification covers workplace processes and is not a product certification. Currently, about 20 certification bodies in Europe, Hong Kong (China), India, Uruguay and the United States have been accredited by SAAS; many of them operate on a global basis. The list and their contact details can be obtained from the SAAS website.

GLOBALG.A.P.

GLOBALG.A.P. certification relates to good agricultural practices and can be obtained for crops, livestock, aquaculture, compound feeds and plant propagation material.

GLOBALG.A.P. certification is provided by more than 100 independent certification organizations in more than 80 countries that have been accredited by the GLOBALG.A.P. organization. In addition, there are about 20 countries that operate what is known as equivalent schemes. They are recognized by the GLOBALG.A.P. organization on the basis of their demonstrated technical capability. Suppliers can apply to any of these organizations, many of which operate in more than one country, for GLOBALG.A.P. certification, The complete list of certification bodies and their contact details can be found on the GLOBALG.A.P. website.

Cost of certification

It is difficult to provide an accurate estimate of the cost of certification. It will depend on the number of days that the auditors will spend on reviewing quality manuals and procedures, auditing on site and evaluating the rectification of non-conformities, and the certification fee that many charge annually. An application fee is usually charged as well and it can be as high as US$ 1,500.00.

It is therefore crucial to obtain a proper and full quotation from the certification body (see also question 70 on choosing a certification body) before signing application forms and contracts for certification.

REFERENCES

Certification for Development (FLO-CERT). www.flo-cert.net

Fairtrade Labelling Organizations International (FLO). www.fairtrade.net

GLOBALG.A.P. Certification. http://www2.globalgap.org/apprcbs.html

Social Accountability Accreditation Services (SAAS). www.saasaccreditation.org/certification.htm

Worldwide Responsible Accredited Production (WRAP). www.wrapcompliance.org

78. What is eco-labelling?

Principles

Eco-labelling is a labelling system to identify consumer products that are manufactured in a way that avoids or reduces detrimental effects on the environment based on life-cycle considerations. It is therefore a type of product certification (see also question 68).

Although eco-labelling was started by NGOs decades ago, it has now become a big business, with a growing number of schemes being offered in the marketplace. EU has even promulgated legislation to bring some order into this growing market. Any type of product can be subject to eco-labelling, but it is more usual to find consumer goods being labelled.

Eco-labelling can be a first-party or supplier's declaration of conformity (see question 57) – also known as a 'green' statement. If the manufacturer or supplier declares that the product is eco-friendly, this is done to promote its image of being sensitive to environmental concerns. Some will even use the international recycling symbol on their packaging, but this is still only a supplier's declaration.

More important from a market perspective are third-party eco-labelling schemes. There are a growing number of certification organizations that have specialized eco-labelling schemes; these are independent from manufacturers or suppliers and the purchasers, and could be of relevance in specific markets (see also question 16 on textile-specific labelling).

ISO has published a number of eco-labelling international standards in its ISO 14000 series for use by eco-labelling certification organizations. They include 'ISO 14020, Environmental labels and declarations – General principles'; 'ISO 14021, Environmental labels and declarations – Self-declared environmental claims (Type II environmental labelling)'; 'ISO 14024, Environmental labels and declarations – Type I environmental labelling – Principles and procedures; and 'ISO/TR 14025, Environmental labels and declarations – Type III environmental declarations' (see also question 17).

Global Ecolabelling Network (GEN)

The Global Ecolabelling Network (GEN) is a non-profit association of third-party, environmental performance labelling organizations founded in 1994 to improve, promote, and develop the 'ecolabelling' of products and services. Currently, it consists of 26 members from Asia, Europe, North and South America, including major organizations such as Good Environmental Choice (Australia), Green Seal (United States), Federal Environmental Agency (Germany), Japan Environment Association (JEA), Nordic Ecolabelling Board (covering five Nordic countries) and the Department for Environment, Food and Rural Affairs (United Kingdom). Their activities include the collection and promotion of information on eco-labelling programmes and participation in the eco-labelling activities of the United Nations Environment Programme (UNEP), the International Organization for Standardization (ISO) and the World Trade Organization (WTO). They also explore mutual recognition programmes and provide a mechanism for information exchange. More information can be obtained from the website of the Global Ecolabelling Network.

EU Ecolabel

The EU Ecolabel is recognized throughout the 27 EU Member States as well as in Iceland, Liechtenstein and Norway. The scheme recognizes environmentally sound goods and services by awarding them a distinctive and easily recognizable symbol of environmental quality – the Flower. The Flower helps manufacturers, retailers and service providers to gain recognition for good environmental standards while helping purchasers to identify products that are less harmful to the environment.

This voluntary scheme covers 26 types of products and services (2010), with other groups being continuously added. The products covered include cleaning products, electronic equipment, paper products, textiles, home and garden products, lubricants and services such as tourist accommodation. The label is awarded only to the most environmentally friendly brands in each product group.

The scheme has recently been revised to simplify procedures for companies applying for the label and increase the number of product groups. Some of the important changes include reduced fees, less administrative burdens for companies, increased synergy with other national labels, and faster criteria development and revision procedures. More information on the EU Ecolabel can be obtained from its websites.

Forest Stewardship Council (FSC)

The Forest Stewardship Council (FSC) is another organization whose projects could be considered eco-labelling. It was founded in 1993 to improve forest conservation and to reduce deforestation. A growing number of wooden products, paper and paper products are available with the FSC endorsement. It operates on a 'chain of custody' principle, the process whereby the source of the timber used in the manufacture of these products is verified against standards for environmentally appropriate, socially beneficial and economically viable management. The timber is tracked through the supply chain to the end product, so that consumers can choose to buy sustainably harvested wood over alternatives that may be contributing to deforestation worldwide. More information on the FSC scheme and the certification bodies involved can be found on the FSC website.

Marine Stewardship Council (MSC)

The Marine Stewardship Council's distinctive blue eco-label enables consumers to identify seafood that has come from a sustainable source. The MSC programme is voluntary and fisheries that are independently assessed and meet the MSC's environmental standard may use the MSC blue eco-label. As of 2010, nearly 4 000 products in over 60 countries around the world carry the MSC eco-label.

The MSC standard is consistent with the 'Guidelines for the Eco-labelling of Fish and Fishery Products from Marine Wild Capture Fisheries', adopted by the United Nations Food and Agriculture Organization (FAO) in 2005. Any fishery that wishes to become MSC-certified and use the eco-label is assessed against the MSC standard by an independent certification body that has been accredited to perform MSC assessments by Accreditation Services International (ASI). The chain of custody certification along the supply chain from boat to point of sale ensures that seafood sold bearing the eco-label originated from an MSC-certified fishery.

Packaging and recycling

There are many recycling schemes that can be considered eco-labelling, especially in the packaging industry. Some are of economic importance only in their country of origin, others have gained wider relevance. Two examples are discussed below.

Green Dot. The Green Dot (German: Grüner Punkt) mark originated in Germany, but has now been introduced throughout Europe as a license symbol of a European network of industry-funded systems for recycling the packaging materials of consumer goods. The logo is trademark protected worldwide. Since its European introduction, the scheme has been rolled out to 27 European countries. The Green Dot is used by more than 170 000 companies and about 460 billion packaging items are labelled yearly with the Dot.

The basic idea of the Green Dot is that consumers who see the logo know that the manufacturer of the product contributes to the cost of recovery and recycling. This can be the recycling of household waste collected by the authorities (e.g. in special bags – in Germany these are yellow), or in containers in public places such as car parks and outside supermarkets. The system is financed by a Green Dot license fee paid by the producers of the products. Fees vary by country and are based on the packaging materials used (e.g. paper, plastic, metal, wood, cardboard) as well as the cost of the collection, sorting and recycling methods used. Each country also has different fees for joining the scheme and ongoing fixed and variable fees. In simple terms, the system encourages manufacturers to cut down on packaging as this saves them the cost of license fees. The use of the Green Dot is overseen by the Pro-Europe Organization. Detailed Information is available on its website.

Resin identification codes. This set of codes developed by the Society of the Plastics Industry (SPI) in 1988 is now used worldwide for the primary purpose of allowing efficient separation of the different polymer types for recycling. The symbols (of which only two are shown in the diagram) used in the code consist of arrows that cycle clockwise to form a rounded triangle enclosing a number, often with an acronym representing the plastic below the triangle. More information on the symbols, their use and design can be obtained from the SPI website.

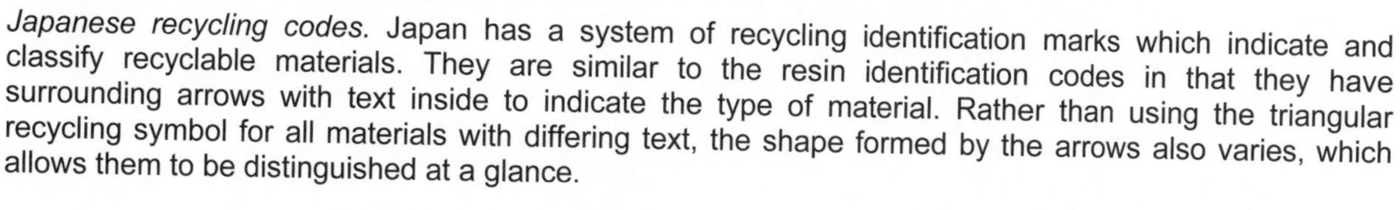

Japanese recycling codes. Japan has a system of recycling identification marks which indicate and classify recyclable materials. They are similar to the resin identification codes in that they have surrounding arrows with text inside to indicate the type of material. Rather than using the triangular recycling symbol for all materials with differing text, the shape formed by the arrows also varies, which allows them to be distinguished at a glance.

FOR MORE INFORMATION

- European Commission. Communication on Sustainable Consumption and Production and Sustainable Industrial Policy Action Plan. http://ec.europa.eu/environment/eussd/pdf/com_2008_397.pdf

  Communication from the European Commission to the organs of the European Union.

- International Trade Centre. *Export Quality Management Bulletin* No. 86, Directory of marks and labels related to food safety, environmental integrity and social equity. www.intracen.org/exporters/quality-management/Quality_publications_index.

- Regulation (EC) No. 66/2010 of the European Parliament and of the Council of 25 November 2009 on the EU Ecolabel. http://eur-lex.europa.eu/LexUriServ/LexUriServ.do?uri=OJ:L:2010:027:0001:0019:EN:PDF

  Original EU regulation on the Ecolabel.

REFERENCES

EU Ecolabel. http://ec.europa.eu/environment/ecolabel

Forest Stewardship Council. www.fsc.org

Global Ecolabelling Network (GEN). www.globalecolabelling.net

Green Dot. www.pro-e.org/

Pro-Europe Organization. www.pro-e.org/

Resin identification codes. www.ides.com/resources/plastic-recycling-codes.asp

The Plastics Web. www.ides.com/resources/plastic-recycling-codes.asp

METROLOGY

79. What is metrology and why is it important in international trade?

Metrology is a technical term meaning all activities and procedures related to measurements. The ultimate goal of metrology, also defined as 'the science of measurement and its application' (*International Vocabulary of Metrology*, 2010), is to ensure correct, comparable and reliable measuring results. Metrology can be subdivided into the following areas:

- *Scientific* or *general metrology.* This part of metrology deals with problems common to all metrological questions irrespective of the quantity itself. For instance, it touches on the general theoretical and practical problems related to units of measurement, the problem of errors in measurement, and the problems of the metrological properties of measuring instruments.
- *Industrial metrology.* This discipline focuses on measurements in production and quality control. Typical issues are calibration procedures and calibration intervals, control of measurement processes, and management of measuring equipment.
- *Legal metrology.* This term relates to mandatory technical requirements. A legal metrology service checks these requirements in order to guarantee correct measurements in areas of public interest, such as trade, health, the environment and safety (*International Vocabulary of Terms in Legal Metrology*, 2000).

Measurement enters into practically all commercial operations, from trading in bulk goods (petroleum, natural gas, metal ores) to the retail sale of goods to the public in the marketplace. In particular, international trade in manufactured goods and production processes using parts and components manufactured in different regions of the world require correct measurements based on an international metrology system. This can be illustrated by the examples below.

- **International trade and the significance of a globally accepted system of units**

  Suppose you want to know the diameter of a pipe. Do you want the dimension in centimetres or inches? What is requested by your customer? The centimetre and the inch are units belonging to two different systems of units. Whereas the centimetre is a submultiple of the metre, the unit of length of the International System of Units (SI), the inch, belongs to the so-called Imperial Measurement System. The SI is the recommended system and is applied worldwide, whereas imperial units are used in a few countries or for specific applications.

- **High-precision measurements as basis of telecommunication and information technology**

  'Time' is the quantity most often measured. With today's technology, the correct time is disseminated via radio, television, the telephone, the Internet and by satellite. One example of ultra-precise time measurements is the global positioning system, GPS, where time signals of atomic clocks from at least three satellites are used to calculate the position of the receiver on the ground with an accuracy of a fraction of a metre. These extraordinarily accurate results can be achieved only under the condition that each clock produces time signals of the same accuracy. This technology helps to make shipment of goods faster and safer, it facilitates and accelerates the exchange and retrieval of information and constitutes the base of electronic trade and commerce (*Secrets of Electronic Commerce*, 2009).

- **Contributions of metrology to conformity assessment and certification**

  In global markets, certificates are often required as evidence of the compliance of products or services with specified standards or regulations. In many cases, conformity assessments and the checking of compliance with standards or regulations require measurements and tests. Measurements and tests must therefore be correct within specified limits, comparable and reliable to ensure confidence in certificates.

In general, the accuracy of measuring instruments is achieved through regular calibrations. Calibration involves comparing a measuring instrument with a more accurate measurement standard. National measurement standards, which usually provide the most accurate measurements in a country, are compared with international or other national standards to ensure the correct dissemination of units worldwide. If an unbroken chain of documented calibrations exists from the highest standard down to ordinary measuring instruments, then the measurements achieved are called 'traceable'.

In many countries, national metrology institutes are responsible for keeping and disseminating the correct units of measurement that are needed by calibration laboratories, legal metrology services and others. The calibration of measuring and test equipment is a responsibility of the user or owner. Official obligatory accuracy checks, verifications, are carried out by legal metrology services for measuring instruments in regulated areas such as commercial transactions.

Each step down in the calibration hierarchy (see figure question 84) is connected with a loss of accuracy or growing uncertainty. Traceability is one prerequisite for ensuring correct measurements within specified measurement uncertainties or, in the case of legal metrology, within tolerable error limits.

International metrology organizations such as the International Bureau of Weight and Measures (BIPM) and the International Organization of Legal Metrology (OIML), in cooperation with international standardization and accreditation organizations, have established procedures to be followed in order to ensure correct measurements and to establish confidence in the competence of those making out certificates. Measurement and test laboratories should therefore be accredited (see question 87). All these measures facilitate international trade and help to avoid duplication of tests.

FOR MORE INFORMATION

- EURAMET. Metrology – In Short, 3rd ed. July 2008. www.euramet.org/. Contact: secretariat@euramet.org

  This booklet contains a comprehensive overview of metrology. It explains important terms, describes international and regional organizations and notes links to them, and gives examples of the impact of measurements.

- Marbán, R.M. and J.A. Pellecer. Metrology for non-metrologists. ISBN 99922-770-1-7. Organization of American States, 2002. (Also available in Spanish). http://www.science.oas.org/OEA_GTZ/LIBROS/METROLOGIA/english/met_cont.pdf

- This book contains comprehensive information on metrology in a language that can be understood by non-metrologists. It provides the most important definitions and covers all measurement units and their main applications. On Legal Metrology and OIML, see: www.oiml.org

  All Recommendations, vocabularies and documents are accessible free of charge. Detailed information is given on the OIML Basic Certificate System and Mutual Acceptance Arrangement for types of measuring instruments.

- On the International Metrology System and the International System of Units, Traceability, Metre Convention, Mutual Acceptance Arrangements, see www.bipm.org.

  This discusses the activities of the International Bureau of Weights and Measures (BIPM) and provides the names of institutes that are signatories to mutual acceptance arrangements.

- United States Agency for International Development (USAID). Standards, Metrology, Conformity Assessment and the TBT Agreement. A Desk Top Reference Handbook. http://pdf.usaid.gov/pdf_docs/PNADP635.pdf

  Detailed explanation of the above topics. Excellent source book for deepening one's understanding of metrology and conformity assessment.

REFERENCES

International Organization of Legal Metrology

- International Vocabulary of Metrology – Basic and General Concepts and Associated Terms (VIM). 3rd ed. 2010. www.oiml.org/publications/V/V002-200-e10.pdf
- International Vocabulary of Terms in Legal Metrology (VIML). English/French. 2000. www.oiml.org/publications/V/V001-ef00.pdf

International Trade Centre. Secrets of Electronic Commerce: A Guide for Small- and Medium-Sized Exporters. Obtainable from http://www.intracen.org/publicationlist.aspx?taxid=233

80. Is metrology essential for me and what should I observe?

Your answers to the questions in the diagram will help you make a metrological decision. The term 'product' includes services. The numbers in the small boxes refer to the remarks further below.

Steps towards a metrological decision

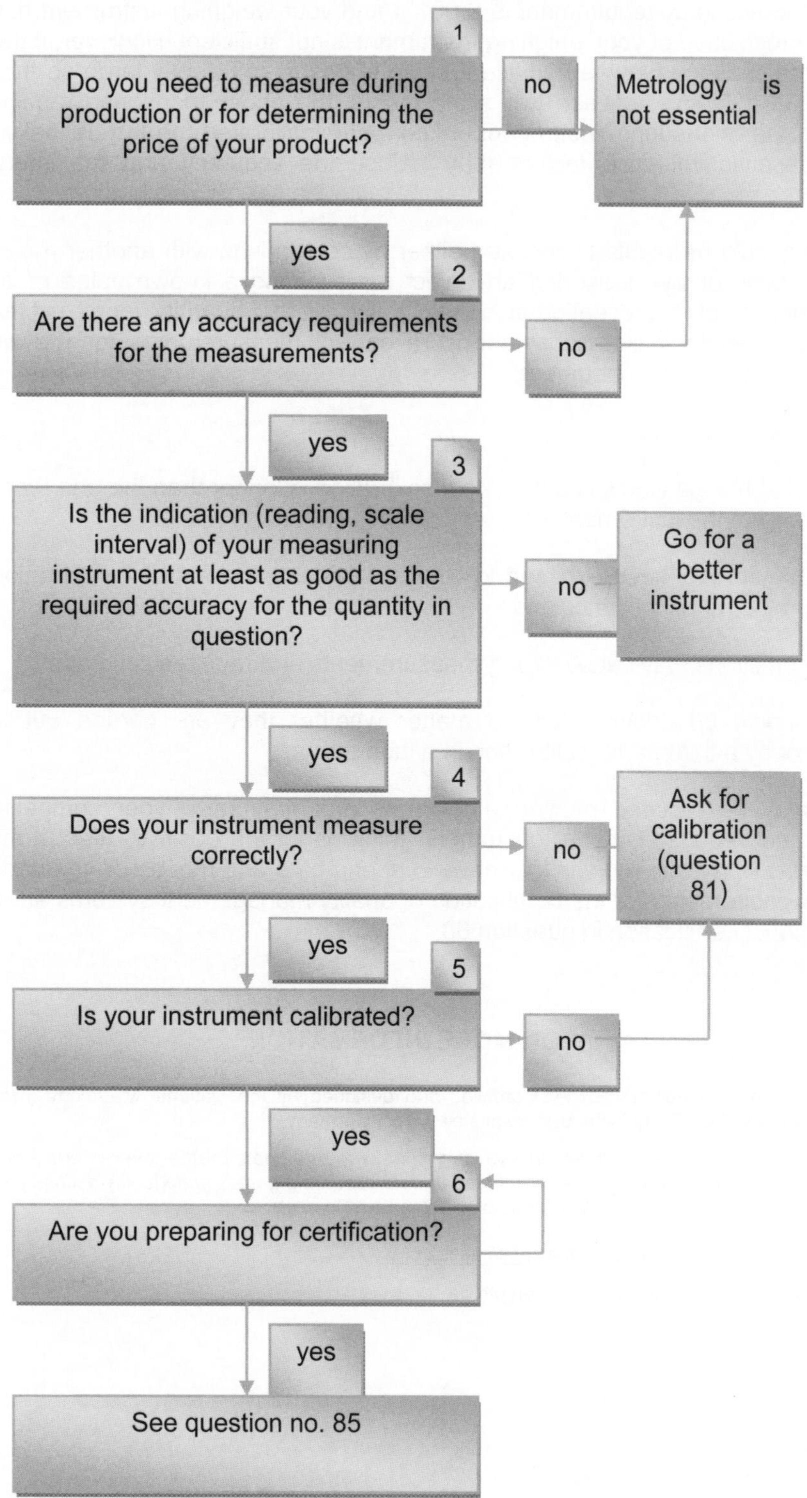

Source: Eberhard Seiler, Germany.

Remarks:

1. Measurements are necessary if you have to meet specifications required by regulations, standards, your customer, or if you sell your product, for example, by mass (kg) or length (m). Of interest here are measurements other than those for inventory purposes, e.g. determining whether sufficient raw material is still available or how many kg have been produced.

2. Of interest here are accuracy requirements like, for example: 100 mm +/- 0.5 mm or 2 000 g + 1 g.

3. Examples: If the accuracy requirement is 0.001 g and your weighing instrument has a scale interval of 0.005 g, the resolution of your weighing instrument is not sufficient. However, if the scale interval is 0.002 g and the distance between adjacent scale marks is sufficiently large so that 0.001 g can be determined as the middle between two scale marks, the above-mentioned requirement is fulfilled, provided that the measuring instrument is correctly calibrated. But it is risky to rely on this assumption because influence factors may reduce the accuracy and the interpolation may be uncertain.

4. The accuracy should be regularly checked either by comparison with another measuring instrument of higher accuracy, or by measuring an object representing a known value of a quantity (e.g. a calibrated gauge block representing a certain value of the quantity length). Measuring and test equipment need regular calibrations to ensure correct measurements for the whole range. You should be suspicious if your instrument:

   - Has not been calibrated;

   - The time that has passed since the latest calibration is longer than the one recommended by the manufacturer of the instrument; or

   - Your instrument has been exposed to overload, mechanical shocks or vibrations, wrong supply voltage or other unusual conditions.

   Any of these conditions may cause wrong measurements and requires calibration.

5. Calibrations should be documented no matter whether they are carried out in-house, by the manufacturer or by a third party (calibration in a laboratory).

6. Certification may be required by your customers and may raise your competitiveness. Even if certification is not required by your customers, think about the positive effect it may have on your competitiveness. However, you will first have to spend time and money on the certification process. Details of the requirements for the certification of quality management systems are given in question 69, and for product certification in question 68.

FOR MORE INFORMATION

- Measurement Practice Improvement Guide. Compiled and designed by the National Metrology Institute of South Africa (NMISA) and the Physikalisch-Technische Bundesanstalt (PTB), Germany.

  The Guide provides several series of statements which you have to rate one after the other to arrive at a self-assessment. It will also help you to consider your performance with regard to measurement rules and identify actions you can take to improve your measurement practice. Also available in French and Spanish. Contacts:

  - NMISA: www.nmisa.org. Email enquiries:info@nmisa.org

  - PTB: www.ptb.de. Email enquiries: presse@ptb.de

81. Which of my equipment should be calibrated and why?

All measuring and test equipment should be calibrated. Calibration is used to:

- Ensure conformity with product specifications and product quality requirements,
- Avoid the risk of scrap and rejects,
- Determine the price, and
- Meet requirements for certification, e.g. according to ISO 9001:2008.

Calibration has to be carried out because the performance of measuring and test equipment may change with time as a result of the influence of the environment to which it is exposed, wear and tear, overload or improper use. The accuracy of the measurement and test equipment should be checked before use and regularly calibrated or after exposure to influence factors (see question 80). Recalibration is not necessary for certain simple types of measuring instruments made of glass such as measuring cylinders, pipettes, burettes, or certain thermometers, if used within the working conditions they were designed for.

During calibration, the value of a quantity measured by the equipment is compared with the value of the same quantity provided by a measurement standard. If you have instruments of different accuracy classes for the same quantity and the same measuring range, at least the instrument with the highest accuracy – also known as 'precision instrument' – should be calibrated by a calibration laboratory, preferably by an accredited calibration laboratory.

The calibrated precision instruments can be used for in-house calibrations of instruments of lower accuracy. Details of the calibration such as a short description of the calibration method and/or a sketch, the standard used, the results obtained, the date and the name of the operator should be documented and stored together with the operation manuals and other documents relevant for the instruments.

Usually, the result of a calibration (or measurement) should include a calculation of the uncertainty. This is a requirement for professional calibration laboratories (see question 84). Since the calculation requires a profound knowledge of the calibration process and of statistics, it might be too complicated and not absolutely necessary for calibrations requiring not too high accuracies (not too low uncertainties). Instead of using methods according to the 'Guide of expression of uncertainty in measurement' (2008), other statements may suffice. For instance, if the accuracy of the standard used is 10 times higher than that of the instrument to be calibrated, a detailed calculation would not be necessary for in-house purposes. But calibration certificates must always indicate the uncertainty (see question 84).

A sticker should be attached to the instrument after successful calibration showing the date of the calibration and an indication of the person who carried it out. It is not recommended to mention the date for the next recalibration because this might lead to the assumption that no calibrations are necessary until this date. This is true only if the instrument has not been exposed to abnormal conditions or if it shows unexpected results. In case the calibration status is no longer valid or the calibration is doubtful, the instrument should be marked as such and not used until a recalibration has been carried out.

Calibration enhances your competitiveness as it helps you to avoid the risk of producing scraps and complaints by your customers.

FOR MORE INFORMATION

- International Laboratory Accreditation Cooperation and International Organization of Legal Metrology. Guidelines for the determination of calibration intervals of measuring instruments. ILAC-G24/OIML D 10) 2007. www.ilac.org/guidanceseries.html or www.oiml.org/publications/D/D010-e07.pdf

  This document identifies and describes the methods that are available and known for the evaluation of calibration intervals. It is intended for use by calibration laboratories. Normal users of instruments should rely on the recommendations of the manufacturers. However, the document contains information of general interest and may be consulted for a better understanding of the requirements.

- International Organization for Standardization. ISO 10012:2003, Measurement management systems – Requirements for measurement processes and measuring equipment. Obtainable from ISO or ISO members (list at www.iso.org).

  This standard provides guidance on the management of measurement processes and actions necessary to demonstrate compliance of the measuring equipment used with metrological requirements.

REFERENCES

International Bureau of Weights and Measures. Evaluation of measurement data – Guide to the expression of uncertainty in measurement. JCGM 100:2008. www.bipm.org/en/publications/guides/gum.html

International Organization for Standardization. ISO 9001:2008, Quality management systems – Requirements. Obtainable from ISO or ISO members (list at www.iso.org).

82. Where can I get my equipment calibrated and at what intervals?

Usually, the equipment manufacturer or his representative in your country can get your equipment calibrated or recommend a calibration laboratory. You may also contact one of the following institutions:

- National accreditation body,
- National calibration service,
- National metrology institute
- National standards body,
- Chamber of commerce and industry, and
- Engineering department of a university.

If no suitable calibration laboratory can be recommended in your country, you should ask for one in a neighbouring country. The names and contact points of accredited laboratories can be found on the websites of regional accreditation bodies (see 'For More Information').

The flow chart below illustrates the steps for choosing the right calibration laboratory.

Steps for choosing a calibration laboratory

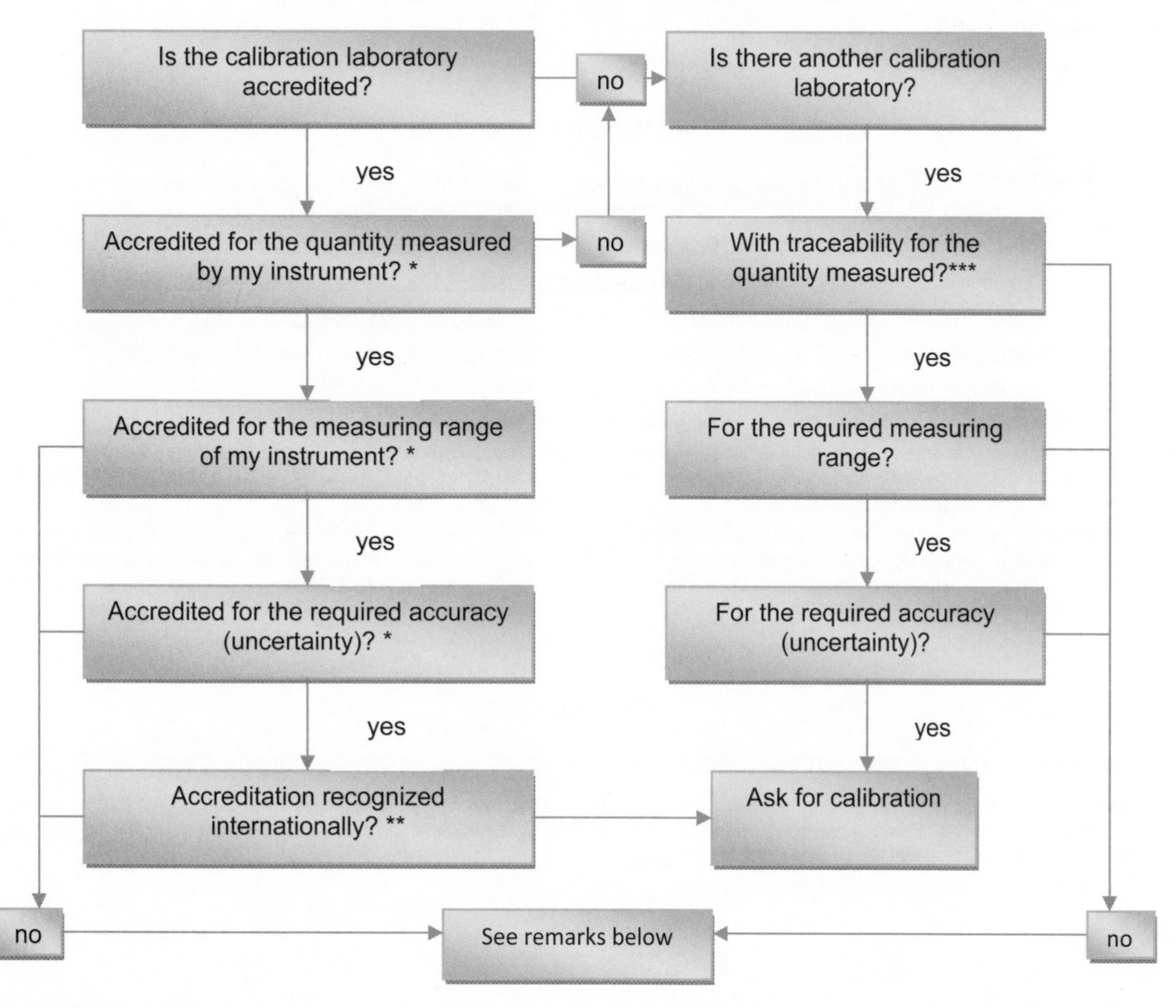

Source: Eberhard Seiler, Germany.

* Accredited laboratories must meet the requirements of the international standard ISO/IEC 17025:2005, which means that they have to operate a quality management system, employ qualified staff, maintain suitable laboratory conditions and use traceable standards for calibrations. Laboratories are accredited for specified quantities, measuring ranges and uncertainties. All three elements should satisfy your requirements. The accreditation certificate should be checked in this regard and also checked if it is still valid. Furthermore, you should check to which national measurement standard the laboratory is traceable. The results and the scope of calibration (measuring range, uncertainty) should be mentioned in the calibration certificate or in an annex, which should be an integral part of the certificate.

** If your customer asks for an internationally acceptable calibration certificate, you have to choose a laboratory that has been accredited by an accreditation body that has signed the Mutual Recognition Arrangement or MRA of ILAC. Called the ILAC Arrangement, it entered into force on 31 January 2001. Even if there is no such requirement from your customer, laboratories accredited by an accreditation body signatory to the ILAC Arrangement should be preferred.

*** See question 84 for an explanation of traceability.

The following should also be noted:

- If you cannot find a calibration laboratory that satisfies all your requirements, you should choose the one that fulfils most of your requirements and look for a laboratory that is better qualified for the next calibration. In addition to technical requirements, cost and time, shipment and customs clearance should also be taken into consideration.
- Calibration intervals are usually recommended by the manufacturer of the measuring or test equipment and should be observed. However, the performance of the instrument depends on its treatment and use. In some situations, immediate recalibration is required – for instance because the measuring result obtained is doubtful or unexpected. Recalibration is also necessary after overloading, improper electrical supply or other instances of mishandling. The user of the instrument is responsible for requesting recalibration in these cases; otherwise, there will be risk of incorrect measurements.

FOR MORE INFORMATION

- Accredited calibration laboratories are listed by national accreditation bodies. ILAC and regional accreditation organizations maintain websites with links to the national accreditation bodies among their members:
  - Asia Pacific Laboratory Accreditation Cooperation (APLAC). www.aplac.org/membership.html
  - European co-operation for Accreditation (EA). www.european-accreditation.org/content/ea/members.htm
  - InterAmerican Accreditation Cooperation (IAAC). www.iaac.org.mx/English/Members.php
  - International Laboratory Accreditation Cooperation (ILAC). www.ilac.org/documents/mra_signatories.pdf
  - Southern African Development Community Accreditation (SADCA). www.sadca.org/documents/SADCA%20contact%20details-English.pdf
- International Laboratory Accreditation Cooperation and International Organization of Legal Metrology. Guidelines for the determination of calibration intervals of measuring instruments. ILAC-G24/OIML D 10) 2007. www.ilac.org/guidanceseries.html or www.oiml.org/publications/D/D010-e07.pdf

  This document identifies and describes the methods that are available and known for the evaluation of calibration intervals. It is intended for use by calibration laboratories. Normal users of instruments should rely on the recommendations of the manufacturers. However, the document contains information of general interest and may be consulted for a better understanding of the requirements.

REFERENCES

International Laboratory Accreditation Cooperation. ILAC MRA and Signatories. www.ilac.org/ilacarrangement.html

International Organization for Standardization and International Electrotechnical Commission. ISO/IEC 17025:2005, General requirements for the competence of testing and calibration laboratories. Obtainable from ISO or ISO members (list at www.iso.org) and from IEC or IEC National Committees (list at www.iec.ch).

83. Who can advise on measurement problems?

Measurement problems can be very complex and need to be contextualized to the environment of the measurement. Therefore, before contacting one of the organizations mentioned further down, you should specify, for example:

- The purpose of the measurement (e.g. determination of the inner diameter of a bore hole);
- The quantity to be measured (e.g. length);
- The measuring range (e.g. 5 mm up to 50 mm);
- The accuracy or tolerable error limits (e.g. + 0.005 mm, – 0.001 mm);
- The location (at the work bench, the point of installation, during production, etc);
- The environment (indoors, outdoors, under certain influence factors, etc);
- The method (continuously, measuring frequency, etc);
- The desired indication (direct reading, analogue, digital registration, electronic data transfer, etc.).

Once these questions have been clarified, the representative of the manufacturer of your measuring equipment should be contacted first because he or she usually has a good understanding of the relevant measurement problems. With the help of search engines, you may find information on, and links to, manufacturers on the Internet. If the measurement problem cannot be solved by the representative or manufacturer of the equipment, then you may choose to contact one of the following organizations or institutions:

- **The national metrology association.** In many countries, metrology professionals have established associations or societies to exchange knowledge in metrology and instrumentation, and to enhance national, regional and international cooperation.
- **The national metrology institute.** This is the national authority for keeping and maintaining the national measurement standards; it may also be called the national bureau of standards or the national bureau of weights and measures. It may be able to provide expertise or may know who else in the country can be contacted.
- **Engineering or physics faculties of universities.** The teaching staff of these faculties may be familiar with your problem, or will perhaps know colleagues who are specialists in your field of interest.
- **Regional or international organizations.** If no national organizations exist, or adequate advice cannot be obtained in the country, regional or international organizations can be asked for help. The main regional organizations are listed under Question 82.

FOR MORE INFORMATION

- International Laboratory Accreditation Cooperation. ILAC MRA and Signatories. www.ilac.org/ilacarrangement.html

  The ILAC Arrangement supports international trade by promoting international confidence and acceptance of accredited laboratory data. Technical barriers to trade, such as the retesting of products each time they enter a new economy, can be reduced.

84. What is measurement traceability and measurement uncertainty?

To explain the concept of traceability, take an equal arm balance as an example. You put the load on one pan and calibrated weight pieces on the other until equilibrium is reached. To ensure the same result with other sets of weights at other locations, traceable calibrated weight pieces are needed. Traceability means that the calibration can be traced back to the international standard, in the case of mass and weights up to the international kg prototype. The kg prototype is realized by a cylinder of platinum-iridium kept at the International Bureau of Weights and Measures in Sèvres, near Paris, France. Copies of this prototype serve as national mass standards and are maintained at national metrology institutes.

Although manufactured with the highest accuracy, the copies show small individual differences when compared with the kg prototype. Repeated comparison measurements differ slightly because of random and systematic (e.g. environmental) influences and add an uncertainty to the result. The complete result of a calibration indicates the deviation from the value of the standard (either plus or minus) and an estimation of the uncertainty of this value (in both directions plus and minus).

Let us now turn to the concept of measurement uncertainty. How to determine the uncertainty is explained in detail in the ISO/IEC 'Guide to the expression of uncertainty in measurement', also known as GUM. According to the GUM method, all important components that influence the uncertainty have to be identified. Each component of measurement uncertainty is then expressed as a standard uncertainty of type A or B.

For type A and B, different probability distributions are applied. For type A, an observed distribution is used (derived from repeated measurements), for type B an assumed distribution is used. The combined uncertainty is calculated by combining the individual uncertainty components according to the law of propagation of uncertainty. In order to compare uncertainties, the coverage factor k must be applied to the combined uncertainty and indicated. For $k = 2$ you can expect about 95% of the results in the interval given by the uncertainty. The measurement uncertainty and the coverage factor must be documented in the calibration certificate together with all details such as the environmental conditions and the calibration procedure.

Here is an example of a result stated in a calibration certificate:

$$R = (1.000\,078 \pm 0.000\,024)\ \Omega$$

Coverage factor: 2

For in-house accuracy checks of measuring instruments, a calculation of the measurement uncertainty is usually not required, but details of the checks should be documented and stored (see question 81).

Traceability generally requires a series of calibrations with standards of different accuracies. This calibration hierarchy for the quantity pressure is shown in the figure below.

Calibration hierarchy using the quantity pressure

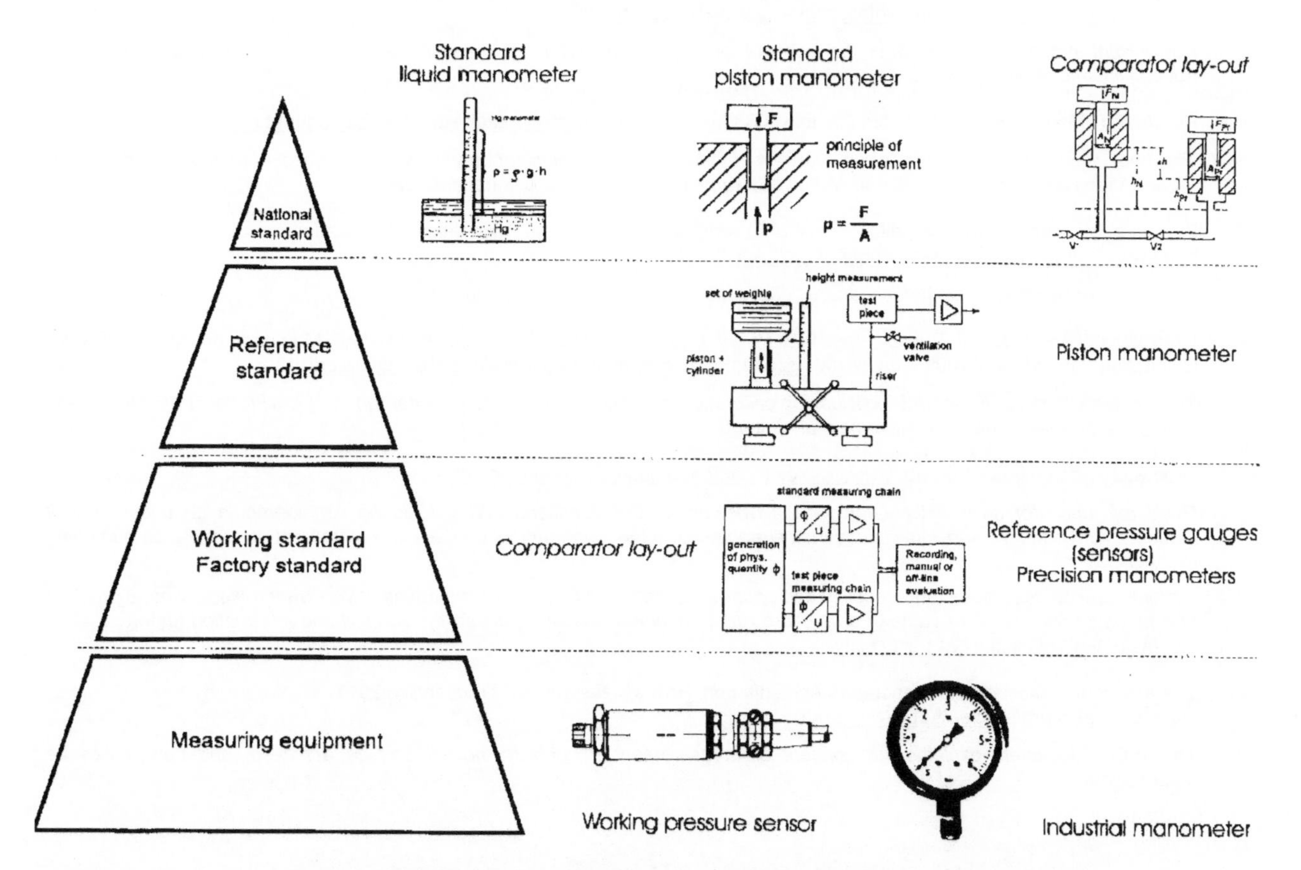

Source: EAL-G12: Traceability of Measuring and Test Equipment to National Standards, November 1995.

Pressure is a derived SI unit with the name pascal, the symbol Pa. It is a measure of force per area and is defined as one newton (N) of force applied over an area of 1 square metre. It is expressed in SI units as N/m^2. It can be stated in SI base units as $kg/(m \cdot s^2)$ (s being second). The national primary standard should be realized according to the definition. This is a device where a force of a known strength acts on a defined area. The realization is a typical task of a national metrology laboratory.

The figure above shows on top two devices which realize the pressure according to the definition and a comparator. Force is created by either liquid or solid masses under the local gravity acting on a surface. The mass, the local gravity and the area need to be determined with the highest accuracy (smallest uncertainty) in order to realize and reproduce pressures of known quantities.

National pressure standards are used to calibrate the so-called reference standards of lower accuracy used by calibration laboratories, often accredited, and also by national metrology institutes to calibrate working standards. Standards that are used for routine calibrations by calibration laboratories are called working standards, or factory standards if used by factories for in-house calibrations.

FOR MORE INFORMATION

- Da Silva, Ricardo Bettencourt. Uncertainty and Metrological Traceability. http://eurachem2011.fc.ul.pt/presentations/IL4%20-%20RBSilva.pdf

  PowerPoint presentation. Presents the concept of traceability, types of measurement references, how to demonstrate traceability and shows some case studies.

- EURAMET. Metrology – In Short, 3rd ed. July 2008. www.euramet.org/. Contact: secretariat@euramet.org

  This booklet contains a comprehensive overview of metrology. It explains important terms, describes international and regional organizations and notes links to them, and gives examples of the impact of measurements.

- European co-operation for Accreditation. List of European co-operation for Accreditation Publications. http://www.european-accreditation.org/n1/doc/EA-1-01.pdf

  Lists EA publications in nine series: general, application, and international, among others.

- International Accreditation Service, Inc. IAS Policy Guide on Calibration, Traceability, and Measurement Uncertainty for Calibration Laboratories. 2009. http://www.iasonline.org/Calibration_Laboratories/policy_guide.pdf

  This document defines the IAS policies for calibration laboratories (internal or external) and calibration traceability, and discusses the estimation of measurement uncertainty.

- Laboratory Accreditation Bureau. www.l-a-b.com/content/measurement-uncertainty

  Good reference for uncertainty. Look for the answers to the questions: 'What is to be considered in an uncertainty of measurement budget?' and 'How is uncertainty applied to a measurement when making a statement of compliance according to ILAC G8?'

  A more detailed description of traceability and uncertainty including figures and examples. If you want to know what a provider of a measurement result or value of a standard must document to claim traceability, you will find information under:www.l-a-b.com/content/measurement-traceability.

- The American Association for Laboratory Accreditation. Policy Measurement Traceability. 2011. http://www.a2la.org/policies/A2LA_P102.pdf

  This policy document explains the concept of measurement traceability, how it can be achieved, and how it can be demonstrated.

REFERENCES

European co-operation for Accreditation. Traceability of Measuring and Test Equipment to National Standards. EAL-G12. November 1995. www.european-accreditation.org. Contact: secretariat@european-accreditation.org

International Organization for Standardization and International Electrotechnical Commission. ISO/IEC Guide 98-3:2008. Uncertainty of measurement – Part 3: Guide to the expression of uncertainty in measurement (GUM:1995). Obtainable from ISO or ISO members (list at www.iso.org) and from IEC or IEC National Committees (list at www.iec.ch).

85. What should I do in regard to measurements if I want to be certified according to ISO/IEC 9001:2008?

Measurements are part of quality management systems. According to clause 7.6 of ISO 9001:2008, you have to determine which measurements are necessary and which measurement devices are needed to provide evidence of conformity of a product to determined requirements. Starting from the product you are manufacturing, you must identify the parameters to be measured and monitored during production. You could begin with the inspection of incoming material and parts or components which should be checked for compliance with specifications.

If, for example, you ordered sheet metal of a certain thickness, you should check it before commencing production. You must decide whether a vernier calliper or a micrometer screw is needed to determine the thickness with sufficient accuracy (see question 80).

In a similar way, compliance with specifications has to be measured during production. Therefore, processes have to be established to ensure that the necessary measurements are carried out in a manner consistent with the requirement.

According to ISO 9001:2008: 'Where necessary to ensure valid results, measuring equipment shall be calibrated or verified at specified intervals, or prior to use, against measurement standards traceable to international or national measurement standards; where no such standards exist, the basis for calibration or verification shall be recorded.' (See question 82.)

Subclauses of clause 7.6 also stipulate adjustments, identification and protection of the measuring equipment. Records of the results of calibration or verification must be maintained. In addition, measurement, analysis and improvement processes shall be planned, implemented and monitored (clause 8). The main goal is to demonstrate that all measuring processes comply with the requirements to demonstrate conformity with specifications, are documented and properly implemented.

FOR MORE INFORMATION

- International Organization for Standardization. ISO 10012:2003, Measurement Management Systems – Requirements for measurement processes and measuring equipment. Obtainable from ISO or ISO members (list at www.iso.org).

  ISO 10012:2003 specifies generic requirements and provides guidance for the management of measurement processes and metrological confirmation of measuring equipment used to support and demonstrate compliance with metrological requirements. It specifies the quality management requirements of a measurement management system that can be used by an organization performing measurements as part of its overall management system and to ensure metrological requirements are met.

REFERENCES

International Organization for Standardization. ISO 9001:2008, Quality Management Systems – Requirements. Obtainable from ISO or ISO members (list at www.iso.org).

86. What are the requirements for the sale of pre-packed goods as regards weights and measures?

Requirements for pre-packed goods offered for sale are regulated in many countries and very often differ. The International Organization of Legal Metrology (OIML) has prepared two recommendations on these requirements: 'R 79, Labelling requirements for pre-packed products' (1997) and 'R 87, Net content in packages' (2004/2008).

Whereas R 79 defines package terms and sets out requirements for labelling, R 87 specifies metrological requirements for goods packaged at a constant nominal content and declared in units of mass or volume. Quantities other than mass and volume (length, area, number) are not part of R 87. The recommendations are published on the OIML website.

The main requirement concerns the average content: the average net content conveyed by any lot of packaged goods available for inspection should equal or exceed the net content as declared on the package. This has to be fulfilled when the goods are ready for sale at the point of pack or, where applicable, at the point of import. Deficiencies from the stated quantity are permitted for individual packages, provided they are not larger than specified tolerances as defined by the OIML recommendations.

OIML member States should use these recommendations as a basis for their national regulations. Information about whether these recommendations were used in national regulations is available on the link provided in the section 'For more information' under the title 'Inquiry on the implementation of OIML International Recommendations'.

However, compliance with the recommendations does not necessarily lead to the acceptance of goods into every country, because it may not be an OIML member or it may apply divergent regulations even though it is an OIML member. Information on the regulations in force can be obtained from the national legal metrology services. The addresses of OIML members and corresponding members (in total about 100) are given in the OIML link cited in 'For more information'.

Currently, OIML is working on the revision of the recommendations and on a voluntary certification system for pre-packages which should facilitate the international trade in pre-packages (see *OIML Bulletin* in 'References').

The regulations of the United States and the European Union are listed below.

FOR MORE INFORMATION

- Council Directive of 20 January 1976, on the approximation of the laws of the Member States relating to the making-up by weight or by volume of certain prepackaged products (76/211/EEC) *(OJ L 46*, 21.2.1976, p. 1). http://eur-lex.europa.eu/LexUriServ/LexUriServ.do?uri=CONSLEG:1976L0211:20090411:EN:PDF

  Amendments:

  - M1 Commission Directive 78/891/EEC of 28 September 1978, OJL 311, 4.11.1978, p. 21.

- M2 Directive 2007/45/EC of the European Parliament and of the Council of 5 September 2007, OJL 247, 21.9. 2007 p. 17. European Cooperation in Legal Metrology, WELMEC: Guide for packers and importers of e-marked prepacked products, June 2005. www.welmec.org/latest/guides.html

  This guide serves as manual for packers using the E-mark who want to have their procedures recognized in connection with E-marking regulations, or who want to modify procedures that have already been recognized. The content is based on legal requirements, their interpretation by WELMEC and practical solutions and recommendations.

- European legislation on prepackages. http://eur-lex.europa.eu/Notice.do?val=455902:cs&lang=en&list=455902:cs,51760:cs,&pos=1&page=1&nbl=2&pgs=10&hwords=76/211/EEC~&checktexte=checkbox&visu=#texte

  Directive 2007/45/EC of the European Parliament and of the Council of 5 September 2007 laying down rules on nominal quantities for prepacked products, repealing Council Directives 75/106/EEC and 80/232/EEC, and amending Council Directive 76/211/EEC.

- International Organization of Legal Metrology

  - Member States and Corresponding Members, Addresses. www.oiml.org/about/membership.html

    OIML database giving addresses of member States or corresponding members.

  - Inquiry on the implementation of OIML International Recommendations, Results. www.oiml.org/inquiries/NR/

    In the past, BIML inquiries on the implementation of OIML international recommendations were organized every four years in conjunction with the OIML Conference. Starting from the 2008 Sydney Conference, this inquiry has now become a permanent survey. Members of the International Committee of Legal Metrology (CIML), representatives of OIML corresponding members and representatives of the countries that requested to participate in the inquiry can fill in their country's responses directly online, and may easily update the information at any time.

- National Institute of Standards and Technology. NIST Handbook 133, Checking the Net Contents of Packaged Goods as Adopted by the 89th National Conference on Weights and Measures (2004), United States regulations. http://ts.nist.gov/WeightsAndMeasures/h1334-05.cfm

  This handbook has been prepared as a procedural guide for the compliance testing of net content statements on packaged goods. Compliance testing of packaged goods is the determination of the conformance of the results of the packaging, distribution and retailing process (the packages) to specific legal requirements for net content declarations.

REFERENCES

International Organization of Legal Metrology

- Labelling requirements for prepackaged products (1997). R 79. www.oiml.org/publications/
- Prepackaged products. OIML Bulletin, vol. LI; Number 3, July 2010. www.oiml.org/bulletin/bulletin_contents.html?x=2010&y=07

Quantity of product in packages (2004/2008). R 87. International Organization of Legal Metrology. www.oiml.org/publications/

ACCREDITATION

87. What is the value of accreditation?

Concept

Accreditation is a formal recognition of competence. It is commonly thought of as being limited to approval by an accreditation body using criteria defined in the guides and international standards published by the International Organization for Standardization (ISO) and the International Electrotechnical Commission (IEC), i.e. the ISO/IEC 17000 family of standards. This can be a rather narrow view in some situations and markets, where other standards may apply. For instance, some countries still 'accredit' using national standards which are not harmonized with the current international standards. For international recognition, however, the application of international standards is strongly recommended.

Application in conformity assessment

From the point of view of conformity assessment, accreditation is applied to laboratories, inspection bodies and certification bodies.

The accreditation process has been applied to laboratories since the 1940s. Users of laboratory services are often familiar with accreditation and have a sophisticated understanding of its value. The accreditation of certification bodies is a more recent activity. While there has been an extraordinary demand for certification, its accreditation is perhaps not so well appreciated. Similarly, accreditation of inspection bodies is a recent development, and it is growing in significance as government inspectorates in many countries are reduced and their activity taken over by the private sector. In these situations accreditation provides assurance of continuing competence and is used by governments as an element of licensing arrangements.

Accreditation adds value to conformity assessment bodies as well as to their managements in a number of ways, as detailed under 'Benefits of accreditation' below. However, its priority for a particular laboratory, certification body or inspection body depends on the perception of its stakeholders and the market conditions within which they operate.

The owner or management of an enterprise may seek reassurance that, having decided to implement a quality management system (QMS) like ISO 9001, the certification body of choice is competent to provide certification services. The accreditation of the certification body reassures both the client and its customers that the certification body is being operated effectively and therefore that the certifications it grants are valid. Accreditation of certification bodies within the QMS framework is given in terms of general industry sectors where the certification body can claim familiarity and some expertise.

The accreditation of a laboratory, in contrast to that of a product certification body or an inspection body, consists of a rigorous investigation into the competence of individual technical staff for particular tests and measurements or products, in addition to an assessment of the management system.

Benefits of accreditation

Users of laboratory services are concerned mostly with reliability and accuracy of test data. Laboratory owners, particularly large corporations or absentee investors, may require their laboratories to be accredited to impose a discipline on their management and thus to assure them that the laboratories are being operated in a technically competent manner and that the data they produce are reliable.

For the laboratory management, the external technical assessment undertaken by experts of the accreditation body provides confidence that the laboratory is working to a best practice standard and that, within the scope of its accreditation, it is judged to be fully competent and well managed to at least the standard of its competitors. It also provides opportunities for improvement in performance and for gaining insights into current developments in its field of work as a result of the interaction between the laboratory staff and the expert assessors.

Accreditation may by itself generate customer confidence in a laboratory's competence and integrity. This is not to say that laboratories that are not accredited are not of a similar high standard, but it does indicate that accreditation can take the place of any other form of assessment that would have had to be conducted by an individual customer. For laboratories, accreditation is certainly less intrusive than multiple appraisals by different customers.

In some markets or for particular customers, special requirements are imposed over and above normal accreditation requirements. These will often be administrative in nature, but they may also have technical elements such as participation in specific proficiency-testing programmes. In these situations, the customer sometimes undertakes an evaluation according to these special requirements and, in so doing, imposes another form of accreditation. In other cases, the customer may ask the accreditation body to cover the additional requirements in its assessment of the laboratories on which the requirements have been imposed. This additional assessment may then be included in the scope of the accreditation. This happens when governments use accreditation bodies for regulatory activities and ask the accreditation body to assess against regulations as well as the normal accreditation standards.

In some countries where, for instance, a particular regulatory regime demands accreditation or where an industry has adopted accreditation as standard practice, it may be difficult, even impossible, to do business without accreditation. In these countries, accreditation becomes a de facto licence to operate. Examples of these situations can be found especially in developed countries. Such policies may cover laboratories, inspection bodies and certification bodies.

It is often stated that accreditation is either an unnecessary cost or too costly. In some circumstances this may be so. However, for most laboratories, the accreditation costs are small compared with the costs of complying with standards which have to be met in any case. The accreditation process imposes a discipline which is a tool for good management. Accreditation also eliminates many of the hidden costs associated with confidence-building in the market and with maintaining that confidence on a continuing basis.

FOR MORE INFORMATION

- International Accreditation Forum (IAF). http://www.iaf.nu/

  The IAF website provides further information on conformity assessment of management systems, products, services, personnel and on similar programmes of conformity assessment.

- International Laboratory Accreditation Cooperation. http://www.ilac.org/

  The ILAC website provides readers with further information about ILAC, ILAC MRA and its signatories, its membership, events, and publications and other resources.

- International Laboratory Accreditation Cooperation. Why Use an Accredited Laboratory? http://biochemspace.ueuo.com/why_use_an_accredited_lab.pdf

  Small brochure on the main reasons for choosing an accredited laboratory to fulfill your testing, calibration or measurement needs.

- International Accreditation Forum and International Organization for Standardization.
  - Expected Outcomes for Accredited Certification to ISO 14001. http://www.compad.com.au/cms/iaf/workstation/upFiles/509680.IAF-ISO_Communique_Expected_Outcomes_ISO_14001.pdf

    Brochure on what to expect from accredited certification to ISO 14001.
  - Expected Outcomes for Accredited Certification to ISO 9001. http://www.iso.org/iso/definitive_expected_outcomes_iso9001.pdf

    Brochure on what to expect from accredited certification to ISO 9001.

- Unger, Peter. Accreditation: A Viable Tool for Import Safety. American Association for Laboratory Accreditation. http://www.a2la.org/press_releases/Import_Safety_100307.pdf

  A six-page paper discussing the benefits of accreditation and the work of the American Association for Laboratory Accreditation (A2LA).

88. What can be accredited?

ISO/IEC 17000:2004 defines accreditation as 'third party attestation related to a conformity assessment body conveying formal demonstration of its competence to carry out specific conformity assessment tasks'.

This means that conformity assessment bodies – inspection bodies, testing laboratories, various forms of certification bodies – product and the various types of system certification bodies, measurement laboratories and design verification bodies can all be accredited.

In its current form, accreditation was introduced in Australia in 1947 and initially focused on laboratories undertaking conventional testing of products and materials in traditional scientific disciplines – biology, chemistry, engineering and physics.

Scopes of accreditation were expressed in terms of a combination of disciplines, products, tests and standards. For example, a laboratory might be accredited for the chemical analysis of steel for carbon and various alloying elements by the methods described in a particular national standard or by using a specific technique.

Accreditation for certification bodies started in the United Kingdom in the early 1980s in response to the development of the Standards Code within the General Agreement on Tariffs and Trade (GATT), the precursor to the WTO. Initially, it was concerned only with product certification bodies whose scopes could be readily defined in terms of products and standards and in relation to safety and performance.

Accreditation of bodies carrying out certification against systems standards (such as ISO 9001) became very active in the 1990s. The definition of the scopes of such certifications is much broader than the very precise definitions used in laboratory or product certification, because they generally relate to industry and activity categories. For more information, refer to IAF ID1:2010 (see "For more information" below).

In recent years, certification programmes have been developed for other system standards such as ISO 14001, HACCP and ISO 22000. This has also happened for the standards prepared by large businesses such as motor vehicle manufacturers and retail shopping chains.

Inspection accreditation is the most recent field within conformity assessment to be widely introduced. As noted in question 65, ISO/IEC 17020 was introduced in 1996. The scopes of inspection accreditation are related to products or services and are defined in terms of standards, codes and regulations.

Laboratory accreditation has also traditionally covered calibration services and, more recently, other supporting services for laboratories such as:

- Proficiency testing providers;
- Reference material providers;
- Research laboratories.

Such organizations may seek accreditation against similar standards derived from the ISO 9001 and ISO/IEC 17025 standards.

In recent years, the same principles have been applied more widely to include:

- Laboratory medicine, where the principal objective is diagnosis and monitoring rather than conformity assessment;
- Diagnostic imaging (medical radiology and others);
- Forensic science;
- Personnel certification;
- Software testing, security-related activities.

While these are not necessarily directly related to conformity assessment, the programmes use the same basic concepts and criteria (technical competence and quality management) and employ peer evaluation processes for the assessment of competence. The word 'accreditation' has a long tradition of use in other fields unrelated to conformity assessment, but, in this area, accreditation is always utilized in an environment where the ISO/IEC 17000 family of standards is applicable.

Personnel certification

This is a recent development that has been gaining popularity lately.

Certification of personnel is related to the recognition of individuals possessing particular knowledge, expertise or skills and able to demonstrate the ability to apply those skills. This is distinct from having acquired academic qualifications although these may be a prerequisite for the certification process.

Personnel certification bodies are subject to the requirements of ISO/IEC 17024. The process of certification must be independent of training programmes intended to lead to certification. As with all forms of certification, the process also includes provisions for monitoring performance and periodic recertification.

Accreditation of common conformity assessment bodies and organizations

Most commonly accredited conformity assessment bodies (CABs)	Standards	
	International standards against which the accreditation of CABs and organizations is carried out	**Requirements and standards for clients of CABs and organizations**
Calibration laboratories	ISO/IEC 17025	Various measurement- and instrument-specific requirements
Testing laboratories (general)	ISO/IEC 17025	Various measurement- and product-specific requirements
Medical laboratories	ISO/IEC 15189	Various diagnostic tests
Inspection bodies	ISO/IEC 17020	Various product and regulatory requirements
Certification bodies		
i. Quality management system	ISO/IEC 17021	ISO 9001
ii. Environmental management system	ISO/IEC 17021	ISO 14001
iii. Food safety management system	ISO/IEC 17021	ISO 22000
iv. Product certification	ISO/IEC Guide 65	Various product-specific requirements
v. Certification of persons	ISO/IEC 17024	Various skill-specific requirements

Source: John Gilmour, Australia.

FOR MORE INFORMATION

- International Accreditation Forum (IAF). IAF Informative Documents. IAF ID 1:2010 Issue 1 QMS Scopes of Accreditation. http://www.renar.ro/modules/accprocess/accprocess/Doc%20IAF/IAF-ID1-2010QMSScopes.pdf

  Informative document developed to facilitate the consistent application of ISO 17021:2006. Contains a list of economic sectors/activities and the correspondent IAF NACE code (division, group, class).

- International Organization for Standardization. Mechanisms for performing conformity assessment. http://www.iso.org/iso/resources/conformity_assessment/mechanisms_for_performing_conformity_assessment.htm

  A three-page document that briefly discusses testing, inspection bodies, certification and management system certification, among others.

- International Personnel Certification Association. www.ipcaweb.org

  IPC provides recognition to individuals who, having demonstrated competence to IPC-approved schemes, can improve the performance of organizations.

- United Kingdom Accreditation Service (UKAS). www.ukas.com

  UKAS assesses and accredits laboratories, certification and inspection bodies, among others.

REFERENCES

Organization for Standardization and International Electrotechnical Commission. ISO/IEC 17000:2004, Conformity assessment – Vocabulary and general principles. Obtainable from ISO or ISO members (list at www.iso.org), and from IEC or IEC National Committees (list at www.iec.ch).

89. What is the difference between certification and accreditation?

Put simply, certification is a statement by a third party that a product or service complies with a standard or specification. Accreditation is a statement by an authoritative body that another body is technically competent to perform certain specified activities.

Both activities rely on standards as the basic benchmarks, but accreditation is supplemented by a process of expert peer review to ensure knowledge and good practice of the particular area of science or technology that is usually impossible to codify in generic standards. Accreditation bodies, where international recognition is required, operate to the requirements of ISO/IEC 17011. Certification bodies work to other appropriate standards (see question 88).

Accreditation is a service that provides supervision and credibility to conformity assessment bodies. It may be used to support trade and commerce or for regulatory purposes. Some accreditation bodies restrict their scope of activities to specialist fields, e.g. testing and calibration laboratories, or may offer accreditation across the broad spectrum of conformity assessment.

As noted in question 88, bodies carrying out any of the various forms of certification are subject to accreditation along with inspection bodies and laboratories performing testing, calibration and measurement. Product certification has a long history and there is no confusion about its place in conformity assessment. The more recent introduction of various forms of management system certification and the lack of a consistent terminology (the use of the term 'registration' for 'certification', for example) has led to some misunderstanding, and indeed misinformation, regarding the relationship between accreditation and certification in these activities.

The problem arose with the widespread adoption of the ISO 9000 series and the misconception that in some way the standard indicated technical competence rather than the management of a quality system, within any context. In the late 1980s and early 1990s, there was the perception that ISO 9001 could replace earlier systems for ensuring competence and integrity within the field of testing and measurement, which were based on the adoption of ISO/IEC 17025. The issue was exacerbated when ISO/IEC 17025 incorporated the system requirements of ISO 9001, introducing substantial overlap between the two activities.

In any particular market, there will be relatively few certification bodies to be accredited while the potential number of laboratories to be accredited will be much higher. However, the profile of the certification bodies will, because of commercial exposure, be much higher in the market. This profile difference sometimes causes confusion in that the terms 'accreditation' and 'certification' are used interchangeably, particularly with respect to ISO 9001 certification. It must be remembered that accreditation follows an assessment of specific technical competence, while certification is the result of a demonstration of compliance with a standard – in the case of ISO 9001, a quality management system standard that is generic rather than product or industry specific.

There have been commercial incentives to promote the view that certification and accreditation are sufficiently alike as to be interchangeable. It is worth noting that in some markets, in the United States in particular, the term 'registration' is used instead of 'certification' for the application of management system programmes, and the audit bodies are referred to as 'registrars' rather than 'certification bodies'. The term 'certification' is limited to bodies certifying products.

To remove some of the ambiguity, and to indicate very clearly the different roles, some governments have either mandated that there be a single national accreditation body (e.g. in countries of the European Union) or given monopoly rights to a single body within defined sectors, as in Australia and South Africa. In other jurisdictions like the United States, a degree of competition is permitted. Accreditation bodies are prohibited from offering competing services where they accredit others to provide such services.

Conformity assessment hierarchy

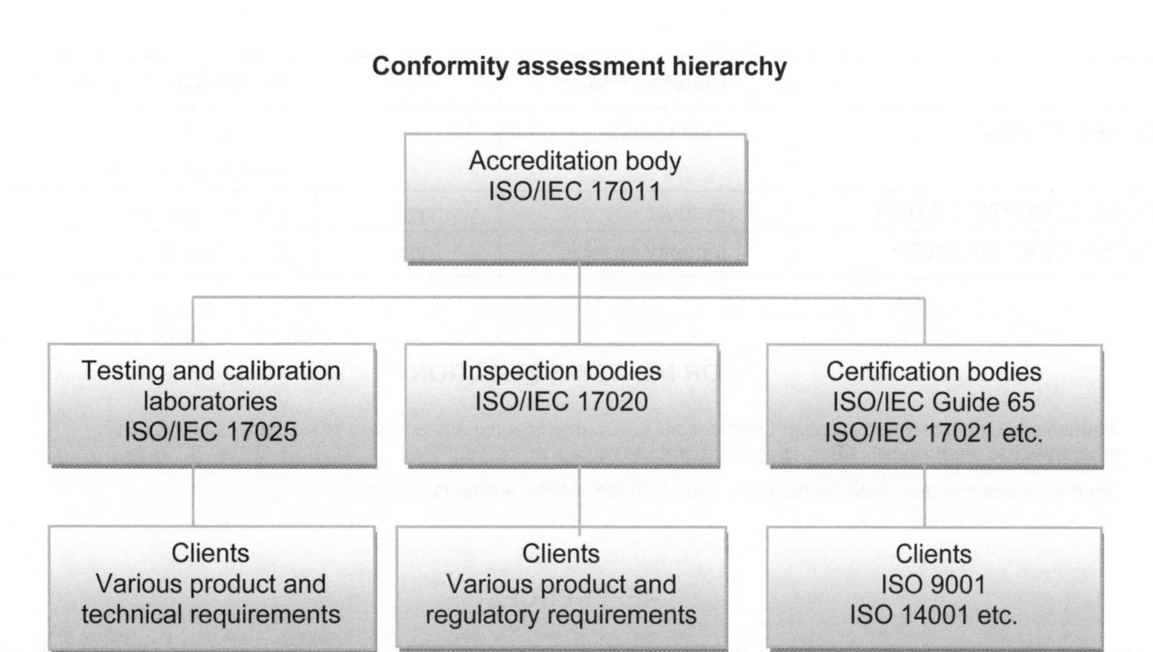

Source: John Gilmour, Australia.

In practice, one of the biggest differences between certification and accreditation lies in the application of the standards as auditable instruments for use by either accreditation bodies (ISO/IEC 17025) or certification bodies (ISO 9001). Here, the focus of the third-party bodies is dissimilar. The accreditation body uses standards to assess a body and to come to a conclusion about the technical competence of the conformity assessment body, while the certification body audits a product or a system to determine compliance with the standard. In this context, the laboratory accreditation body is also interested in the application of methods of test and the skill of individuals in making certain measurements and engages technical experts to assess these elements of a laboratory's operations. The quality management elements of the two standards are harmonized and both laboratory accreditation bodies and QMS certification bodies use similarly qualified auditors or assessors to assess the implementation of those elements.

There has been considerable debate about the need to accredit a laboratory when it is part of an organization that has been certified to ISO 9001. To a large extent, this depends on the customer, but some users of test data will almost always insist on the laboratory being separately accredited.

An audit of a company against ISO 9001 compared to an assessment of a laboratory against ISO/IEC 17025 may be compared to the difference between a road map and a street directory. The laboratory assessment is much more probing on the laboratory operations and is concerned with issues of technical competence. A quality system audit of a large organization will see the laboratory as a small element of the whole.

Even if the organization is a stand-alone laboratory, an audit against ISO 9001 does not consider the knowledge of the scientists, technicians and operators. The example given in question 64 for the way and level of detail in which accreditation is defined (measurement, range and uncertainty) illustrates the technical nature of accreditation whereas an ISO 9001 certificate might express this simply by reference to the industry sector for electrical instrumentation.

Both ILAC and IAF have done much work to clarify these issues, with the result that there is now very little debate on the subject at the technical level and within the conformity assessment user community. However, misconceptions continue to be common in the wider community.

	COMPETENCE	QMS	ASSESSORS/AUDITORS
ACCREDITATION	Test specific	yes	QMS qualified Technical experts
PRODUCT CERTIFICATION	Product specific	yes	Product experts
SYSTEM CERTIFICATION	Industry specific	yes	QMS qualified

FOR MORE INFORMATION

- International Laboratory Accreditation Cooperation (ILAC). International Accreditation or ISO 9001 Certification? http://www.ilac.org/documents/Bro_english/Laboratory_accred_or_cert.pdf

  Small brochure that discusses the benefits of having a laboratory certified to ISO 9001.

REFERENCES

International Organization for Standardization. ISO 9001:2008, Quality management systems – Requirements. Obtainable from ISO or ISO members (list at www.iso.org).

International Organization for Standardization and International Electrotechnical Commission

- ISO/IEC 17011:2004, Conformity assessment – General requirements for accreditation bodies accrediting conformity assessment bodies. Obtainable from ISO or ISO members (list at www.iso.org) and from IEC or IEC National Committees (list at www.iec.ch).
- ISO/IEC 17025:2005, General requirements for the competence of testing and calibration laboratories. Obtainable from ISO or ISO members (list at www.iso.org) and from IEC or IEC National Committees (list at www.iec.ch).

90. Does accreditation automatically lead to the recognition of my test reports and certification?

The simple answer is no. See also the response to question 60.

International recognition of any form of attestation of conformity is extremely varied from country to country and even within different geographical and technical jurisdictions within a country.

WTO regards the lack of acceptance of test reports as a major barrier to trade, and there is no universal answer to the question posed here. It is a market-by-market and, indeed, a regulator-by-regulator question, for which the manufacturer must determine an answer before seeking entry into a particular market. Large or complex markets such as the United States and Japan have the most varied approaches, but some developing countries also have some unique features.

A regulatory body or a commercial buyer may:

- Accept any test report.
- Accept a test report from a laboratory that has established a good reputation with a particular regulatory authority or customer.
- Accept a test report from a laboratory accredited by the national accreditation body in the importing market, provided the test report is endorsed by that accreditation body.
- Accept a test report from a laboratory accredited by one of the mutual recognition partners where mutual recognition arrangements exist between accreditation bodies. Accept a report from any of the few laboratories it has itself recognized.
- Accept test reports only from the laboratory operated by the relevant regulatory authority.

In all the above cases, except the last, the acceptance body will sometimes require the testing laboratory to be independent of the manufacturer. The use of the manufacturer's own test facilities may be acceptable only sometimes.

It is increasingly acknowledged that the key issue is competence, not ownership. This is the reason for the acceptability of the manufacturer's own facilities. As mutual recognition arrangements between accreditation bodies develop and mature, some of the old barriers are breaking down. However, some regulatory authorities are reluctant to discard processes and policies that have served them well for long periods.

A number of government-to-government agreements determine the conditions for bilateral trade in a limited range of products. Some of them allow testing to be done in the country of origin and often specify acceptable laboratories. The European Union has negotiated a number of such agreements with Australia, Canada, New Zealand, Switzerland and the United States, among others. Similar agreements also exist within the Asia-Pacific Economic Cooperation region for such items as food and electrical equipment.

On occasion, governments unilaterally recognize certain international certification arrangements. Among the agreements of the type described are the Australia-European Community Agreement on Trade in Wine, bilateral agreements on aircraft airworthiness, and agreements according recognition to the IECEE CB scheme on the safety of electrical equipment.

In most markets, individual regulatory authorities are responsible for determining entry requirements, and it is not uncommon to find in one country different approaches to the acceptability of test reports from foreign laboratories. Regulatory authorities with different areas of responsibility are free to define their own conformity assessment requirements without taking into account the policies of other regulators. The final decision always remains with a particular regulatory authority, and manufacturers must determine the requirements of each market before trying to obtain entry for their products.

FOR MORE INFORMATION

- World Trade Organization. Committee on Technical Barriers to Trade. Second Triennial Review of the Operation and Implementation of the Agreement on Technical Barriers to Trade. G/TBT/9. http://www.wto.org/english/res_e/booksp_e/analytic_index_e/tbt_02_e.htm.

  Full text of the second triennial review of the TBT Agreement. Annex 5 provides an indicative list of approaches to facilitate acceptance of the results of conformity assessment.

91. What are mutual recognition agreements (MRAs)? How do they facilitate trade?

As the name implies, MRAs are agreements between two or more parties to recognize the competence of each other to provide certain specified services. In the context of this question, agreements can exist between governments, between accreditation bodies or even between conformity assessment bodies. They can be bilateral (limited to two parties) or multilateral (any number of parties).

It is important to note that two terms are used internationally to describe mutual recognition agreements or arrangements – MRA and MLA. In Europe, the agreement among the accreditation bodies of the European co-operation for Accreditation (EA) is referred to as the EA Multilateral Agreement or EA MLA. A similar agreement between the member bodies of the Asia-Pacific Laboratory Accreditation Cooperation (APLAC) is called the Mutual Recognition Arrangement or MRA. The agreement among members of the International Laboratory Accreditation Cooperation (ILAC) is known as the ILAC Mutual Recognition Arrangement or the ILAC Arrangement in short. An agreement exists at the international level for certification bodies through the International Accreditation Forum (IAF), and at regional level through bodies such as EA and PAC (Pacific Accreditation Cooperation). The IAF Multilateral Recognition Arrangement is referred to as the IAF MLA.

Some governments have the view that the term 'agreement' should be restricted to government-to-government relationships, although there is no legal basis for this approach. For this reason, however, agreements between accreditation bodies are usually called 'arrangements' to avoid any difficulties for their government accreditation body members. Irrespective of the term used, the substance of both types of document is the same.

Government-to-government agreements are almost all bilateral, whereas those between accreditation bodies were initially also bilateral but are now almost all multilateral. This leads to another terminological confusion in which some multilateral mutual recognition arrangements are called MLAs but in other cases, MRAs. Again the substance is unchanged.

The purpose of this particular mutual recognition activity is to facilitate trade by enabling conformity assessment performed in the country of origin to be accepted in the country of import without any unnecessary duplication of such activities.

Government-to-government MRAs are negotiated in the context of ensuring that WTO obligations are met. They are always limited to specified regulated product sectors and may acquire treaty status. They define the conditions under which conformity assessment carried out in one country will be accepted in the second country. They may invoke accreditation as the process for giving confidence in the competence of conformity assessment bodies in either country or they may stipulate other confidence-building measures. They apply only to products sold in the territories of the two signatories and may also be limited to products manufactured and subjected to conformity assessment in those territories. For instance, such agreements may sometimes prohibit acceptance of a product manufactured in a third country but tested in an approved laboratory in the territory of one of the signatories to the agreement without some substantial transformation in that territory.

MRAs/MLAs developed within the accreditation environment are more broadly based and are intended to facilitate trade and other data exchanges in any circumstances. They have been developed within the institutional frameworks of ILAC and IAF and are heavily dependent on the work of two international standards writing bodies, ISO and IEC. For participation in the ILAC and IAF MRAs/MLAs, compliance with the relevant ISO/IEC 17000 family of standards is essential.

These ILAC/IAF arrangements proclaim that the accreditation processes of all signatories are harmonized by the application of the relevant standards and that each accreditation has equivalent validity. The concept is that users of documents of conformity assessment who recognize accreditation in one jurisdiction may therefore have confidence in accreditations granted in a different jurisdiction by a different body.

Essentially, the MRAs are only binding on signatories and it is up to the end users, be they regulatory authorities or commercial users, to accept the accreditation process or not.

Initially there was considerable scepticism about the efficacy of such a system but its recognition is developing very strongly. EU and countries such as Australia, New Zealand and South Africa, which have long used accreditation as the preferred mechanism for accepting attestations of conformity internally, have been very willing to use the model of the ILAC and IAF Arrangements to satisfy their international needs. Other countries are increasingly using the system and commercial users, such as the large retail chains, are also recognizing the efficiencies of the system.

An important development during the past decade has been the MRA within the metrology community under the auspices of the International Bureau of Weights and Measures (BIPM). National measurement institutes compare calibration and measurement capabilities (CMCs), the results of which are published on the BIPM website. This initiative greatly strengthens the credibility of ILAC Arrangement and other MRAs in the calibration and testing areas.

FOR MORE INFORMATION

- European Co-operation for Accreditation. The EA MLA: What are the Benefits?
  http://www.european-accreditation.org/content/mla/what.htm

  Discusses the benefits of EA MLA for government and regulators and for industry and the business community, and provides a checklist for the accreditation process.

- IAF/ILAC Multi-Lateral Mutual Recognition Arrangements (Arrangements): Application of ISO/IEC 17011:2004.
  http://www.ilac.org/documents/IAF-ILAC_A5_03_2011.pdf

  Contains a description of the application of ISO/IEC 17011:2004, including terms and definitions, normative references, and responsibilities of the accreditation body.

- International Accreditation Forum (IAF). Certified Once, Accepted Everywhere.
  http://www.dar.bam.de/pdf/IAF_CorpBrochure_Print_version_Mar06.pdf

  Discusses the mission, objectives and structure of IAF, and contains an explanation of MLAs and MRAs.

- International Laboratory Accreditation Cooperation

  - Success stories from ILAC Signatories. http://www.ilac.org/successstories.html

    The ILAC Marketing and Communications Committee (MCC) has been asking its members to provide 'good news' stories that emphasize the benefits accreditation and the ILAC Arrangement have brought a variety of stakeholders. A collection of good news stories is available on the ILAC.

  - ILAC Mutual Recognition Arrangement (Arrangement). http://eng.cnas.org.cn/extra/col1/1186657815.pdf

    This document describes the elements of a mutual recognition arrangement for the accreditation of a testing and calibration laboratory.

- Trans Atlantic Consumer Dialogue (TACD). TACD Briefing Paper on Mutual Recognition Agreements (MRAs). March 2001.
  http://tacd.org/index2.php?option=com_docman&task=doc_view&gid=102&Itemid=

  Discusses concepts and the context of mutual recognition agreements and the legal basis for MRA authority; analyses MRAs in relation to consumer issues.

WTO AGREEMENTS ON TBT AND SPS

92. What are the WTO Agreements on TBT and SPS and what are the main differences between these Agreements?

Introduction to WTO

The World Trade Organization (WTO) was established in 1995 after the Uruguay Round of multilateral trade negotiations, which took place from 1986 to 1994. Its overriding objective is to help trade to flow smoothly, freely, fairly and predictably. It does this, inter alia, by administering trade agreements and rules, monitoring Members' trade policies, settling trade disputes and assisting developing countries on trade policy issues through technical assistance and training programmes.

WTO is a forum for governments, and businesses can be represented only through their governments. Although businesses cannot obtain direct assistance from WTO, they can participate in the training programmes that the organization promotes. WTO Members agree by consensus on the rules and regulations that are to be applied multilaterally. They do not lose their sovereignty when they take decisions with their partners on these rules.

The WTO Agreements take into account the different levels of economic development in member countries, and the differing commercial and economic policies of their governments.

Background to the WTO Agreements on TBT and SPS

There has been an increase in non-tariff measures such as standards (see question 13), technical regulations (see question 18), conformity assessment procedures (see question 55) and sanitary and phytosanitary measures (see question 19) in most countries following the reduction in tariff barriers. Because non-tariff measures can constitute barriers to trade, WTO Members established the Agreement on Technical Barriers to Trade (the WTO Agreement on TBT) and the Agreement on the Application of Sanitary and Phytosanitary Measures (the WTO Agreement on SPS) to lay down international rules for the establishment and application of standards, technical regulations, conformity assessment procedures, and sanitary and phytosanitary (SPS) measures.

A provision of the Agreements calls for WTO Members to use international standards as a basis for their technical regulations and SPS measures unless the use of international standards would be an inappropriate or ineffective means of achieving the desired policy objective or desired level of protection. Where international standards have been used as a basis for technical regulations and SPS measures, it is presumed that these do not create unnecessary obstacles to trade. Although both Agreements are signed by governments, their goal is to help business obtain market access for regulated products by providing a framework to ensure that non-tariff measures dealing with technical requirements will not create arbitrary or unnecessary obstacles to trade.

Because the Agreements impose similar but not identical requirements on importing countries, it is critically important to sort out which are SPS and which are TBT measures. SPS measures are those that conform with the definitions in Annex A of the SPS Agreement, covering, for instance, such matters as pesticide residues in fruits and aflatoxins in peanuts. All other technical barriers to trade come under the TBT Agreement.

The WTO Agreement on TBT

The premise of the WTO Agreement on TBT is that WTO Members are allowed to adopt technical regulations, standards and conformity assessment procedures for legitimate objectives like protection of the environment, prevention of deceptive practices, protection of human, animal or plant life or health, provided they do not constitute unnecessary obstacles to trade. It applies to both industrial and agricultural products but excludes SPS measures and services. It imposes the following obligations on WTO Members:

- To use international standards as a basis for technical regulations and international guides or recommendations for conformity assessment procedures, wherever relevant standards are available, as long as they are not an ineffective or inappropriate means of pursuing the national policy objectives (i.e. legitimate objectives);

- Not to discriminate between imported products by their origin (most-favoured-nation or MFN principle) and between imported and domestic products (national treatment principle) in the application of technical regulations and conformity assessment procedures;
- Not to require retesting or recertification if the technical regulation in the exporting country has been recognized as equivalent or the results of conformity assessment procedures are covered by a mutual recognition agreement;
- To notify WTO and consider comments from other WTO Members before finalizing technical regulations or conformity assessment procedures that would affect international trade if relevant international standards, guides or recommendations do not exist or do not cover the technical content of the technical regulations. Members are required to provide adequate time (at least 60 days) for other Members to comment on the notified measure. Additionally, the TBT Committee recommends a minimum of six months between publication and entry into force of a technical regulation, to allow exporters, particularly those from developing and least developed countries, time to adapt to the regulation and comply with its requirements. WTO Members are allowed to impose technical regulations immediately in response to urgent situations.

The WTO Agreement on TBT has established a Code of Good Practice for the Preparation, Adoption and Application of Standards to ensure that standardizing bodies which adhere to this code:

- Accord the same treatment to national and foreign products in their standards;
- Ensure that their standards are not prepared to create unnecessary obstacles to trade;
- Participate in the development of international standards;
- Publish a work programme every six months;
- Usually allow a period of at least 60 days for comment on draft standards and take into account these comments before finalizing the standards.

The WTO Agreement on SPS

The premise of the WTO Agreement on SPS is that WTO Members have the right to adopt SPS measures to protect human, animal or plant life or health but these must not constitute unjustifiable discrimination between Members or a disguised restriction on international trade. It applies to SPS measures associated with food and agricultural products, but not with quality issues, e.g. grade and weight, which are dealt with in the WTO Agreement on TBT. It obliges regulatory bodies:

- To base their measures on international standards, international guides or recommendations developed by the Codex Alimentarius Commission, the International Office of Epizootics, and under the auspices of the Secretariat of the International Plant Protection Convention (see question 15);
- To accept measures of exporting countries as equivalent if they achieve the same level of SPS protection;
- To base measures on science and an appropriate assessment of risks, and inform WTO and consider comments from other WTO Members before finalizing them if international standards, guides or recommendations are not available or a higher level of protection is needed and the measures being drawn up would affect international trade. Members are allowed to impose SPS measures immediately in response to urgent situations.

Main differences between the Agreements

The main differences between the SPS and TBT Agreements are detailed below.

- The TBT Agreement deals with technical regulations and conformity assessment procedures for industrial and agricultural products, except for regulations specifically dealing with food safety, animal health and plant health which are covered by the SPS Agreement.
- The SPS Agreement makes reference to specific standards-setting bodies, i.e. the Codex Alimentarius Commission (CAC), the International Office of Epizootics (OIE) and the organizations

operating within the framework of the International Plant Protection Convention. The TBT Agreement does not make reference to specific international standards-setting bodies. However, during the second triennial review of the operation and implementation of the Agreement on TBT, the TBT Committee laid down principles for the development of international standards, guides and recommendations.

- There is a significant difference in the importance given to 'scientific evidence' in the two Agreements. There is an unequivocal obligation to base sanitary and phytosanitary measures on scientific evidence in the Agreement on SPS. In contrast, in the case of TBT, the use of scientific evidence would depend on the objectives of the technical regulations in question, and would be considered along with other sources of evidence (e.g. religion or public morals, occurrences of deceptive practices).

- There is also a significant difference in the MFN (Most Favoured Nation) treatment in the two Agreements. There is an unequivocal obligation in the WTO Agreement on TBT for technical regulations to apply to all imported and domestic products indiscriminately. SPS measures, particularly those which aim at preventing animal or plant-borne diseases from entering a country, may be more or less demanding depending on the level of prevalence of specific diseases or pests in a country or in a region of that country. Imports may be allowed without any restrictions from countries that are free from certain types of pests and diseases, while those from countries where such pests and diseases are widespread may be prohibited or subjected to quarantine or measures like fumigation. However, SPS measures aimed at ensuring the safety of food products would have to be applied generally on an MFN basis.

- Both Agreements allow Members to deviate from international standards in their measures under certain circumstances. In the WTO Agreement on TBT, a WTO Member may adopt a national standard which is different or higher than the international standard if it is considered necessary for 'fundamental climatic or geographical factors or fundamental technological problems', or if the international standard would be inappropriate or ineffective in achieving the desired policy objective. In the WTO Agreement on SPS, Members have the right to introduce measures that result in a 'higher level of protection' than would be achieved if they were based on international standards if one of the following conditions is met:

  - There is a scientific justification. Where a Member determines on the basis of the assessment of risks that a higher level of sanitary or phytosanitary protection is appropriate.

  - Provisional SPS measures may be applied on the basis of available pertinent information in cases where relevant scientific evidence is insufficient. This information may include that from relevant international organizations as well as from SPS measures applied by other WTO Members. Technical regulations and conformity assessment procedures are not applied on a provisional basis.

- The determination of compliance with standards and technical regulations is called 'conformity assessment' in the WTO Agreement on TBT whereas it is called 'control, inspection and approval' in the WTO Agreement on SPS.

FOR MORE INFORMATION

- International Trade Centre. 'The SPS Agreement: WTO Agreement on the Application of Sanitary and Phytosanitary Measures.' *International Trade Forum Magazine*, Issue 3, 2010. http://www.tradeforum.org/The-SPS-Agreement-WTO-Agreement-on-the-Application-of-Sanitary-and-Phytosanitary-Measures/

  Explains how developing countries can fully benefit from the SPS Agreement and the work of the SPS Committee.

- United States Agency for International Development. Standards, Metrology, Conformity Assessment and the TBT Agreement: A Desk Top Reference Handbook. http://pdf.usaid.gov/pdf_docs/PNADP635.pdf

  Detailed explanation on the topics above. Excellent source for a deeper understanding of metrology and conformity assessment.

- World Trade Organization
  - The WTO Agreements Series – Sanitary and Phytosanitary Measures. Downloadable from the WTO website at http://www.wto.org/english/res_e/booksp_e/agrmntseries4_sps_e.pdf

    Explains the basic structure of the WTO Agreements; gives an overview of the SPS Agreement, answers frequently-asked questions on the Agreement and gives its legal text.

  - Technical information on technical barriers to trade. http://www.wto.org/english/tratop_e/tbt_e/tbt_info_e.htm

  Explains the background to, and the reason for, the Agreement, as well as the principles contained in it.

REFERENCES

International Trade Centre and Commonwealth Secretariat. Influencing and Meeting International Standards – Challenges for developing countries, vol. 1 – Background Information, Findings from Case Studies and Technical Assistance Needs. 2003. http://www.intracen.org/about/e-shop/

World Trade Organization. Committee on Technical Barriers to Trade. Second Triennial Review of the Operation and Implementation of the Agreement on Technical Barriers to Trade. G/TBT/9. http://www.wto.org/english/res_e/booksp_e/analytic_index_e/tbt_02_e.htm

93. How can the business community benefit from the WTO Agreement on Technical Barriers to Trade?

The TBT Agreement is designed to help the business community. It gives countries the right to adopt technical regulations, standards and conformity assessment requirements, but these must not constitute unnecessary obstacles to international trade.

From a business perspective, enterprises benefit in a number of ways from the TBT Agreement as detailed below.

Information on technical requirements in export markets

The first thing you need to know before deciding to export is to obtain information on the technical requirements for your product in your target market (see questions 23 and 24). This can be a daunting task; however, it is facilitated by the obligation of WTO Members to establish enquiry points for TBT, which are required to provide information on technical regulations, standards and conformity assessment procedures to other WTO Members and interested parties. You can obtain this information directly from the TBT enquiry point in your target market or through your national TBT enquiry point if your country is a WTO Member[6].

Monitoring mandatory technical requirements in export markets

If you do not keep up to date about developments in technical requirements in your target market, you run the risk of your product not being accepted as it may not meet new requirements. You can benefit from the obligation of WTO Members to notify other WTO Members through the WTO Secretariat about proposed technical regulations and conformity assessment procedures when these are not based on international standards and may have a significant effect on trade[7].

In many countries, the notifications on technical regulations and conformity assessment procedures are monitored by a designated organization such as the TBT enquiry point, and are screened and communicated to stakeholders according to their area of interest. In addition to making you aware of the proposed technical requirements, the system enables you to comment on these proposals through the relevant governmental organization in your country and to make your comment known to the notifying WTO Member for consideration, provided that your country is a WTO Member.

Monitoring voluntary technical requirements in export markets

Tracking changes in the mandatory requirements for your export product is not sufficient. Changes in the voluntary standards in your target market can drive you out of that market if you do not adapt your product to the new requirements since many buyers expect products to meet these standards even if they are voluntary. For example, in Germany, there were many producers of PVC pipes when the technology for their manufacture became available; the number of producers fell considerably following the establishment of a national standard on PVC pipes as many pipe manufacturers could not meet the national standard.

How can you keep track of changes in standards of interest to you? You can take advantage of the obligation of standardizing bodies in WTO Members to publish their work programmes (list of standards under preparation) at least once every six months according to the 'Code of Good Practice for the Preparation, Adoption and Application of Standards' (see question 92)[8]. You can contact the relevant standardizing body directly or ask your national standards body to do so.

---

[6] Information on TBT enquiry points is available here: http://tbtims.wto.org/web/pages/settings/country/Selection.aspx

[7] The WTO Secretariat repository of TBT notifications is housed in the TBT Information Management System (TBT IMS): http://tbtims.wto.org/

[8] See the following links on notifications of work programmes and other information about standardizing bodies: http://www.standardsinfo.net/info/inttrade.html, http://www.standardsinfo.net/info/docs_wto/SCD_Update_EN.pdf, http://www.standardsinfo.net/info/docs_wto/UpdateList_2011-08-22.pdf

Harmonization of technical regulations

You could be baffled by the differences in technical regulations in the countries you wish to export to. However, Members are trying to comply with the requirement in the TBT Agreement to base their technical regulations on international standards, as this will generally prevent disputes with their trading partners. Furthermore, regional blocks such as the European Union and the Association of Southeast Asian Nations work to harmonize their technical regulations. Examples are the EU directive on toys and the ASEAN directive on cosmetics. Harmonized technical regulations allow you to have economies of scale and avoid the hassles associated with redesigning your product to suit divergent technical regulations.

Access to foreign conformity assessment procedures

In a number of countries, the national standards body operates a national product certification scheme which was available only to domestic producers before the WTO was established. They thus had a comparative advantage vis-à-vis foreign producers, especially if the mark was well-known and recognized.

However, this advantage has disappeared as the TBT Agreement requires WTO Members to treat the products of domestic and foreign producers alike in as far as conformity assessment procedures are concerned. If you are exporting your product to India, you can apply for the product certification mark of the Bureau of Indian Standards and you can affix that mark on your product if it fulfils the requirements of the certification scheme. The same would apply to your exports to other markets.

Mutual recognition of conformity assessment procedures

If you are exporting to a country with which your country has a mutual recognition agreement covering your product (see question 91), the test report or certification obtained in your country would be accepted in the importing country without retesting or recertification. This will avoid additional expenditure and delay in marketing the product. Mutual recognition agreements exist in some regional blocs such as EU and the East African Community. There are also such agreements between countries and between regional blocs and countries.[9]

Equivalence of technical regulations

Even if the technical regulation in your target market differs from that in your country, you need not redesign your product if the two countries have considered these technical regulations as equivalent. The TBT Agreement requires WTO Members to give positive consideration to accepting as equivalent the technical regulations of other Members, even if these regulations differ from their own, provided that they are satisfied that these regulations adequately fulfil the objectives of their own regulations.

Trade disputes

If you feel that your product is being denied entry into your target market because of an unnecessary technical barrier, you can take up this issue with your sector association or chamber of commerce and industry. If you succeed in convincing them about the validity of your claim, they can take it up with the ministry responsible for WTO matters in your country.

Your technical barrier to trade could be discussed on a bilateral level with the government of the importing country. If that does not result in a satisfactory outcome, the matter could be taken up under the agenda on 'Specific trade concerns' in the WTO Committee on TBT, which meets three times a year. There your country may get the support of other WTO Members.[10] In a number of instances, trade disputes have been resolved in that forum.

---

[9] The following link enables users to search for MRAs that have been notified to the WTO: http://tbtims.wto.org/web/pages/search/notification/agreement/Search.aspx

[10] Information on TBT-specific trade concerns can be found here: http://tbtims.wto.org/web/pages/search/stc/Search.aspx

Only if efforts to settle the trade dispute through consultation on a bilateral basis have failed, can your country have recourse to the WTO dispute settlement mechanism. This is lengthy and expensive but can be effective.

One example of a successful resolution of a trade dispute under the dispute settlement mechanism is the sardines case of Peru versus EU. Sardines from Peru were not allowed to be labelled with the trade description 'sardines' in the EU market. The matter was taken up through the dispute settlement mechanism and EU had to change its technical regulation on sardines to adjust it to the Codex standard and allow sardines from Peru (scientifically known as *Sardinops sagax sagax*) to be labelled as such.

FOR MORE INFORMATION

- International Trade Centre. Business Briefing.
  http://www.intracen.org/trade-support/wto-updates-for-business/business-briefing/

  A complete list of the 'Business Briefings' published by WTO on a range of topics related to SPS and TBT measures.

- World Trade Organization
  - Dispute settlement case between Peru and the European Union on sardines.
    http://www.wto.org/english/tratop_e/dispu_e/cases_e/ds231_e.htm

    Gives details of the dispute settlement case between Peru and EU on the trade description 'sardines'.
  - Technical Information on technical barriers to trade.
    http://www.wto.org/english/tratop_e/tbt_e/tbt_info_e.htm

    Explains the background to, and the reason for, the TBT Agreement, as well as the principles contained in it.
  - Technical barriers to Trade, national enquiry points.
    http://www.wto.org/english/tratop_e/tbt_e/tbt_enquiry_points_e.htm

    Lists names and contact details of enquiry points; provides additional information.

94. How can the business community benefit from the WTO Agreement on the Application of Sanitary and Phytosanitary Measures?

The SPS Agreement is designed to help the business community. It was negotiated in order to protect international trade flows from arbitrary or unjustified restrictions in the form of food safety and biosecurity regulations in importing countries, while allowing trading countries to implement legitimate protections against threats to human, animal or plant health.

In order to maximize the benefits of the Agreement for trade, the business community must work closely with their governments to identify SPS measures in importing countries that may be inconsistent with the provisions of the Agreement. Business can assist efforts to reduce or eliminate such restrictions by providing relevant information and advice based on practical knowledge and experience and on information available from commercial trading partners. Business can offer valuable guidance to government on priorities for the use of government resources in negotiating with other countries on lowering trade barriers.

From a business perspective, enterprises benefit in a number of ways from the SPS Agreement as detailed below.

Information on SPS measures in export markets

The transparency provisions of the SPS Agreement give access to essential information needed by traders – for example, on the conditions that must be met by exported commodities in order to be allowed access to the importing country. The enquiry points mandated by the Agreement provide a convenient means of accessing information from the relevant authorities of importing countries (see question 23).[11] The transparency provisions also enable the governments of exporting countries to express concerns in advance of the introduction of trade-restrictive SPS measures by importing countries (see question 25).

Harmonization of SPS measures

The SPS Agreement facilitates trade by encouraging the use of the international standards established by the Codex Alimentarius Commission, the International Office of Epizootics and standard-setting organizations operating within the framework of the International Plant Protection Convention (IPPC). For instance, the adoption of ISPM 15 on 'Regulation of wood packaging material in international trade' by a number of countries facilitates the trade in products using wood packaging. ISPM stands for International Standards for Phytosanitary Measures, which are issued by IPPC.

Risk assessment

When a WTO Member adopts SPS measures which differ from international standards or where international standards do not exist, it has to carry out an appropriate assessment of the actual risks involved. If requested by another WTO Member, it has to make known the factors taken into consideration, the assessment procedures used and the level of risk determined to be appropriate. The benefit to both exporters and importers are that SPS measures are not established or revised in an arbitrary manner and exports and imports would not be halted arbitrarily.

[11] Information on SPS enquiry points and notification authorities is available here:
http://spsims.wto.org/web/pages/settings/country/Selection.aspx

Adaptation to regional conditions, including pest- or disease-free areas and areas of low pest or disease prevalence

The adoption of the concept of pest- and disease-free areas maximizes the scope for trade. SPS risks do not correspond to national boundaries and this is recognized by the SPS Agreement. In a country, there may be areas that have a lower risk than others. The SPS Agreement recognizes that pest- or disease-free areas may exist in countries with specific pests and diseases, determined by factors such as geography, ecosystems, epidemiological surveillance and the effectiveness of SPS controls. One example concerns the areas free from foot-and-mouth disease (FMD) within countries that do not have an FMD-free overall status.

Equivalence

WTO Members are required to accept the SPS measures of other WTO Members as equivalent to their own, even if these measures differ, if the exporting Member objectively demonstrates that its measures achieve the same level of SPS protection as those in the importing country. An example is the recognition of United States SPS systems and related regulatory systems for meat, poultry and poultry products and all other processed products (including milk products) for human or animal consumption by Panama. Importers of such products from the United States in Panama benefit from simplified import procedures as these products do not have to undergo controls under the SPS measures applicable in Panama.

Market access strategy

The formal regime of rights and obligations makes it possible to plan and implement a coherent market access strategy (see question 95).

Trade concerns

The forum provided by the SPS Committee for the discussion of specific trade concerns benefits business by allowing exporting countries to raise their concerns about particular impediments to trade in a very direct way with importing countries. This procedure offers significant prospects that mutually acceptable solutions will be found.[12]

It is important to note that countries can use the dispute settlement mechanism of WTO (see question 93); however, one should bear in mind that trade disputes are costly to all parties.

REFERENCES

Henson, Spencer and others. Impact of Sanitary and Phytosanitary Measures on Developing Countries. University of Reading, Department of Agricultural & Food Economics, April 2000.

International Plant Protection Convention. Regulation of Wood Packaging Material in International Trade. https://www.ippc.int/index.php?id=1110798&frompage=13399&tx_publication_pi1%5BshowUid%5D=133703&type=publication&L=0

World Trade Organization. Understanding the WTO Agreement on Sanitary and Phytosanitary Measures. http://www.wto.org/english/tratop_e/sps_e/spsund_e.htm

[12] Information on SPS-specific trade concerns can be found here: http://spsims.wto.org/web/pages/search/stc/Search.aspx

95. How can a market access strategy be developed by using the WTO Agreement on SPS?

In general, successful trading depends on exporters meeting the specifications of importers, including official SPS requirements, in a reliable way. The national enquiry points that are part of the transparency mechanisms under the SPS Agreement provide a channel through which exporters can obtain information about the importing country's food standards and the measures it imposes to protect animal and plant health, such as quarantine provisions, vaccination and fumigation procedures, and so forth.

Sometimes, however, exporters are faced with a variety of import controls that appear unduly to restrict their trading operations for multiple products in multiple markets. In such situations it may be useful for the traders and the government of an exporting country to cooperate in the development and implementation of an SPS export market access strategy. The purpose of such strategies would be to address market access restrictions systematically, taking into account priorities and therefore making the best use of the limited resources that governments have available for negotiation on trade issues.

The development of a market access strategy begins with consultation between the prospective exporters and relevant authorities (ministry of trade, ministry of agriculture, animal and plant health specialist agencies, etc.) of the exporting country. The purpose is to draw up a list of matters on which action is to be initiated, taking into account priorities. The highest priority should go to matters that offer the highest likelihood of successful negotiations and prospects for the highest increase in the value of trade.

The first step is to identify situations where technical barriers to trade applied by importing countries are inhibiting exports. These technical barriers may be either measures that are subject to discipline under the SPS Agreement or measures subject to the TBT Agreement. Because the Agreements impose similar but not identical requirements on importing countries, it is critically important to sort out which are SPS and which are TBT measures. SPS measures are those that conform with the definitions in Annex A of the SPS Agreement; all other technical barriers to trade come under the TBT Agreement. This section focuses on SPS measures that are causing barriers to trade.

The development of a strategy cannot proceed until the measures under consideration are well understood. In particular, it is important to know the rationale for the application of the measure, and (in circumstances where the measure is not based on a relevant international standard), whether that rationale is supported by scientific evidence and a risk assessment. Usually, such issues are addressed through dialogue between the relevant agencies of the importing and exporting countries, but private sector contacts may also be very useful in helping to clarify a potential dispute.

The next step is to study the export impediments that have been identified and to assign priorities to them. The aim is to work out how best to allocate the finite government and private sector resources in the exporting country to the task of getting importing countries to reduce or eliminate their technical barriers to trade.

Priorities should be assigned on the basis of the following considerations:

- It is better to use the resources available for market access negotiations on issues that offer a higher chance of success.
- It is better to use resources on issues where the successful removal of market access barriers will result in the biggest increase in the value of exports.
- Some problems may take a long time to resolve; others may be dealt with (whether successfully or unsuccessfully) quite quickly. A balance of effort between these two categories is desirable.

Both government agencies and the business community have a contribution to make to the prioritization process.

Then, taking these priorities into account, a coherent market access target list or agenda can be drawn up. For each market access objective, there should be an associated programme of activities designed to achieve the objective as efficiently as possible.

Typically, the programme of activities aimed at achieving market access will include the development of a market access case for submission to the relevant authorities of the importing country. In some circumstances, the market access case may consist essentially of statements and supporting arguments to the effect that the measures being objected to are inconsistent with the SPS Agreement. In other cases, scientific or technical studies or data collection may be necessary to establish the validity of the claims being made by the exporting country.

Importing countries often have to deal with many different access requests simultaneously. Notwithstanding their obligations as WTO Members, they may be unwilling or unable to deal at once with any particular request from an exporting country. In such a situation, immediate resort by the exporting country to WTO dispute settlement procedures might be thought by the importing country to be excessive and provocative. Through discussions and negotiations between the relevant authorities of the countries involved, a solution is usually found along the lines of a best-endeavours commitment by the importing country to deal with an access request as soon as possible and within a reasonable period of time.

Once dialogue begins on an access request, it is important for the authorities of the exporting country to ensure that there are no avoidable delays in the process, for example in responding to requests by the importing country for clarification or additional information.

Either after, or in parallel with, bilateral discussion of a market access issue, an exporting country may elect to take the matter up in the multilateral forum of WTO. This can be done in an incremental way, beginning with informal discussions at the initiative of an exporting country in the margins of a meeting of the SPS Committee. This initial negotiation aims to alert the importing country that is maintaining technical barriers to trade that the issue may be taken up in the forum of the Committee if a solution is not reached.

If the problem is not solved in private, the SPS Committee has as a regular agenda item the discussion of issues of specific trade interest. In essence, through this procedure, the Committee is providing its 'good offices' to facilitate the resolution of issues. Under this heading, affected exporting countries may raise their concern about particular access impediments. In the past, some of the discussions along these lines had apparently a strong influence on the development or revision of policy in an importing country.

If an agreement cannot be reached between the parties, the WTO dispute settlement procedure is available, starting with formal consultations. Some disputes are resolved early in the process, but those which go through the whole process of panel hearings, draft and final reports, and appeal may take a long time to settle (several years, possibly). The process is also expensive for participants because of the need to commit expert resources, and it may exacerbate relations between trading partners. However, on the evidence of the small number of disputes on SPS issues that have gone through the dispute settlement procedure, it is a very effective mechanism.

FOR MORE INFORMATION

- Implementation of science-based risk analysis for application of SPS measures in Australia: A case study – Importation of Ya pear from Hebei Province, People's Republic of China. World Trade Organization.
  http://www.wto.org/english/tratop_e/sps_e/risk00_e/risk00_e.htm

  A useful PowerPoint presentation made by D. Gascoine at the WTO Risk Analysis Workshop on 29-30 June 2000 on the implementation of science-based risk analysis for the application of SPS measures in Australia.

APPENDICES

Appendix I

ITC survey to update *Export Quality Management: An answer book for small and medium-sized exporters*

A. Letter of invitation to prospective participants

Dear Colleague,

The International Trade Centre (ITC) published 'Export Quality Management: An answer book for small and medium-sized enterprises' in 2001. This book has been customized to serve as a practical reference guide for SMEs in 18 countries.

In order to reflect new developments in the field of Quality Infrastructure (technical regulations, sanitary and phytosanitary measures, standards, conformity assessment, metrology and accreditation), and corresponding changes in the queries and concerns of exporting SMEs, ITC will be updating the present edition of the guide. ITC will undertake this update in partnership with PTB, the German National Metrology Institute.

We are seeking views from organizations and partners based on which we will undertake the update. From your experience with challenges faced by exporters to meet technical requirements in export markets and overcome technical barriers to trade, we seek your response to the following, with particular emphasis on the utility of information and practical relevance to SMEs in particular:

1. From the list of questions in the current guide in Section 1, please indicate questions you would like to maintain in the second edition of the guide, and those you consider should be removed.
2. In Section 2, please suggest new questions that should be included.
3. In Section 3 provide the 3 prime concerns/constraints of exporting SMEs to meet technical requirements in export markets.

Please provide comments on the proposed new structure of chapters in Section 4

For a complimentary copy of the guide, you may send us a request to quality@intracen.org. Please send your response to the survey to quality@intracen.org before 15 September 2009.

SECTION 1: Indicate which questions should be kept in the second edition, and which should be removed

Technical regulations and standards

1. What is a technical regulation?

   ☐ Keep ☐ Remove

2. What is the relationship between a technical regulation and standard?

   ☐ Keep ☐ Remove

3. Are standards and technical regulations barriers to trade?

   ☐ Keep ☐ Remove

4. Where do I find information on technical regulations individual countries?

   ☐ Keep ☐ Remove

5. Where can I get information on standards?

   ☐ Keep ☐ Remove

6. Can I influence the preparation of standards and technical regulations?

   ☐ Keep ☐ Remove

7. How can I keep abreast of developments of interest to me?

   ☐ Keep ☐ Remove

8. Are technical regulations same from country to country?

   ☐ Keep ☐ Remove

9. Is quality management a requirement for complying with technical regulations?

   ☐ Keep ☐ Remove

10. What aspects of product do technical regulations deal with?

    ☐ Keep ☐ Remove

11. Which are the major international standards bodies

    ☐ Keep ☐ Remove

12. What work is going on to harmonize standards? How do equivalence and comparability between different national standards

    ☐ Keep ☐ Remove

13. Can we expect more international standards to be developed for use in technical regulations?

    ☐ Keep ☐ Remove

14. What are the packaging requirements for my products?

    ☐ Keep ☐ Remove

15. What is eco-labelling?

    ☐ Keep ☐ Remove

Product certification

16. What is product certification? How does it differ from quality system certification?

☐ Keep ☐ Remove

17. What are the criteria for selecting certification bodies?

☐ Keep ☐ Remove

18. What type of certification is required to prove compliance with technical regulations?

☐ Keep ☐ Remove

19. Will my certification be accepted in another country?

☐ Keep ☐ Remove

20. Are there international certification systems for products?

☐ Keep ☐ Remove

21. Where can I get information on certification bodies operating in various countries?

☐ Keep ☐ Remove

22. How does inspection relate to other forms of conformity assessment and what is its place in international trade?

☐ Keep ☐ Remove

23. What are the European Union's New Approach to product regulation and Global Approach to conformity assessment?

☐ Keep ☐ Remove

24. What is a 'supplier's declaration of conformity?

☐ Keep ☐ Remove

Testing

25. What is testing? Why is it important in international trade?

☐ Keep ☐ Remove

26. Where can I get my products tested to find out whether they comply with standards and regulatory requirements?

☐ Keep ☐ Remove

27. How do I ensure that the test report on my product will be accepted overseas?

☐ Keep ☐ Remove

28. How do I go about setting up my own testing laboratory?

☐ Keep ☐ Remove

29. Are there any standards for laboratory design?

☐ Keep ☐ Remove

30. Where can I obtain information on testing equipment for quality control in my company?

☐ Keep ☐ Remove

31. What role do inspection and testing play in a quality management system?
☐ Keep ☐ Remove

32. What is the difference between ISO/IEC 17025 and ISO 9001?
☐ Keep ☐ Remove

33. What proficiency testing programmes are available to laboratories in developing countries?
☐ Keep ☐ Remove

34. What are appropriate measurement standards for specific tests?
☐ Keep ☐ Remove

35. What is an acceptable demonstration of traceability?
☐ Keep ☐ Remove

36. Where can laboratory assessors receive relevant training?
☐ Keep ☐ Remove

Metrology

37. What is metrology?
☐ Keep ☐ Remove

38. Why is metrology important in international trade?
☐ Keep ☐ Remove

39. Why should I have my testing and measuring equipment calibrated and at what intervals?
☐ Keep ☐ Remove

40. Where can I get my equipment calibrated?
☐ Keep ☐ Remove

41. What factors should I consider in selecting a laboratory for calibrating my equipment?
☐ Keep ☐ Remove

42. Should I calibrate or verify all my measuring equipment?
☐ Keep ☐ Remove

43. What is the meaning of 'accuracy' and 'uncertainty' in a measurement?
☐ Keep ☐ Remove

44. What is the meaning of traceability?
☐ Keep ☐ Remove

45. What is a measurement standard?
☐ Keep ☐ Remove

46. What is the difference between calibration, verification, adjustment and gauging?
☐ Keep ☐ Remove

47. Who can advise on measurement problems?
☐ Keep ☐ Remove

48. What are common pitfalls and problems encountered in impl. ISO 9000 as regards inspection, measuring and test equipment?
☐ Keep ☐ Remove

49. What are the international organizations dealing with metrology?
☐ Keep ☐ Remove

50. What is the International System of Units (SI)? Are there other systems in use?
☐ Keep ☐ Remove

51. What are the requirements for weights and measures in the sale of pre-packed goods?
☐ Keep ☐ Remove

52. Are there regulatory requirements for measuring instruments?
☐ Keep ☐ Remove

Quality management

53. What is the relationship between quality control, quality assurance and quality management?
☐ Keep ☐ Remove

54. What is the concept of the 'triple role' in quality management?
☐ Keep ☐ Remove

55. Will a quality product cost more, and what are the benefits of manufacturing quality products?
☐ Keep ☐ Remove

56. Is quality management an issue only for management?
☐ Keep ☐ Remove

57. What is meant by the 'quality policy' of a company/organization and how does it promote quality management?
☐ Keep ☐ Remove

58. How do I know if my existing resources are sufficient to implement a quality management system?
☐ Keep ☐ Remove

59. What level of technical skills is required to implement a quality management system?
☐ Keep ☐ Remove

60. How do I make my customers aware of my achievements in quality management?
☐ Keep ☐ Remove

61. How do I ensure that my raw materials and purchased components (inputs) are fit for use?
☐ Keep ☐ Remove

62. Why are statistical techniques important in quality management?
☐ Keep ☐ Remove

63. How can I motivate my subordinates to achieve quality?

☐ Keep ☐ Remove

64. How do I keep abreast of developments in quality?

☐ Keep ☐ Remove

ISO 9000

65. What are the ISO 9000 series of standards and how widely are they used? Do they help the export trade?

☐ Keep ☐ Remove

66. What standards make up the ISO 9000 family? What are the major differences between the 1994 and 2000 versions of the standards?

☐ Keep ☐ Remove

67. Is ISO 9000 applicable to both the manufacturing and the services sectors?

☐ Keep ☐ Remove

68. What are the costs and benefits of obtaining ISO 9000 certification?

☐ Keep ☐ Remove

69. What does my company need to do if it is currently certified/registered to ISO 9001:1994, ISO 9002:1994 or ISO 9003:1994?

☐ Keep ☐ Remove

70. How do I set up an ISO 9000 quality management system?

☐ Keep ☐ Remove

71. What are common pitfalls and problems encountered in implementing ISO 9000?

☐ Keep ☐ Remove

72. Will an SME be able to implement ISO 9001:2000?

☐ Keep ☐ Remove

73. What is the role of internal audits in ISO 9000 and how are they conducted?

☐ Keep ☐ Remove

74. Is it necessary to have automatic/semi-automatic equipment to be certified to ISO 9001 or are manual operations adequate?

☐ Keep ☐ Remove

75. What are the requirements to become quality auditors?

☐ Keep ☐ Remove

76. What procedures do companies need to document for certification to ISO 9000? Can they use electronic media to do so?

☐ Keep ☐ Remove

77. What are the steps taken by certification bodies following an application for certification after the grant of a certificate of registration to ISO 9000?

☐ Keep ☐ Remove

78. Will implementation of ISO 9000 always result in acceptable products? If not, how do certification bodies address the situation?

    ☐ Keep ☐ Remove

79. What are the sector-specific versions of the ISO 9000 quality management standard?

    ☐ Keep ☐ Remove

Other Management Systems

80. What other management system standards exist besides ISO 9000?

    ☐ Keep ☐ Remove

81. What factors should I consider when choosing a management system for my company?

    ☐ Keep ☐ Remove

82. What is HACCP and why is it important for SMEs in the food sector?

    ☐ Keep ☐ Remove

83. How does HACCP fit in with ISO 9000?

    ☐ Keep ☐ Remove

84. How is HACCP implemented? What are some cost-saving measures that SMEs can take?

    ☐ Keep ☐ Remove

85. What is ISO 14000? Is it applicable to both the manufacturing and services sectors?

    ☐ Keep ☐ Remove

86. How does ISO 14000 help SMEs to increase the acceptability of their export products?

    ☐ Keep ☐ Remove

87. Is it necessary to have the best pollution control technology to implement ISO 14000?

    ☐ Keep ☐ Remove

88. How can the ISO 14000 EMS be integrated with the ISO 9000 QMS?

    ☐ Keep ☐ Remove

Accreditation

89. What is the value of accreditation?

    ☐ Keep ☐ Remove

90. What are the accreditation organizations at the international level?

    ☐ Keep ☐ Remove

91. What are MRAs, and how do they facilitate trade?

    ☐ Keep ☐ Remove

92. Why is it so difficult for laboratories in developing countries to be accredited?

    ☐ Keep ☐ Remove

World Trade Organization

93. What requirements does the WTO Agreement on Technical Barriers to Trade impose on technical regulations?

    ☐ Keep ☐ Remove

94. How can the business community benefit from the TBT Agreement?

    ☐ Keep ☐ Remove

95. What are the requirements for conformity assessment procedures in the TBT Agreement?

    ☐ Keep ☐ Remove

96. In what circumstances does the SPS Agreement apply?

    ☐ Keep ☐ Remove

International Trade Centre

97. What type of market information is available from ITC?

    ☐ Keep ☐ Remove

98. How can ITC help SMEs in the area of quality management?

    ☐ Keep ☐ Remove

99. What services does ITC offer to help small businesses trade electronically?

    ☐ Keep ☐ Remove

100. What tools can SMEs obtain from ITC?

    ☐ Keep ☐ Remove

SECTION 2: Suggested new questions to be included in the second edition

1
2
3
4
5
Other...

SECTION 3: Top three concerns/constraints for small and medium-sized exporters to meet technical requirements in export markets

1
2
3

SECTION 4: Comments on the proposed new structure of the publication

CURRENT STRUCTURE OF THE PUBLICATION	PROPOSED STRUCTURE OF THE PUBLICATION
1. Technical regulations and standards 2. Product certification 3. Testing 4. Metrology 5. Quality management 6. ISO 9000 7. Other management systems 8. Accreditation 9. World Trade Organization 10. International Trade Centre 11. Appendices i. ITC survey on quality management ii. Websites in the world of standardization, quality assurance, accreditation and metrology	1. Quality infrastructure at a glance 2. Technical requirements *Standards* *Technical regulations* *Sanitary and Phytosanitary Measures* 3. Quality management *Including ISO 9001* 4. Food safety management systems *Including ISO 22000* 5. Management system for the environment and social accountability *Including ISO 14001* *Social accountability* *WRAP* 6. Metrology 7. Testing 8. Product certification and inspection 9. Accreditation 10. WTO Agreements on TBT and SPS

B. Survey Participants

ITC gratefully acknowledges the participation of the individuals, enterprises and trade support organizations listed below in its 2009 survey for the revision of the Trade Secrets publication *Export Quality Management – An answer book to small and medium-sized enterprises*.

Trade support organizations

Enrique S. Mantilla, President, Argentine Chamber of Exporters, Argentina

Ferdaus Ara Begum, Additional Secretary (R&P), Dhaka Chamber of Commerce & Industry, Bangladesh

Michael W. De Shield, Director, Food Safety Services, Belize Agricultural Health Authority, Belize

Keeper Morgan, Director, Commercial Enterprises, Botswana Bureau of Standards, Botswana

Nancy Samir Hathout, Training Director, Foreign Trade Training Centre (FTTC), Egypt

Mengistu Bessir, Manager, Business Support Services, Addis Ababa Chamber of Commerce & Sectoral Association, Ethiopia

Theresa L. Adu, WTO/TBT National Enquiry Point Manager, Ghana Standards Board, Ghana

B. Venkataraman, Director, National Accreditation Board for Certification Bodies (ABCB), Quality Council of India, India

Terry Kawamura, Senior Chief Expert on Business Excellence, Japanese Standards Association, Japan

Khemraj Ramful, Director, Mauritius Standards Bureau, Mauritius

Maria Isabel Lopez, Executive Director, Mexican Accreditation Body (Entidad Mexicana de Acreditación – EMA), Mexico

Bijaya Bahadur Shrestha, Chairperson, Productivity & Quality Committee, Federation of Nepalese Chambers of Commerce & Industry (FNCCI), Nepal

Rosa Cabello Lecca, Head in charge of Technical Cooperation and International Affairs, INDECOPI, Peru

Ma. Flordeliza C. Leong, Senior Manager, Philippine Exporters Confederation, Inc. (PHILEXPORT), Philippines

Gabit Mukhambetov, Chairman, Committee for Technical Regulation and Metrology, Ministry of Industry and Trade of Republic of Kazakhstan, Kazakhstan

Roshen Weereratne, Consultant – Membership Services, International Affairs Division, Sri Lanka

Mustafa Aghbar, General Director, Specialized Technical Services Ltd., Syrian Arab Republic

Consultants

S. C. Arora, India

Basudev Bhattacharya, India

Francisco Blaha, New Zealand

Navin Shamji Dedhia, United States

Ivar Foss, Norway

John Gilmour, Australia

John Landos, Australia

Manfred Kindler, Germany

Pradip V. Mehta, United States

Eberhard Seiler, Germany

Rajinder Raj Sud, Malaysia

International organizations

Gabriela Ehrlich, Head of Communications, International Electrotechnical Commission, Switzerland

Gretchen Stanton, Senior Counselor, Agriculture and Commodities Division, World Trade Organization, Switzerland

Melvin Spreij, Counselor, Secretary to the Standards and Trade Development Facility (STDF), Agriculture and Commodities Division, World Trade Organization, Switzerland

Pierre de Ruvo, Executive Secretary, International Electrotechnical Commission for Electrical Equipment, Switzerland

Appendix II

Useful websites

African Organisation for Standardization	www.arso-oran.org
American Society for Quality	www.asq.org
Asia Pacific Laboratory Accreditation Cooperation	www.aplac.org
ASTM International (formerly known as the American Society for Testing and Materials)	www.astm.org
Australian Wool Innovation Limited	www.wool.com
British Retail Consortium	www.brc.org.uk
Centre for the Promotion of Imports from developing countries	www.cbi.eu
Chartered Quality Institute	www.thecqi.org
Codex Alimentarius Commission	www.codexalimentarius.net
European Association of National Metrology Institutes	www.euramet.org
European co-operation for Accreditation	www.european-accreditation.org
EFQM (formerly known as the European Foundation for Quality Management)	www.efqm.org
European Organization for Quality	www.eoq.org
European Proficiency Testing Information System	www.eptis.bam.de
Export HelpDesk	www.exporthelp.europa.eu
Fairtrade International	www.fairtrade.net
Food and Agriculture Organization of the United Nations	www.fao.org
FSSC 22000	www.fssc22000.com
Global Food Safety Initiative	www.mygfsi.com
GLOBALG.A.P.	www.globalgap.org
Global Organic Textile Standard	www.global-standard.org
Independent International Organisation for Certification Limited	www.iioc.org
InterAmerican Accreditation Cooperation	www.iaac.org.mx
International Accreditation Forum	www.iaf.nu
International Bureau of Weights and Measures	www.bipm.org
International Electrotechnical Commission	www.iec.ch
International Federation of Standards Users	www.ifan.org
International Laboratory Accreditation Cooperation	www.ilac.org
International Measurement Confederation	www.imeko.org
International Organization for Standardization.	www.iso.org
International Organization of Legal Metrology	www.oiml.org
International Personnel Certification Association	www.ipcaweb.org
International Plant Protection Convention	www.ippc.int
International Register of Certificated Auditors	www.irca.org
International Telecommunication Union	www.itu.int

International Trade Centre	www.intracen.org
International Trade Forum Magazine	www.tradeforum.org
Iseal Alliance	www.isealalliance.org
Juran Institute	www.juran.com
Malcolm Baldrige National Quality Award	www.nist.gov/baldrige
Network on Metrology, Accreditation and Standardization for Developing Countries	www.dcmas.net
Oeko-Tex	www.oeko-tex.com
Organisation for Economic Co-operation and Development	www.oecd.org
Physikalisch-Technische Bundesanstalt	www.ptb.de
Social Accountability International	www.sa-intl.org
Standards and Trade Development Facility	www.standardsfacility.org
Standards Map	www.standardsmap.org
United Nations Conference on Trade and Development	www.unctad.org
United Nations Economic Commission for Europe	www.unece.org
United Nations Environment Programme	www.unep.org
United Nations Industrial Development Organization	www.unido.org
World Bank	www.worldbank.org
World Health Organization	www.who.org
World Intellectual Property Organization	www.wipo.int
World Organisation for Animal Health	www.oie.int
World Standards Services Network	www.wssn.net
World Trade Organization	www.wto.org
Worldwide Responsible Accredited Production	www.wrapcompliance.org